UNDER SIX REIGNS

By the same author

Courts and Cabinets
Studies in Diplomacy and Statecraft
Frederick the Great
Studies in German History
Maria Theresa and Other Studies
Catherine the Great and Other Studies
History and Historians in the Nineteenth Century
   Revised edition, with a new introduction, 1952
Louis XV
The Second Empire

Under Six Reigns

G. P. GOOCH
C.H., D.LITT., F.B.A.

Give me liberty to know, to utter and to argue freely, according to conscience, above all other liberties. MILTON

Les révolutions changent tout sauf le cœur humain. PASCAL

What men have done and said, above all what they have thought, that is history. MAITLAND

LONGMANS

LONGMANS, GREEN AND CO LTD
6 & 7 CLIFFORD STREET, LONDON WI
THIBAULT HOUSE, THIBAULT SQUARE, CAPE TOWN
605–611 LONSDALE STREET, MELBOURNE CI
443 LOCKHART ROAD, HONG KONG
ACCRA, AUCKLAND, IBADAN
KINGSTON (JAMAICA), KUALA LUMPUR
LAHORE, NAIROBI, SALISBURY (RHODESIA)
LONGMANS, GREEN AND CO INC
119 WEST 40TH STREET, NEW YORK 18
LONGMANS, GREEN AND CO
20 CRANFIELD ROAD, TORONTO 16
ORIENT LONGMANS PRIVATE LTD
CALCUTTA, BOMBAY, MADRAS
DELHI, HYDERABAD, DACCA

First published 1958
Second Impression 1959
Third Impression 1960

*Permission has been given for this book to be transcribed
into Braille.*

PRINTED IN GREAT BRITAIN BY
JARROLD AND SONS LTD NORWICH

PREFACE

WRITERS of reminiscences fall into two main categories—those who have made history and those who have watched it in the making. While the former provide essential material for the political historian, the latter furnish testimony to students of social life and literary taste, changes in atmosphere and religious beliefs. Lord Pethick-Lawrence, an old friend from Eton and Trinity, entitled his autobiography *Fate Has Been Kind*. My own tale could be summarized in the same smiling formula. The greatest privilege of a young man is to shape his career as the deepest urges of his mind and heart dictate. *Was man in der Jugend wünscht davon hat man im Alter die Fülle*.[1] Unfortunately that is not always the case, but it was true of Goethe and it has been true of myself. Nature fashioned me for study and reflection, not for action. This record is a testament of gratitude for my good fortune and for the friendships which have enriched a happy life.

Bishop Creighton used to say that he would have liked to live in the majestic century of Innocent III and Aquinas. Sir William Harcourt would have preferred the age of Walpole. I am satisfied to have been born in mid-Victorian England, the golden age of the middle classes, and to have lived far into the century of the common man. My vivid memories begin with the death of Gordon, the Home Rule split, the acclamations of the first Jubilee, the cold douche of the great dock strike, the shoddy Boulanger intermezzo, the eviction of the Iron Chancellor and the calamitous collapse of Parnell. I have seen Queen Victoria and heard Gladstone speak in the House of Commons. I have always thought and felt as a responsible citizen of the world, ever mindful of the underlying unity of the vast and quarrelsome human family. The classics in which I was bred have bequeathed to us nothing finer than the familiar words: *Homo sum, humani nihil a me alienum*

[1] What one wishes in early days one obtains in full measure in old age.

v

puto. No one can repeat that resonant confession of faith with deeper conviction than an octogenarian historian.

The first seven and the fourteenth chapters were published in the *Contemporary Review*. My thanks are due for permission to reprint.

G. P. G.

CONTENTS

I

ENGLAND IN THE EIGHTIES

VICTORIAN England was a pleasant place for a middle-class family. Unlike the sixteenth, seventeenth and eighteenth centuries with their respective religious, political and economic revolutions, the nineteenth was a period of tranquil growth. The Reform Bill of 1832 transferred political power from the landed aristocracy to the *bourgeoisie* which ruled without a rival till 1914. No wonder the Victorians with few exceptions were optimists. Heirs to a great estate, they witnessed its rapid development with unalloyed satisfaction and knew the world was watching them with envious admiration. Justly proud of their liberties and their strength, they faced the future without a tremor. With their coal and their factories, their empire and their navy, their ancient Constitution and their Queen, they feared nothing in the world. National solidarity was assured, not only by the habit of compromise which had grown into an instinct, but by a general acceptance of institutions and ideas—peace, free enterprise, free trade, the two-party system, a large fleet and a small, voluntary army. The stately edifice appeared so firmly based that its residents might almost be pardoned for cherishing the illusion of finality. A little money went a long way, for everything was cheap—food and clothing, rent and coal, labour, education and travel. Income tax was well under a shilling in the pound, death duties and super-tax were unknown. Till the United States forged ahead after the Civil War and Germany after unification, England—with her far flung Empire at her back—was generally regarded as the strongest, freest and richest country in the world. Only gradually did I realize in my sheltered home that capitalism had its victims as well as its winners and that not all that glittered was pure gold. In the

1

Hungry Forties Disraeli had spoken in the greatest of his novels of The Two Nations; Dickens and Mrs. Gaskell, the Christian Socialists and Carlyle had lifted a corner of the curtain which hid an abyss of misery and stunted lives. Charity there was in plenty, but even as late as the eighties poverty was sometimes accepted as almost an ordinance of nature. A Welfare State and a minimum standard of life for the manual worker were hardly even a distant dream. Canon Scott Holland used to speak of the comfortable and the uncomfortable classes. I was one of the lucky ones.

Born in London in 1873 I must begin with an explanation of my name. George Peabody, the famous American financier and philanthropist, had died four years before my arrival, but his memory was still green and his bust stood in the hall. When I grew up I learned more than the bare fact that I was called after him and that he had played a decisive part in my father's life. After opening stores in various American cities he migrated to London in 1837, merchants and manufacturers on both sides of the Atlantic sending their wares through his hands. Some of them secured advances on articles in his possession before they were sold, while others left large sums in his keeping after the sales, knowing that they could obtain them at need and that meanwhile they were earning good interest. Thus the merchant grew into the banker, the banker into the financier of American railways and other enterprises. Needing a young partner he revisited Boston in 1854, and was recommended Junius Morgan as the best business brain in the city. The firm now became George Peabody & Co. Ten years later the senior partner retired, nominating Junius Morgan as his successor but declining to allow the use of his name. The business, however, was so solidly established that the substitution of the titles of J. S. Morgan & Co. made no practical difference and the founder continued to tender advice. He received the Freedom of the City of London and declined a knighthood. When he died in London in 1869 his body was sent home in a British man-of-war. A year later occurred the most dramatic incident in the history of the firm. At the end of October, 1870, Junius Morgan was summoned to Tours, whither the French Government had fled before the German invaders, and was asked if he could raise ten millions and, if so, on what terms. 'Six per cent at eighty' was the reply, and the agreement was promptly concluded. A few days later it was announced that bonds guaranteed by the French Government were available at eight-five. The loan was readily taken up and at the end of the war the bonds were at par. The profit was substantial, the increase of prestige greater still. The house of Morgan now became the chief agent, next to the older firms of Rothschild and Baring, in raising foreign government loans in the English market. The next great move was the refunding of the American Civil War debt, and the New York branch made rapid advance under Pierpont Morgan who inherited his father's *flair* for business and capacity for quick resolves.

My father, a Suffolk man born in 1811, entered the London firm of George Peabody as a clerk in its earliest days, rose to a junior partnership before the retirement of the founder, and remained a partner when Junius Morgan reigned in his stead. A letter of George Peabody in April 1868 to my grandmother, congratulated her on her daughter's engagement. He enclosed a cheque for £100 for 'some article or articles of ornament or use', and the diamond jewel which was always called the Peabody brooch kept alive the memory of one of the most generous of men. The Peabody Dwellings for poor families, a project suggested to him by Lord Shaftesbury, and the statue behind the Royal Exchange perpetuate his name in London, while it is commemorated by numerous educational and philanthropic institutions in the land of his birth.

My mother, the daughter of a Norfolk clergyman, was born in the year of the Queen's accession. The village of Bramerton near Norwich was typical of the old order that has now almost passed away. The elder brother lived as Squire at the Hall while the younger reared a family of ten at the Rectory. In those days there was no machinery for the higher education of women even had the family resources been equal to the strain. Percy Lubbock has painted an exquisite picture of country life in Norfolk in his study of the Gurneys of Earlham, limited of course in comparison with the manifold opportunities of today but very far from stagnant or dull. The large broods then in fashion meant troops of relations and a stream of visitors, and the eldest daughter at the Rectory was Chief of Staff to the Rector's wife. Occasional visits to London brought glimpses of a wider world, and among her cherished memories were public readings of Dickens and Kingsley's sermons in Westminster Abbey. She read the novels and poems of the great Victorians as they appeared. She preferred Thackeray to Dickens and loved George Eliot better than either, partly because she wrote of rural England which was a closed book to the giants of Fleet Street and Pall Mall. She enjoyed Kingsley, Charlotte Brontë and Trollope. Among the poets Tennyson was first and the rest nowhere. The Laureate seemed like Queen Victoria, all-pervading, unique, monumental, a national institution. The primacy of *In Memoriam* in one field was as incontestable as that of *Vanity Fair* in another. The *Idylls of the King* were as popular as Mendelssohn's *Songs without Words*. Browning came later into the lives of my mother's generation, and his wife was rated slightly above her deserts though we still enjoy the *Sonnets from the Portuguese*. Swinburne's *Poems and Ballads* would have seemed out of place in a country Rectory, but the reflective verse of Matthew Arnold found the welcome it deserved. She loved all good literature, but to the end of her life at the age of eighty-seven Tennyson and George Eliot retained a special place in her heart.

My father had formed a typical mid-Victorian library, consisting mainly of what were regarded as the classics of English history and literature. Gibbon was there, of course, and Robertson's *Charles V*, and Hume's *History of England* with the continuation by Smollett, and the letters of Horace Walpole. Alison's best-seller on the Napoleonic era claimed a whole shelf to itself, and Macaulay's complete works were supplemented by his nephew's delightful biography. America was represented by Bancroft's complacent *History of the United States*, Prescott's entrancing narratives of the Spanish Empire in the New World, and Motley's epic on the Rise of the Dutch Republic. It was the golden age of the amateurs who secured a far wider public than their more scholarly successors. In the field of literature the principal items were complete editions of the Waverley Novels, Dickens, Thackeray, George Eliot and Kingsley. Among miscellaneous items I recall such solid fare as *The Wealth of Nations* and the *Greville Memoirs*. My father, though not much of a reader, enjoyed political biographies and reminiscences. He was a judge of pictures, and he purchased a number of flower-pieces by

Fantin-Latour before he was discovered by a wider world. George Christie, the head of the famous firm, was an old friend and neighbour of my mother's family, and the auctions in King Street were an unfailing interest.

My father retired from business at the age of sixty-six. Owing to the great difference in our ages he seemed to me more like a grandfather than a parent, and I was too young to inquire much about the experiences of his busy life. He had come of age in the year of the Reform Bill, travelled to London by stagecoach, and visited the United States soon after the Civil War. He looked back with special admiration to Peel, preferring his solid sanity to the coruscations of Gladstone and Disraeli. He paid frequent visits to the Royal Institution, his children sharing in the privileges of membership by admission to the Christmas lectures for juveniles. My lifelong interest in science dates from the discourses of Tyndall, Dewar and Robert Ball. The latter made the strongest appeal, for astronomy was easier to grasp, and the genial Ulsterman was perhaps the most popular lecturer of his time. It was a red-letter day when my father brought home a three-inch telescope, which revealed to our delighted eyes the mountains of the moon, the rings of Saturn and satellites of Jupiter. If I owed my introduction to science to my father, it was my mother who led me into the enchanted land of music. She was an accomplished pianist and a regular attendant at the Saturday Pops at St. James's Hall, where she preferred Mme Schumann to any other artist. I grew up to the sound of Beethoven's sonatas, and the vogue of Mendelssohn was still at its height. Beginning like other juveniles with Gilbert and Sullivan, I was led forward by loving hands to the classics and taught to play the piano.

The most stimulating of my parents' friends was Dr. Boyd Carpenter, Vicar of Christ Church, Lancaster Gate, where my parents worshipped with Victorian regularity. I was never to hear a more eloquent preacher than the little Ulsterman with his mobile features and musical voice, and never to meet a man of more irresistible charm. We loved to hear him read poetry aloud and enjoyed his lectures on Dante. He was already chaplain to the Queen and Canon of Windsor, and when one Sunday morning in 1884 Gladstone was noticed in the congregation, we sensed that his hour had come. The Prime Minister sat close to my parents' pew, and I vividly remember his fine head, white hair and wonderful eyes. Shortly afterwards our beloved vicar was appointed Bishop of Ripon, and for the last thirty years of his life he was one of the ornaments of the Church. Queen Victoria could never have enough of his company, and he was chosen to preach the Jubilee sermon in 1887. He was a valued friend of the Empress Frederick and of William II, whom he visited in Berlin and who used to read his sermons to his long-suffering wife. Ripon Hall at Oxford commemorates the debt of Anglican Modernists to one of the earliest Broad Churchmen on the Episcopal Bench.

Being destined for Eton, I was sent to Hawtrey's well-known preparatory school at Slough in my tenth year. Having been an Eton master he had pitched his tents within sight of the Round Tower. The curriculum was modelled on that of Eton, which means that the classical languages and mathematics claimed most of our time. Two years later, being head of the school, which had migrated to Westgate, I left for Eton, which I entered at an unusually early age, shortly before my twelfth birthday.

Eton in the eighties and nineties has been painted by many brushes, by nobody with such artistry as Percy Lubbock. The foreground is occupied by the Headmaster—'our huge magnificent Warre, endowed with the majesty of Jove. He was greatness manifest and unquestioned, so vast was he, so dominant. When he came striding into a division for a visit of inspection, sweeping and rustling in his robes, it was a drama that never lost its grandeur. When he came down in wrath the earth shook, and his great voice was a trumpet, shattering the air.' His sermons, adds Percy Lubbock, were ineffective and his intellectual influence nil. 'He was broad and safe and massive. An air of the world was about him—or if not of the world, an air of England, a large-limbed, high-coloured Victorian England, seated in honour and plenty. His idea of education was that it should produce solid and honourable Englishmen after the country's heart.' I can confirm every trait in this portrait. There were no subtleties, no unplumbed depths, no philosophic background, no wings. Though a good classic he was not an intellectual. His mind was static and tradition was his guide: that the curriculum needed bringing up to date never entered his head. His authority, resting on his office and personality, inspired awe in the masters scarcely less than in the boys. The Oxford historian Fletcher has done his best to convey what he rightly calls an indefinable greatness in the official biography, but we approach closer to the man in Sargent's portrait of Jupiter tonans in his robes.

During my three years at Eton I sat at the feet of several teachers who afterwards rose to fame. My first form-master was Inge, afterwards the celebrated 'gloomy' Dean of St. Pauls and one of the finest intellects of our time, then a shy young man of twenty-five. No one was less fitted for the drudgery of teaching little boys Greek and Latin than this fastidious scholar. Next in distinction was 'Monty' James, destined to win fame by his medieval studies and his ghost stories, to return to his old school as Provost, and to receive the Order of Merit. A third was Arthur Benson, son and biographer of the Archbishop of Canterbury, a perfect physical specimen of the Nordic type. He was an ideal form-master and later one of the most popular of house-masters, but after a quarter of a century he moved to Cambridge whence he poured forth a stream of popular essays 'from a College Window'. A fourth celebrity, Bourchier, a gifted Irishman, left in 1888 to become *The Times* Correspondent in the Balkans, where as the unwavering champion of Bulgaria he helped to make history. I was to see more of him during my years in Parliament. A fifth was Edward Lyttelton, the handsomest member of a distinguished family and himself a future headmaster of the school. Of these and other pundits we may read in Eric Parker's *Eton in the Eighties*.

No school in England could boast such a distinguished staff, but its energies were largely sterilized by the dead hand of the past. Lovers of classics and mathematics were happy enough, but boys like myself who craved a more varied diet were almost starved. A small concession was made in a course of elementary science; but though the chemical experiments were a welcome diversion, the teaching was of an amateur kind for the teacher was himself an amateur. French was imparted by a little Frenchman whose unmerited sufferings at the hands of his unruly class fill me with sympathy after the lapse of seventy years. Our form-master, himself a classical scholar, was expected to take history in his stride, which meant that he contented himself with reading out of a text-book. Literature was not taught at all. I never saw a

newspaper, and information about current affairs we were left to
pick up in the holidays. Eton was a dignified relic of the Middle
Ages, a little island screened from the tides by a stout breakwater
of tradition. So long as it continued to turn out Prime Ministers
and Viceroys, Field-Marshals and Archbishops, no change appeared
to its Headmaster and Governors to be needed and reform had
to wait till the twentieth century. Delicate, studious and caring
nothing for games, I never fitted into the system. There was a
good deal of bullying, swearing was almost universal, and there
were pockets of immorality. Daily chapel and Sunday sermons
made little impression on the life and thought of a thousand carefree lads. The idea of confiding in my house-master, an irritable
bachelor, never occurred to me. Among my Eton acquaintances
who rose to be Cabinet Ministers I may mention Lord Balcarres,
the handsomest boy in the school, Lord Beauchamp, and Lord
Pethick-Lawrence. I left without regret in the summer of 1888 in
my fifteenth year. I had recently lost a good deal of time through
ill health, and since little was done at school in those far off days
for the care of the body my parents concluded that I should fare
better at home.

For the next three years I attended the General Literature
Department of King's College in the Strand. The Centenary
History by my Cambridge friend Professor Hearnshaw, published in 1929, describes the fortunes of this Church of England
riposte to the undenominational University College in Gower
Street. The Anglican atmosphere penetrated every corner and the
Principal had always been an ecclesiastic of high standing. Dr.
Wace, later Dean of Canterbury, was not only a prominent
theologian but had been on the staff of *The Times* in the spacious
days of Delane. The College could not compare in numbers or
distinction with its rival, but both staff and students had contributed their quota to the roll of fame. Its greatest ornament was
Lord Lister, who first applied his antiseptic methods in King's
College Hospital, at that time only a couple of hundred yards
away. Confessional limitations impeded the growth of the College
till, at the turn of the century, they yielded to the bracing principle
of the open door and membership of the new London University,
the Theological Department living on as a confessional enclave.
When I entered King's in 1888 it was a quiet litte place.

Teachers and students alike, we were all members of the Established Church. The lecture-rooms and spacious corridors, now crowded with youths and maidens, were half empty. The boys of King's College School before its removal to Wimbledon were tucked away in the basement and we had no contact with them. The College remained what it had been since its foundation, an Anglican fortress in the eyes of its friends, an Anglican backwater in the eyes of its critics; but after Eton it appeared to me deliciously up to date. I found myself promoted from an antediluvian curriculum to a place where the classics were fully honoured but modern subjects also received their due. Since the classes were small the professors gave us an amount of individual attention unknown in public schools. Though I was the youngest member of the department, I felt that I had escaped from the fetters of school life into a wider world. Lessons were a delight and the Saturday holiday kept us from getting stale. The Theological Department occupied the pride of place. We began with Chapel every morning, and our curriculum included an amount of theological instruction rare even in those far-off days; but of this I had no cause to complain, for our teachers knew how to arouse and maintain our interest.

The College was dominated by the formidable personality of the Principal. The countenance of Dr. Wace was hard and dry, our intercourse wholly official, but he inspired deep respect. We knew him to be a leading Hebrew scholar and one of the pillars of the Church. His famous controversy with Huxley in successive numbers of the *Nineteenth Century* took place during my time at King's, and we gazed at him with awe as he marched slowly along the corridor in cap and gown. I was too immature to read the articles with a critical eye, but I felt the power and skill of both the gladiators as their swords crossed. Wace was an Evangelical to whom Modernism was anathema, yet I never heard anything in a lecture-room more impressive than his discourses on the Old Testament. My copy of Hooker's *Ecclesiastical Polity*, which I won as a prize for Divinity, recalls the harsh strong voice of the Principal dilating on the Prophets. The New Testament we studied in Greek under the guidance of the Vice-Principal, later a Canon of Durham, from whom I first learned of what used to be called the Higher Criticism. In belabouring Baur and the Tübingen

2

School he unwittingly taught us that there was more than one approach to the problems of inspiration and miracles.

More challenging than the Fundamentalism of our theological instructors were the lectures of Dr. Momerie on Philosophy. His carefully prepared utterances were remarkable for point and pungency. So greatly did he interest me that I read his books and occasionally attended his sermons on Sunday morning at the Foundling Hospital, of which he was chaplain. No discourses could have been more unsuited to the poor little mites sitting in their charity uniform in serried rows in the grim old chapel, no longer existing, where Handel had played the organ. Brought up in the narrow circle of a nonconformist minister, Momerie soon threw dogma to the winds and distinguished himself in philosophy at Edinburgh and Cambridge. Despite his sceptical views he was ordained and appointed to the Chair of Logic and Metaphysics at King's. For such a man to enter the Ministry and to accept a post in an Anglican institution was hardly playing the game, for he made no attempt to bridle his tongue. The College authorities had no wish for a second Maurice campaign, but the publication of a volume entitled *Inspiration and other Sermons* in 1889 brought matters to a head. Among the members of the Council was Gladstone, who, despite his impeccable orthodoxy, pleaded for compromise. The knot was untied by his transfer from the Department of Theology to that of General Literature, involving the exchange of a large audience of candidates for the Ministry for a small gathering of youths destined for secular professions. I owe the awakening of my life-long interest in philosophy to these lectures.

Though our theological instructors were borrowed from the Theological Department, we could boast stars of our own. The brightest luminary was Sir John Laughton, the leading British authority on sea power and founder of the Navy Records Society. His lectures were rather uninspiring, for he conceived of history as a record of events rather than a panorama of the many-sided life of humanity. I should doubtless have chosen history as my life-work in any case, but his encouragement came at a formative time. He lived long enough to witness the emergence of Admiral Mahan in the United States and the growth of a vigorous school of British naval historians with himself and Julian Corbett at their head. When his books are forgotten the scores of naval articles he wrote for the *Dictionary of National Biography* will keep his name alive. To King's I trace the beginnings of my intellectual life, for there was a University atmosphere long before I reached University age. Greek, Latin and mathematics retained their rightful place, but history, English and French literature, philosophy and theology were taught by scholars who communicated their own enthusiasm to their pupils.

Literature beckoned almost as persuasively as history. I had begun my initiation, like most schoolboys of that remote age, not with British authors but with Greeks and Romans, and I am grateful for being nourished on the classics. Homer, in particular, is untranslatable, and I never grudged a moment spent in looking up words in the dictionary. The best plan, I think, when learning a language is to begin with a masterpiece which creates the enthusiasm needed to overcome the initial difficulties. Many a schoolboy has stuck fast in second-rate writers like Xenophon, Ovid or Nepos, and has asked himself if it is really worth while to work so hard for so little reward. Let him start in Greek with the death of Hector, the Periclean Oration and the Sicilian expedition, the apologia of Socrates and the closing scene of the *Phaedo*; in Latin with the *Aeneid* and the Odes of Horace, Livy's story of Hannibal's invasion of Italy and the grim picture of Tiberius in the *Annals* of Tacitus. In an industrial and scientific age compulsory Greek was bound to disappear, but Latin and French should be thoroughly learned in our public schools.

During my three years at King's I discovered the glories of English literature from Chaucer onwards. Scott I never fully enjoyed till I left the University and could realize the splendour of his finest scenes. It was lucky for me that the little volumes of *Cassell's National Library*, costing fourpence halfpenny apiece, were beginning to make their weekly appearance, well printed, tastefully bound, each of them furnished with an introduction by Professor Henry Morley. It was in this series that I studied Shakespeare, the essays of Bacon, Addison and Macaulay, the shorter poems of Milton, Pope's *Essay on Man*, Burke *On the Present Discontents*, and many another pearl of great price. It was a feast in which course followed course without a break for four years. My library began with these little volumes and with the

English Men of Letters, the delightful series edited by John Morley.
Dumas I had enjoyed in my schooldays, and I now fell in love
with Molière and Victor Hugo. *Les Misérables* I thought must
surely be the greatest novel in the world till I read *War and Peace*.

My juvenile historical studies fostered an uncritical admiration
of men of action, and I paid my tribute to the greatest of them in
papers read to the Essay Society at King's. Creasy's *Decisive
Battles* and Lockhart's *Napoleon*, which I had brought home as
prizes in my schooldays, were read and re-read before turning to
later authorities; and I conceived a boyish enthusiasm for Caesar
from Froude's spirited biography and the superb closing volume
of Mommsen's *History of Rome*. The fever was over before I was
out of my teens, but it raged fiercely while it lasted. I loved
Plutarch's Lives, and my apprenticeship to Carlyle began with
Heroes and Hero Worship, a book for the young and only for the
young. I may add in partial self-defence that I did not confine my
homage to the conquerors, for Motley's glowing record of the
life and death of William the Silent stirred my imagination.
Concerts were no less keenly enjoyed, among them Henschel's
spirited rendering of the ballads of Schubert, Schumann and
Loewe at the recitals given by himself and his first wife. My
memories of the old St. James's Hall include Joachim and Piatti,
Sarasate and Ysaye, Paderewski and Pachmann. *Lohengrin* was my
first opera, a happy choice, and I advanced with growing eager-
ness to *Tannhäuser*, *Tristan* and the *Meistersinger*. Among the star
performers at Covent Garden the brothers de Reszke stand out
in my memory.

My first taste of the theatre was the exquisite performance by
Irving and Ellen Terry of *The Vicar of Wakefield* at the Lyceum,
which brought tears to many eyes, and for the next decade I
applauded that incomparable pair in almost every piece. His
mannerisms were rather a trial and he was not equally successful
in all his parts. As Hamlet he could not compare in intellectuality
with Forbes Robertson, and the senility of his King Lear was
overdone. In *The Bells*, his first success, in Tennyson's *Becket*, as
Shylock, and as the Master of Ravensworth in *The Bride of Lam-
mermoor*, to name only a few of his famous roles, he was magnificent. Ellen Terry was at her best in such parts as Portia and
Beatrice: never have I seen such rippling grace on the stage in

England or elsewhere. Tragedy was beyond her, and it was a mistake to attempt Lady Macbeth. The fame of Ibsen was just beginning to reach London, and time was needed to discover his shining merits. I remember performances of *Hedda Gabler* and *The Doll's House* when the audience was small and cold. *Ghosts* we were forbidden by the Lord Chamberlain to see till many years later.

I had no party colour till I settled down in Cambridge, when I realized that my sympathies were in the Liberal camp. My father, like most City men, had followed Gladstone till he began to advocate Home Rule. Henceforth my parents, my relatives and our visitors were either Conservatives or Liberal Unionists, the latter soon to become indistinguishable from the former. After the defection of Bright, Chamberlain and the Whigs the Liberal party had to be rebuilt, a process gravely retarded by agrarian outrages and boycotting in Ireland and by the squalid divorce proceedings of Parnell. For the last time in English history the sovereign took sides in a political controversy and made no attempt to conceal her political and personal dislike of the Grand Old Man. I have lived through three periods of almost pathological party strife—the opening phase of the Home Rule struggle, the polemics of the South African War, and the Lloyd George budget of 1909, in all of which social relations were strained. In the field of foreign affairs we thought of Germany, Austria and Italy as friends, France and Russia as potential foes. The United States, anchored in its traditional isolationism, seemed too far away to count for much in the fortunes of the Old World. I was nurtured on *The Times* and *Punch*, then and now regarded as national institutions. No evening or Sunday paper ever entered the house.

In the latter part of my time at King's I began in a boyish way to think about life. Tolstoi's trilogy, *My Religion*, *My Confession*, and *What to do*, stirred me more than anything except *Sartor Resartus*. Edwin Arnold's *Light of Asia* introduced me to Buddhism, and a Theosophical friend took me to the headquarters of the Society in Hampstead where I heard Annie Besant lecture for the first time. I read Renan's *Vie de Jésus*, the weakest as well as the most famous of his books, and Strauss's *Life of Christ*, but neither the sentimentalism of the one nor the chilly rationalism of the other brought satisfaction. I preferred the deeper notes of Seeley's *Ecce Homo* and the reflective poems of Matthew Arnold. Regular church-going and family prayers were still the rule in households like ours, but under the impact of Darwinism and the study of comparative religion the dogmatic crust was beginning to crack. I sometimes attended a church in Marylebone where Haweis, best known for his delightful writings on music and musicians, discoursed on subjects of the day. He was for many years a leading figure in the Broad Church world, and his lecture-sermons on new books and thinkers attracted the same sort of undenominational congregation as that which later flocked to hear Dr. Campbell at the City Temple. My horizon was widening, and in my eighteenth year I was ready for a new flight. My three years at King's had been a period of untroubled happiness, and I think of the College which was later good enough to make me an Honorary Fellow with affectionate gratitude.

2

CAMBRIDGE IN THE NINETIES

HAVING passed the 'Little-Go', which in those remote days included a play of Euripides and Paley's *Evidences of Christianity*, I entered the greatest college in the world in 1891. Christ's is proud of Milton, St. John's of Wordsworth, Jesus of Coleridge, Peterhouse and Pembroke of Gray, Sidney of Cromwell; but Trinity College alone could proudly boast of such a galaxy as Bacon and Newton, Byron and Macaulay, Thackeray and Tennyson, to say nothing of the innumerable statesmen who had dreamed dreams and seen visions within its ancient walls. If the crowning architectural glory of Cambridge is the Chapel of King's, the Great Court of Trinity, with the gateway of its founder Henry VIII, the chapel and the dining hall, is not far behind.

The reign of Dr. Montagu Butler has been chronicled in a charming memoir by his distinguished son. Unlike other colleges, where the Master is chosen by the Fellows, Trinity is a Crown appointment. The most distinguished name on the list was Richard Bentley, greatest of England's classical scholars. The omniscient Whewell—philosopher, scientist, historian, divine— had been the outstanding figure not only in Trinity but in the University during the first half of the Victorian era. Thompson his successor, Regius Professor of Greek, was remembered for his caustic wit. The sharpest of his arrows—'We are none of us infallible, not even the youngest'—was aimed at Gerald Balfour, whose academic career was much more distinguished than that of his brother Arthur. No greater contrast could be imagined between that formidable censor of human frailties and the kindly old man of benevolent aspect and gentle voice who followed him in the Master's Lodge. After ruling Harrow for a quarter of a century, Butler returned to his old College in 1886. The statutes of 1882 abolished the rule that the Master must be a clergyman, and some of the Fellows would have preferred Lord Rayleigh the physicist or Henry Sidgwick the philosopher. The latter described the appointment as 'a snub to academic work'. Though Butler was a brilliant classical scholar he was not an academic star of the first magnitude.

The wisdom of the choice was vindicated in the thirty-two years of his rule. No Master of Trinity—perhaps no Master of any Cambridge College—has been so beloved. If to reserved natures he sometimes appeared a trifle effusive, his friends were aware that his gracious manner was the natural expression of a loving heart. He was a great gentleman of the old school. He looked older than his years, and we regarded him not merely as our head but as the father of the College. It used to be said with humorous exaggeration that he would shake hands with the humblest undergraduate as if the trembling youth were the only friend he had in the world; and though he enjoyed the society of celebrities he was unstinting in encouragement to starters in the race. He showed me unfailing kindness, ever ready to congratulate when academic honours came my way. Though his heart was in the classics, he had a fair knowledge of English political history since Chatham and Burke. His sermons were simple in structure, exquisitely delivered and carefully phrased. He was perhaps the most polished after-dinner speaker of his time except Rosebery. He was at his best as a host discoursing on the portraits and traditions of the Master's Lodge. His second marriage in 1888 to Miss Ramsay, who had been placed alone in the first division of the first class of the Classical Tripos in the previous year, had brought him a new spring-time and filled his stately home with the prattle of happy children.

It was exciting for a newcomer to view the celebrities in Hall or Chapel. Aldis Wright, Vice-Master, Senior Bursar and editor of the *Cambridge Shakespeare*, was dignified but remote. Philosophy was strongly represented by Sidgwick, James Ward and Mac-Taggart, all three belonging to different schools of thought, classics by Henry Jackson and Verrall, mathematics by Cayley and Forsyth, science by J. J. Thomson who was destined to succeed Butler in the Master's Lodge. Attendance at Chapel was required on Sunday and twice in the week, and markers stood at the entrance like division clerks in the House of Commons. If the record was unsatisfactory, the recalcitrant was summoned to the rooms of the Senior or Junior Dean, both of them clergymen, where a discussion of intellectual difficulties sometimes ensued.

The provision for students of history at Trinity was meagre. Though there were sixty Fellows, not a single historian had been admitted into that circle of the elect: even the illustrious Maitland had tried and failed. The Historical Tripos dated only from 1875, and the claim of classics and mathematics to the lion's share of the spoils was unchallenged. Our Director of Studies was a classical scholar whose acquaintance with events after the fall of the Roman Empire was far from profound. Except for being advised to attend certain lectures we were left to ourselves. There was no *Seminar* and we were not taught to write essays. The only test of our progress was to be found in the college examinations at the end of our first and second year and in the University Tripos at the end of the third which procured a degree. My 'Tutor' or academic guardian played an even smaller part than the Director of Studies, and our relations were confined to a formal breakfast party once a year. His principal task was to forward the College bills to our parents.

The leader of historical studies in Trinity was Cunningham, whose *Growth of English Industry and Commerce* was published in 1882 and repeatedly revised. A mass of information was contained in his stout volumes, and he shared with Thorold Rogers the distinction of inaugurating the study of economic history in the British Isles; but he lacked charm of style and skill in arrangement, and we lamented that Ashley's delightful survey never advanced beyond the Middle Ages. For two years I sat at his feet: no other subject except English Constitutional History was so intensively studied. He had no sympathy with the Free Trade and *laissez-faire* doctrines of Victorian liberalism, and he used to quote with gusto Adam Smith's famous aphorism: 'Defence is greater than opulence'. Like Ashley he had much in common with the German School of List, Roscher and Schmoller. When Chamberlain unfurled the banner of Tariff Reform in 1903 Cunningham, unlike most of our economic oracles, rallied to his support. Though I shared neither his political nor his economic views, I was indebted to him for his writings, lectures and personal kindness.

I approached economic problems from a different angle in a course of lectures by Alfred Marshall, whom Keynes described as our greatest economist since Adam Smith. The Professor of Political Economy was a Liberal and a Free Trader and, like Ricardo, Mill and Jevons, regarded economics as an independent science rather than a branch of statecraft. Economic theory formed no part of the Historical Tripos, except in so far as the study of economic history involved some acquaintance with the development of ideas; but I realized that a theoretical grounding was essential to an understanding of concrete questions. Marshall's massive *Principles of Economics* was a hard nut to crack but well worth the effort. Though I was not a member of his flock he received me in his home with his usual kindness. He was a great citizen no less than an eminent thinker, and generations of students derived inspiration from his teaching.

The dominating figure in the Cambridge historical world was the Regius Professor of Modern History. Though the Chair had been founded in 1724 no expert held the post till 1869 when, on Kingsley's resignation, it was offered by Gladstone to Seeley. He had gained notoriety as the author of *Ecce Homo* and had been Professor of Latin at University College, London; but he was a diligent student of history, and his twenty-five years at Cambridge won for it a place equal in status to the older studies. His utilitarian view resembled that of the founders of the Professorship. 'Why should history be studied?' he asked in his Inaugural. 'Because it is the school of statesmanship. Our University is and must be a seminary of politicians.' It was much the same gospel that Freeman was proclaiming from the sister Chair at Oxford: 'History is past politics and politics is present history.' This limited conception was not due to a narrow range of interest, for Seeley was a man of varied erudition; but he believed in the division of labour and reserved for the historian the political aspect of the story of mankind. His dominant interest was the rise and fall of modern states and their relations to one another. His most ambitious effort, *The Life and Times of Stein*, presented the Napoleonic era from a new angle, and invited admiration for Prussia's heroic struggle against her oppressor. Its reception was disappointing, but the two courses on *The Expansion of England* published in 1884 carried his name across the world. Victorians were at last waking up to the importance of their colonies, and the book ranks with Dilke's *Greater Britain* as a political event. As the Regius Professor had only to deliver one lecture a week, it was customary to write out his discourse. He loved large surveys, international problems, comprehensive generalizations. In the lectures on the struggle with Louis XIV to which I listened, and in *The Growth of British Policy*, to which he devoted his closing years, he made us visualize the diplomatic unity of Europe as no one except Ranke had done. He believed that the fortunes of a state depended less on its institutions than on its place in the world.

Seeley was eager to train the minds of his students. It was mainly owing to his initiative that Political Science had been included in the curriculum of the Historical Tripos, and he held conversation classes in his own house. It was not a *Seminar*, for we were given no texts to study and no paper work: students had merely to walk into his dining-room on a certain morning in the week. The numbers were small, most of us were rather shy, and the Professor was a weary old man; but there was no lack of grip, no waning of his contempt for slovenly thinking. He employed the Socratic method, and we were invited to explain precisely what we meant by the State, Liberty, Equality, Democracy and other elastic terms. Then we were cross-examined, and finally he would state his own views. It was a searching discipline at a time of life when the student is apt to run before he can walk. He never established the delightful relations with students which made Acton's Professorship memorable in many lives, but we all felt his power. Though his view of history was far too narrow to satisfy my demands, I owe him gratitude for his endeavour to relate learning to citizenship.

English Constitutional History was taught by George (later Sir George) Prothero of King's and James Tanner of St. John's. The former had studied under Sybel at Bonn, had written a life of Simon de Montfort, was preparing his selection of Constitutional Documents of Elizabeth and James I, and was editing the *Cambridge Historical Series* which was designed to cover the world of the last four centuries. In 1894 he accepted a Professorship at Edinburgh and a few years later became Editor of the

Quarterly Review. His lectures were clear and business-like, and he honoured me with a friendship which lasted till his death. Tanner's lectures were more colourful, for they were carefully phrased and were read with dramatic effect. He was at his best on the constitutional struggles of the seventeenth century and was beginning his researches on Pepys which prepared the way for Sir Arthur Bryant. Hallam's *Constitutional History*, from which Queen Victoria and the Prince Consort learned the duties of an English sovereign, I had studied at King's. Now I learned to reverence Stubbs, not only in his masterpiece and in the *Select Charters* but in his illuminating Introductions to our medieval chronicles in the Rolls series. For the later centuries we read Erskine May, then and now the supreme authority on Parliamentary procedure. The classical treatises of Bagehot, Anson and Dicey explained the underlying assumptions of the Victorian era which witnessed the simultaneous decline of the power of the Crown and the House of Lords. After mastering British interpretations it was a stimulating experience to grapple with Gneist, the great German jurist, and to note his admiration for our system of local government by unpaid country gentlemen, a conception unfamiliar to bureaucratic Germany.

Political Science formed an essential portion of our curriculum, and there was none in which I took keener delight. Our instructor was a man who wrote next to nothing but was a suggestive teacher. I digested the classics of political science from Plato and Aristotle to Machiavelli and Hobbes, Locke and Montesquieu, Rousseau and Burke, Bentham and Mill. Neither Fitzjames Stephen's slashing attack *Liberty, Equality, Fraternity*, nor Maine's *Essays on Popular Government* shattered my allegiance to the thoughtful Liberalism of which Mill was the oracle, for I have always remained more apprehensive of the dangers of the concentration than of the fragmentation of power. Systematic instruction in European history was unknown, a glaring defect long since remedied. Partial compensation was found in Special Subjects, which were changed every few years and from which the student could make his choice. I seized the opportunity of boring holes into the Middle Ages. My first selected period was the age of Theodoric and Justinian, illumined by the voluminous eyewitness records of Procopius. My second special subject was

Germany after the collapse of the Carolingian Empire. There is no quicker road into the heart of the Middle Ages than in such intensive study of the political institutions, social life and ideology of selected periods with the aid of contemporary authorities.

In the summer of 1894 I was placed in the first class of the Historical Tripos and decided to stay on for a fourth year. Much as I had enjoyed my undergraduate days, the zest and profit of the final stage surpassed them. I saw more of the Master and the Fellows, and it was my duty as a Major Scholar to take my turn in reading the lessons in chapel. Holders of major scholarships were also invited to the annual Commemoration Feast, and the festivities of 1894 were graced by the presence of Harcourt, himself a Trinity man, and Goschen. The past and present Chancellors of the Exchequer spoke well, but the Master carried off the prize. His dignity and benignity found a worthy setting in the glorious old hall built, like my rooms in the Great Court, while Shakespeare and Bacon were alive.

My chief task was in reading for the annual Lightfoot prize in ecclesiastical history, the examination for which took place during the summer term of 1895. Theological students still spoke with awe of the great Cambridge triumvirate, Lightfoot, Westcott and Hort; and the greatest of the three was Lightfoot, editor of *The Apostolic Fathers* and Bishop of Durham. The prize of £100 which commemorated his association with the University was designed to encourage the study of Church history; and indeed the programme was comprehensive enough to satisfy the keenest appetite, combining as it did a working knowledge of the whole field with intensive study of two selected periods. Reading Gibbon from the first page to the last I discovered that the first half is incomparably finer than the second, that the further he moves away from Imperial Rome the weaker he becomes, that the mysticism and ecstasies of the medieval Church were a riddle to him and the later Byzantine Empire a bore. It was equally obvious that the chapters on the Antonines, Constantine, Julian, Justinian and Mohammed are as immortal as Thucydides and Tacitus, that the plan of building a bridge from the old world to the new was an inspiration, and that his style is a perpetual delight. The nine volumes of Milman's *History of Latin Christianity*, in comparison, lacked distinction, but the edifice was solidly built. The Dean of St. Paul's was more of a statesman than a theologian, and he envisaged the Church as an institution rather than, like Neander, an instrument for the winning of souls. Bishop Creighton's *History of the Papacy at the close of the Middle Ages* was no less impressive in its cool detachment and sound scholarship. Ranke's *History of the Popes* and *The Reformation Era in Germany* taught me to understand why he was reckoned the greatest of the professionals, as Gibbon remains the greatest of the amateurs.

I was fortunate in the special subjects selected for intensive study. The reign of Constantine was one of the decisive moments of history, when the victorious Emperor adopted Christianity and transferred the capital of the Roman Empire, while the Council of Nicaea formulated the creed under which Christendom has lived ever since. The chief sources were the historical narratives of the courtly Eusebius and the theological treatises of Athanasius himself, and I studied with equal diligence the chief guides through the labyrinth of the early heresies. Hefele's monumental *History of the Councils* and Harnack's *History of Dogma* increased my respect for German scholarship. I enjoyed Newman's early work on the Arians and his less known but more profound analyses in his *Select Treatises of Athanasius*.

The second special subject was religious life and thought in the England of Bishop Butler and John Wesley. I plunged into the *Analogy of Natural and Revealed Religion*, of which the younger Pitt declared that it raised more doubts than it solved, and which, however we react to the argument, must impress every reader by its power and sincerity. The *Sermons*, hardly less striking in their unadorned simplicity, have their place not only among theological classics but in the literature of ethics. The Deist controversy, which formed the starting point of his apologetics and was as much a philosophical as a theological issue, had been fully described in Leslie Stephen's *English Thought in the Eighteenth Century*, the most enduring of his many works. Wesley was a simpler theme, best approached through his journal and sermons. I won the prize, and the principal examiner was kind enough to say in his whimsical way: 'You make a good Lightfoot scholar: we are not ashamed of you.'

Next to my studies in Church history, none of the occupations of my fourth year proved more stimulating than MacTaggart's lectures on Hegel. I knew the latter's *Philosophy of History*, which is full of suggestive ideas, but I had never attempted his purely philosophical treatises. Our leading British Hegelian announced a course on the *Logic* to be held in his own rooms. Half a dozen of us, including his future biographer, Lowes Dickinson, sat round the table with a translation of the smaller *Logic* in front of us, while the lecturer had the larger *Logic* open before him in German for reference in case of need. The *Logic* is a majestic structure, and the dialectic process—from thesis to antithesis and synthesis—carries us steadily forward from the first simple category of Being to the distant goal of Absolute Spirit. Few people nowadays trouble about the Hegelian dialectic, but his application of the conception of development to various departments of thought proved an inspiration to workers in many fields. In a striking essay entitled *Darwin and Hegel* Ritchie worked out the relationship between the two very different men who had done most to popularize the idea. Though I never enlisted under the Hegelian banner I was attracted to the philosophic idealism which, deriving for the most part from Kant and Hegel, dominated British Universities during the closing years of the century. I was born just early enough to breathe the cool dry air of mid-Victorian empiricism associated with the names of Mill, Herbert Spencer, Lewes and Bain, but by 1895 their reign was almost over. I had been impressed by the broad sweep of Spencer's *First Principles* and interested by his writings on ethics and political science, education and sociology, but he knew nothing about metaphysics. A remarkable transformation occurred when the teaching of Kant and Hegel reached our shores in the closing decades of the century. Idealism once again raised its head in the writings of T. H. Green, John and Edward Caird, Bradley, Bosanquet, James Ward, Andrew Seth and MacTaggart. I owed something to them all, but the books that made the deepest impression on me were Green's *Prolegomena to Ethics* and Bradley's *Ethical Studies*, both of which covered a wider field than their titles suggest. Seth's searching criticisms of Hegel were a useful antidote to the enthusiasm of MacTaggart, and James Ward's treatise on Psychology unlocked a world to which the Associationists possessed no key. The New Realism of Bertrand Russell and George Moore was soon to invade the University Chairs, for philosophy is ever in a state of flux.

The outstanding personality in the Cambridge philosophical world was Henry Sidgwick, and the Professor of Moral Philosophy was perhaps the most distinguished figure in Trinity. To look at him, with his white hair, pink complexion, well-cut features and air of benevolent wisdom was to understand what the Greeks meant when they spoke of a man as *Kalos K'Agathos*, the combination of beauty and virtue. Like Leslie Stephen he had been a clerical Fellow under the old dispensation, but they had long ago given up their Orders and their orthodox beliefs. He disapproved the attitude of men like Rashdall who, though drifting far away from their old dogmatic moorings, remained officials of the Anglican Church. He was untouched by the idealist revival and cared little for metaphysics. *The Methods of Ethics*, the best of his books, was as powerful an exposition of empiricism as Bradley's *Ethical Studies* of the rival intuitionist creed, but his *History of Ethics* revealed a curious blindness to the significance of idealist interpretations. Lacking wings of his own he distrusted those who soared into the sky. His treatise on Political Economy did not compare in originality with Jevons and Marshall, and his *Elements of Politics*, which we diligently studied for our course on Political Science, struck me as rather thin. He was better to read than to hear, for his stammer was incurable; but when he read a paper at the Moral Science Club I was relieved to notice his lack of embarrassment. Mrs. Sidgwick, the gifted sister of Arthur Balfour, was his intellectual comrade. Their services to the cause of women's university education were beyond praise, and the Psychical Research Society owed much to their support. Since the Creightons left Cambridge there was no such distinguished couple as the Mistress of Newnham and her husband.

For a young man with a healthy appetite there was an almost bewildering choice of fare among the lectures or courses of distinguished visitors. Among the former Creighton's Rede Lecture in the Senate House on Aeneas Sylvius, Pope Pius II, was perhaps the most striking. Though the Professor of Ecclesiastical History had become a Bishop, he remained a zealous humanist to the end. He would have felt quite at home with

Erasmus and the scholars of the Renaissance, and he had as little use for Luther as for Rome. Another visiting lecturer much to my taste was Edward Dowden, who delivered the Clark Lectures on English Literature. His subject was *The French Revolution in English Literature*, and the six discourses appeared shortly after in one of the best of his books. I was in my Shelley phase, and I delighted in his full-length biography of the most ethereal of our poets. The lectures on the Lake poets in their hot youth, Burke and Godwin, were skilful interpretations. Dowden stood midway between literary critics like Gosse and Saintsbury, who cared most for form, and the more philosophic school of Matthew Arnold and Leslie Stephen whose deepest interest was in personality and ideas.

The University Sermon was delivered by a different preacher every Sunday afternoon in Great St. Mary's at two o'clock. It was impossible to fill the pulpit every week with supermen, for there were not enough to go round; but in the course of four years I formed a fair notion of what was going on in the Anglican Church —High, Low and Broad. If Bishop Lightfoot used to instruct his prospective hosts to look out for the ugliest face on the railway platform, Westcott, his successor at Durham, had he not been the humblest of men, might have bidden them seek the most spiritual countenance they ever knew. While Dante was said to look as if he had been in hell, Westcott might well have seen the Holy Grail. Next in impressiveness in the pulpit was Gore, then at the height of his fame as leader of the younger High Churchmen. Though he had frightened Liddon by his theology, he came to rank as a pillar of orthodoxy and to accept a bishopric. I had read *Lux Mundi*, which had made such a stir a year or two earlier, and his Brampton Lectures on the Incarnation; and, like everyone else, I felt his flaming sincerity and profound piety. I was less impressed by Farrar, whose sermons were overloaded with adjectives. He had been for a generation the best-seller among Anglican divines, but his sermons, which filled Westminster Abbey, struck me as lacking the highest distinction. My first sight of General Booth, looking like an Old Testament patriarch, was at a Salvation Army service in the Town Hall.

For a hundred years active politicians have visited Oxford and Cambridge to put their case before the debating societies or to encourage their disciples in the party associations. The most impressive of such birds of passage during my time was John Redmond, who spoke at the Union in favour of Home Rule while the Bill was ploughing its weary way through Parliament in 1893. Though at that time merely the leader of the little Parnellite group on the Irish benches, he could speak for Irish nationalism with no less authority than Dillon, O'Brien or Tim Healy; but though he made a deep impression on his audience, the motion for Home Rule was lost, for 'the senior partner', as Rosebery described England, remained predominantly Unionist till after the First World War. After the Celtic eloquence of a born orator Lord Ripon's address to the Liberal Club was a very tame performance. The Colonial Secretary was nearly seventy, the oldest member of the fourth Gladstone Cabinet after the octogenarian Premier himself, and he seemed to have lost his elasticity. Among younger Liberals Haldane and George Russell, of whom I was to see a good deal in later years, were welcome visitors. The former, still a private member, was rapidly moving into the front rank. His interest in German philosophy was well known, and I met him for the first time in the congenial atmosphere of Henry Sidgwick's rooms. George Russell, justly proud of the greatest of Whig families, was the author of the best short biography of his hero Gladstone and an accomplished raconteur, many of whose anecdotes appeared in his delightful *Collections and Recollections*. His chief concern was the plight of the Christian subjects of the Sultan. His heart was in religion rather than party warfare, and after 1895, on losing his seat, he exchanged politics for literature. No Liberal visitor produced such a flutter as Sir Charles Dilke, and the invitation brought protests and resignations from some of our Cambridge Liberals. I felt no temptation to follow their example, for after several years in the political wilderness he had returned to Parliament. His permanent exclusion from office seemed a sufficient penalty to those who believed in his guilt, and he remained a conspicuous figure in the House, a specialist alike in Imperial, foreign and domestic affairs. His speech, though packed with information, lacked colour and charm. Ten years later, as a young Member of Parliament, I learned to appreciate his kindness and his unflagging zeal for the oppressed at home and abroad.

In the early nineties England was ruled by the middle class, and the Labour movement was in its infancy. There was therefore a certain thrill in hearing authentic tidings from leaders of the army that was soon to march on to the stage. In England as else-where Socialism was formulated by bourgeois thinkers long before it was adopted and proclaimed by a political party. Having read the *Fabian Essays* I was interested to see and hear Sidney and Beatrice Webb, then newly married, at a little meeting in the rooms of a Professor. I was struck by their robust self-confidence and the tireless efficiency of their brains. They made a striking couple in the identity of their ideas and the difference of their persona-lities, and the firm of Webb was to leave an enduring mark on our ideology and institutions. A greater thrill was provided when Tom Mann, at that time one of the leading spirits of the 'New Unionism', addressed a large meeting in the hall of King's. His later career was an anti-climax, for he was passed in the race by Keir Hardie and other men of more solid qualities; but in the early nineties he was a very live wire and could hold his audience.

My first visit to Parliament was in 1893 when the Home Rule Bill was in Committee, and I was lucky enough to hear Gladstone intervene. He was eighty-four, and I was struck by his extreme fragility. The voice had lost its resonance, and it was difficult to catch every word in the Strangers' Gallery; but I am glad to have seen the Grand Old Man in the last of his sixty sessions. Within a year he resigned, after uttering a warning to the House of Lords, and Rosebery took his place. The latter's life had been roses, roses all the way. He was welcomed with plaudits by his party, with respect by the Opposition, and with an audible sigh of relief at Windsor, but the honeymoon was soon over. At an Eighty Club reception in London I was struck by his youthful appearance at the age of forty-eight and the lack of colour in his eyes.

My University years produced a fair crop of celebrities, and I had the good fortune to know most of the winners. The greatest was General Smuts, then a slim, reserved, thoughtful student at Christ's, which he loved and revisited to the end of his days. He kept close to his work, and his performance in the Law Tripos was the talk of the University. He was not easy to know well, and nobody expected him to win fame as soldier, statesman and philosopher. In my own College George Trevelyan, later Regius

Professor of Modern History and Master of Trinity, followed in the literary footsteps of his father and his father's celebrated uncle. A great worker, reader and walker, he overflowed with physical and mental vitality, loving poetry not less than history. He was to pay his debt many years later in his brief Autobiography and in his little volume on the history of the College. Bertrand Russell, philosopher and mathematician, displayed a maturity that marked him out among his contemporaries. His friend George Moore, afterwards Professor of Philosophy and author of *Principia Ethica*, possessed a mind with no less keen an edge and was soon to influence Keynes and a host of lesser men. All four—Smuts, Trevelyan, Russell and Moore—were destined to receive the Order of Merit.

Other friends seemed equally likely to make their name. Maurice Amos, later Sir Maurice, legal adviser to the Egyptian Government, who entered Trinity at the same time as myself, chose the History Tripos, but after a few weeks he transferred his allegiance to Moral Science in which he found more scope for his nimble brain. A formidable debater, he was more mature when he came up than most of us, for he had escaped the dull routine of the Public School. His father's connection with Egypt decided his career, but what was gained by law was lost to philosophy. Equally unexpected was the evolution of Barnes, the future Bishop of Birmingham, pugnacious champion of the Modernists and hammer of the Anglo-Catholics, from the quiet mathematical student for whom a Professorship seemed the likeliest destiny. An even greater surprise was in store for the friends of Andrews, a classical scholar of Pembroke. The son of an Irvingite Minister, his ardent spirit was kindled by the idealism of Westcott, Scott Holland and Gore who combined High Church sympathies with democratic convictions, had recently launched the Christian Social Movement, and proclaimed their gospel in the little monthly *Commonwealth*. On taking Orders he plunged into the slums of South London as head of the Pembroke College Mission and a few years later joined the Cambridge Mission to Delhi. Little did he or I imagine that the East would lay such a spell upon him as to wean him from his Church and Trinitarian creed. Charlie Andrews, as he was familiarly known in three continents, became a teacher in the Bengal school of Tagore, the champion of the rights of Indians in Africa and the Fiji Islands, and in later years the bosom friend of Gandhi. At the close of his life he described his spiritual pilgrimage in his striking book *What I Owe to Christ*. No Englishman of our time won so much of the affectionate confidence of Indians, and no one with a white skin ever loved them more. It was a triumph of personality, which enabled the friend of the two greatest Indians of their generation to win the respect of successive Viceroys.

I can only refer to a few other friends and acquaintances who were to make their name. Edmund Whittaker, later Sir Edmund, who had come up to Trinity from a Scottish Grammar School and won a mathematical Fellowship at his first attempt, was appointed Royal Astronomer of Ireland at the age of thirty-three and became one of our leading physicists. Frederick Lawrence, a friend from Eton days, who added the name of Pethick after his marriage, had a *flair* for mathematics and economics, entered Parliament, accepted a peerage, and as Secretary of State for India in the third Labour Government shared in the courageous decision in 1947 to terminate British rule after nearly three and a half centuries. I must close the list of Cambridge friends with Professor Hearnshaw, historian and publicist; Professor Sir John Clapham, our leading economic historian and President of the British Academy; Bertram Hopkinson, later Professor of Engineering and a civilian victim of the First World War; Charles Roden Buxton, inheritor of the passion for service which has distinguished his family for generations; and John Cowper Powys, the West country novelist, who recalls our lively talks on literature in his autobiography. 'Eddie' Marsh, later Sir Edward, patron of poets and painters, was a classical scholar of Trinity, but his heart was in English and French literature.

Since the three academic terms only account for half the year, the Long Vacation plays its part in the University years, and I visited the shrines of some of the Immortals. It was a delight to hear *Parsifal* at Bayreuth at a time when the Master had been dead for a decade, and Cosima, Liszt's clever daughter, was still active; his imperious spirit seemed to brood over the old town with its memories of Wilhelmina, favourite sister of Frederick the Great. Despite Nietzsche's complaint that he had become soft in his old age, and that the Christian accents of *Parsifal* were a deplorable reaction from the healthy realism of the *Meistersinger* and the paganism of the *Ring*, I never doubted that his last work deserved its enduring fame. The performances went with a swing, and though I have seen the operas elsewhere, they produced their maximum effect in the Festspielhaus built for him by King Ludwig of Bavaria of tragic memory.

Next to Bayreuth no place of pilgrimage in my University years was more inspiring than Weimar. Carlyle had led me to Goethe, and his life by Lewes was one of my favourite biographies. Eckermann's *Conversations* were and still are my companion. *Faust* I only knew in the English versions which convey the story but not the magic. Carlyle's translation of *Wilhelm Meister* accompanied me, but despite purple patches I enjoyed it less than *Werther*, and I understood why Niebuhr described it as a menagerie of tame animals. Goethe's house had recently been opened to the public after the death of his youngest grandson in 1887, and it was only sixty years since he had passed away. The portraits of his friends round the walls brought the Augustan age of German literature to life, and the venerable grandson of Karl August ruled the little Duchy from the neighbouring Schloss. Jena spoke to me of Schiller, the Wartburg of Luther. At Ferney I went over the home of Voltaire's old age, and read the celebrated inscription on the Church—*Deo erexit Voltaire*.

My four years at Trinity passed like a sunny day in spring. Though the joys of the mind are ageless the first rapture can never recur. When I arrived I was already in love with history and literature and had begun to explore the world of ideas. When I left I knew something of the imperishable achievements of the human spirit in many fields. For two years more my Alma Mater occupied a leading place in my thoughts. I was awarded the University essay prize when the subject was Daniel Defoe. The author of *Robinson Crusoe*—novelist, pamphleteer, historian, poet, moralist—is one of the most voluminous writers in our literature. The novels—*Moll Flanders*, *Roxana* and the rest—were available in Bohn's Library; and the more popular miscellaneous writings, such as the *Essay on Projects* and the *History of the Plague*, were obtainable in one or other of the cheap series which sprouted in the closing years of the century. Larger works such as the *History of the Union with Scotland* and *History of the Devil* were on the shelves of the London Library, while *The Review*, a periodical written almost entirely by his own untiring hand, had to be studied in the British Museum. The Member's Prize—so called because the thirty pounds were provided by the two Members for the University—was expended on books chosen by the winner, handsomely bound and stamped with the University arms.

In 1897 my book *English Democratic Ideas in the Seventeenth Century*, which won a prize named after Bishop Thirlwall, the historian of Greece, was presented before publication as a Dissertation for a Trinity Fellowship. I had been encouraged by the College authorities to compete, though no Fellowship had as yet been awarded to a student of history. In addition to the Dissertation we were examined in Moral Science and in a Special Subject of our choice. For the former we were expected to master a number of solid works including Mill's *Logic* and *Political Economy*. For the latter I chose the reign of the Emperor Barbarossa. The task of adjudication in a large College like Trinity is exceptionally difficult since the experts who speak with authority on candidates in their own field know nothing either of the subjects or the merits of the rest. In 1897 the two vacancies were filled by a mathematician and a physiologist, the future Lord Pethick-Lawrence and Sir Walter Morley Fletcher. I was told that if a third Fellowship had been available it would have fallen to me, and that I was supported by the Master, Lord Acton and Henry Sidgwick. In a report to Dr. Butler Acton was good enough to say that he thought not only highly of my Dissertation but very highly indeed. It was a disappointment at the time, but in the light of subsequent events I can only rejoice. Anchored in Cambridge I should have enjoyed an academic career to the full, but I should have missed the wider opportunities and experiences of London life. A year later George Trevelyan secured the first History Fellowship at Trinity with *England in the Age of Wycliffe*, and henceforth students of history have had a fair chance. Many years later my beloved College enrolled me among its Honorary Fellows at the same time as my distinguished contemporary Vaughan Williams.

3

BERLIN IN THE NINETIES

I FIRST trod German soil in 1889 on returning from Italy through Munich and the Rhineland from Strasbourg to Cologne. A second visit in 1894 took me to three famous shrines, Weimar, the Wartburg and Bayreuth. A third and longer sojourn followed in 1895, when I attended lectures in the University of Berlin. I told my teacher that I wished to pick up grammar and syntax as I went along. We started with *Wilhelm Tell*, for Schiller is easier for beginners than the ordinary novel with its innumerable nouns, and the splendid rhetoric carries one along. *Faust* was a harder nut to crack. I discovered that the translations reproduced the splendour of the original as little as a plaster cast conveys the full message of Pheidias and Praxiteles. Poetry is the magic of words, and the magic evaporates when the mould is broken. Compared with *Faust* the newspapers were simple enough, and I was soon ready for the adventure that had beckoned me to the capital.

'Your Majesty,' observed Hardenberg to Frederick William III when the yoke of Napoleon lay heavy on Prussia, 'we must make up in spiritual values what we have lost on the material plane.' The new University fostered the national revival which culminated in the War of Liberation. The spacious palace in the Linden of Prince Henry, the gifted brother of Frederick the Great, stood ready for use, for its childless owner had died in 1806. The project was launched by Wilhelm von Humboldt, the greatest Education Minister of whom Prussia or Germany can boast, and from 1810 till the coming of Hitler it possessed a staff without a rival in the world. To teachers and students alike academic freedom is the breath of life. Its growth may be studied in the monumental history by Lenz and in Harnack's bicentenary record of the Prussian Academy.

As my time in Berlin, which was limited to three months, was too short to specialize, I sampled the celebrities. Since Ranke and Droysen had died in 1886 and Mommsen had ceased to lecture, the lion of the historical department was Treitschke, 'the Bismarck of the chair'. He had espoused the Prussian cause with a crusader's conviction in the war of 1866, and he would have preferred a unitary solution of the German problem to the federal structure which Bismarck inherited and transformed. Though he was only sixty-one he was an almost legendary figure, seeming to embody the triumphs and exaltation of the heroic age. He looked more like a man of action, as indeed he was, than a Professor. His enormous head and flashing eyes rendered him a conspicuous figure in any gathering, and his class-room was crowded with students who had come to see him as much as to learn. The most brilliant of German historians, past or present, was a disappointing lecturer and for a foreigner difficult to understand, since he had been deaf since childhood. His strident discourses on *Politik*, published after his death from his notes and the reports of his pupils, appeared in English dress during the First World War with a critical introduction by Lord Balfour. I was only just in time for he died in the following year, leaving his monumental *History of Germany in the Nineteenth Century* unfinished. The German Macaulay confessed that his blood was too hot for the work of a historian, and it was deafness alone which debarred him from following his father into the Saxon army. A materialist in his worship of force, he was an idealist in his devotion to his country, for which he would have been proud to lay down his life. W. H. Dawson, author of instructive works on modern Germany, who attended his lectures a little earlier, saw his eyes fill with tears when he spoke of patriotism. 'Treitschke,' reported Austen Chamberlain from Berlin in 1887, 'has opened to me a new side of the German character—a narrow-minded, proud, intolerant Prussian chauvinism. And the worst of it is that he is forming a school.' I too felt the emotional impact of the greatest and the last of the Prussian School, the most politically influential German scholar who ever lived.

Another veteran whom I was just in time to hear was Ernst

Curtius, author of the first readable history of Greece in the German tongue, in his eightieth year and too weak to stand up while lecturing. He had accompanied Otfried Müller to Greece in the thirties, and since the death of Boeckh he had been the Nestor of German Hellenists. Unlike Grote he was much more interested in culture than politics, and his idealization of the Athenian Commonwealth was soon to be toned down by Beloch. But his enthusiasm for classical literature and art was a spiritual asset in the iron age of Sadowa and Sedan, and the refined little figure with its snow-white hair seemed like a messenger from the city of the violet crown. He was lecturing on his excavations at Olympia of which the Hermes of Praxiteles was the supreme reward.

Among the younger Professors no one had climbed the ladder of fame so rapidly as Harnack. In his middle forties he gave an impression of limitless vitality. There was an excellent practice by which an Ordinary Professor on one day in the week delivered a lecture adapted to the needs of students of other faculties. In my *Semester* he had chosen the Lord's Prayer as the subject of his popular course, and he addressed the largest audience that I encountered in any class-room. My German was still too limited to seek out any of the celebrities at whose feet I sat, but on my next visit I brought an introduction from our common friend Bailey Saunders, the translator of his famous *Wesen des Christentums*. The impression derived from the spacious Aula was confirmed in the quiet of his library. Here was a man to whom every moment of the day was precious, and to whom life meant unresting endeavour. No German scholar since Mommsen has approached him in world-wide fame or surpassed him in the value of his work. Forty years later I enjoyed the admirable biography by his daughter.

To pass to the class-room of Pfleiderer was to breathe a more restful atmosphere. While Harnack was a man of the world, a friend of the Kaiser, a *persona grata* in political and diplomatic circles, a star performer at international congresses, Pfleiderer was content to be a scholar. I had admired his *History of the Philosophy of Religion since Spinoza* which had appeared in English dress, and I was happy to find him expounding his favourite Schleiermacher. On my next visit I brought an introduction from

Philip Wicksteed, theologian, Dante scholar and economist. He was then busy with his encyclopaedic survey of *Primitive Christianity*, in which he related the new faith to contemporary creeds. We talked of Harnack, for whose keen intellect and mastery of Christian origins he expressed admiration, adding that he possessed little knowledge of contemporary faiths.

Economics were authoritatively represented by the veterans Adolf Wagner and Gustav Schmoller. The former, on whose rather stodgy text-books generations of students had been reared, was a dour Prussian, whose lectures, for all their solid worth, lacked colour and verve. Schmoller, who came from the warmer south, had a livelier manner and a wider scope. Though the author of an encyclopaedic treatise on Political Economy, his most enduring work was accomplished in economic and administrative history and as an editor of the *Acta Borussica*. He was the oracle of the so-called Historical School, the antithesis of the *laissez-faire* liberalism of Brentano, and his *Seminar* turned out as many competent scholars as in earlier decades had sprung from the loins of Ranke and Sybel, Giesebrecht and Waitz. He summoned the State to show a vigorous lead in social reform, and in the early days of the Empire he had been denounced by Treitschke as a Socialist of the Chair. He replied in a spirited little book entitled *Der Kathedersozialismus*, in which he expounded the ideology which subsequently found expression in Bismarck's insurance legislation and is now known all over the world as the Welfare State.

None of the Professors except Treitschke looked so imposing as Gierke, the latest of the apostolic succession of German jurists which began with Eichhorn and Savigny and added the honoured names of Gneist, Ihering and Brunner as the century advanced. I have never seen a scholar's head at close quarters which created such an impression of Doric simplicity and strength. It was the perfect Nordic type of which the race fanatics such as Gobineau, Houston Stewart, Chamberlain and Rosenberg loved to dream. He spoke with deliberation, weighing thoughts and words. His profound interpretations of the political and legal ideas of the Middle Ages were conveyed to English readers by Maitland, from whom I carried a letter of introduction. In certain ways he seemed to belong to an earlier generation. A son of the north

German countryside, he disliked big cities. He thought with Carlyle that the most precious of the rights of man is the right to be firmly and wisely ruled, and he disliked Bülow's readiness to compromise with a democratic age. The latter used to say that Imperial Germany represented a happy blend of the hard Prussian north with the softer and more liberal south. Of such a fusion there was in the great jurist no trace.

A gentler and more modern type was represented by Paulsen, the leading philosopher of the University, who deserves the eulogy in Wickham Steed's *Through Thirty Years* and whose friendly welcome in response to an introduction from an old pupil I recall with gratitude. His book on Kant was the first German interpretation of the greatest of modern thinkers that I read; but he was not himself a strikingly original thinker, and his massive *Geschichte des gelehrten Unterrichts in Deutschland* is a more enduring monument than his well-known *System der Ethik*. Though none of the Berlin Professors could be called Liberals in the political sense, Paulsen was modern in his outlook; as patriotic as his colleagues, he was no slavish believer in the gospel of force. There was indeed no more wholesome influence in the academic world of Berlin than this large-hearted scholar.

The capital provided the opportunity to sample the press, to hear the leading preachers, to attend a session of the Reichstag, and to see the Kaiser. If in *Wissenschaft* the Germans were in the van, in political maturity they lagged far behind. Though the anti-socialist law of 1878 had lapsed in 1890, the Social Democrats under Liebknecht and Bebel were still regarded by the government as beyond the pale. *Vorwärts*, their official organ, was not on sale at the bookstalls of the State railways, and on the twenty-fifth anniversary of the battle of Sedan the ebullient ruler denounced a party numbering millions of his subjects as a traitorous gang. Except for a few of the leaders the members were working men from the towns of the Protestant north. Socialism was at least as distasteful to the *bourgeoisie* as to the nobility, the Junkers, the great industrialists and the Court. Moreover the gulf between the *laissez-faire* Radicals under Eugen Richter and the Socialists was too deep to form an effective Opposition. The triumphs of Bismarck had paralysed the Liberal party in Prussia, and the economic doctrines of its few survivors confined its appeal to the middle class. As a Gladstonian Liberal I found none of the parties to my taste.

Nothing so forcibly struck an English student of the political scene as the impotence of the Reichstag, irreverently described as a fig-leaf to cover the nakedness of autocracy. Though elected by manhood suffrage, it was limited in its functions and paralysed by the rivalries of its groups. The government floated complacently on the prestige of the Bismarckian era, and except among the Socialists there seemed little desire for a larger freedom. The middle class were much more interested in literature and the arts than in public affairs. In Bülow's phrase, the Germans were an unpolitical people. In a remarkable volume of lectures entitled *Regierung und Volkswille* Hans Delbrück, editor of the *Preussische Jahrbücher*, described the Bismarckian constitution as the ideal blend of a powerful executive with adult male suffrage, a free Press and Parliamentary control of finance. William II commanded neither the reverence nor the affection which his grandfather inspired, but his charm—when he cared to exercise it—and versatility were universally recognized. With Bismarck in sulky retirement at Friedrichsruh and the aged Hohenlohe in the Chancellor's Palace in the Wilhelmstrasse, the last of the Hohenzollerns had the stage to himself. Critics had to be careful about *lèse-majesté*, but Maximilian Harden, the most intrepid journalist of his time, helped to keep the waters moving. His pungent little weekly *Die Zukunft* was everywhere on sale, and I became a diligent reader. The *Vossische Zeitung*, commonly known as *Tante Voss*, the favourite organ of the middle-class Intelligentsia, was mildly—very mildly—liberal in politics but admirable in the cultural sphere. While the *Kreuz-Zeitung* voiced the views of the Junkers and *Germania* spoke for the Catholics, the *Berliner Tageblatt*—soon to reach its zenith under Theodor Wolff—catered for a left centre *clientèle*. The illustrated weeklies—the *Fliegende Blätter* and *Simplicissimus*—allowed themselves audacities which the dailies feared to display. The mutiplicity of parties suited the government which could always play them off against each other at the cost of some trifling concession, and none of the Chancellors was more skilful in the management of the Reichstag than the supple Bülow, always referred to as 'the eel' by Kiderlen, a rough-tongued Württemberger. The Reichstag debates struck me as a sham fight since the government could not be overthrown and could always get its way in the end, if necessary by a dissolution.

In addition to politics and *Wissenschaft*, Berlin had a stronger claim than any other German city to be called the home of the arts. Menzel, *die kleine Excellenz* as he was called from his diminutive stature, perhaps the greatest German painter since Holbein, might be seen in his favourite corner in a *café* on the Potsdamer Platz. Lenbach lived in Munich, but his superb portraits of Bismarck, Moltke and the old Emperor were familiar in the north. Joachim taught in the Hochschule at Charlottenburg, and I could enjoy his famous Quartet for a shilling or two. Weingartner was in the first blush of his fame as a conductor, and at the Opera a Wagner performance was to be heard almost every week. For a music-lover like myself Berlin was the Promised Land. The repertory at the Schauspielhaus included Goethe and Schiller, Lessing and Kleist, Grillparzer and Hebbel among the classics, while Gustav Freytag's *Die Journalisten*, the historical dramas of Wildenbruch who had Hohenzollern blood in his veins, and the problem plays of Wedekind were popular items. New pieces could be tested at the Deutsches Theater and the Lessing Theater.

The brightest stars in the literary firmament were Hauptmann and Sudermann, whose best work for the stage was done by the time they were forty. Hauptmann's *Die Weber*, a grim study of bygone strikes and starvation in his native Silesia, had flustered the authorities for a moment; but the patient workers needed the horrors and privations of the First World War to goad them into revolution. *Die Versunkene Glocke*, in a very different *genre*, was a favourite with romantic youth. There was no romance in Sudermann's tragedy of *Heimat* (better known as *Magda*), and *Johannisfeuer*, with the author's stark Ostpreussen background. Among foreign dramatists Ibsen reigned supreme years before London audiences took him to their heart. Oscar Wilde stood some way behind; Bernard Shaw reached the German stage only in the new century; Shakespeare was always in season. French plays were not often given, though the *Dame aux Camélias*, *La Tosca* and *L'Aiglon* were occasionally heard. Among novels Gustav Freytag's lengthy series *Die Ahnen*, so popular in the seventies and eighties, was losing its appeal as the epic of German unification became a memory, but *Soll und Haben* was still widely read. Fontane's Wanderings in the Mark were as popular as his evocation of the War of Liberation in *Vor dem Sturm*. Felix Dahn's *Ein Kampf um Rom* and Georg Ebers' *Eine Aegyptische Königstochter* stood together and without rivals among historical novels. In the field of poetry people were beginning to talk of Stefan George, and Nietzsche's *Zarathustra* was the bible of impetuous youth.

Though the Lutheran Church, like the Orthodox Church in Russia, seemed to the Social Democrats little more than a buttress of the political and economic *status quo*, there were some earnest men in the pulpits and the Inner Mission carried on its beneficent activities. The most remarkable of the Lutheran divines was Stöcker, who had won fame as the champion of a mild brand of Christian Socialism and had enjoyed the patronage of the Kaiser before his accession to the throne. His hour had been brief, for he slid into anti-Semitism. He was now little more than the shadow of his former self, but he remained an inspiring preacher, though his congregation was small. Very different was Dryander, the Court Chaplain, whose sermons were more conventional and whose church was always full. He was sometimes considered too much of a courtier, but his visits to the exile at Doorn many years later showed that he was not a mere fair-weather friend. His memoirs leave a pleasant impression, and it is a feather in his cap that he was *persona grata* both at Potsdam and Friedrichsruh. The Kaiser was a Liberal in theology, as he showed by his friendship with Harnack and in his remarkable declaration on Delitzsch's *Babel und Bibel*.

My three autumn months in Berlin in 1895 gave me an elementary knowledge of the people and institutions. I had begun to get the feel of the country, to learn how Germans looked at the world, to realize their energy and thoroughness, to note their pride in their new-found unity, their delight in their growing prosperity, their confidence in their embattled strength, their worship of efficiency, their zeal for education, their respect for learning, their strange indifference to politics and tacit acceptance of authoritarian rule. Above all I had lifted a corner of the veil from the inexhaustible treasure-house of German learning, the intensive exploration of which was to be one of the most rewarding occupations of my life. I left the capital a few days before the Jameson Raid and the Kruger telegram opened a new and unhappy chapter in Anglo-German relations. The founding of the Reich had been welcomed in England where France had never been a trusted friend. Now for the first time there was talk of war.

4

LORD ACTON

I HAVE sometimes been called Lord Acton's pupil, even—without any justification—his favourite pupil. If that flattering label is intended to indicate that I sat at his feet in my formative years and derived my conception of history from him, it is incorrect. I never saw him till the day I left Cambridge in 1895, when I had formed my own ideas without being particularly influenced by any of my teachers. If, on the other hand, my name is thus honourably associated with his, it is because none of my contemporaries received more personal kindness from him, none entertained a warmer admiration for his writings, and none shared with deeper conviction his hatred of coercion and regimentation from whatever quarter it might come—from an omnipotent state, an intolerant Church, or a Parliamentary majority. He had grateful debtors but not a single disciple. We differed, of course, in our religious beliefs, for there were no Catholics in the University; but he also differed in many ways from members of his own communion, and his closest English friends were found outside the Roman obedience. He was that *rara avis* a Catholic Liberal, fearlessly proclaiming his views on the limits of ecclesiastical authority, and exalting the individual Christian conscience above any institution as the final arbiter in public or private conduct. Anyone less resembling the principal converts among his English contemporaries it was impossible to conceive. Had he not been the child of Catholic parents this impenitent individualist would never have entered the totalitarian camp. While Newman accepted the Vatican Decrees reluctantly, and Ward and Manning greeted them with a cheer, Acton deplored the centralization of power. He never referred to this painful topic and of course we never brought it up. In his two courses of Cambridge lectures there is not a word to indicate the communion to which he belonged. So far from feeling like a fish out of water in a Protestant University, he enjoyed its society to the full, for nowhere had he been so warmly appreciated. His six years as Regius Professor were his Indian Summer, one of the happiest periods of a life which had known many disappointments.

No one could have felt keener satisfaction than myself when the nomination was announced. I had hoped for it and talked of it without expecting it, for no Catholic had ever been considered for the post. Grateful though I felt to Seeley and much as I admired his writings, I yearned for a broader and deeper interpretation of history than the political school could provide. Early in 1895 my old London teacher Sir John Laughton walked into my room in the Great Court of Trinity, telling me that he had come to sound opinion as to the chances of his appointment. I could not wish him success, for his approach was even narrower than that of Seeley. By a curious coincidence Rosebery was called upon during his brief Premiership to select the Regius Professors of History at the sister Universities, and the wisdom of the Cambridge choice was quickly recognized. We all felt that he brought an international atmosphere into the University. His descent through his father from the Prime Minister of Naples during the Napoleonic era, and through his mother from the ancient German house of Dalberg, secured from his birth the entry into a cosmopolitan circle which was enlarged by the marriage of his early widowed mother to Lord Granville, a pillar of the Whigs throughout the Victorian era.

Döllinger, his revered Munich teacher, had said that if Acton did not write a big work before he was forty he never would. The forecast was fulfilled, and one of the most learned men of his time passed away at the age of sixty-eight without having published a book. His treasures—and treasures they were—had to be sought in the pages of periodicals. He took little interest in metaphysics and science, *belles-lettres* and the arts, but in his knowledge of European ideologies since the Middle Ages he has never been surpassed in England or anywhere else. His massive article on German Schools of History inaugurated the first number of the

English Historical Review in 1886, and was described by Creighton, the editor, as taking his breath away. His tribute to Döllinger, written after his aged master's death in 1890, was scarcely less impressive. His reviews of such classics as Lea's *History of the Inquisition*, Creighton's volumes on the Renaissance Papacy, and Bryce's *American Commonwealth* were little treatises in themselves, and his contributions formed the most striking feature of the opening phase of that famous journal like Macaulay's essays in the *Edinburgh Review*.

A crowded audience gathered to hear the Inaugural which in its opening phrases struck off the fetters in which Seeley had bound himself and attempted to bind his pupils. 'Politics and history are interwoven but are not commensurate. Ours is a domain that reaches farther than affairs of state. It is our function to keep in view and to command the movement of ideas, which are not the effect but the cause of public events.' Passing from the scope of history to the spirit which should govern our inquiries, Acton emphasized the sanctity of the moral code. 'I exhort you never to debase the moral currency but to try others by the final maxim that governs your own lives, and to suffer no man and no cause to escape the undying penalty which history has the power to inflict on wrong. If we lower our standard in history, we cannot uphold it in Church and State.' It was a striking performance, and the deep tones of his voice added weight to his confession of faith.

In the hierarchy of British historians Acton occupies in one respect a place below his predecessor Seeley and his successors Bury and Trevelyan, all of whom have bequeathed to us enduring monuments of scholarship; but in force of personality and width of outlook, in the stimulus of his conversation and the suggestiveness of his writings he surpasses all holders of the Cambridge Chair. To Seeley history was a school of citizenship, to Acton a spiritual discipline. 'In judging men and things ethics go before dogma, politics and nationality. The inflexible integrity of the moral code is to me the secret of the authority, the dignity and the nobility of history.' Reviewers of the Inaugural, which was published with a wealth of annotations, rejected its ethical rigorism while saluting the power and suggestiveness of the discourse. No other historian has declined to attribute at least some share of the guilt of a sinner to the ideology and practice of his time, and for once the majority were right.

In my first talk with Acton at the Athenaeum in the following January, after my return from three months in Berlin, we exchanged memories of the leading German University. He recalled the lectures of Ranke and Boeckh in the fifties, and sought my impressions of Treitschke and Harnack. Our main topic, however, was the volume on the political ideas of seventeenth-century England which was beginning to fill my thoughts. The arresting work of Figgis on *The Divine Right of Kings* had stated the case for that un-English doctrine, and it was my ambition to present the democratic ideology of the same controversial era in competition for the annual Thirlwall prize. He entered warmly into my scheme and proceeded, as was his way, to recommend a list of French and German monographs, among them Gierke's *Althusius*, which he described in his oracular way as the best book on modern political thinking.

Acton was lavish—too lavish—with his superlatives both in praise or blame. Profoundly English in his passion for ordered liberty, he was utterly un-English in his scorn of compromise. As a young Member of Parliament he confessed that nobody agreed with him and he agreed with nobody. He was later to find a leader after his own heart in Gladstone, but in the Church of his birth he ploughed a lonely furrow till the end. Though he accepted its theology this prince of individualists spent many years of his life denouncing its past misdeeds. He fought at Döllinger's side against the mounting tide of Ultramontanism, flagellated the Jesuits who, in his opinion, pulled the strings to which Pio Nono danced, fulminated against the Inquisition, and pronounced the Massacre of Saint Bartholomew the greatest crime of modern times. Indifference, casuistry, compromise on moral issues seemed to him not failings but sins against the inner light which meant as much to him as to George Fox. If he could satisfy his conscience he cared little what his ecclesiastical superiors said or thought. After the Vatican Council he expected to be excommunicated like Döllinger, but as a layman he was spared. Neither of them joined the Old Catholics though they remained in touch with their friends who did. Many years later Baron von Hügel, the friend of Father Tyrrell, confided to me that he too would have got into trouble had he been a priest.

For the next five years I enjoyed the friendship and encouragement of the Regius Professor, visiting him at the Athenaeum, in his room in Trinity, or in his spacious home on the Trumpington Road. Gladstone, according to Lord Morley, could never have enough of his company. The same authoritative witness at the close of his life told me that if he could summon one of his old friends from the grave, and only one, it would be Acton. If I were thinking in terms of intellectual stimulus I should make the same choice. To boundless knowledge of books he added an unsurpassed knowledge of celebrities who played a part in the political, religious and academic life of Europe and America for half a century. He had sat in the Commons when Palmerston was at the helm and later in the Lords, though he rarely intervened in debate. Having spent half his life abroad, he was equally at home in England and Germany, Italy and France. He had challenged the formidable triumvirate—Newman, Manning and Ward—in an unsuccessful attempt to introduce the critical standards of German scholarship into English Catholic circles. In politics he was a convinced Home Ruler, an opponent of the South African war, and a foe of Imperialism wherever it reared its ugly head, in other words a Gladstonian.

Greatly as I admired his learning I never regarded his verdicts as final. Though it was always of interest to receive his oracular pronouncements, some of them struck men of cooler blood like myself as too severe. Döllinger's ethical relativism, his readiness to make allowances for human frailty and the varying standards of different ages, wounded him to the heart: since the coming of Christ, he declared defiantly, there was no excuse for anyone to say that he did not know the difference between right and wrong. While most historians content themselves with trying to describe 'how things really were', to use the familiar formula of Ranke, he had struck without fear or favour. 'The greater the sinner the greater the sin.' To hush up crimes was almost as grave an offence as to commit them. Hence his celebrated onslaught on Creighton's leniency to the Renaissance Popes—the first and last instance of a Catholic scholar censuring an Anglican Bishop for whitewashing the Vatican. The man with the sponge, he declared, was almost as bad as the man with the dagger.

If the categorical imperative of the conscience was the first article of Acton's ideology, the second was the promotion of liberty in all its forms through the cutting up of power into little bits so that no mortal man or group of men or institution should possess too much of it. The oft-quoted aphorism in a letter to Creighton—'all power tends to corrupt and absolute power corrupts absolutely'—is his legacy to mankind. He declined to make an exception for the Pope whose claim to infallibility in matters of faith and morals was rebutted with a wealth of erudition in the most celebrated of Döllinger's writings, *The Pope and the Council*. Acton's ideal constitution was a federation on the Swiss or American model, a system of wheels within wheels. Though he was born in Italy of a German mother, educated in France and Germany, and spent a large part of his life abroad, he had enough English blood in his veins to love political and spiritual liberty with a passion never exceeded by any of its island champions from Milton to Mill. For him it was literally the breath of life.

It was Acton's lifelong opposition to totalitarianism in every form which accounts for the spectacular revival of interest in the man and his writings in the middle decades of the twentieth century. Fifty years after his death the lonely scholar has come into his own. 'He is of this age more than of his,' declares Gertrude Himmelfarb in her striking volume *Lord Acton: a Study in Religion and Politics*; 'he is indeed one of our great contemporaries.' It is above all as an apostle of liberty that his name and influence survive. He ranks with Locke and Jefferson, Humboldt, Mill and Croce among the leading Liberal standard-bearers of the modern world. He agreed with Gladstone that the price of liberty is eternal vigilance, and with Goethe's couplet that 'He and he only merits liberty who conquers it afresh from day to day.' He demanded much more than national and political self-determination. 'By liberty I mean the assurance that every man shall be protected in doing what he believes his duty against the influence of authority and majorities, customs and opinion. It is better to be the citizen of a humble commonwealth in the Alps than the subject of the superb autocracy that overshadows half of Asia and Europe.'

Since liberty was the greatest prize of civilized mankind and indeed the hall-mark of civilization, its evolution appeared to Acton the most significant theme in the whole range of historical research. 'We have no thread through the enormous intricacy of modern politics,' he declared in his *Lectures on Modern History,* 'except the idea of progress towards more perfect and assured freedom and the divine right of free men.' The dream of his life—to write the history of liberty—was unfulfilled, for his words on Döllinger are applicable to himself: 'He would not write with imperfect materials, and to him the materials were always imperfect.' Happily we can reconstruct the outlines from the crumbs which fell from his table. The first step on the long road was the Stoic recognition of 'the law of nature', the second the proclamation of the spiritual independence of the individual by the Christian Church, the first great institution which dared to tell the state: 'thus far and no further'. The third was the British invention of representative government in the thirteenth century, the fourth the proclamation of the Rights of Man by the Founding Fathers of the United States and the men of 1789. While almost every Catholic speaks with horror of the French Revolution Acton salutes its opening phase with a cheer. The Declaration of the Rights of Man is welcomed as 'the triumphant proclamation of the doctrine that human obligations are not all assignable to interest or to force. This single page of print is stronger than all the armies of Napoleon.' Yet democracy, like all forms of government, needs to be watched, for no class is fit for a monopoly of power. 'The law of liberty tends to abolish the reign of race over race, of faith over faith, of class over class.' The emancipation of conscience, he declared, was the main content of modern history.

Acton's principal occupation during his closing years was the planning of the *Cambridge Modern History.* He accepted the invitation of the University Press with alacrity, 'because such an opportunity of promoting his own ideas for the treatment of history has seldom been given to any man. We shall avoid the needless utterance of opinion or service of a cause. Contributors will understand that our Waterloo must satisfy French and English, Germans and Dutch alike.' He had drawn up a list of contributors and secured the acceptance of the greater number when in the spring of 1901 he had a stroke. Though he gradually rallied, his work at Cambridge was over and he retired to his wife's home at Tegernsee in the Bavarian Alps. On the evening before I started for Egypt in January, 1902, I received a long letter in pencil asking me to look up various queries in the British Museum. I promised to comply after my return, but then it was too late. He died shortly before the appearance of the first volume. The Introductory Chapter on the legacy of the Middle Ages which he had intended to write was entrusted to Bishop Creighton. It was my privilege to contribute to four of the twelve volumes, to review his posthumous lectures, essays, and correspondence before the First World War, and to welcome the monographs which have appeared after the close of the Second. An even more enduring monument to his connection with Cambridge is the magnificent library purchased by Andrew Carnegie and presented to Lord Morley, who in turn presented it to the University. There students young and old may consult his vast collections of notes and extracts, bricks for a mighty edifice which his habits of work and the brief span of human life forbade the architect to construct. *Qui trop embrasse mal étreint.*

5

PARIS IN THE NINETIES

M Y autumn in Berlin in 1895 was followed a year later by an autumn in Paris. I lodged with a family the head of which had been born a Catholic but was now studying for the Protestant Ministry. There was none of the usual bellicosity of the convert about him, and his sweetness of temper attracted both Catholic and Protestant friends to his home in Passy. The Protestants of France are a small community, numbering scarcely more than half a million and scattered in little groups which had survived the massacre of St. Bartholomew and the savage fury of the *dragonnades*. But their importance, like that of the Quakers, is out of proportion to their numbers, for they represent one of the most valuable elements in the national life. It is almost as rare for a French Protestant as for an English Quaker to find himself a prisoner at the bar. I was well aware that either a Catholic or a freethinking family would have been far more representative of the main sections of French society, but I had every reason to be content with my lot. My host was full of stories of the celebrities he used to see in Versailles which the victorious Germans made their headquarters during the siege of Paris and which remained the seat of government during the opening phase of the Third Republic. By the time of my visit in 1896 France had recovered her resilience and had found a friend in Russia after two decades of impotent isolation.

Knowing the chief sights of Paris from previous visits it was the academic world which I had come to explore. The University has been a beacon light since the Middle Ages, and the French capital is unique in possessing a sister institution of scarcely inferior prestige in the College de France. The celebrated foundation of Francis I, beginning with chairs of Theology, Hebrew and Greek, had grown into a corporation where almost every department of learning was represented. While the University lectures were only for students, the class-rooms of the College de France were open to the public and in some cases were filled to the door. I was too late to hear Renan, but it was a familiar story how visitors attracted by his world-wide fame would take their seats beneath his desk and crawl away when he proceeded to elucidate a Semitic text. A more flagrant example of lion-hunting was to occur a few years later when Bergson's *Evolution Créatrice* was the talk of the town, and *tout Paris*, including the fair sex in the latest creations of the Rue de la Paix, crowded the corridors to catch a glimpse of the little Jew who looked like an intelligent bird.

It was a delight to see and to hear the celebrities, particularly when I was familiar with some of their works. The leading figure in history at the Sorbonne was Lavisse, joint editor with Rambaud of the *Histoire Générale* and sole editor of the still greater *Histoire de France*. He was lecturing on the age of Louis XIV, to which he devoted the most enduring of his writings. His were the only lectures I ever attended where the door was locked to exclude late-comers and early-goers. In ancient history Maspero the Egyptologist towered above his fellows, while the veteran Gaston Boissier addressed a crowded class-room on his favourite theme of Roman society. For the Middle Ages I found no one more attractive than Emile Gebhardt, author of that delicious book *L'Italie mystique*. In philosophy Boutroux reigned supreme till the arrival from a provincial University a few years later of Bergson, his most brilliant pupil. Paul Leroy-Beaulieu discoursed on economics, his brother Anatole, author of the monumental *L'Empire des Tsars*, on his favourite theme of Russia. Emile Faguet, whose high-pitched voice had earned him among the students the nickname of the eunuch, interpreted the treasures of French literature with the same penetrating clarity that keeps his writings alive.

In addition to the University and the College de France, Paris could boast of the Ecole Libre des Sciences Politiques. The calamities of 1870 and the carnage of the Commune suggested to some thoughtful Frenchmen that a better training for the higher grades of the public service at home and abroad was required. No

one held this conviction with greater fervour than Taine, who
was chiefly instrumental in the foundation of the school and whose
bust stood in the hall. He found an ideal collaborator in Emile
Boutmy, known to English readers by his studies of our Constitution, who became the first Director and was still at his post
in 1896. I explained to him that it was not my intention to enrol
myself as a student, but that I desired to attend some of the
lectures during my brief stay. He kindly acceded to my request,
and I listened to the leading specialists in history, finance and
international law. The dominating figure was Albert Sorel, who
had served his apprenticeship in the Foreign Office but withdrew
from diplomacy after the war of 1870. Thenceforward as an
intimate friend both of Boutmy and Taine he had devoted his
talents to the school and to the composition of his majestic
L'Europe et la Révolution Française, the most considerable historical
work produced under the Third Republic. It was a privilege to
hear the greatest master of diplomatic history since Ranke discourse on the development of the European system in the nineteenth century. French Professors are almost invariably masters
of the technique of lecturing, for the study of 'rhetoric' is a prominent feature of secondary education. In addition to attendance
at these three famous seats of learning I heard Giry, the learned
medievalist, in the Ecole des hautes Etudes, and Auguste Sabatier,
brother of the biographer of St. Francis and author of that
inspiring book *Les Religions de l'Autorité et la Religion de l'Esprit*,
in the Faculty of Protestant Theology. My kind host, who had
opened the way to the class-room of his friend Sabatier, the
intellectual leader of the Liberal Protestants, also procured my
admission to a lecture on dogmatic theology in the Institut
Catholique. Unfortunately, having been reared on the English
pronunciation of Latin, I understood hardly a word.

In Paris as in Berlin Sunday mornings were employed in samp-
ling the leading preachers of the day in St. Sulpice, the Madeleine,
and other famous shrines. There was no star of the first magnitude like Lacordaire or Dupanloup. Loisy, scholar and rebel, had
not yet emerged, and Mgr. Duchesne, the first critical Catholic
historian of the Early Church, adorned the Ecole Française at
Rome. The sermons were earnest and eloquent, but dogmatic
and institutional religion seemed to be regarded by the majority

of Parisians with indifference or contempt. On one occasion I was shocked to witness a preacher stop in the middle of a sentence at the shrill warning of a time bell and walk rapidly down the pulpit stairs. Where is the English divine of any denomination who would submit to such discipline? The services in the Protestant church at Passy, to which I occasionally accompanied my host and his family, were simple to austerity: to one accustomed to the Anglican ritual they seemed colourless and cold. Only when one has attended Protestant services on the Continent does one realize to the full how unique an institution is that typically English compromise the Anglican Church, situated as it is midway between Rome and Geneva.

French thought and literature were still dominated by positivism and realism. The two supermen who had ruled the Third Republic almost without challenge had recently passed from the scene, Renan in 1892 and Taine in 1893. Both had outlived the storms of their early manhood and had been enrolled among the glories of France. I already knew many of their books, delighting in the limpid style of the one and the rude vigour of the other, but I now read *Les Origines de la France contemporaine*, Taine's political testament in six large volumes. Neither of them entertained a rosy view of human nature in general or French democracy in particular; but while Renan surveyed the motley pageant of life with a tolerant smile, Taine witnessed the struggle with despondency in his heart. He distrusted the masses as deeply as he detested Napoleon and other autocrats, and the horrors of the Commune convinced him that French civilization was a veneer beneath which seethed the passions of primeval savagery. Man he compared to a chained gorilla, France to a vicious horse mounted by a bad rider: since 1789 the French had acted and thought partly like madmen, partly like children. England, by contrast, was the home of ordered liberty. One of the noblest characters of his age was also the most incorrigible pessimist. Like Clemenceau, he believed neither in God nor man, but Clemenceau at any rate believed in France. The gloomy picture seemed to be confirmed by the novelists, Flaubert, Zola, Maupassant, Daudet, Anatole France. In his exquisite book *Le Roman Russe* the Vicomte de Vogüé contrasted the 'ethical realism' of the great Russian and British novelists with the soulless naturalism of France which he denounced. No English reader of French fiction in the nineties could miss the atmospheric difference in the life they depicted— an entire absence of the Puritan tradition and a scanty respect for the fundamental pieties. A change of literary taste was to come a few years later with Maurice Barrès, Péguy and other crusaders of the Right, but in 1896 France seemed in the main content with what Zola called 'le roman expérimental'.

In continental capitals, where state-aided theatres are a matter of course, the visitor may rely on a varied menu. It was a liberal education to see a seventeenth-century masterpiece or a nine-teenth-century favourite at the Comédie Française; and at the Odéon, which was also under the supervision of the state, a classic was staged once a week at popular prices for the benefit of students. On certain occasions a *Conférence* was delivered from the stage of the latter before the performance. I had the good fortune to hear such a discourse by Jules Lemaître, marked by the same delicate distinction and lightness of touch which made him the leading impressionist critic of the time. I enjoyed Coquelin *aîné* in *Le Bourgeois Gentilhomme* and Sarah Bernhardt in *La Dame aux Camélias*; some years later I saw them together, an incom-parable pair, in Rostand's *L'Aiglon*, the finest historical drama produced in modern France. Molière was my favourite among French writers, and the bright memories of *Tartuffe* and *L'Avare*, *Le Médecin malgré lui*, *Les Précieuses Ridicules* and *Les Fourberies de Scapin* have never dimmed. Racine's *Britannicus* left a deep impression, but even Sarah Bernhardt could not reconcile me to the monotonous horror of *Phèdre*. Having seen her in Paris and London in most of her celebrated parts—*Hamlet*, Alfred de Musset's *Lorenzaccio* and Sardou's *La Tosca*—I confess that I preferred *La Dame aux Camélias* which she was said to have played over a thousand times. She seemed to me the greatest tragic actress of her time; for Duse, whom I admired in *Magda* and *Francesca da Rimini*, spoke in Italian, which I was unable to follow when rapidly declaimed. 'The divine Sarah' never shone in the part of a good woman or Duse in that of a sinner. The opera was inferior to the theatre, but the Lamoureux concerts were up to the stan-dard of London and Berlin.

The old quarters of Paris and its environs were a source of inexhaustible interest. Malmaison and Chantilly, which I was to visit some years later, were not yet on view, but I was privileged to see one or two historic buildings which foreigners rarely entered. My host obtained permission for himself and 'a friend' to visit the fortress of Vincennes, with its memories of Condé, Mirabeau and the martyred Duc d'Enghien, and I was cautioned not to reveal my identity as an Englishman as our countries were not on very friendly terms. The ruins of Port Royal, a symbol of the bigotry of Louis XIV, told a tale of Jansenist piety, learning and sufferings. In the Cité nothing fascinated me more than the Conciergerie, with its searing memories of the twenty-two doomed Girondins, Mme Roland and Marie Antoinette.

French politics were rather flat during the period between the collapse of Boulanger and the reopening of the Dreyfus case. Félix Faure had recently succeeded the murdered Carnot at the Elysée; and though the 'tanner' of Havre was scorned by the disgruntled Noblesse of the Faubourg Saint-Germain, he played his part with reasonable success. The President of the Republic is merely the first citizen and there is no halo round his head. It was not till the later years of his term that he began to take himself a little too seriously for Republican tastes and that scandal became associated with his name. I only saw him arrive at an official function; but I heard Loubet, his more estimable successor, at that time President of the Senate, speak at the burial of Challemel-Lacour in the cemetery of Père La Chaise. On the same occasion Hanotaux, then Foreign Minister and the renowned biographer of Richelieu, delivered a finely phrased tribute to the man who, like himself, was both a scholar and a diplomatist. Another difference between England and France peeped out on this occasion in the absence of all religious ceremonies, though the final breach with the Church was still to come. It was interesting to contrast the tumult of the French Chamber, which the President's bell made fitful efforts to subdue, with the decorum of St. Stephen's. I read the *Temps* every day and the *Revue des deux Mondes* every fortnight as in duty bound, and the other papers sufficiently often to grasp where they stood. A leader in the *Temps* or the *Débats* was up to the standard of *The Times*, but anyone who trusted to the French press alone for his knowledge of what was going on in the world would be politically starved. A large staff of Foreign Correspondents was beyond its resources.

My two months in Paris were crowded with stimulating experiences, and I gained some idea as to how France looks at the world. Though Bodley's classical interpretation of his adopted country did not appear till a year or two later, my studies of French history provided a framework into which I could fit my impressions. The main lines of foreign policy, as Sorel had shown, had been inherited from the *ancien régime*, the political structure from the Revolution. The Nobility and the Church had been knocked off their perch, royalism died with the childless Comte de Chambord, and Bonapartism was buried at Sedan. The supremacy of the thrifty and rather limited *bourgeoisie* was unchallenged. The urban workers counted for little, for they were balanced by the peasantry to whom socialism made no appeal. French politics were a wearisome game of musical chairs. The Ministries which rose and fell with the regularity of the tides represented the sceptical, democratic, individualist France which was born in 1789. In the witty aphorism of André Siegfried the Frenchman's head is on the Left, his pocket on the Right. 'La République,' declared Thiers after the fall of the Second Empire, 'c'est ce qui nous divise le moins.' It remained true in 1896 and it is true today.

6

VICTORIAN SUNSET

WHEN the verdict was delivered that I was not to be a
Trinity don, Dr. Butler, with his usual fatherly kindness, advised me to apply for a Fellowship at one or
other of the smaller colleges where Trinity men with a First were
occasionally in demand. He seemed anxious to keep me within the
academic fold. When I confessed that I might perhaps some day
try my luck in public life, he observed a little deprecatingly that
the strongest of his contemporaries, such as Henry Sidgwick, had
been satisfied with a scholar's career. I was offered a post as
University Extension Lecturer, and not long afterwards I was
sounded by Sir Adolphus Ward in regard to a position in Manchester University; but I preferred to live at home as I was
fortunate enough to possess independent means. My main
occupation of course would be historical study, but I could never
be content with a purely academic career. I hoped to be of some
little use in social work and thus to repay some small part of my
debt for a lucky dip in the lottery of life.

My first book, *English Democratic Ideas in the Seventeenth Century*,
won the Thirlwall Prize in 1897, was published by the Cambridge
University Press in 1898, appeared in a pirated edition in America,
reappeared with additional notes and appendices by Harold Laski
in 1927, and was reprinted once again in 1955. Meanwhile the
chapter on the Communists of the Commonwealth era was translated into Russian without seeking permission from author or
publisher. I was first attracted to the subject by my admiration
for Milton's prose treatises and my interest in Harrington's *Oceana*,
which argued for the first time in the history of political thinking
that power ultimately depends on the distribution of property and

thereby anticipated Marx. Though the two crowded middle decades of the century formed the core of the book, my sketch of democratic thought extended from the Reformation to the opening of the eighteenth century. It was a rewarding task to watch the gladiators of different classes, parties and creeds struggling to secure, retain or regain what they believed to be their inalienable rights.

No one could work at seventeenth-century England without intensive study of the writings of Gardiner, who was as ready as Acton to share his treasures with young students like myself. There was something heroic in the record of this modest scholar, caring nothing for fame or fortune, who toiled for forty years at the enterprise which is his enduring monument. Earning his living by writing text-books and delivering popular lectures, he declined the Oxford Chair on the death of Froude in 1895 in order to bring his slowly moving narrative a few years nearer to its goal in 1660. He was always to be found at the same desk in the British Museum, surrounded by a pile of books. He had no gift of style, but his knowledge of the printed and unprinted materials of his period was unique. It is his glory to have narrated the most critical and controversial era of our history for the first time with relative detachment, and to have understood antagonists who could never understand each other. The path of deliverance from the Whig and Tory dog-fight had been opened in Ranke's monumental *England in the Seventeenth Century*, to which, except for the writings of Gardiner, I owed more than to any other large-scale work on the period.

To breathe the atmosphere and understand the controversies of the period the enormous Thomason collection of pamphlets in the British Museum was at my disposal. The London bookseller, scenting revolution in the air, began to collect books and pamphlets, newspapers and sermons in 1640, and persevered till the Restoration twenty years later. No such quarry exists for any period of our history before the foundation of the British Museum in the eighteenth century with its statutory rights as this corpus of 30,000 items bound up in over 2,000 volumes. No one had set sail on this ocean of faded print to illustrate the history of political ideas except Eduard Bernstein the German socialist during his years of exile in England in the eighties. Among the most interesting of my themes were two pioneers: Winstanley the Communist, and Lilburne the Leveller, the rise of the sects and the debates in the Army Council. A new Cromwell, cautious and conservative, had emerged from the Clarke Papers recently published by Firth, standing midway between royalists and radicals, exposed to abuse from both camps. No man of action was less of a doctrinaire. Several years later I accepted an invitation to write a second book on the same fermenting age.

An Easter visit to Rome in 1897 and a longer sojourn in 1898 were only less stimulating to a young historian than student days in Berlin and Paris. It was the obvious opportunity to learn Italian, a language too full of vowels for my taste and lacking the majesty of its Latin mother. I devoured the Classic *Storia della Letteratura* by Francesco de Sanctis, greatest of Italian literary historians before Croce. Having read Dante in the Temple Classics, with a translation on one side of the open page and the original on the other, I now sampled the minor deities from Petrarch, Tasso and Michaelangelo to Leopardi and Carducci. Italy is a land of poets rather than of dramatists or novelists. The tragedies of Alfieri struck me as machine-made, but I delighted in Manzoni's *Promessi Sposi*, which received the enthusiastic praise of Walter Scott. D'Annunzio was still at the beginning of his meteoric career, and Fogazzaro had not yet written *The Saint*.

All roads lead to Rome, and I prepared for the pilgrimage to the best of my ability. I devoured the eight stout volumes in German of Gregorovius on the *History of Rome in the Middle Ages* which I had chosen as a Cambridge prize, the panoramic surveys of the Renaissance by Burckhardt and Symonds, Vasari's *Lives of the Painters*, Goethe's *Italienische Reise*, Lanciani's archaeological studies of Ancient Rome, Furtwängler's superbly illustrated *Masterpieces of Greek Sculpture*, and many other works old and new on Italian history, literature and art. I heard Lanciani lecture in excellent English, attended a debate in the Chamber on the Cretan crisis, and saw King Humbert driving unattended through the streets. I found myself among 50,000 pilgrims in St. Peter's on Easter Day who had gathered to witness the entrance of the octogenarian Leo XIII, whose face seemed as white as his raiment, and to hear the silver trumpets peal. On both my visits to the Eternal City I received the hospitality which the historian Count Balzani, the friend of Freeman and Hodgkin, Creighton and

Bryce, extended to British students. Despite wars, revolutions and vandalism Italy remains the greatest museum in the world. The deserted streets of Pompeii, the opulent beauty of Amalfi on its rocky perch, the lonely temples of Paestum, Assisi, Perugia and Siena basking on their hillsides, the Byzantine glories of Ravenna, Giotto's tower in Florence, the Cathedral, Baptistery and leaning tower at Pisa: these and other enchantments were carried home to dream about for the rest of my life. Nowhere else have cities such beautiful names. I had seen Titian at Venice, and Raphael could be studied elsewhere, but for the fifteenth-century Tuscans we must go to Tuscany. Fra Angelico, Botticelli and Lippo Lippi have always kept a special corner in my heart. Since Leonardo's *Last Supper* is only a ghost of its former splendour, no single picture in the peninsula seemed to me so marvellous as Velazquez's portrait of Innocent X in the Doria Palace in Rome.

No sooner was my first book launched than Acton was ready with plans for another. A chronological handbook was required, he argued in a long letter, which would present the growth of modern civilization in tabular form. I was to be surrounded and supported by auxiliary experts; he himself would give all the assistance in his power, and the book should be published by the Cambridge University Press. He proceeded to demonstrate why various works in French, German and Italian were too limited in scope to satisfy his demands. Numerous handbooks had dealt with politics alone and a few with *Kulturgeschichte*, but no sustained attempt had been made to combine them. The suggestion harmonized with my conviction that history embraces the whole life of mankind, and we agreed that I should start with Columbus. Politics were to fill the left-hand page and culture the right, so that the student might see at a glance what was going on in the world. He was good enough to read the greater part of the proofs and to furnish a brief Foreword in his usual pregnant style.

> History embraces ideas as much as events, and derives its best virtue from regions beyond the sphere of state. No previous writer has grasped this fundamental truth with deeper conviction and understanding than Mr. Gooch. Viewing Modern History as a whole he does justice to its several elements, to thought as well as action, to the mass of influences which constitute opinion and govern the life of nations and the progress of civilization.

In such a wide field a young scholar needed advice, and the pundits responded in the friendliest way. I need only recall such distinguished names as Sir Richard Jebb for classical scholarship, Dr. Richard Garnett for Italian literature, and Sir Edmund Gosse for Scandinavia. The book, which was finished in 1900 and published in 1901, came down to the end of 1899. Reprinted in 1906 with a few corrections, it continued to sell steadily for many years.

On settling down at home after my adventures in Berlin and Paris, I began the practice of popular lecturing which was to continue into old age. Among Seeley's achievements was the foundation of the Social and Political Education League, designed to convey something of the culture of the Universities to the masses. While the University Extension movement involved paid lecturers, paying students and regular classes, the S.P.E.L., as it was called, offered single addresses by unpaid speakers in and near London. The Cambridge Secretary, who had been my instructor in Political Science, invited me to join the panel. Seeley's object was the training of citizens, and his dream was interpreted in the broadest way. Almost every aspect of life except party politics was embraced in the lecture list which was circulated to Settlements and Literary Societies, chapels and clubs. I spoke a good deal on the countries I had visited, and there was a brisk demand for a lecture on Tolstoi, then at the height of his fame. For less educated audiences lantern lectures were provided, and my illustrated talks on London, Paris and Rome were in request. The annual Presidential Address was delivered during half a century by leading Intellectuals, among them Bishop Creighton, Oliver Lodge, James Bryce, Herbert Fisher, Professor Pollard and Julian Huxley.

More systematic teaching claimed many evenings at the University Settlements. I was associated with Mansfield House in Canning Town, in the heart of dockland, almost from its infancy. The Settlement had been founded by Mansfield College, Oxford, then under the guidance of Principal Fairbairn, one of the most learned theologians of the age and a man of warm human sympathies. The first Warden was Percy, later Sir Percy, Alden, who had come from Balliol to the East End fired with the faith of Arnold Toynbee and T. H. Green, and who quickly won a leading place in the life of West Ham. A fine residence had been

erected in which lectures, concerts and At Homes were held; a
Women's Settlement, with a hospital of its own, was only a few
streets away. The charge of bourgeois complacency had some
foundation in the earlier decades of the reign of Victoria, but the
creation of Toynbee Hall and other University Settlements would
alone suffice to rebut any such accusation in its closing phase.
Young men fresh from College, clerks and manual workers
mingled happily on a basis of simple human equality.

For some years I took a class in economic history—the only
kind of history for which there was a demand in dockland—and
printed a detailed syllabus for its use. Men who had been working
their muscles all day could hardly be expected to read solid books,
but they followed with interest the story of the workers from
serfdom and the medieval guilds to the Trade Unions and Co-
operative Societies of the nineteenth century. West Ham was the
cradle of the Labour Party, for it had returned Keir Hardie to
Parliament in 1892. The uncouth demagogue of popular imagination proved on personal acquaintance to be a man of exceptional
refinement, with a tender heart and a love of beautiful things. I
liked him from the first, and the Labour Party can be proud of its
founder whose soul was fired by the vision of a fairer life for the
common man. A very different type was the rough diamond Will
Thorne, the other political celebrity of the district. He had been
present at the burial of Karl Marx, and his burly figure seemed to
embody the cause of unskilled labour. Nowhere in London could
I have obtained a better insight into the mentality of the urban
worker. Socialism was in the air in West Ham, for the dwellers
in its mean streets could hardly be expected to applaud a capitalist
society.

The name of Canon Barnett had long been familiar at Cambridge as indeed throughout the English-speaking world, and
scores of young graduates found their way to Whitechapel to
offer their services or to consult him about their careers. Toynbee
Hall was the earliest and remains the most celebrated of the
University Settlements which have sprung up in the great cities
on both sides of the Atlantic; the residents and lecturers who won
fame as statesmen and civil servants, economists and social
workers, form an imposing list. Its influence on inquiring minds
in the East End was illustrated in the autobiography of my valued

friend Thomas Okey, translator of Dante, who rose from the making of baskets to the Chair of Italian literature at Cambridge.

The life of Barnett by his gifted wife portrays one of the most original figures of his time. The launching of the Settlement movement was no mean achievement, but the man was greater than his work. What attracted old and young, rich and poor, was above all his mellow wisdom: to this day I think of him as one of the wisest men I ever met. What Barnett was to young men starting out in life, declared Alfred Spender, could never be told. The Canon, testifies Lord Beveridge, was an infinitely wise creature with a strong temper controlled and directed by love of God and man. The blend of a warm heart and a cool head rendered him an ideal counsellor. This quiet Whitechapel clergyman possessed the mind of a statesman. Clemenceau declared in the eighties that he was one of the three really great men he met in England. Hyndman, a well-to-do bourgeois Marxist, used to say that the middle-class reformer wished to help the poor in their poverty but not out of their poverty. The sneer would have had no effect on Barnett, who, though eager for well-considered political and economic change, based his philosophy on the training of character and tested proposals by their ultimate effect on the self-respect of the beneficiaries. Not even the Charity Organization Society offered more inflexible opposition to all forms of pauperization than the Vicar of St. Jude. His gospel was not the early Victorian formula of self-help—a mockery for the vast army of men and women who never had a chance—but the provision of opportunity, physical, mental and spiritual, for healthy growth. The Whitechapel Art Gallery, with its annual exhibitions and volunteer guides, was as dear to his heart as the Children's Country Holiday Fund. He was a left-wing Gladstonian Liberal, not a Socialist, preferring local initiative and collective supervision to wholesale nationalization. The Barnetts are as inseparable in the memory of their friends as the Webbs. They belonged to the noble profession of Servants of Humanity, but identity of thought and aim was combined with a striking diversity of temperament. Though there was nothing in the least flabby or sentimental about him, the Canon was almost feminine in his gentleness and tenderness, whereas the inflexible will of his wife was suggestive of the stronger sex. The one seemed born to persuade, the other to command. I received nothing but kindness from them both, but I occasionally heard rumours of ruffled feathers when Dame Henrietta had been on the war-path. Despite their differing natures it was a perfect partnership. The Warden used to say that the whole work of the Settlement revolved round his wife's tea-table, meaning that it was the human touch which made Toynbee Hall a living institution. Her brain was as constructive as his, and it is to her that we owe Hampstead Garden Suburb and the better provision for 'the children of the State'. Two houses called Balliol and Wadham were separated by a concrete tennis court from the Settlement buildings. They were designed for young men who, while earning their living as clerks, school teachers or minor civil servants, desired to continue their studies. At the time I offered my services a scheme was being launched to prepare such of them as desired help for the London Matriculation, and I was invited to undertake their instruction in history. Organized adult education is among the best inventions of the modern world.

The Working Men's College was located in Great Ormond Street in a house once inhabited by Lord Thurlow, the grim old Tory Chancellor of George III. Though an art-school had been added at the end of the garden we were terribly overcrowded, and we soon moved north to Crowndale Road where the present spacious edifice was built. For some years I took classes in history, and like many another who has taught in that temple of good-fellowship I became wedded to it for life. Though its founder, Frederick Denison Maurice, had been dead for a quarter of a century, his gracious spirit seemed to brood over his creation, and his beautiful face gazed down at us from the walls. The title was a misnomer, for manual workers were very rare birds, but the young men who filled our classrooms were equally worth teaching and no less grateful for our help. Most of them, as was natural, patronized the courses which prepared them for examinations or a business career; but it was the aim of the founder to build up a miniature University where the Humanities would also be taught as an end in themselves. His programme had been faithfully carried out with the aid, not only of Oxford and Cambridge men fresh from their degrees, but of celebrities like Ruskin at the height of their fame.

When I began to attend the Annual Suppers in the later nineties the so-called Founders were still alive. The outstanding personality among these veterans was Furnivall, founder of the Early English Text Society, who occupied a place in the life of the College which has never again been filled. Though he died at eighty-five he remained an *enfant terrible* to the end, bubbling over with vitality, cocksure and aggressive. I have never known a man with a tenderer heart and a sharper tongue, more quiveringly alive, more quick in the uptake, more ready to spend himself for causes in which he believed. The memorial volume published in 1911, containing a biography and fifty appreciations from pupils, colleagues and friends, preserves the features of a unique personality. On the occasion of the Annual Supper he invariably made the same speech, boosting his sculling club at Hammersmith and their Sunday morning row and parading his aggressive rationalism. From anyone but Furnivall such slashing attacks on the beliefs of many of his hearers would have aroused bitter resentment, but we all knew his little ways. The collection for the Ormond Street Hospital for Sick Children, for which he always pleaded, revealed the gentler side of the old gladiator.

The life and soul of the College in the nineties was George Tansley, founder of the Old Students' Club, whose name in the hierarchy stands immediately below that of Maurice himself. He had entered as a student in the first year, sat at the feet of Maurice and Ruskin, and became a teacher himself. Retiring from business in middle life he gave his time, money and brains to the College which he loved with the devotion of a mother for her child. He knew every student, and he welcomed with almost embarrassing gratitude young volunteers like myself. Rarely have I seen such selfless dedication, such touching humility, such a passion for service. Well might Sir Charles Lucas in the Jubilee history of the College answer the question 'What good has the Working Men's College done?' with the words: 'For one thing it produced, or helped to produce, George Tansley.'

Maurice had been succeeded as Principal by Tom Hughes, author of *Tom Brown's Schooldays*, who in turn was followed by Sir John Lubbock, later Lord Avebury, banker and scientist. The fourth Principal, who reigned when I arrived, was Dicey, author of the classical treatise, *The Law and Custom of the*

Constitution, the best of its kind since Bagehot. Knowing him only from his books and vehement campaign against Home Rule, I was pleasantly surprised to find a kindly old scholar with gentle voice and ways. The Professor was always ready to come up from Oxford, and his speeches at the Annual Supper were full of mellow wisdom and quiet humour. The most effective speaker on these occasions, however, was Sir Charles Lucas, then Vice-Principal and later Dicey's successor. As Permanent Under-Secretary at the Colonial Office and author of the indispensable *Historical Geography of the British Colonies*, he was not only an eminent Civil Servant but an active worker for Imperial consolidation. After Tansley's death he was the chief personage in the College, and his speeches were a cascade of jokes and puns that kept the tables in a roar. I should rank him with Labouchere, Birrell, Bernard Shaw, Guedalla and A. P. Herbert among the wittiest speakers I have heard. There was nothing of the buffoon about Lucas, who would pass in a moment from gay to grave. He was succeeded by General Sir Frederick Maurice, the gifted grandson of the Founder. During my early years at the College I took weekly classes, substituting at a later date addresses at the Saturday evening public lectures and at meetings of the Old Students' Club.

In my fourth year at Cambridge I had been invited to serve on the committee of the local Charity Organization Society, and had learned its austere method of inquiry. It was unfortunate in its name, which it has wisely changed, and the unbending individualism of its founder exposed it to attack. Yet it is possible to hold a broader social philosophy than Sir Charles Loch and yet to realize how much valuable work it has achieved in the relief of genuine distress and in the exposure of pestilent parasites, a list of whom was confidentially circulated to subscribers. A connecting link between Cambridge and London was provided by Cambridge House, a Settlement in the Walworth Road, where I occasionally lectured, and the Trinity College Mission, which had assumed responsibility for a vast parish of twenty thousand souls in the neighbouring borough of Camberwell. For several years I was closely associated with the work of a parish carved out of the territory of the Trinity Mission. From time to time we had distinguished visitors from the north side of the river, among whom

I recall Lord Hugh Cecil and George Russell, who addressed crowded men's meetings with impassioned eloquence. The parishioners were what property agents describe as 'respectable working-class', equidistant from the squalor of the riverside and the quasi-gentility of the outer suburbs: the eye was caught less by what they suffered than by what they lacked. Their lives were drab and the manifold recreations of today were unknown. A revealing picture of South London as I knew it at the turn of the century was painted by Alexander Patterson, the well-known prison reformer, in his moving study *Across the Bridges*. The parochial system of the Church of England is a friend in need to men and women of all denominations or none. I explored police courts, workhouses, asylums and other items of the vast administrative machine of the capital. I stood as an Independent without success for the Camberwell Board of Guardians, and I was not surprised that the manual workers preferred to be represented by a member of their own class who knew best where the shoe pinched.

Shortly after leaving the University I became associated with the social work of the Church Army at the invitation of its founder. Wilson Carlile, the son of a well-to-do City merchant, had started on a business career when in early manhood he was 'converted' and ordained. While serving as a curate in a wealthy parish of South Kensington, he had begun open-air mission work in the reeking slums between Victoria Street and the river. He was knocked down by roughs and badly ruptured, but the work grew rapidly and in 1882 he established the Church Army. Like the Salvation Army, of which it was the Anglican equivalent, it developed a network of redemptive agencies, and within ten years it was entrenched in every diocese in England. Its theology was evangelical in its simplest form, what Americans such as Dr. Graham called fundamentalism—the utter unworthiness of man and the infinite mercy of God. It suited the 'down and out' in the street, the prison and the public-house among whom the devoted officers, male and female, spent their days. With people of this type conversion is sometimes an instantaneous experience.

Carlile was the greatest optimist I have ever known. His faith was strong enough to move mountains, for he discerned the finger of Providence in every occurrence of daily life. Gastritis was a slow job, he wrote to me, but it was a good training. 'God's presence has been very real.' When he sprained his leg in a cycling accident it was so arranged that he might have a little more leisure to think. When his wife died he told me that he felt she was nearer to him than when on earth. For him no sinner was beyond the pale: it was never too late to mend. Among his treasures was a set of burglar's tools presented to him in gratitude. The divine spark was glimmering in the drunkard and the prostitute, and it only needed a determined effort by a man or woman of rock-like faith to kindle it into a steady flame. After a visit to the Mint I told him of a machine which weighed every golden sovereign, automatically ejecting those which fell below the required standard and which were melted down for a second trial. Out came his pocket book, and he jotted down a useful illustration of the doctrine that every offender has another chance. Realizing that conversion was only the beginning, he dotted the country with labour homes where a man could work under supervision for a few months, and cheap lodging homes where he could live when he regained his feet. A special lodging home was available for educated men who had slipped and who were employed in addressing envelopes instead of chopping wood. The Church Army set its face against indiscriminate almsgiving as firmly as the C.O.S., and the public were urged to buy work-tickets which could be exchanged for food after the allotted task was performed. The Chief was a born organizer, and his nimble brain was always planning ahead. The Friends of the Poor, which started as a branch of the Church Army, soon hived off as a separate organization and has recently celebrated its jubilee.

Carlile's mental and physical energy was extraordinary. Appointed Rector of St. Mary-at-Hill in 1892 he transformed an empty City Church and Rectory into a busy hive of social and spiritual redemption. On Sundays he would stride through the streets with his choir in their surplices, singing rousing hymns to the strident accompaniment of trombones and shepherding the swelling crowd into evening service. After the sermon, brief and unconventional in form and substance, he invited members of the congregation to stay and tell him their troubles at the communion rail. Though stories of misery and degradation poured into his ears all day long, his buoyancy was inexhaustible. Unlike Lord

Shaftesbury who was obsessed by the thought of suffering and sin, there was always a smile on his face, for there was perpetual sunshine in his heart. Cope has portrayed him in his surplice with the familiar trombone in his uplifted arm as if he were singing 'Onward Christian Soldiers' at the top of his voice. As such we remember him, a prophet proclaiming not the wrath but the inexhaustible mercy of God.

For several years before I was elected to Parliament in 1906 I was a member of the Executive Committee of the Church Army, where the most prominent figure after the Chief was Edward Clifford, painter and evangelist, the friend of men so different as the Duke of Westminster, Burne-Jones and Father Damien. I became acquainted with every aspect of the work, appealing for funds in smart drawing-room meetings, roaming the Embankment late at night where the homeless crowds shivered under the bridges, and shepherding them if they were willing into Church Army Homes. My special assignment was in the vagrancy department, which was designed to supplement the soulless machinery of the casual wards. The Poor Law was merely a relieving agency, not an instrument of redemption, and hundreds of men tramped from one workhouse to another with the regularity of a policeman's beat. It was Carlile's dream to provide a chain of centres where food was provided in return for wood-chopping, and where the officer in charge looked out for a chance of lifting a man off the road. The task proved beyond the strength of a private society, for some tramps were so wedded to nomadic life that they had lost the taste for settled work. Not till the era of full employment after the Second World War did the professional vagrant disappear.

If the founder of the Church Army was the greatest optimist of my acquaintance, Dr. Paton ran him close. Himself a Congregational Minister and head of a training college at Nottingham for Congregational clergy, he had long grown into a national figure when I learned to know and love him at the turn of the century. He had studied the work of the Inner Mission in Germany and liked to talk of its founder Wichern. He was the parent of more societies for what Americans call social uplift than any man of his time. His farm colonies for epileptics are perhaps the most widely known of his creations, but he was as zealous for the normal citizen as for the afflicted and those who fall by the way-side. He maintained that the organization of leisure was as vital as the organization of work, and the National Home Reading Union was one of his schemes. I was associated with him in the Social Institutes Union, a body for the provision of recreational facilities for adults in school buildings after the children had left, and in the British Institute for Social Service, a bureau of infor-mation and research of which Percy Alden, his friend and mine, was in charge. He worked at full steam till his death at the age of eighty-one, his faith in human nature undimmed. His biography by Sir James Marchant may be recommended to anyone who cares to make acquaintance with a practical idealist and latter-day saint.

The most dynamic and colourful of Victorian philanthropists was General Booth, whose commanding air, white hair and Semitic nose marked him out in any gathering as a born leader of men. I had heard him at Cambridge and was introduced to him at a rally at the Crystal Palace, where the sight of a woman con-ductor of a huge orchestra illustrated the equality of the sexes in his world-wide organization. *Darkest England and the Way Out* had recently appeared, and the old man was full of his schemes. 'I take the waste land, the waste lives, and the waste money out of the pockets of the rich,' he said to me, 'and I churn them all up together.' As he spoke he swung his right arm round and round as if he were churning milk. Huxley described the methods of the Salvation Army as 'corybantic Christianity', and its crude fundamentalism was not to my taste; but long acquaintance with its work at home and abroad—its self-sacrificing officers who renounce the amenities of life, its shelters, its workshops, its farm colonies—fills me with admiration and gratitude. I was particularly attached to Commissioner David Lamb, who was in control of the emigration department and continually travelling about the world, and whose views on social policy were frequently ex-pounded in *The Times*.

Founders of religious and social organizations are usually autocrats, and Benjamin Waugh was no exception to the rule. As a Congregational Minister and an original member of the London School Board he had become interested in neglected and ill-treated youth, and in 1884 he founded the Society for the Prevention of Cruelty to Children. I had become attracted to the work through a zealous Cambridge friend, and I was deeply impressed by the commanding personality of the Chief. The principal obstacle in the establishment of a branch office, he declared, was the complacent conviction that in that particular locality at any rate cruelty was unknown. It was a gripping experience to hear him at a public meeting telling story after story from his store of memories, passing from pathos to sarcasm and from sarcasm to righteous indignation. The Act of 1889 and its more stringent successors were the first-fruits of his campaign. When he died in 1908 he had improved the position of the English child, both in law and in fact, out of all recognition.

Among other Servants of Humanity—surely the noblest of all professions—with whom I came in contact I may mention Sir John Kirk, Secretary of the Ragged School Union, and Lady Henry Somerset, temperance apostle and founder of the colony for inebriate women at Duxhurst in Surrey. My knowledge of the poor was further increased by life-long experience as Trustee of a branch of the London City Mission in the dingy little streets tucked away behind Paddington Station, and crowded with unskilled, unemployed, under-employed and unemployable labourers. It was impossible to see so much of the dark shadows of the mighty city without continually reflecting both on the inequality of fortune and on possible remedies—education, evangelization, emigration, temperance teaching, home colonization, socialism, housing, public health and land reform. No one dreamed at the turn of the century of a national system of insurance against unemployment and sickness. I felt the power of *Progress and Poverty* without becoming a disciple of Henry George, for I have never believed in single-track remedies. I listened to Sir Charles Loch on one side and to the Fabians on the other, but I was never tempted to enlist under the banner either of *laissez-faire* or collectivism. Like most Englishmen, whatever their party colour, I preferred the middle of the road. The gigantic problem of social betterment, as revealed in the survey of London by Charles Booth and his associates, could only be tackled by the combined activites of the state, the local authorities, the voluntary associations, the churches, and the individual citizen; but for the integration of effort on a broad front which we call the Welfare State we had to wait till the Century of the Common Man.

7

THE SOUTH AFRICAN WAR

THE closing years of the Victorian era found England in a
buoyant mood such as she had scarcely known since the
reign of Elizabeth. The Home Rule split in the Liberal party
in 1886 installed the Unionists in power for twenty years. The
Jubilees of 1887 and 1897 focused the eyes of the world on a vast,
prosperous and powerful realm. A spirit of almost intoxicating
self-confidence prevailed. In the words of Alfred Spender,
Chamberlain was the conductor of the big brass band playing the
new imperial tunes, in which Kipling supplied incomparable
solos. Rhodes and Kitchener were the heroes of the hour. The
high-water mark of national complacency was reached in 1898,
when the Sudan was conquered and the French flag hauled down
at Fashoda. 'Take up the white man's burden.' There was a widespread conviction that no task was beyond our power; that our
share of the earth's surface could never be too large; that there
was something almost impious in resistance to our aims and arms.
Never had John Bull felt so sure of himself. In his penetrating
study *Victorian England* G. M. Young testifies that the British
public had grown more excitable and more easily satisfied with
material values at the close of the reign.

It was a difficult time for Liberals. The majority had no use for
our wares, and the party was discredited by the quarrels of its
chiefs. Rosebery resigned the leadership in 1896 on the ground of
contested authority, and two years later Harcourt and Morley,
his chief Gladstonian rivals, followed suit. Campbell-Bannerman,
who shouldered the thankless burden, was no match in debate
for Balfour. The prospects of Home Rule, which had not been
very cheerful since the collapse of Parnell, were further injured by

the squalid feud of Parnellites and anti-Parnellites, and weak-kneed Liberals of the Rosebery type lost faith in the principle of Irish self-government. Welsh Disestablishment and Local Option, the other main planks in 'the Newcastle Programme', were regarded by the mass of the nation with hostility or indifference. In the field of social reform the party had as little to offer to the common man as the Conservatives, for its creed remained predominantly political and economic democracy was still far away.

After Omdurman and Fashoda the British Government turned its attention to South Africa. What Lord Selborne, Under Secretary for the Colonies, called 'that accursed Raid', the mysterious failure of the Parliamentary Committee to probe the conspiracy to the bottom, the white-washing of Rhodes in Parliament by Chamberlain, and what Lecky, an ardent Unionist, described as the trail of finance, diminished our moral standing in the world and stiffened the backs of the Boers, sturdy and stubborn as their ancestors who had challenged the might of Philip II. The ten years of Unionist supremacy between 1895 and 1905 witnessed some valuable achievements at home and abroad, but in the eyes of most Liberals—and not a few Conservatives as well—their South African record was deplorable from beginning to end. The appointment of Milner, who had done so well in Egypt under the eye of Cromer and as Chairman of the Board of Inland Revenue, was a major error, for he seemed to the Dutch to embody the arrogance of a conquering race. Though the Boer farmers, with their fundamentalist theology and their contempt for the native, were not of the type to appeal to English Liberals, we inherited from Gladstone a belief in the right of little nations to live their own lives.

I had been distressed by the Armenian massacres, the Cretan revolt of 1896, and the Greco-Turkish war to which it led, but I was far more deeply stirred in the spring and summer of 1899 when England was no longer a mere spectator. It is much easier to judge the South African struggle with calmness of spirit after more than half a century, for the sterling qualities of the Boers have long been recognized and the superiority complex from which we suffered in the closing phase of the Victorian era has happily disappeared. With Milner and Kruger in the ring it would have been almost a miracle if the problem of the Uitlanders had been settled by peaceful means. Though neither of them wanted a war, both were resolved to fight for their principles in case of need—Kruger for the preservation of his untrammelled independence, Milner for British paramountcy in South Africa.

Two wholly antagonistic systems—a medieval race oligarchy and a modern industrial state recognizing no difference of status between various white races—cannot permanently live side by side in what is one country. Race oligarchy has got to go and I see no sign of it removing itself.

To the High Commissioner the British Empire was a religion. Judged by our European standards the Transvaal régime was an anachronism, but since the Raid Kruger had become the symbol of national survival. He remembered the Great Trek when the Boers had marched away from British rule into the uncharted interior in order to live their own life, and it was natural that he should yield as little as he could to the cosmopolitan throng which swarmed into his country in search of gold. 'If I put the English-man on the box,' he observed in his homely phraseology, 'he will drive my carriage into Queen Victoria's stables.' 'It is our country you want', he exclaimed when he and Milner met at the decisive Bloemfontein Conference; 'I am not ready to hand over my country to strangers.' Whether a tolerable compromise on the franchise could have been secured by more skilful negotiations at an earlier stage we cannot be sure, but by 1899 the atmosphere was poisoned by the shrill complaints of the Outlanders and the deepening suspicions of the Boers. The Transvaal had begun to arm on a considerable scale after the ominous warning of the Raid, the Orange Free State—though it had no Uitlander problem—was resolved to share its fortunes, and the British Empire was never in a less yielding mood.

After taking time to look round, and after the re-election of Kruger as President of the Transvaal with an increased majority in February 1898, Milner reported that there was no way out of the political troubles of South Africa except reform in the Trans-vaal or war, though he did not expect the final smash for several years. His correspondence with the British Government during the two and a half years of crisis fills the first massive volume of

6

The Milner Papers published in 1931. Here we may read his denunciations of 'the dishonest despotism in Pretoria', 'the despotic oligarchy armed to the teeth'; and here we find reiterated warnings from Chamberlain that with trouble in the Nile valley and in the Far East it was essential to go slow in South Africa. 'The Raid has placed this country in a false position, so let the irritation pass away before we resume pressure on the Transvaal.' And perhaps the old President might die. Yet when Sir William Butler, Commander of our small forces in South Africa, declared that the country needed rest, not a surgical operation, there was a shout of anger. The General, complained Milner, was a violent Krugerite; 'he or I will have to go'. So Butler was recalled.

The summer of 1899 is one of the most harrowing memories of my life. After the desperate struggles of 1914 and 1939 the South African war may look like a storm in a tea-cup, but it was our first major conflict since the Crimea. When Chamberlain declared that the sands were running out we could almost hear the roar of the avalanche. Were the disabilities of the Outlanders, who had gone to the Rand for their own purposes and made large fortunes, worth a war—not one of the minor colonial expeditions against 'lesser breeds without the law', as Kipling called our various foes, but a stern struggle against white Christians as civilized as ourselves? The notion that the Boers had been stealthily plotting for many years to drive us out of South Africa was one of the slogans belligerents invent to justify an appeal to arms: all they had wanted was to be left alone. When the guns went off the question of supremacy was inevitably raised, but during the negotiations which preceded the catastrophe the concrete issue was the political claims of the immigrants whose status was compared by the High Commissioner to that of helots. In his *Transvaal from Within*, which we all read in the autumn of 1899, Sir Percy Fitzpatrick painted a lurid picture of the corruption, inefficiency and deliberate hostility of what Milner described as the Pretoria gang. Yet the moral problem remained. Even assuming that indictment by one of the most respected of the Uitlanders to be approximately correct, had we a legal and moral right to coerce a state which in domestic affairs possessed the same unfettered sovereignty as England or France at the point of the bayonet? That was the question every citizen had to decide for himself.

When a quarrel is mounting towards a crisis critics are informed that they must hold their tongues lest a hint of national disunion should stiffen the potential enemy. On the other hand, unless the warning voice is raised in good time there is no possibility of altering the course of the ship. To look on in silence when momentous issues are at stake is the negation of 'government by discussion' which is the essence of democracy, and I rejoiced when two powerful voices rang out from Manchester on 15 September.

You may carry fire and sword into the midst of peace and industry: it will be wrong. A war of the strongest government in the world with untold wealth and inexhaustible reserves against this little republic will bring you no glory: it will be wrong. It may add a new province to your empire: it will still be wrong.

Such was the stirring message of John Morley and of Leonard Courtney, the most independent of Liberal Unionists. Never had I read two public speeches with more heartfelt gratitude. 'I envy you the honour of having led the Liberal host into action,' wrote Harcourt to Morley, 'and rejoice that I am now able to bring up the reserves in your support.' Unfortunately the quarrel had gone too far for speeches to count. An Army Corps was on its way to the Cape, and on 9 October the Transvaal Government, as expected, anticipated its arrival by an ultimatum. Salisbury spoke of it as 'Joe's war'. It would be more correct to speak of Milner's war and Kruger's war, though the ultimate cause was the discovery of gold on the Rand.

No problem in the ethics of citizenship is more difficult than the duty of men and women who disapprove a conflict in which their country becomes engaged. Shall they content themselves with registering a protest and then stand aside till the storm is over, or shall they strive to combat the agencies and ideologies which in their opinion helped to produce the catastrophe? If the latter course be adopted, it is mainly with the desire to prepare the way for the settlement that lies ahead. It was clear that there could only be one end to the duel between the giant and the dwarf. Stead's *Stop the War* campaign was worse than useless, and had I been in Parliament I should not have joined the six intransigents who opposed the estimates, for our men at the front could

not be let down. On the other hand I thought it worth attempting
to keep the thermometer below boiling-point. The man in the
street knew little of the past and present of South Africa, and he
greedily swallowed the noxious beverage poured down his throat
by the *Daily Mail*, then in the first flush of its career. In a brochure
The War and its Causes, published a few weeks after the outbreak
of hostilities, I outlined the story of the Dutch in South Africa
and endeavoured to explain why they acted as they did. I no longer
possess a copy, and I should, doubtless, find it crude and one-
sided, but I do not regret that my political début was an essay in
comprehension. Today British Imperialism is as dead as Queen
Anne. What little was left of it after the Second World War
disappeared when our rule in India ended in 1947. The British
Empire has given place to the British Commonwealth.

Most of the Liberal leaders were opposed to the war, and even
the minority condemned Chamberlain's technique. Within a
month of the outbreak the South Africa Conciliation Committee
was established under the auspices of Selous, the big-game hunter
who knew the Boer farmer better than any other Englishman and
had marched north with Rhodes to found Rhodesia in 1890.
Leonard Courtney was elected President and Frederick Mackarness, a lawyer with intimate knowledge of South Africa, Chairman of the Executive Committee. Its object was to supply
accurate information wherever obtainable and to look beyond the
passions of the moment to the means by which our foes might
ultimately be reconciled. The Committee was a rallying point for
politicians, journalists, publicists, preachers and pacifists who were
labelled Little Englanders and 'friends of every country but their
own'. Some who sympathized with its objects held aloof on the
ground that efforts at conciliation in time of war are wasted. Had
not Cobden exclaimed after his experiences in the Crimean war
that he would never again attempt to separate two mad dogs?
Here was a first-class political issue of the dimensions of Protection and Home Rule, an issue grave enough to sever old friendships and party ties. The two leading spirits of our Committee
already mentioned were Liberal Unionists, who had left their old
friends in the eighties on the Irish question and were before long
to return; for Home Rule seemed a long way off, and the immediate peril, as they read the situation, was Imperialism. Twenty

years later I was destined to write their lives. Nothing draws men more closely together than co-operation in an unpopular cause, and the 'Pro-Boers' were linked by a freemasonry which lasted up to the First World War and in some cases beyond it.

Courtney had specialized in South African questions for many years, and no Member of Parliament had more resolutely denounced the Jameson Raid. When the Report of the Parliamentary Committee was debated, and Chamberlain declared that Rhodes had done nothing inconsistent with his personal honour, he rejoined that Rhodes was steeped in deceit. 'It is necessary that we should clear ourselves absolutely of the past. If you wish to establish the reputation of this country, if you wish to make unsullied the honour of our statesmen, you ought to show that in the judgment of this House and of this nation it is not to be tolerated that his name should remain on the Privy Council.' The second task, he argued, was to summon Rhodes's solicitor to the bar of the House and compel the production of the telegrams which would indicate the relations of his client with the Colonial Office. When his advice was rejected, a bad day's work was done for the prestige of the British Empire and the peace of South Africa. A man of such knowledge, foresight and courage made an ideal President of the Conciliation Committee. For twenty years he had been a prominent actor on the political stage, and the South African war made him a national figure. Those who detested his principles and those who shared them agreed in the recognition of his utter disinterestedness. It was a triumph of character and personality. 'I wish there was more Cornish granite like you in the world', remarked his old friend Earl Grey in 1902; and a younger friend aptly testified that he was a man for all weathers. That he was denounced as a Pro-Boer and Little Englander, a crank and a doctrinaire, troubled him not at all. When I gave him one of my books and wrote in it *Victrix causa deis placuit sed victa Catoni* he seemed flattered by the comparison.

I was welcomed to his home in Cheyne Walk which was to mean so much to me for twenty years, and I learned to love the sturdy old host. Though I was neither a Unionist nor as yet a convert to Proportional Representation, minor differences melted away in our common detestation of the South African record of the Government. When the harmony of many homes, my own included, was strained by divergent views on the war, he was a tower of strength. There was nothing flabby or nebulous about him, for his mind had a keen edge. He was interested in everything except trifles. He loved poetry, of which he held inexhaustible stores in his memory; he was something of a connoisseur in pictures; he had travelled in many parts of the world; and he revealed a deep though undogmatic piety in his thoughtful little book, *The Diary of a Churchgoer*. Born in 1832 he had followed public events since the revolution of 1848. His wife, one of the nine Miss Potters and an elder sister of Mrs. Sidney Webb, stood with unflinching courage at his side, and helped to make their home a social centre of the Pro-Boers.

While Courtney's knowledge of the historical relations of Boer and Briton was unrivalled, the Chairman of the Executive was a mine of information on recent developments. A son of a Bishop of Oxford and a nephew of Chief Justice Coleridge, Mackarness had practised as a lawyer in Cape Colony where he met the leading figures of both races. To him, as to old Richard Hooker, law was 'the voice of God'. After his return he appeared before the Privy Council in South African cases, and learned of every move on the chess-board through such friends as Merriman and Sauer, Sir Henry de Villiers and Schreiner, Sir James Rose Innes and Sir Richard Solomon. His opposition to the war arose not merely from the respect he had formed for the Dutch but from his conviction that the grievances of the Outlanders, though real and vexatious, were limited in extent. Where Milner discovered 'panoplied hatred, insensate ambition, invincible ignorance', Mackarness saw only the natural reluctance of a little farming community to enfranchise immigrants who had recently plotted the overthrow of the Republic. His pamphlets and letters to the press throughout the struggle were courteous in tone and packed with knowledge. History, he believed, would condemn the South African war as it had condemned the struggle in the Crimea. He loved England so tenderly that he could not bear to see a blot on her scutcheon. It was indeed the greatest sorrow and trial of his life. He was ready for any personal sacrifice, and his campaign ruined his legal practice. I used to call him the bulldog, for once engaged in a struggle of principle he never let go. The members of the Conciliation Committee had not to wait many years before we learned from the lips of Botha and Smuts that the bitterness of defeat had been in some degree assuaged by the knowledge that Chamberlain and Milner did not speak for the whole of Great Britain.

The argument for the war was presented by St. Loe Strachey with remarkable power in the *Spectator*, which I read diligently every week. Equally striking were the leaders in the *Daily News* by Sir Edward Cook, an ardent Liberal Imperialist and author of *The Rights and Wrongs of the Transvaal War*, the best defence of the Chamberlain-Milner policy ever written. On my side of the fence the most gifted journalistic champion was Massingham. He had made the *Daily Chronicle* the expression of his Gladstonian Liberalism, but he resigned his editorial chair without hesitation when the proprietors invited him to support the war. A similar misfortune befell the Liberal Ulsterman, Crook, editor of the *Echo*, who accepted his fate with the same uncomplaining philosophy. These evictions left the *Morning Leader* the only London paper in open opposition. The *Westminster Gazette*, believing that the war was 'unnecessary but not unjust', strove to prevent the two sections of the Liberal Party from drifting irrevocably apart, and usually shared our views on specific misdeeds of the Government. The cool temperament of Alfred Spender, the eldest and ablest of three brothers, was a national asset in those days of boiling passion; and though I felt more hotly about the whole affair I was grateful for the balanced comments of the only Liberal journalist who kept in touch with both wings. My chief comfort in the daily press came from the *Manchester Guardian*, in which its proprietor and editor, C. P. Scott, Member of Parliament till the dissolution of 1900, and Leonard Hobhouse, as eminent in journalism as in philosophy and sociology, expounded the Gladstonian tradition.

The South African war brought me my first taste of journalism. A group of young Oxford Liberals, all of whom were to make their name, assumed control of the *Speaker*, a Liberal weekly. Its editor J. L. Hammond, later our leading social historian, had derived his principles from Fox and Gladstone. To him and his colleagues the conflict represented the domination of some of the least desirable elements in our national life. His principal comrade was Francis Hirst, subsequently editor of the *Economist*, formerly his collaborator in the well-known *Essays in Liberalism* which also contained contributions from Gilbert Murray, Hilaire Belloc and John Simon. Though the ship was thus mainly manned by an Oxford crew, it carried cargo supplied by other hands such as Chesterton and Hobson. My contributions were reviews. When the worst of the Imperialist tornado was over Hammond exchanged journalism for historical research, but his spirited campaign contributed to the Liberal triumph of 1906.

I took a deeper plunge into journalism when the *Echo* came into the market. Under Passmore Edwards it had enjoyed a wide circulation as a Liberal organ, but there were too many evening papers in London and it was now on the down grade. The Liberal case, however, was so inadequately represented in the Press that the paper was purchased by my old Eton and Trinity friend Lawrence, then at the beginning of a distinguished career. He was prospective Unionist candidate for a London borough when the war drove him into the opposite camp. He invited me to help in the enterprise, and I contributed occasional leaders, interviews and reviews. Though the war dominated everything, the *Echo* stood for a more advanced social programme than was usual at that time. When it changed hands we invited and obtained the blessings of many leading opponents of the fashionable Imperialism, among them the octogenarian Herbert Spencer, who, however, deplored any departure from the *laissez-faire* doctrines of his youth. The chief leader-writers were Hammond and Percy Alden, the former specializing in foreign and colonial affairs, the latter a recognized authority on social reform. Lawrence was bursting with energy, but not even he could save a moribund journal with an unpopular policy.

Though the Unionists possessed a large majority and the Septennial Act was still in operation, they suddenly dissolved Parliament in September, 1900. Proclaiming that the struggle was nearly over, they asked for a mandate to finish the job. It was Chamberlain's election, and he campaigned with the raucous slogan that every vote for a Liberal was a vote for the Boers. A born fighter, like Lloyd George and Churchill, 'Joe' always fought with the gloves off. The result of what was called the khaki election was never in doubt, and the Government was returned in undiminished strength. I had addressed meetings for the Eighty

Club, a Liberal organization dating from the victory in 1880, but I had my first experience of electioneering at Lincoln, where Charles Roberts, temperance reformer and later Under-Secretary for India, was the candidate. The first intoxication of the war was over, and we received a fair hearing. In spite of their deplorable divisions Liberals lost no further ground, and we knew our time would come.

During the war years I learned to know nearly all the active opponents of the Government policy. It was a special privilege to meet John Morley, with whom I had a bond of union in our affection for Lord Acton. He was immersed in his biography of Gladstone and for a time his voice was seldom heard in Parliament. His rare appearances were an event, and he never slackened in his denunciations of 'uncompensated mischief and irreparable wrong'. I was soon to renew acquaintance in the House of Commons, but it was not till some years later after his retirement from active politics that I became an intimate friend. Lloyd George, on the other hand, whose acquaintance I also made in those stormy days, was a fiery crusader, for in 'the Welsh wizard' the native hue of resolution was never sicklied o'er by the pale cast of thought. Though he had been in Parliament for nine years, it was only during the South African struggle that he became a national figure. His passionate love for 'the little land among the hills' helped him to understand the nationalism of the Boers and their devotion to their own way of life. While most of the Pro-Boer leaders—Campbell-Bannerman, Harcourt, Morley, Ripon, Spencer, Bryce—were veterans of the Liberal army, Lloyd George represented youth with its punch and scorn of compromise. Massingham compared him to the leading character in a well-constructed play coming on the stage at the psychological moment. He was the great discovery of the Liberals at the end of the nineties, as Balfour had been acclaimed by the Conservatives at the end of the eighties. Having worked his way up from the bottom of the social ladder the penniless orphan had brought with him an abiding sympathy with the poor. Now it became clear to friend and foe that he would go far and perhaps fill the post of radical leader vacated by Chamberlain's secession over Home Rule.

Among the younger standard-bearers in the Pro-Boer army

was Ramsay MacDonald. At an early period of the war I climbed
the stairs to his flat in Lincoln's Inn Fields and found a friendly
welcome. Margaret MacDonald was scarcely less of a personality,
but she was cast in a very different mould. It was a perfect partnership to which the bereaved husband was later to pay touching
tribute in two books, one for the general reader, the other privately
printed, for intimate friends. She possessed sufficient means to
enable them to live in modest comfort and to travel; and she
introduced him into the world of scientists in which her father,
Stephen Gladstone, the friend of Faraday, and her uncle Lord
Kelvin were shining lights. He loved literature and the arts and
was a diligent student of economics and sociology. No one at that
time except himself foresaw his rise to the Premiership, but we all
felt his power. With his rich Highland voice he was already one
of the most moving speakers of the time, and he wrote almost as
well as he spoke. The At Homes at Lincoln's Inn Fields described
in Lord Elton's biography and other books were a meeting place
for Pro-Boers only second to that of the Courtneys in Cheyne
Walk. Margaret MacDonald combined the radiance of a happy
child with the thoughtful tenderness of mature womanhood. No
one cared less for the pomps and vanities of the world, and she
was one of the few whom high place could never have spoiled.
She was full of 'good works', interesting herself in politics mainly
as an instrument of social betterment. Among her numerous
activities was her campaign against the employment of girls in
public houses, which she believed to be detrimental to their
health and potentially dangerous to their morals. For many years
she was one of the leading spirits in the Women's Industrial
Council which sought to promote the welfare of women in
industry. Few women I have known were so deeply mourned.

The South African war lasted far longer than anyone anticipated. The initial failures of our troops were quickly retrieved
when Roberts and Kitchener arrived at the opening of 1900 and
overwhelming forces were hurried to the front; yet for two years
after the tide turned the Boers fought on doggedly, not for
victory but for honour. The guerrilla warfare imposed upon them
by the paucity of their numbers and the vastness of the terrain
frayed the nerves of the British authorities and led to the employment of methods of which systematic farm-burning was the

worst. Such measures merely steeled the resolution of the commandos in the field. When it was proclaimed in the summer of 1901 that leaders who had not surrendered by a certain date would be banished for life, it was clear that the Government had lost its poise. For Milner, convinced as he was of 'the eternal duplicity of the Boers', the only terms were unconditional surrender; but as the conflict dragged on the sterling qualities of our foes and their Generals, Botha and Smuts, Delarey and De Wet, began to be realized. Kruger had fled to Europe on the capture of Pretoria, and the men under arms were determined to hold out till they could yield without humiliation. In a celebrated speech at Chesterfield, Rosebery, sometimes described as 'the Orator of Empire', suggested a meeting 'at some wayside inn'.

Kitchener entertained a steadily increasing admiration for the enemy, and when the end came in the spring of 1902 it was the soldier who favoured generous terms while the High Commissioner held out for his pound of flesh. The long chapter on the Peace of Vereeniging in the second volume of *The Milner Papers* is filled with denunciations of his colleague. 'I don't at all relish the idea of an interview between Kitchener and the Boer delegates. . . . He is fearfully wrongheaded sometimes. . . . Kitchener's policy I think a wholly mistaken one. . . . I distrust all negotiations. . . . My great difficulty is Lord Kitchener. He does not care what he gives away. . . . All he is doing is to paralyse me. . . . I hate all negotiations.' Such was the mentality of the High Commissioner. Happily for South Africa the magnanimity of the Commander-in-Chief prevailed over the die-hard champion of a dictated peace who regarded concessions as a betrayal of the loyalists whose cause he had espoused with passionate devotion. Courtney once spoke of Milner as a lost mind. It would be fairer to say that he was sent to the wrong place. Though he possessed some fine qualities, above all complete personal disinterestedness, and was adored by his 'kindergarten', he was temperamentally unfitted to deal with a proud race that could be broken but never bent. Even his old friend Haldane, the stoutest of his supporters among the Liberal Imperialists, conceded many years later that he was not the best man to handle the situation in South Africa.

While the Liberal supporters of the war, captained by Rosebery and his three lieutenants, Asquith, Grey and Haldane, drifted away from the main body of the party and formed the short-lived Liberal League, the struggle had stirred the easy-going Campbell-Bannerman to the depths and his utterances became increasingly critical. The two sections of the party were engaged in what F. C. Gould, the inspired caricaturist of the *Westminster Gazette*, wittily described as war to the knife and fork. The climax was reached at a public dinner at which the Liberal Leader denounced some recent coercive measures as 'methods of barbarism', and Morley claimed that he and his associates were 'in the main stream of Liberalism'. I still think of that dinner as perhaps the most memorable I have attended. We were certainly not carried away by oratory, for Campbell-Bannerman and Harcourt read their speeches, and Morley was at all times more impressive than eloquent. All three, however, let themselves go, giving rein to their detestation of a policy and a spirit which they regarded as unworthy of our best traditions.

No aspect of the struggle aroused such feeling as the concentration camps in which Boer families were herded when their homes were destroyed. The technique of winning the war by devastating the terrain and burning farms necessitated some provision for the women and children, but the camps proved death-traps for the young. That there was deliberate cruelty or callousness was never suggested, but ignorance and carelessness were scarcely less lethal. It was the achievement of Emily Hobhouse, sister of the Professor, to reveal the alarming conditions and thereby to secure their amelioration. That she was denounced as an enemy of her country for saving thousands of innocent lives was a striking illustration of war hysteria. She told her story in *The Brunt of the War*, and it is summarized in her biography by Ruth Fry. Her health never recovered from the strain, but her name is linked with that of C.-B. in the grateful memory of the losing side. It is one of the ironies of history that two of the persons most vehemently attacked by their countrymen were those who did most to reconcile our foes to their new life within the Empire. When the struggle was over she returned to South Africa and aided recovery by establishing domestic industries. The gratitude of the Boers took practical shape in the presentation of a sum with which to buy a house. She was the Florence

Nightingale of the Boer War, though she ministered not to wounded soldiers but to women and children in distress.

My views on the war were shared by most of the young Liberal recruits no less than by the Gladstonian veterans. Among my intimate friends at the turn of the century was Charles Masterman, whose meteoric career may be studied in the biography by his wife. We were the same age and had met at Cambridge where he had studied science, but it was not till we were both busy with social work in London that we were thrown together. The 'model dwelling' in the East End in which he first pitched his camp proved to be verminous and required fumigation. He was for some time Secretary of the Children's Country Holiday Fund, for he loved children, and it was always a happy moment when he saw batches of them off at the station. He was a radiant figure in those days—slim, refined, ascetic, a brilliant talker and writer, a practical idealist. He was one of the standard-bearers in the Christian Social Union, an intimate friend of Bishop Gore and Canon Scott Holland, a frequent contributor to *The Common-wealth*, into which the latter distilled his rich personality every month. Like his leaders Masterman was a High Church Radical, finding in the New Testament the mandate for far-reaching social reform. His experiences and reflections were set forth with compelling eloquence in his little book *From the Abyss*, in a collection of essays entitled *In Peril of Change*, and later in his comprehensive survey *The Condition of England*.

Masterman was always talking of the 'condition of the people question', and he was far more anxious to raise their standard than to enlarge the Empire. At the height of the war he planned a volume of essays to be written by a group of young Liberals. The problem of the title was happily solved by George Trevelyan, who suggested *The Heart of the Empire*. Masterman provided the Preface and opened with a comprehensive survey entitled Realities at Home. Lawrence followed on Housing, Bray (the editor's comrade in the 'model dwelling') on the Children of the Town, Noel Buxton on Temperance Reform (with inside knowledge of the brewing trade), Philip Wilson, later a Member of Parliament, on The Distribution of Industry, Pigou, soon to succeed Marshall as Professor of Political Economy at Cambridge, on The Problem of Charity, and Head, a Cambridge History don, on The Church and the People. The volume closed with a lengthy study of Imperialism by myself, and a conclusion by George Trevelyan entitled The Past and the Future. The book, which was published in 1901 by Fisher Unwin, son-in-law of Richard Cobden and an ardent 'Pro-Boer', sold astonishingly well, and a cheap edition appeared in 1902. Perhaps we could claim some modest share in feeding the rills which swelled the Liberal torrent of 1906. Three of our contributors were to become Cabinet Ministers, one an Archbishop, and one to receive the Order of Merit.

'A discussion of Imperialism in theory and practice,' wrote the editor in the Preface, 'forms a natural pendant to a volume that attempts to deal with the problems that face us at the Heart of the Empire.' That seemed natural enough to us but not to some reviewers who denounced me as the black sheep of an otherwise respectable flock. My colleagues were as impenitent as myself, and Masterman held his shield over me in his Preface to the cheap edition.

> Adverse criticism has mainly concentrated itself upon regrets that the discussion of the difficult problems of Social Reform should be incorporated with a more or less controversial examination of modern Imperialism. The authors are unable to accept this sharp delimitation of home and foreign affairs. Every day is exhibiting how closely the two problems are intertwined. On deeper examination forces that make for unrest abroad are found to be the same forces that are stifling progress at home. Lack of sympathetic imagination, materialism and the spirit of mastery: these form the trinity which have to be strenuously fought in both spheres of political activity.

I took advantage of the new edition to add a few pages bringing the story of the struggle to the opening of 1902 when the end of the struggle was in sight.

Re-reading my dissertation on Imperialism after an interval of half a century I find my opinions essentially unchanged, though I should naturally express them with greater restraint. On the relation of politics to ethics, on national and racial arrogance, on the glorification of force, on credulity in wartime, I think today as I thought in my youth. In a survey of the dependencies I pleaded for the Ripon touch in India as against Curzon's superiority complex, and I anticipated 'the gradual transference of the machinery of administration to native hands, retaining only the supreme direction in our own.' At the close of a discussion of the causes and incidents of the South African war I urged the Government to use its brains as well as its guns.

> Liberals will continue to believe and assert that the problem before British statesmen is at least as much political as military. The most complete success of the policy of unconditional surrender is better calculated than anything else to leave on our hands an insoluble political problem—the problem of reconciling to our rule one of the toughest and bravest races in the world, smarting under defeat and bound neither by pledges nor by interest to respect a settlement in the formation of which they have had no part.

The Treaty of Vereeniging in May 1902, marked the abandonment of Milner's short-sighted policy of unconditional surrender. Everyone was sick of the struggle, and it was no longer the test of patriotism to assert that the South African Dutch were a cruel and treacherous race. Yet the process of enlightenment at home had been slow, for war fever had raged with devastating intensity. I was aware of the fortunes of the peace party in the Crimean war, of the popular conviction at that time that the Russians were brutal barbarians, of the naïve credulity which suspected the loyalty of the Prince Consort himself. Now I learned from direct experience the spiritual demoralization which war brings in its train, the clouding of the mind, the paralysis of the critical faculties. The enemy became a fearsome monster with horns and hoofs against whose vices and crimes our own shining virtues stood out in bold relief. There was nothing peculiar to England in these pathological phenomena. Social psychology was in its infancy, though valuable pioneering work had been done in France by Tarde and Le Bon and was soon to be carried further by Graham Wallas's masterpiece *Human Nature in Politics*. It was the distinction of John Hobson—economist, sociologist, journalist—to review the political and economic features of the era of expansion in his classical treatise on Imperialism. He had visited South Africa as a correspondent when the storm was blowing up in the summer of 1899, and on his return I began a friendship of forty years. While the younger generation of today have only known their country as the pillar of peace—which it became after the South African war when we possessed as much of the earth's surface as we desired—those with longer memories recall the time when our territorial appetite was as keen as that of our rivals. All the Great Powers of Europe except the Austrian Empire suffered from the same urge.

The conflict of 1899–1902 was a turning point in my life. Hitherto I had specialized in social questions: henceforth problems of empire and international relations occupied the foremost place in my thoughts, and the idea of entering public life ceased to be a far-off dream. Having been in contact with men who were making history, I felt myself no longer a mere onlooker but a regular soldier in the Liberal ranks. My party, which had been marking time since the retirement of Gladstone in 1894, had found a fresh inspiration and an inspiring chief. 'Imperialism!' exclaimed C.-B.; 'I hate the name and I hate the thing.' So did I. Looking back half a century later I rejoice that, so far as my country is concerned, it has disappeared.

8

EDWARDIAN SPRINGTIME

THE passing of Victoria, the accession of Edward VII, the end of the South African war, and the retirement of Salisbury, inaugurated a new era in politics and society. After the long twilight of the widowed Queen the doors and windows of Windsor Castle were flung open and the Court was filled with the throb of life. The Unionist Government seemed almost as strong, if not quite so impressive, under 'Prince Arthur' as it had been under the banner of his majestic uncle; but the tide was beginning to turn, and Chamberlain was meditating the crusade which was to turn the political situation upside down. At the close of hostilities in 1902 public attention was once more focused on the home front. The war had ended in victory but hardly in triumph, for the struggle had revealed grave flaws in our armour. It was a period of stocktaking and introspection, but also of eager planning and reviving hopes. Liberalism was on the up-grade, though office still appeared far away.

During the opening years of the new century I was privileged to enlarge my acquaintance with foreign countries. On a visit to Vienna in 1900 I gained my first insight into the nationalities problem of the Hapsburg Empire. At the moment the chief trouble arose from the Czechs, and as a Home Ruler I sympathized with their feelings, though without the slightest hostility towards Austria whose modest ambition was merely to continue to exist. Though the growth of nationalism was slowly sapping her strength, she remained a Great Power and a shining cultural influence. The city of Beethoven and Schubert, Brahms, Johann Strauss and Hugo Wolf, was like a beacon light in central Europe. Schnitzler was at the beginning of his career, Hugo von

7

Hofmannsthal and Stefan Zweig were trying their wings, and the opera was a joy. My most enduring memory was of the pictures in the national collection and the scarcely less resplendent treasures of the Lichtenstein Palace.

I returned home via Prague, where Czech nationalism could be studied from the other end. Bohemia, like all the provinces of cis-Leithan Austria, possessed a provincial diet, and the Czech University, founded in 1881, proved a concession of the utmost political significance. Francis Joseph, however, was still widely regarded as an alien ruler, and the Czech majority fretted under Teutonic domination. The lovely capital made the impression of a purely Czech city, and it was disconcerting to find the names of streets and the routes of trams in an unfamiliar tongue. A question in German addressed to a passer-by was sometimes ignored, though all educated Czechs knew both languages. It was my first experience of the deep-seated antagonism of the Teuton and the Slav which was soon to plunge the world into war.

The outstanding figure on the political stage was Kramarz, leader of the Young Czechs and spokesman of the national aspirations in the Reichsrat; but a far more remarkable personage was Masaryk, to whom I had brought an introduction from the well-known Vienna journalist Sigmund Münz. The Professor of Philosophy and Sociology at the Czech University was already famous among the Slav races of the monarchy as a scholar and teacher, though he was little known to the outside world. Ardent as was his Czech patriotism, his love of truth was stronger still; for he had exposed as impudent modern forgeries the Königinhof manuscripts which uncritical historians had used to prove the lofty civilization of their country in the Middle Ages. He had displayed even greater courage by denouncing the monstrous superstition that the Jews indulged in the ritual murder of Christian children. He was to become a European celebrity some years later, when from his place in the Reichsrat he denounced the forgeries employed in the bitter conflict with Belgrade; but it was not very difficult as early as 1900 to discover that the Professor with his grave scholar's face and quiet voice was a personality to be reckoned with. He possessed an astonishing knowledge of political and cultural conditions in almost every country of Europe, Russia above all. He had studied in Leipzig as well as

Vienna, and he owed too much to German scholarship to share the prevalent racial bias against the masterful Teuton. He gave me his latest work, *The Philosophical and Sociological Bases of Marxism*, a massive volume in German analysing the teaching of Marx with unrivalled thoroughness and displaying a mastery of nineteenth-century ideologies. He visited me in London a year or two later, en route to lecture in America, and again in the testing years of war. I watched with eager interest the philosopher emerging from his study to challenge Aehrenthal to his face and later risking his life in the cause of Czechoslovak independence.

In 1902 I had my first glimpse of the East. Egypt was passing through the quietest phase of the British Occupation, for the Sudan had been reconquered and the revival of militant nationalism had not begun. The finances were at last in excellent order, and it seemed as if the anomalous spectacle of a European Power squatting uninvited in a Turkish province might continue indefinitely according to the principle *ce n'est que le provisoire qui reste*. Lord Cromer, the greatest of our proconsuls, who possessed the patience and insight which Milner and Curzon lacked, sat firmly in the saddle. I had read his annual reports with admiration and pride, and I had no desire to see British troops march out and Turkish troops march in. The young Khedive, who felt like a caged bird, had begun his reign by beating his wings against the bars; but he was scarcely more a native product than ourselves, for he was descended from an Albanian chief. The country was ruled by the 'British Agent and Consul-General', not by Abbas II, and for the time being it was the wisest arrangement. Though Cromer was past sixty, he looked strong and well. There was a touch of severity in his fine face and of command in his voice, but he was immensely respected and his devotion to the interests of Egypt was beyond challenge. Though a fine classical scholar he never attempted to master Arabic.

I brought an introduction to Wilfrid Blunt, former champion of Arabi, persistent critic of Cromer, and friend of the few Nationalists who survived. I had been struck by his book *The Future of Islam*, though I shared his enthusiasm neither for the faith nor for the civilizations which it had helped to create. It was disappointing to find him away, and I did not meet him till the Egyptian question boiled up in Parliament in 1906. There were at that time no outstanding representatives of native opinion. Arabi was an exile in Ceylon, and most of the wealthy and educated class were Turks or Armenians. Leonard Courtney had given me an introduction to Tigrane Pasha, a rich and highly cultivated Armenian who had been Foreign Minister in the eighties, of whom Cromer was to paint an elaborate portrait in his *Modern Egypt*. He was not altogether satisfied with the British régime, but no Armenian could wish for the restoration of Turkish rule. The unofficial British view I learned from an old Trinity friend, at that time an instructor in the Law School and destined as Sir Maurice Amos to become legal adviser to the Egyptian Government. Everyone in Cairo seemed to agree that the British had come to stay.

I prepared myself by extensive reading in history and archaeology, and took with me old authorities such as Herodotus and new ones such as Erman's admirable *Life in Ancient Egypt*. The superb collections in the Cairo Museum made the treasures of Herculaneum at Naples seem like things of yesterday. It was impressive to gaze upon the features of Rameses II, the Louis XIV of the ancient world, as he lies in his glass case, as recognizable as when he closed his eyes over three thousand years ago. While the Cairo area witnesses to the Early Kingdom, at Luxor the traveller is in the heart of the Later Kingdom, with the glorious temple of Karnak on the right bank of the river and the tombs of the kings on the left. At Philae we were just in time to land on the island before the completion of the Assouan Dam drowned the Ptolemaic temples in a vast reservoir behind the First Cataract. In the valley of the Nile the old world and the new jostle each other at every turn, while the fellah pursues his unchanging course and man and beast live on the bounty of the mighty stream born in the highlands of Abyssinia and the Great Lakes three thousand miles away.

A visit to Greece on the way home introduced me to the cradle of European culture, and I rejoiced more than ever that I had been reared on the classics. The Athens of today is larger than Constantinople, but in 1902 it made a provincial impression. The road from Piraeus was full of holes, there was no through railway to the north, and people spoke of going to Europe when they set out on their travels. The country had been a derelict Turkish province less than eighty years before and its development had been handicapped by poverty. In so barren a land only a hardworking and abstemious race could thrive, and the Greeks had been so chastened in the Turkish war of 1897 that they hardly counted on the Balkan chessboard. I discussed the political situation with the British Minister, Sir Edwin Egerton, and with Bourchier, the famous *Times* Correspondent whom I was to know so well in after years. King George, brother of our Queen Alexandra, lived quietly in the vast square palace in the centre of the town, a tactful constitutional ruler, respected rather than beloved. The Orthodox Church was as closely identified with the national cause as the Catholic Church with the Home Rulers in Ireland, for in both cases the clergy had borne a leading part in the fight against alien domination.

No one can be disappointed with the Parthenon and the view from the Acropolis over sea and land, but the museum at Athens contained nothing to approach the Elgin marbles in the British Museum. A coasting boat brought us through the Corinth canal to the little village of Itea in the spacious gulf, whence we drove up through the olive groves to Delphi where French archaeologists had been clearing the historic site. It was a perfect spring day for the most romantically situated shrine in the world. I have enjoyed the panorama from the Alhambra at Granada and from the Palace of the Prince Bishops on its rocky height at Salzburg, but the view from Delphi across the Gulf of Corinth to the mountains of Peloponnesus stands alone. Mycenae and Tiryns, where the name of Schliemann was still a household word, were visited from Nauplia, and we were about to start for Olympia when typhoid hurried me back to the capital. It was a disappointment to miss the Hermes of Praxiteles by a few hours. Weeks of illness followed in an Athens hotel, enlivened at Easter by the shooting in which the Greeks express their uninhibited rapture at the resurrection of Christ.

In the following year, 1903, I married Else Schön, an art student whom I had met during my first visit to Berlin, and we chose Spain for our wedding trip. The country was slowly recovering its breath after the knock-out blow of 1898. The loss of Cuba and the Philippines proved a blessing in disguise, for the nation could now devote itself to internal problems, freed from a financial and

military burden which it was no longer able to bear. But dominant
impressions were the vastness, the emptiness, the isolation, the
stagnation and the poverty of the peninsula. While Italy stood in
the main current of European life, Spain seemed like a quiet backwater behind the rampart of the Pyrenees. There was something
melancholy in the spectacle of a state which had once bestrode
the world and was now the shadow of a great name. King Alfonso
was only seventeen, and little was known of him except that he
had been carefully brought up by his respected Austrian mother.
Canovas and Sagasta, the Conservative and Liberal chiefs who
had alternated in office since the restoration of the Monarchy in
1874, had recently died, and there was no outstanding figure on
the political stage. I picked up the threads from *The Times*
Correspondent in Madrid, Moreton Fullerton, later so well known
by his stimulating book *The Problems of Power*. Spanish socialism
was still in its infancy, but I sought out its leader Iglesias, a
thoughtful intellectual whom Spanish socialists of today revere
as their French comrades revere Jaurès. The working-class movement was strongest in the coast towns, for Castile was still the
fortress of Church and King.

Entering the country from the Biarritz end of the Pyrenees we
approached the capital through Burgos, with its noble cathedral,
Avila, the walled city of St. Theresa, and the Escurial, a pile as
forbidding as Wormwood Scrubs. It was Philip II in stone; and,
though I had emancipated myself from the invective of Motley
and had learned from Martin Hume to regard him with more
tolerant eyes as 'a good man according to his lights', he remained
a chilly figure. We felt very close to him in the dark chamber
where he lay patiently waiting for the end, his eyes fixed through
an opening on the high altar. We were informed by the guide that
only one niche remained in the burial chamber of the kings. In
the Prado at Madrid Velasquez and Goya are seen in all their
glory. The vogue of El Greco, which now draws tourists to
Toledo scarcely less than the cathedral, was not so great in 1903
as it afterwards became. Murillo can be seen almost as well in
other countries as in his own. Spanish Gothic, though a little
florid for northern taste, seems to suit the exuberant south.

In Seville as in Toledo examples of Christian and Moorish art
stand side by side. The cathedral and its tower are a joy for ever,

and the Moorish palace fascinates by its delicate grace. After the rather mediocre Islamic architecture of Cairo it was refreshing to see the exquisite workmanship of the Spanish Moors. The mosque of Cordova with its thousand columns is a curiosity, and Granada deserves its undying renown. The courts of the Alhambra, so bare without and so elaborate within, must have seemed an earthly paradise to the Africans whose expulsion by Ferdinand and Isabella was a gain to the Church and a loss to the culture of Europe. Our last glimpse of the peninsula was Barcelona, which throbbed with vitality and seemed the half-way house between conservative Castile and democratic France. A short run from the Catalonian capital brought us to Montserrat, the romantic shrine among the rocky hills where Ignatius Loyola resolved to found the Society of Jesus and enrolled himself among the makers of modern history.

The visit to Spain provided the necessary stimulus to learn the language. I had reserved *Don Quixote*, as I had reserved Borrow's *Bible in Spain*, for such an adventure, and I enjoyed the most famous novel in the world in its country of origin. Among contemporary writers I was attracted to Perez Galdos, the Spanish Scott, whose *Episodios Nacionales*, recounting the history of his country from Napoleon onwards in two score volumes, were to be seen in the windows of every bookshop. Scarcely less interesting were his widely read anti-clerical novels *Dona Perfecta*, *Gloria* and *Leon Roch*, and his much discussed play *Electra*; for though the hold of the Church on the Spanish people as a whole seemed unshaken, a cold draught of anti-clericalism had filtered in from France. The campaign was continued by Blasco Ibañez, then at the beginning of his brilliant career, whose novel *The Cathedral* denounced the selfishness and obscurantism of the Church in vibrant terms. Intellectually no less than politically Spain continued to lead a hermit life. The honoured names of Unamuno, Ortega y Gasset and Madariaga had not yet become familiar in the world debate. Though we felt no temptation to sample a bullfight, it was impossible to see the gigantic bull-rings in every city without realizing how strongly entrenched is this disgusting and degrading cult of blood.

In the following year, 1904, I joined a small party of social workers arranged by Percy Alden for the study of reformatory institutions in Belgium, Germany and Holland. In a penal colony near Antwerp we found hundreds of delinquents busily employed on the needs of the army and the public. So far as possible the inmates plied their own trades, and if they had none they were taught. There were no elaborate precautions against escape, for convicts were easily tracked. The system was better than confinement in a city prison, for they lived in healthy surroundings and there was plenty of skilled work to be done. The superintendent, however, did not pretend that this temporary segregation of the black sheep, however beneficial to the rest of the flock, was of much ethical value.

To pass from the crowded penal community of Belgium to a German labour colony was a welcome relief; for at Lühlerheim, on the east bank of the Rhine near Wesel, we found a cheerful family rather than a soulless institution. The inmates, who numbered only about two dozen, were neither criminals nor professional vagrants, but for the most part men of weak physique and slender skill who found it difficult to get and keep a job. The farm colony was under the kindly direction of a Father, corresponding to a Church Army captain. The men were treated as individuals, and every effort was made to restore their self-confidence during a stay of about four months. Though many turned up again and again at the different colonies, some were nursed back into self-supporting citizenship, and all must have gained from the healthy work and kindly discipline. From Wesel we journeyed east to Bielefeld in Westphalia, the 'Colony of Mercy' described in Julie Sutter's book which had attracted wide attention in England. Here were gathered about two thousand epileptics from all parts of Germany, and here too was a labour colony of the Lühlerheim type. The *genius loci* was Pastor Bodelschwingh, one of the outstanding figures of Protestant Germany at the turn of the century. His father had been Minister of the Interior under Frederick William IV, and the Pastor himself, who gave us a friendly welcome, was born to command. Bethel, as the community was called, represented old Germany at its best—simplicity, piety, discipline and hard work. Our tour closed with a visit to a quasi-penal colony in Holland, where the inmates were employed in fruit growing; but we found nothing so hopeful and helpful as the labour colonies of Germany with their human touch.

In 1905 I visited Denmark to study the institutions which had given the little country a new lease of life after the territorial amputation in 1864. Among them were the High Schools founded by Bishop Grundtvig for adults who came for a winter course when labour was least needed on the land. Their object was not to teach people how to earn but how to enrich their lives. The same belief in national planning was visible in the co-operative system which had raised Denmark to the position of one of the leading food exporters in Europe. The first sight that greeted the traveller was that of the cows grazing with coverings on their backs, and the unusual size of the eggs showed what breeding can achieve. The eggs collected from the farms were stamped with their date and place of origin, arranged in frames and tested by powerful electric light, offenders being promptly tracked down and complaints lodged at the farm. The state railways contributed to the national effort by low freights to the towns and the ports. Though the soil is no better than our own and the winter is more severe, brains and perseverance had raised agriculture to a height which at that time shamed their opposite numbers in England. Among the public institutions of the capital I found nothing so arresting as the Old Age Home which combined cheerfulness, comfort and economy. Copenhagen is above all the city of Thorvaldsen. Though his talent, like that of Canova, was imitative rather than creative he gave the world some exquisite works. The chief ornament of the University was our old friend Professor Höffding, the most eminent thinker in the Scandinavian world since Kierkegaard. The vitality of Denmark enhanced the sense of the value of little nations in the life of a continent dominated by Great Powers armed to the teeth.

Though travel was a delightful incident, historical study remained my principal task. The production of the *Cambridge Modern History* was taken over by a triumvirate consisting of Sir Adolphus Ward, who had recently retired from his Chair at Manchester; my old Cambridge teacher Sir George Prothero; and Sir Stanley Leathes, afterwards First Civil Service Commissioner; but every volume bore the legend on the title page 'Planned by the late Lord Acton'. My contributions were my main historical task during the opening years of the century. For the volume on the French Revolution I attempted a birds-eye view of its impact

on the ideology and institutions of the countries of Europe. In
the Napoleonic volume I was allotted the domestic history of
Great Britain and Ireland during the Great War, in which I found
the Grattan Parliament and the Union the most interesting part
of my theme. To the volume on the Restoration era I contributed
a survey of the domestic history of the British Isles from the
Reform Bill of 1832 to the fall of the Whigs in 1841, and I wound
up the whole enterprise by a chapter on historiography, later
expanded into my *History and Historians in the Nineteenth Century.*
The twelve stout volumes, which contained contributions from
specialists in many lands, was an immediate success, and a Spanish
translation carried its message to South America.

Social work continued as usual. At the invitation of Mrs.
Humphry Ward I joined her committee for organizing play centres
for the children of London. The author of *Robert Elsmere* was an
ardent social worker, as readers of her Autobiography and of
Mrs. George Trevelyan's life of her mother are aware. She
associated herself with the Passmore Edwards Settlement, which
after her death was given her name. The spacious building with
its quiet garden was an ideal spot for boys and girls of working-
class Holborn and St. Pancras to spend their leisure and their
August holidays. Play was organized and included the simple
crafts which children love. If her novels have ceased to be widely
read, her memory lives as the fairy godmother of the London
child.

The Sociological Society, instituted in 1904, provided a new
interest. Its founder Victor Branford, a business man of original
mind, wide learning and retiring disposition, never obtained the
public recognition he deserved. His books were written in an
involved style which limited their appeal, but he was an excellent
lecturer, and he helped the cause with his purse as well as his
brains. For the first year or two a good deal of effort was expended
in defining the nature of sociology, the discussions appearing in
the annual volumes of *Sociological Papers,* and the work was continued in the *Sociological Review.* In later years Branford presented
the Society with a habitation in London, named by himself Leplay
House, for among his services was the rediscovery of the French
sociologist. His closest ally was Sir Patrick Geddes, who approached sociology through biology. I have never known anyone

quite so prodigal of ideas as this brilliant Scotsman who left
his mark in science, sociology, and the organization of universities.
The outstanding figure in our group was Leonard Hobhouse, one
of the finest intellects of his time. He had exchanged the sheltered
life of an Oxford Don for the busy world of journalism, and had
denounced the South African policy of the Government in the
Manchester Guardian. When the struggle was over he migrated to
London, where, except for a brief interlude as editor of the short-
lived Liberal daily *The Tribune*, he spent the rest of his life in
writing and teaching. He was the first editor of the *Sociological
Review*, and the first occupant of the Chair of Sociology in the
University of London. His range was encyclopaedic. He had an
astonishing gift of clear and rapid statement both with tongue and
pen, and he could dictate a leading article to Manchester on the
telephone. His philosophical writings in their quantity, quality
and variety, formed a *corpus* to which there was no parallel since
Mill and Herbert Spencer. No task brought him deeper satisfaction than his chairmanship of Wages Boards in sweated
industries.

No living English thinker appealed to me so much as William
James, brother of America's leading novelist, whose *Psychology* I
had studied at Cambridge, whose *Will to Believe* I had enjoyed at
the end of the century, and whose entrancing Gifford Lectures on
the *Varieties of Religious Experience* were an outstanding event in
the opening years of the new. The chief gift of these years for
students of the unseen world was the appearance of Frederick
Myers' *Human Personality and its Survival of Bodily Death*, published
in two immense volumes in 1903 and abridged for popular use
many years later. Unlike his friend Henry Sidgwick, Myers was a
mystic to whom belief in survival was no effort. I had joined the
Psychical Research Society after leaving Cambridge and followed
the discussions in its Journal with eager interest. The Annual
Presidential Addresses, which I sometimes heard and always read,
kept amateurs like myself in touch with the latest speculations
and results. Though I felt no urge to attend a *séance*, I was grateful
to Sir Oliver Lodge, Sir William Barrett, Mrs. Sidgwick and other
experts for testing the celebrated mediums and striving to extract
their secret. The Society, which never officially expressed opinions,
was too cautious for such adventurous spirits as Conan Doyle,

but every student of the problem of survival must be grateful for
the accumulation and analysis of material.

When the South African war was over, Liberals in the constituencies began to look round for prospective candidates, since
the by-elections indicated that the long reign of the Conservatives
was nearing its end. Bath had returned two members of Parliament for centuries, among them the elder Pitt. Donald Maclean
and a colleague had put up a plucky fight in the khaki election of
1900, and the former decided to stand again. He required a steed
to run in double harness, and in the early summer of 1903, on
returning from my honeymoon, I was adopted as the junior
candidate. No budding politician could have desired a more
congenial constituency. 'The British Florence' was favoured both
by nature and by art, for nowhere in England is such stately
Palladian architecture to be seen. The Abbey, the Assembly
Rooms and the Pump-room, the Circus and the Crescent, Milsom
Street and Prior Park, had seen the rank and fashion, statesmen
and writers, triflers and adventurers of Georgian England come
and go. There were Roman remains in the baths where the warm
springs gushed up. The eighteenth-century streets and squares
were full of ghosts, most of whom returned to earth in the
pageant organized during the time that we represented the city.
It was also peopled by warm-hearted men and women who cared
intensely how their country and the British Empire were ruled.
Though the city was absurdly over-represented by two Members,
the anomaly enabled candidates and constituents to know one
another in a way no longer practicable with the enormous
electoral lists of today.

The social pillar of the Liberal cause was Lady Tweedmouth,
widow of the first holder of the title and mother of the second.
Living in one of the fine old houses in the Circus, she was always
ready to entertain celebrities who came to assist our campaign.
She was a *grande dame* to her finger-tips, proud of her son, who had
been Chief Whip in Gladstone's last Ministry, and of her daughter
Lady Aberdeen who, with her husband, was often in Bath. Lord
Aberdeen, who had been Governor-General of Canada and was
soon to be Viceroy of Ireland, possessed the sweetness of temper
which had distinguished his grandfather, the Prime Minister, and
there was no more modest or unselfish figure on the public stage.

The Aberdeens were as unwearying in good works as in the political arena. Lord Tweedmouth, a more forceful personality and a better speaker than his brother-in-law, was clearly destined for high office, and nobody could foresee the tragic ending of his career.

I was no less fortunate in my colleague than in my constituency. Donald Maclean, who ultimately rose to be President of the Board of Education, was one of the happy people whom everybody likes. He was extremely modest about his abilities, kindly, cheerful, energetic and absolutely straight. Though he was often called 'Fighting Mac', he fought without bitterness and never made an enemy. Our views on the leading issues of the hour were identical, and both of us had been 'Pro-Boers'. A solicitor by profession, he made time for social work as well as for politics, particularly in connection with the Society for the Prevention of Cruelty to Children. Our respective experiences among the poor of Cardiff and London had made us active supporters of the Temperance cause. Though he was a Scot and a Presbyterian and I had been brought up in an Anglican household, we were equally critical of the treatment of Nonconformists under the Education Act of 1902.

The political situation was transformed overnight when, in April 1903, Chamberlain unfurled the Protectionist banner. Though Balfour declared for retaliation as a possible means of reducing foreign tariffs, he rejected the taxation of food and announced that no changes would be made during the existing Parliament. In September the storm burst. The dynamic Colonial Secretary resigned because the Prime Minister had not gone far enough and three other Ministers because they felt he had gone too far. A fortnight after 'the September massacres' the veteran Duke of Devonshire, whose mind moved slowly, followed suit. The Protectionist flurry disunited the Unionists and reunited the Liberals, and by the end of 1903 it was clear that the tide which had been running ever since 1886 had begun to ebb. For the two and a half years of my candidature tariffs were the principal subject of debate, for it concerned every household in the land. Bath was a favourite resort of people living on pensions or small fixed incomes for whom the Conservative party was the obvious spiritual home; but let the purchasing power of the pound be threatened by a rise in the cost of living and their allegiance was gone. The attitude of the Free Trade Unionists exerted a profound influence on middle-class voters whom Liberal propaganda failed to impress. The manual worker was wooed by the promise of more work from the Tariff Reformers and by warnings of higher prices from the Free Trader. Never since the Anti-Corn Law League of the forties had such an intensive educational campaign been carried on. While never suggesting that Free Trade was the best system for every individual or that tariffs would not benefit selected industries, we contended that the existing system produced the greatest happiness of the greatest number.

Next to tariffs no subject was so continuously and so hotly discussed as the Education Act of 1902, for Bath, a 'cathedral city' in miniature, was crowded with churches and chapels. In the election of 1900 Liberal support had been invited by Unionist Ministers on the understanding that the only issue was the South African war; but despite these assurances the School Boards were abolished and the control of elementary education was transferred to County and Town Councils. The Act proved a useful administrative simplification and few tears were shed over the passing of the old authorities, but it contained provisions which roused many Nonconformists to fury. Denominational schools were put on the rates; and though the public authority controlled the secular education, the head teacher was compelled to belong to the denomination and a permanent majority of denominational managers was guaranteed. The grievances of the Nonconformists were that public support was unaccompanied by complete public control, and that, while Anglican teachers had equal chances of employment in the Board Schools, Nonconformist teachers were excluded from almost every village in the land. A passive resistance campaign was organized by Dr. Clifford, the most eloquent of Free Church divines, and sales of furniture belonging to defaulting rate-payers became a feature of the time. While my colleague and I disapproved resistance to the law, we desired to amend it.

The tide that was flowing against the Government was swelled by other rills. Trade Unionists were incensed by the Taff Vale judgment which deprived them of power they believed themselves to possess. Temperance workers resented the Licensing

Act of 1904 which gave licence-holders a right to compensation from a fund levied on the trade if the licence were not renewed, since, though no public money was involved, a formidable obstacle was thus placed in the path of local option or state purchase. The introduction of thousands of Chinese coolies into the Johannesburg mines to remedy the shortage of labour, without their wives and under restrictions which existed nowhere else in the British Empire, was widely condemned as degrading to the workers immured in their compounds and dangerous to the white inhabitants of the Rand if they broke out. I doubt if the cry of 'Chinese slavery'—a slogan never adopted by my colleague or myself—changed many votes, but it helped to sicken the country of the record of the Government. Home Rule as an issue for the next Parliament was explicitly or tacitly excluded from the Liberal programme, for the veto of the House of Lords blocked the way. The duty of the hour, as Liberals saw it, was to save Free Trade, push on with social reform, and reconcile the Dutch in South Africa.

The latter problem, in which I was particularly interested, was insoluble so long as Milner remained High Commissioner, and he knew it. Like Curzon, he lacked the human touch. He had laboured unselfishly, heroically and fruitfully at the material reconstruction of the shattered country, but a different spirit was needed to heal the gaping wounds of war. He had vainly urged Chamberlain to suspend the constitution of Cape Colony on the ground that the executive must be kept in loyal hands for the next few critical years, and self-government for the former Boer Republics seemed to him unthinkable until a loyalist government could be guaranteed.

> You must give us time thoroughly to Anglicize the Transvaal. We must increase the British population first. We cannot afford to risk the experiment of self-government under conditions which make a most bitter Boer government in the Orange River Colony a certainty and a Boer government of sorts a probability even in the Transvaal. To sacrifice your friends in the hope of winning over your enemies has never seemed to me the height of statesmanship. Yet it has an irresistible attraction for some minds.

It was precisely the same argument that is employed by the Kremlin today to deny self-determination to East Germany and

the other unhappy satellites. On Milner's retirement in 1905 Sir
Percy Fitzpatrick voiced the feelings of the triumphant Johannes-
burgers in a revealing sentence: 'Of course the Boers hate you; it
is their certificate of your success.' On his voyage home Milner
wrote to his successor Lord Selborne with his usual bitterness
about the political Boers and the Afrikander party: 'You may
always rely on them to be perfectly charming in their duplicity.'
Very different was the spirit of his old antagonist General Smuts
who wrote:

> Bon voyage! I am afraid you have not liked us; but I cherish the hope
> that as our memories grow mellower and the nobler features of our
> respective ideals become clearer we shall more and more appreciate
> the contribution of each to the formation of that happier South
> Africa which is surely coming and judge more kindly of each other.

What the departing proconsul replied we are not told in *The
Milner Papers*.

Having studied the evolution of Parliament for many years in
books I found it instructive to test the working of democracy in
the constituencies. By indoor meetings, parlour and doorstep
conversations, it was possible not only to learn the hopes and
fears of individual voters but to visualize the mentality of the
average citizen. The result was reassuring. Convictions were
strong, but there was very little bitterness in our controversies
and rowdyism was almost unknown. Many electors listened to
both sides and made up their own minds.

9

THE LIBERAL PARLIAMENT OF 1906

THE Liberal victory of January 1906, to which Bath made its double-barrelled contribution, was decisive beyond our dreams. An able team of veterans adorned the Treasury bench, and among the Under-Secretaries were Winston Churchill, Herbert Samuel, Reginald McKenna and Walter Runciman. It was the end of the Chamberlain, Kipling, Milner, Curzon era. In its political aspect it was above all a mandate for Free Trade and social reform, in its personal aspect a triumph for the Prime Minister. After years of disparagement and contested authority Campbell-Bannerman had come into his own. When Rosebery—who, like Curzon, was his own worst enemy—withdrew from the fray in terror of Home Rule and Lord Spencer succumbed to a stroke, there was no competitor for the first place. No Liberal leader since Gladstone has inspired such devotion as this courageous, unassuming, shrewd old man. Though an exceptionally poor speaker and debater he dominated the new House of Commons, trusted not only by the serried ranks behind him but by the Irish Nationalists and the new Labour contingent some thirty strong. The premiership, in the words of Alfred Spender, made a new man of him; there was never a more miraculous change. Most of us were Gladstonians in foreign affairs, but in the domestic field we desired measures more far-reaching than Gladstone, a typical Victorian individualist, would have approved. The Rosebery section quickly revised its estimate of our leader's worth, and, like other young Members, I was won by his kindness and unaffected simplicity. Having been in the House since 1868 he was full of anecdotes of the Grand Old Man, Dizzy and other giants of the past. He loved France and liked French memoirs without quite realizing their limited value, and on one occasion I had to break it gently to him that those of the Marquise de Créqui which he was enjoying were a fake.

Since Balfour had lost his seat at Manchester, the acting Leader of the Opposition was Joseph Chamberlain, anchored in the unwavering loyalty of Birmingham when the national tide was racing the other way. Chamberlain and C.-B. were in their seventieth year, but the former, with his dark hair and erect figure, looked many years the younger. When he was in good humour his voice was soft and melodious; his intonation was clear as crystal and there was never a superfluous word. I was soon to see him in another mood, but the first impression was an agreeable surprise that the terrible gladiator of Home Rule and Boer War days could be as mild as milk. Till the cruel shears of Fate cut the thread during the celebrations of his seventieth birthday he was unquestionably the most arresting figure in the House. That he had more love in his heart than the world realized we learn from the massive volume of Austen's letters from Westminster to the stricken parent he adored.

The most spectacular performance in the debate on the Address was that of a young barrister who leapt into fame within the space of an hour. F. E. Smith was unknown to the great majority of his audience when he rose to attack the Government in the most astonishing maiden speech of our time. Asquith's *début* in 1886, we were told, had revealed no less promise, but there was a calculated truculence in the new recruit which placed him in a class by himself. It was precisely the tonic which the shattered nerves of his party required, and every barbed arrow was greeted with rapturous applause. I was writing letters in the lobby when the noise drew me back to the crowded chamber. His son's biography reveals his awareness how much was at stake. It was a superb theatrical performance, carried through with the gusto and *sang-froid* of arrogant youth, which lives in Parliamentary tradition like the *début* of Disraeli. F.E. was soon to show that he could provide more than fireworks, and he was wise enough on the next occasion to divest himself of cap and bells. He was the first of the new members to score; but though his amazing talents were recognized by friend and foe, his authority was never to equal his fame. That he missed the first place to which he felt his powers entitled him was the major disappointment of his meteoric career. The rise of John Simon, a miniature Asquith, occurred much more slowly than that of his old Oxford friend.

Next in importance to the Prime Minister and the Leader of the Opposition was the Chancellor of the Exchequer. 'Asquith will get on, he is so direct,' was the verdict of Jowett, a connoisseur of youthful talent, in his Balliol days. Many years later Lord Haldane revealed in his autobiography the pact of 1905 by which Asquith, Grey and himself decided to demand their price for joining a Liberal government if the coming election returned the Liberals to power: C.-B. was to take a peerage and leave the leadership of the Commons to Asquith. When the Prime Minister, fortified by his wife's emphatic injunction: No surrender! decided to defy the Liberal Imps as he called them and to stay in the Commons, the pact was very rightly tossed into the waste-paper basket. After Asquith had accepted the Exchequer his two friends surrendered and received high posts. That Asquith's turn would come we were all well aware. He proved a loyal Chief of Staff, and his debating power was rivalled by Chamberlain alone. 'Send for the sledge-hammer,' exclaimed C.-B. when his services were particularly required. I had heard him in public meetings, where he was not particularly effective and never aroused enthusiasm: only in the House could one fully realize his consummate mastery of speech, words and sentences seeming to arrange themselves without effort in patterns of intricate perfection. 'In Parliament,' testifies Lord Samuel in his Memoirs, 'though not the most eloquent or brilliant, he was, I think, the most impressive speaker of his day.' There was none of the hesitation which sometimes marred the performances of Balfour and Churchill, and nothing of Gladstone's prolixity. Alone of the famous performers of his time, with the possible exception of Chamberlain, he was always at his best. C.-B. described his mind as a faultless piece of machinery. It was impossible to imagine him committing one of Salisbury's 'blazing indiscretions', playing to the gallery, indulging in personalities, hitting below the belt or wooing the press. Too uncreative, unimaginative and undynamic for a place among the Immortals, he was a supreme Parliamentarian. Disdaining the tricks of the rhetorician, he preferred light to heat, logic to emotion, argument to invective. The official biography by his

devoted friend and admirer Alfred Spender, with contributions
by one of his gifted sons, conveys the impression of his effortless
superiority. Adored by his family and by intimate friends such as
Lady Horner, he was too reserved to inspire personal affection
among the rank and file.

The return of Balfour at a by-election within a few weeks of
the opening of Parliament restored its official leader to the
Opposition, and after the disappearance of Joseph Chamberlain
he carried his burden with a smile. The subtleties in his first
speech provoked C.-B. to his celebrated outburst: Enough of this
foolery! That the two men annoyed each other no one could fail
to observe. Yet the Conservative chief gradually won the admiration of our Liberal battalions by his debating skill, his intellectual
and personal distinction, and his unfailing pluck. Now Chamberlain was gone he was universally regarded as the brightest ornament of the Mother of Parliaments. He was an uncertain speaker,
but at his best he was unsurpassed. There was nothing of the
sledge-hammer or the battle-axe about him: it was rather the
Toledo blade. He possessed an analytical mind worthy of a
medieval schoolman, but he had displayed constructive power in
Ireland and the Great War was to reveal his latent strength. Like
his uncle Lord Salisbury he was far too much of an aristocrat to
care whether he satisfied his party or the public, and politics never
claimed more than a portion of his capacious mind. An eager
student of philosophy and science and a keen lover of music, he
was in the great tradition of our Scholar Statesmen. Though often
called a dilettante he was a great deal more than that, both as
statesman, thinker and master of English prose. I had enjoyed his
Foundations of Belief, written in a style as limpid as that of William
James, Bergson and Bertrand Russell. I met him for the first time
at a dinner-party at the Sidney Webbs, and like most other people
surrendered to his charm. The gods had been very kind to him,
and his tall figure, delicate features and exquisite voice were a
fortune in themselves. Younger generations can make his
acquaintance in the affectionate official biography by his niece.
None of his political contemporaries derived more refined enjoy-
ment from good society and the intellectual life. Though he
wished the common man well, he took little interest in his thoughts
and needs. Austen Chamberlain and Bonar Law were useful

lieutenants, but Prince Arthur towered over them all. Walter Long, the typical Tory squire, was intellectually a light-weight.

There was no more attractive figure on the Treasury bench than Edward Grey, but he was too busy to be often in his place. Though he had emerged as one of Rosebery's henchmen and had approved the South African war, he banished every thought of Liberal dissensions and party differences when he returned to the Foreign Office as its chief in December 1905. Tall, slim and athletic, he looked amazingly fit, and the level tones of his voice reflected a soul at peace with itself. He hated extremes, exaggeration, appeals to sentiment, passion or prejudice. It was difficult to believe that he had ever been young and immature. He was not interested in popularity and never strove for applause. His devotion to country life, to the sights of nature and the song of birds, seemed to act as a moral breakwater against the wear and tear of public life. 'I hate politics as much as ever,' he confessed to a friend in 1903. During the four years in which I listened to every debate on foreign affairs I never heard him raise his voice. In the simple words of Lord Samuel he was always serene. As a speaker he was cool, clear, direct, rather colourless and un-inspiring. Never letting himself go, he suited the House far better than the platform, for he never caused the pulse to quicken. Disdaining epigram and purple patches, he regarded speech as a tool, not an art. Though he had always been interested in foreign affairs and was determined to perform his arduous task as well as he could, he dreamed of the time when he could honourably retire from public life. In the words of his affectionate biographer George Trevelyan, 'If to be wholly without ambition is a fault in a states-man, he was guilty indeed.' Public service was a family tradition, not an urge.

This most unusual quality of political selflessness set Grey in a class by himself, and his flawless integrity came to be recognized as a national asset. Inheriting and developing the policy of continental attachments inaugurated by Lansdowne and Balfour, he enjoyed more unqualified support on the Opposition than on the Liberal benches, where some of us Gladstonians needed time to discard the last shreds of suspicion surviving from the antagon-isms of the Boer War. No one who knew him even as slightly as myself could doubt that his mind was set on peace, not merely because we had all we wanted but because he abhorred the thought of war. Unlike Churchill, he had no fighting blood in his veins. Foreign testimonials may be found in the dispatches not only of Paul Cambon and Walter Page but of Count Metternich and Prince Lichnowsky. Too reserved to be widely beloved, he was immensely respected. No man of his time suffered so many cruel blows of fate, and no one bore sorrow with more unfailing courage. In range of interests and intellectual power he was surpassed by half a dozen of his colleagues, but in elevation of character he was the noblest Roman of them all and one of the few mortals whom the world cannot spoil.

A few days after my election I received a letter from James Bryce, the new Chief Secretary for Ireland, inviting me to become his Parliamentary Private Secretary. In addition to their paid secretaries Ministers need a junior *aide-de-camp* for odd jobs such as receiving visitors, looking up references for a specch, and carrying messages. I had learned to know him during the dark days of the South African war, and like everyone else I admired *The Holy Roman Empire* and *The American Commonwealth*. A year later, to his intense satisfaction, he was appointed Ambassador to the United States; but during the long session of 1906 I was initiated into the working of a government department, made the acquaintance of the Irish leaders, and mastered the intricacies of Land Purchase and the University problem.

Though Bryce had coveted the India Office, he threw himself into his task with his usual thoroughness. With the possible exception of Dilke he was the best informed man in the House of Commons, and as an Ulster Scot his knowledge of Ireland and her history was particularly intimate. He found in the Permanent Under-Secretary a colleague with whom it was a delight to work. Sir Antony Macdonnell, an Irish Catholic and Home Ruler who had won high reputation as Civil Servant in India, sacrificed the prospect of the Governorship of Bombay at the wish of his old friend the ex-Viceroy Lord Lansdowne who recommended him for Dublin Castle. It was understood that a man of such long and distinguished services was to be a partner rather than a subordinate of the Chief Secretary; and George Wyndham, at that time at the summit of his brief career, welcomed his assistance on those terms. After launching the great Land Purchase scheme of

1903 the two men discussed the possibilities of devolution at which Lord Dunraven, an independent Unionist, was working with a circle of friends. When a rumour of these talks leaked out Carson, leader of the Ulster die-hards, put his foot down and Wyndham resigned, lamely explaining that he had not fully grasped the significance of Sir Antony's Indian analogies. A more orthodox Chief Secretary was appointed in the person of Walter Long, and devolution was dismissed as a word unsuitable to chaste Unionist lips. Though Sir Antony remained at Dublin Castle his wings were clipped, but with Bryce he regained his earlier status and resilience. The two men took to each other, and the Chief Secretary told me with a smile that he foresaw some future historian poring over their voluminous correspondence. I used to meet him in the Minister's room behind the Speaker's chair and in the Irish Office and liked him from the first.

Though Home Rule was barred for the 1906 Parliament, Bryce and Macdonnell were anxious for some modest measure of devolution, and a committee sat at the Irish Office in London to hammer out a scheme. The Bill was not introduced till the following year, but it was constantly in our thoughts. A second line of advance was attempted in the appointment of a commission under the chairmanship of Sir Edward Fry to report on Trinity College and Dublin University, but no unanimous recommendation was forthcoming. The plan worked out by the Chief Secretary and Sir Antony found little favour, and the solution of the problem of higher education for Catholics adopted by his successor proceeded on other lines. Lord Dudley's acceptance of the chairmanship of a commission on the claims of evicted tenants gave the Minister keen satisfaction, for the ex-Viceroy, himself a wealthy landlord, was *persona grata* in Ireland. The most satisfactory achievement of Bryce's year of office was the provision of 25,000 labourers' cottages with half an acre of land apiece. In one direction, however, a costly error was committed. Ireland was so peaceful in 1906 that the Nationalist demand for the dropping of the Arms Act of 1881 from the annual Expiring Laws Continuation Act was conceded. I was interested to learn many years later from Herbert Fisher's official biography of Bryce that the decision, so far from being urged on the Cabinet by the Chief Secretary, was reached against his advice. He gave way because its continuation would have required the help of Conservative votes against the Nationalists, the Labour men and the Liberal left wing.

Bryce had been a Home Ruler before Gladstone, and his conviction of the inevitability of the change was confirmed by his official control of the creaking machine. So long, however, as the Union remained it was his desire to hold the balance fairly between the contending groups. That the Executive should stand above the battle was not at all to the taste of the Nationalists. His independence was illustrated by his steady support of Sir Horace Plunkett against the Irish members, who could never forgive the expression of his desire to side-track Home Rule by economic prosperity. I was attracted to the quiet, unselfish man who gave his time, money and expert agricultural knowledge to the country he loved. It was his misfortune to stand between the parties and to receive the fire of both sides. He had retained his post as head of the Department of Agriculture when he lost his seat in 1900, and the Nationalists expected that a Liberal Chief Secretary would eject him. Bryce kept him in office pending an inquiry into the working of his Department, and it was left to his successor Birrell, who found him rather a bore, to drive him out. It was only in later years that his worth was universally acclaimed. Bryce's departure for Washington in 1907 was regretted by Plunkett and Macdonnell much more than on the Irish benches.

John Redmond made an admirable Commander-in-Chief of the Irish Nationalists, for he was an impressive speaker and a first-rate Parliamentary tactician. Like Cecil Rhodes he was sometimes compared to a Roman Emperor in looks. The notion prevalent in certain Unionist circles that he was a dangerous rebel was grotesque: had he been born an Englishman this Irish landowner would have been a Conservative, and when the storm burst in 1914 we at last realized his pride in the British Empire. He was too reserved to inspire general affection, and my relations with him were purely official; younger generations may study his character and career in Stephen Gwynn's *Redmond's Last Years* and in the official biography by Denis Gwynn. With Dillon, his chief lieutenant, on the other hand, I was on very friendly terms. He was a Gladstonian Liberal and his sympathies were as wide as the world: no suffering race, no struggling nationality, appealed to him in vain. His capacity for righteous indignation was unlimited, and on a major moral issue he was perhaps the most impressive speaker in the House. Words poured from his lips in a torrent, and I pitied the reporters in the press gallery as they strained at their task. The third member of the triumvirate, T. P. O'Connor, universally known as T.P., was as different from both his colleagues as they were from one another; though of lighter metal he was a general favourite. He was the only member of the party who represented an English constituency, the Irish quarter of Liverpool. Despite the sincerity of his belief in Home Rule the flame burned less fiercely within his bosom, though he pleaded the cause of Catholic schools persuasively enough. Like Dillon he was interested in the affairs of all the world, and the Armenians and Greeks had no better friend. Like Dillon and unlike Redmond he read widely, and we talked of books as often as of politics.

Only less prominent than the three leaders was Swift McNeill, described to me by one of his colleagues as a bundle of emotions. He was easily affected, and any tale of cruelty and distress roused him to white heat. It had long been his custom at the opening of Parliament to denounce flogging in the army, and it was an intense delight to him that at last his goal was reached. I was soon on terms of affection with this lovable man which lasted till his death. He was the scholar of the party and had lectured on constitutional history at Dublin. His knowledge of our Parliamentary traditions and precedents was almost as great as his mastery of Irish history, and none of the Nationalists was oftener on his legs. At Oxford he had sat at the feet of Bryce, then Professor of Civil Law, and he retained an almost filial reverence for his old teacher. Among the most active and attractive of the younger members of the party I may mention two other Protestants, Hugh Law, the son of a Lord Chancellor of Ireland, and Stephen Gwynn, author of a shelf of delightful books. Another young Intellectual was Kettle, who, like John Redmond's younger brother, volunteered and perished in the First World War. The most forceful of the juniors was Devlin, a representative of the Nationalist quarter of Belfast, and one of the most brilliant orators in the House. The wits of the party were Willie Redmond and Jeremiah—always called Jerry—McVeagh, whose impromptu sallies caused ripples of merriment and sometimes a roar.

Two veteran Irish Nationalists stood outside the official ranks, but they were a host in themselves. It was distressing to see William O'Brien and Timothy Healy sitting like pariahs on the Irish benches, surrounded by old associates who were comrades no more. This cantankerous pair could work neither with their fellows nor with each other. There was something of a poet and a dreamer in O'Brien, and the story of his marriage in middle life to Sophie Raffalovich was a romance. The old campaigner of the eighties had mellowed into a Moderate, eager to co-operate with Lord Dunraven and the little group of progressive Unionists who, during the Wyndham régime, came half-way to meet him. Thus the ex-colleague of Parnell and Dillon was heard denouncing the official party for rejecting what he described as the olive branch. His rare interventions in debate were notable occurrences. His whole manner revealed his highly strung temperament, and his voice quivered with emotion. To read his moving autobiography is to realize the passionate devotion of the old Home Rulers to their cause.

If O'Brien's great Parliamentary days were over, Tim Healy remained as effective as ever. He had a tongue like a razor and made little attempt to keep it in control. He would pour forth a stream of vituperation which was relieved from monotony by its unexpected sallies and its mordant wit. He seemed to care more about his Church than about Home Rule, and on the familiar theme of Catholic schools his combination of pathos and passion produced an extraordinary effect. The Speaker, James Lowther, pronounced him the finest orator in the House. How this political Ishmael blossomed into a genial Governor-General of the Irish Free State was one of the miracles wrought by the grant of Dominion status after the First World War.

The Irish Nationalists sat on the Opposition side of the House whichever party was in office, and in the 1906 Parliament only the gangway divided the Ulstermen from their foes. I was just in time to see and hear the redoubtable Colonel Sanderson whose intransigence in no way diminished his personal popularity. The Commander-in-Chief of the Ulster forces was Carson, who, though not an Ulsterman himself, surpassed them all in bitterness of invective, for he had the roughest tongue in the Conservative party. He seemed to be living in the seventeenth century, looking down on Catholics and Home Rulers as an inferior breed. His dark and rather sinister countenance on the front Opposition bench formed a striking contrast to the florid distinction of George Wyndham and the homely features of Walter Long. Our sympathies went out to Wyndham as he sat muzzled during Irish debates; for his successor in office, who cared far less for Ireland, was now the official spokesman of his party. Though Wyndham, a gay and gifted Elizabethan who had strayed into the drab modern world, gradually regained something of his resilience in the later years of his short life, the opening phase of the Parliament of 1906 suggested a broken man. Though untouched by the modern spirit, Long was free from the acrimony which was the curse of Irish politics.

My knowledge of Irish Nationalism was enlarged by frequent visits to the hospitable house in Chelsea of Mrs. Green, widow of the historian and a distinguished historian herself. The love of her native land was a flame that could scorch as well as warm. She ranked with Beatrice Webb and Mrs. Humphry Ward, Mrs. Creighton and Lady Frances Balfour, all of whom I knew, among the cleverest women in London. In addition to Irish M.P.s and English supporters of their cause, intellectuals such as Douglas Hyde, founder of the Gaelic League which strove for the revival of the Gaelic language, were often among her guests. The most striking figures in her circle were Sir Roger Casement and E. D. Morel whom the world at that time knew only as ardent champions of native races. Her volume on *Irish Nationalism* in the Home University Library is still worth reading as an exposition of what nationalism means to such ardent temperaments. In later years she migrated to Dublin and became an honoured member of the Irish Senate.

In the summer recess of 1906 a small party of newly elected Liberal members visited Ireland chiefly to study the congested districts which George Wyndham had described as agricultural slums. Sir Antony Macdonnell received us at the Castle, Lord and Lady Aberdeen at the Viceregal Lodge, Sir Horace Plunkett in his beautiful new house at Foxrock, destined to be burned in the troubles that lay ahead, and John Dillon in his home in Mayo. We were accompanied on our tour by Hugh Law, the Ulster Home Ruler, who knew every inch of the ground. The admirable work of the Congested Districts Board, the most enduring monument of Arthur Balfour's rule as Chief Secretary, was explained to us by the authorities on the spot, and our journey-ings along the west coast were facilitated by the steamer placed at our disposal by the Board. We inspected the carpet factories and lace centres, the fishing stations and other methods of helping a struggling population of half a million souls to keep alive. The Board had done its best to raise the economic level of Connaught, but its poverty had to be seen to be believed. The standard of life remained deplorably low, with the hovels filled by the smoke of the turf fire in the middle and the scanty potato patch outside. To inhabitants of Connemara America might well seem the Promised Land. Among the brighter features of this desolate region were Lady Dudley's nurses, devoted women who added the work of doctors to their own professional tasks. I wrote some articles on our tour for the *Daily News* which had the good fortune to please my chief.

Bryce's departure for Washington at the opening of 1907 ended my semi-official connection with Ireland. Though I regretted the loss of a Minister with whom it had been an education to work, described by C.-B. as the most accomplished man in the House of Commons, I was glad of the opportunity of taking part in Irish debates from which I had hitherto been debarred. Throughout my remaining years in Parliament I followed the changing phases of the Irish drama with eager attention, and at Bryce's wish I sent him occasional bulletins. The Irish Council Bill of 1907, inherited by Birrell from his pre-decessor, was damned with faint praise by the Nationalists at Westminster and rejected by a specially summoned meeting in Ireland as totally inadequate: better to wait for the whole loaf, they felt, than to say thank you for a slice. The University problem, on the other hand, which had baffled Balfour and Bryce, was settled by Birrell; the financial weakness of Wyndham's Land Purchase Act was rectified and grievances of the evicted tenants were removed. We would have been glad to satisfy the demand for autonomy, especially after the success of our South African experiment, but Home Rule had formed no part of the party programme. The Unionists needed rebellion and civil war for their conversion, and they finally accepted larger concessions than would have sufficed before the rise of Sinn Fein. It was the familiar story of the Sibylline books: the longer we wait the more we have to yield. I contributed essays on the evolution of the Home Rule movement and the Grattan Parliament to co-operative volumes edited respectively by Professor Basil Williams and Professor J. H. Morgan.

In his speech at the Albert Hall on taking office Campbell-Bannerman announced that no further importation of Chinese labour into South Africa would be allowed. The declaration was hailed with enthusiasm by the crowded audience and by Liberals throughout the country, for the party longed to see the end of that ill-starred experiment. The coolies were repatriated at the end of their contracts without damage to the mining industry, and native labour, which is always available on reasonable terms, again supplied the need. Equally welcome to Liberals was the grant of self-governing institutions to the Transvaal and Orange River Colony. The timid compromise of the Lyttelton Constitution was swept aside, and C.-B., with his deeper insight into the character of the Boers, decided to win them by a dramatic exhibition of trust. 'We wish to make those who hate us love us,' he had declared, and he proceeded to apply the familiar Liberal remedy. Good government, in his famous phrase which might have come from Gladstone's lips, was no substitute for self-government. Balfour, who never understood the feelings of little nations, denounced the grant of autonomy as the most reckless experiment in the history of our colonial empire; and in the House of Lords Milner characteristically exclaimed that if the British people knew what was being done in their name they would spit it out of their mouth. By this time the stern Proconsul, like Rosebery, had lost all his supporters in the Liberal camp. In the words of George Trevelyan, Grey had discovered that Milner and he had never meant the same thing; the former had always intended British racial supremacy while the latter wanted equal rights for Boer and Briton. Since no legislation was required, the Upper House was fortunately unable to thwart the healing process which Milner in a letter to a friend in April 1907 described as sheer lunacy. British and Dutch began to co-operate in the development of their common home. The two new colonies combined in 1909 with the Cape and Natal to frame a constitution and form a United South Africa; and in 1910 Botha, the George Washington

of his country, captained the first Union Cabinet. Thus South
Africa, thanks to the courage and foresight of a 'Little Englander',
passed out of party controversy, and when the testing-time
arrived in 1914 the world witnessed the fruits of Liberal statesmanship. Of the Unionist leaders Austen Chamberlain alone had
the generosity many years later to confess that his opposition had
been a mistake.

As Lord Elgin, the Colonial Secretary, an ex-Viceroy of India,
sat in the Upper House and was temperamentally the most silent
of men, the brunt of the fight for the pacification of South Africa
fell on the Under-Secretary in the Commons; and gallantly did
he discharge the duties of his first ministerial post. Winston
Churchill combined the confident dogmatism of youth with the
irrepressible vitality of a mountain stream. Loving the smell of
powder, adventure and romance, he would have been a welcome
recruit to the little band of *Les Trois Mousquetaires*. Though he was
now thirty-two and had crowded a series of thrilling experiences
in many parts of the world into his early years, which he described
in the most delightful of his many books, he looked like a boy.
Fully aware of his amazing powers, he confided to Violet Asquith
at a dinner-party: 'We are all worms, but I think I am a glow-
worm.' The earliest of his biographers declared that this *enfant
terrible* advertised himself as easily as he breathed. The brilliant
apostate was the *bête noire* of the Opposition, and to rebuke him,
complained Alfred Lyttelton, was as useless as to rebuke a brass
band. The most effective unofficial champion of Liberal policy in
South Africa was another former Unionist. Like Churchill, Major
Seely, subsequently Minister of War, had left his old party on the
issue of Free Trade. Having distinguished himself as a combatant
in the Boer War he could speak with authority, for he had learned
that the Dutch were men whose friendship was worth winning.
The chief spokesman of the Opposition on South African
questions after the disappearance of Chamberlain was the former
Colonial Secretary, Alfred Lyttelton. The admiration he had
received in society and in the cricket field had left him unspoiled,
and he enjoyed the affectionate regard of the whole House. He
was the soul of honour and he was free from the bitterness which
often tarnished the utterances of Milner and Chamberlain. No
other statesman of his time received finer tributes on his too early

death than Asquith's moving commemoration of the Happy Warrior and his widow's exquisite biography.

The discovery that Milner, now merely a private individual, had authorized flogging in the Johannesburg mines led to a debate on one of the private members' evenings when the winner in the sessional ballot can select his theme. The luck had fallen to Sir William Byles, a lovable old Radical, who gave notice of a resolution of censure on the late High Commissioner 'for authorizing the flogging of Chinese labourers in breach of the law, in violation of treaty obligations, and without the knowledge of the Secretary of State.' The incident aroused almost pathological excitement and the passions of the Boer War flamed up again. After the motion had been moved by Byles and seconded by my old friend Mackarness, Chamberlain defended Milner in a speech vibrating with emotion. Never before nor after did I see him so worked up. He testified that he had never known a greater man and denounced as ungenerous an attack 'for a single error of judgment'. Though most members of the Cabinet sympathized with the resolution, it was decided to substitute a milder formula condemning flogging without mentioning names. What Balfour described as the 'insulting protection' of Churchill, the spokesman of the Government, aroused even greater resentment on the Opposition benches than the frontal attack by the 'Pro-Boers', for he criticized the Byles resolution on the ground that it was not worth while to pursue a retired Civil Servant and that the Ministerialists were strong enough to be generous. Milner's many admirers throughout the country promptly retaliated by organizing an imposing counter-demonstration of confidence.

No factor was so potent in allaying the terrors of the Opposition as the personality of General Botha, who played an active part in the Imperial Conferences. Among the Dominion Premiers whom I have met three men stand out above their fellows— Laurier, Botha and Smuts. The bilingual Canadian statesman looked like a French diplomat of the *ancien régime*, an aristocrat to his finger-tips. Smuts had broadened out from the slim Cambridge student into a sturdy figure, his countenance lit up by light blue eyes and a winning smile. Perhaps the most impressive was the broad-shouldered Dutch farmer, soldier and statesman who never fully mastered English and at all times was sparing of speech. To see Botha was to trust him, and indeed no public figure of my time except Eisenhower has inspired such universal confidence at home and abroad. There was something elemental about him, and his instinctive wisdom was most admired by those who knew him best. Utterly unpretentious and always at peace with himself, he greeted one with a grave smile. Something of his secret may be gleaned from the memoir by Lord Buxton, who, as Governor-General, stood at his side in the formative years of the Union, and from the moving tribute at the graveside from his closest colleague and friend Field Marshal Smuts.

It proved easier to bring peace to South Africa than to remove the grievances of Free Churchmen under the Education Act of 1902, for here the House of Lords stood like a lion in the path. The Minister in charge of the Education Bill of 1906 was *persona gratissima* to the Nonconformists who formed a large and well-organized Parliamentary group. Augustine Birrell, lawyer by profession and man of letters by taste, was one of the wittiest men of his time. Morley thought him the best talker in London, and no one was in greater demand on Liberal platforms; but behind the graceful *façade* of 'Birrelling' lay serious purpose. Though sprung from Nonconformist stock with the tradition of religious liberty in his blood, he was free from the animosity entertained by many Nonconformists of the older generation against the Anglican Church. Deeply versed in the religious history of the British Isles and respecting piety in every camp, he made an admirable pilot on this perilous voyage; and though the Lords killed the Bill by unacceptable amendments he emerged with enhanced prestige. Subsequent attempts by his successors at the Board of Education met with no better fortune; for though Archbishop Davidson played a helpful part, High Church opposition wrecked all attempts to extend the area of unde-nominational teaching. Passive Resistance gradually died away and the Balfour Act of 1902 remained in possession of the field. It was the most conspicuous failure of the Parliament of 1906, illustrating afresh the cynical witticism that the most dangerous political problems are religion and drink.

The Conservative case was in the hands of Balfour, who was fighting for his own offspring, and Sir William Anson, the constitutional pundit who had been his Minister of Education. In these debates new members learned to admire the dialectical skill of the Leader of the Opposition, to whom the cause of Church Schools so strongly appealed. The speeches that Lord Hugh Cecil would have made had he not lost his seat were delivered with equal conviction by his elder brother. One of the thrills of a new Parliament, particularly after a large invasion of fresh faces, is to watch for the emergence of talent. On the Conservative side F.E. was the most dynamic of the new recruits; next to him came Lord Robert Cecil, whose fidelity to Free Trade made him rather a lonely figure in his party. By the end of our first session the latter had secured not only 'the ear of the House' but a recognized place in our public life. On one occasion he and a little band of High Churchmen kept us up till six in the morning in opposing a Bill authorizing marriage with a deceased wife's sister; but we bore him no grudge for the loss of a night's rest, knowing that for him it was a matter of principle. Though incapable of the soaring flights of his brother he was a more useful Member, keenly interested in social questions such as co-partnership.

The attack on the Education Bill was reinforced by a solitary representative of High Church principles on the Liberal benches. Nothing affords a talented speaker such a chance as disagreement with his party on a leading issue, and Speaker Lowther allowed Liberal dissentients unlimited scope. My old friend Masterman pleaded for what he called the neutrality of the state, leaving religious instruction to representatives of the various Churches. Though a logical case could be made out for separating the children into pens, it rested on the fallacy that Protestant as well as Catholic parents desired a particular confessional brand. These High Churchmen seemed unable to realize the indifference of the masses to theological distinctions. In this respect the Archbishop of Canterbury, who valued the undenominational teaching imparted in the Board Schools, was a truer representative of national opinion. Masterman's maiden speech was a brief protest on the first reading, but on the second reading he climbed the first rung of the ladder which led towards Cabinet rank. He knew that he had arrived, and he told me next day that he had lain awake till six in the morning after the effort.

A second controversial measure restored to the Trade Unions the powers they had possessed before the Taff Vale judgment.

Though the Labour Party was only thirty strong it succeeded in extending the scope of the Bill, for the demand of the Trade Unionists was so unanimous that the House of Lords shirked a fight. The chief spokesman for the new party was David Shackleton, a big, gentle, fatherly man who was soon to exchange the lime-light of St. Stephen's for the anonymity of the Civil Service. Keir Hardie, the sessional leader, had won the respect and in many cases the affection even of those who rejected his political creed; but it is no disrespect to the memory of a noble figure to say that his heart was greater than his head. Four other Labour leaders played a significant part from the first. Ramsay MacDonald, the future Prime Minister, described by Balfour as a born Parliamentarian, captured the ear of the House without an effort; and from time to time his simple old Highland mother, accompanied by his wife, watched the performances of her brilliant son from the Ladies' Gallery. Less eloquent but even more impressive was Philip Snowden, whose deep sincerity and argumentative power gripped the House. The future Chancellor of the Exchequer was already the party expert on finance, and a little book entitled *The Socialist Budget*, in which he advocated a five shilling income tax, sent cold shivers down Edwardian spines. Arthur Henderson and George Barnes, soon to become Cabinet Ministers, could always be relied on for serviceable speeches, and their standing in the House steadily increased. The general favourite of the party was Will Crooks, the workhouse child with a heart of gold whom to know was to love. The Labour contingent, despite its limited dimensions, played an influential part, for its leaders were men of experience, character and ability of whom any movement might be proud. The co-operation of Liberalism and Labour functioned without difficulty since all our measures commanded their support.

Though the main legislative venture of our first session was lost, a few sheaves were gathered into the barn. Millions of new workers were added to the categories entitled to compensation for accidents, and rate aid for feeding necessitous schoolchildren was allowed. On the other hand a measure to abolish plural voting was rejected by the Lords. Since the Unionist Peers treated our huge majority fresh from the polls with as little consideration as they had treated the anaemic government of 1892-5, the constitutional issue of the relations of the two Houses began to loom up. It was not cricket, as the phrase went, that all the Bills of one party, even if they had never been discussed by the electorate, should be automatically passed, while those of the rival team, after the authorization of their plans by a decisive verdict, should be rejected or mangled at will. The theory of trusteeship of the nation's abiding interests advanced by the Lords and their supporters sounded unconvincing in the light of their tactical decision to swallow the unwelcome Trades Disputes Bill. A practice grew up by which the minority in the Commons signalled to the majority in the Lords, and we could forecast the fate of our measures from the closing sentences of the Leader of the Opposition.

The session of 1907 was far less exciting, for the main business was the creation of a Territorial army in which the old Volunteer associations were merged. If 1906 was the year of the President of the Board of Education, 1907 was the *début* of the Minister of War. Haldane had come rapidly to the front during the decade of Unionist rule as statesman, lawyer, philosopher and educationalist. He hoped for the Lord Chancellorship, as he confesses in his Autobiography, but had to wait nearly twenty years. The glittering prize fell to 'Bob' Reid, promoted to the Upper House as Lord Loreburn, who had stood close to his leader during the party tensions of the South African war. C.-B. had as little love for the Liberal Imperialists as they for him, and he liked 'Master' Haldane, as he called him, least of all. 'He is always climbing up and down the backstairs,' he remarked, 'but he makes such a clatter that everyone hears him.' He was an ardent Rosebery man, and in 1905, when a change of government seemed imminent, he wrote to Lord Knollys, the King's Private Secretary, 'one longs for Rosebery'. But when that brilliant but erratic chief retired like Achilles to his tent Haldane accepted what was offered him without complaint. Though his direct knowledge of military affairs was limited to membership of a committee on explosives, he picked up the threads with astonishing rapidity, worked out a comprehensive scheme of army reform, and earned Lord Haig's compliment in 1918 that he was the greatest Secretary for War England had ever had. 'What is Schopenhauer doing among the Generals?' C.-B. queried. Schopenhauer, as Curzon dubbed him —a misnomer, for he was an ardent Hegelian—was soon perfectly at home in Whitehall, where the soldiers realized that they had to deal with a born organizer, an indefatigable worker, and a first-class brain.

The debates in Committee on the Army Bill were technical in character, but we listened attentively to the lengthy exposition in which the Minister unfolded his scheme to the House. As John Morley remarked, there were no paragraphs in Haldane's speeches. He was the most prolix speaker on the Treasury Bench, as Asquith was the most concise, but the mastery of his complicated theme was complete. His predecessor Arnold-Forster found little to praise in the plans of his successor; but his death left Wyndham, who had been Under-Secretary for War during the South African conflict, the front bench military expert of the Opposition. He was assisted by Balfour, founder of the Committee of Imperial Defence, who took an unsleeping interest in the problems of national security. On the Government side our leading unofficial expert was Dilke; and Hilaire Belloc, who had served in the French artillery, made the best speeches of his brief political career on the Bill. One of the surprises of the Parliament of 1906 was the failure of that brilliant figure to make his mark at Westminster. The most arrogant mortal I ever knew felt boundless disdain for Protestants and Puritans, Jews and Germans; the latter he regarded—a hangover from the 1870 war— with such detestation that he declined to learn their language. That England was governed by moneyed interests and the Jews was one of his strangest delusions. Unlike his disciple Chesterton he never really understood the tolerant and individualistic English character to which we owe our liberties.

The death of C.-B.'s wife after a long illness sapped his vitality. In the autumn of 1907 he addressed a great meeting at Bristol and suffered a severe heart attack a few hours later. The Liberal members of the surrounding districts, including Maclean and myself who had journeyed from Bath, heard the last platform speech of our beloved chief. Though he reappeared at the opening of the session of 1908 his strength ebbed rapidly. He resigned at Easter and was soon in his grave. He had led the Liberal host out of the wilderness to its most resounding victory, had reconciled the Boers, and had won the affection of his followers. The little group of Liberal Imperialists quickly discovered that they had undervalued his gifts. In a letter which gave him keen pleasure Grey, who had been extremely reluctant to serve under him, paid him an unsolicited tribute. C.-B., testified Haldane long afterwards, was an admirable chief when one had secured his confidence, and the veteran Premier congratulated the War Minister on his services in 1907. He was *persona grata* with Edward VII, who greatly preferred him to Balfour, who was too much of an Intellectual, and to Asquith, who was too reserved. His brain was not of the first order, but he had the real stuff of Liberalism in him. Less of a Whig than the elder Harcourt, more approachable than Asquith, more dependable than Lloyd George, he brought a certain generosity of spirit to the problems of the day when those qualities were most urgently needed at home and abroad. His faith in the common man was justified again and again. 'I hope that when you draw up a calendar of empire-builders,' declared General Smuts in 1917, 'you will not forget the name of Campbell-Bannerman—a wise man with profound feeling and profound political instinct, who achieved one of the wisest political settlements in the history of this nation.'

10

IMPERIAL AND FOREIGN AFFAIRS

THE Liberal Government inherited a tangled situation in India and strove to clear it up. Though Curzon, the greatest of our Viceroys since Dalhousie, had spent himself in the service of the country which he loved, he failed to realize that it was coming of age. The Partition of Bengal, which had grown by increase of population to an unwieldly size, appeared to him a purely administrative question; but the indignation it aroused among Indian Nationalists revealed once again that the expert who is merely an expert is often a false guide. Despite his splendid abilities he lacked the human touch which had made India regard Lord Ripon as a friend, and which was to win affectionate confidence for more than one of his successors. His attitude in the conflict with Kitchener, which is explained in the second volume of Lord Zetland's official biography, failed to commend itself to the Balfour Cabinet, and the Viceroyalty which had opened to a flourish of trumpets in 1898 closed in the summer of 1905 in anger and gloom. Lord Minto exchanged Ottawa for Simla, and a few months later John Morley succeeded Brodrick at the India Office.

Though Morley had written about Warren Hastings in his biography of Burke, he was as ignorant of modern India as most of our statesmen before it became his official concern. He was notoriously indifferent to the glamour of empire, but he seemed also unaware of the rapid growth of nationalist sentiment of the last two decades. His first speech, delivered on an amendment to the Address, suggested a man groping his way through the fog. It was a striking illustration of our British practice of setting an amateur to tasks which more logical communities would entrust to a specialist. The time-honoured tradition, however, vindicated itself once again at both ends of the telegraph wire, and the Morley-Minto partnership opened a fruitful chapter in the annals of Imperial rule. The letters of the veteran Liberal Minister to the Conservative Viceroy form the most arresting portion of his *Recollections*, and Minto's replies are utilized in John Buchan's biography of his friend. Morley and Minto had never met, and intellectually they stood at opposite poles; but they brought fresh minds to their task, consulting representative Indians whom Curzon had ignored.

The House of Commons was never without its Anglo-Indian contingent, and the Parliament of 1906 could boast of more than the usual share. Our leading expert on the Liberal side was Sir Henry Cotton, whose striking little book *New India* had passed through several editions; but he was ineffective on his legs and his lengthy speeches emptied the House. He was reinforced by half a dozen other veteran administrators who shared his dislike of the partition of Bengal and his desire for constitutional advance. These experts formed the nucleus of a large India Committee to which I and other amateurs belonged. We were confident that the venerable Home Ruler at the India Office would grow into a great Secretary of State, and we rejoiced that the Under-Secretary John Ellis, the veteran Quaker and campaigner against the opium traffic, stood at his side.

Morley felt unable to cancel the partition of Bengal though he was aware of its devastating effects; but he consented to terminate the export of opium to China and thereby to remove an old blot on our record. Moreover we soon learned that he was considering an extension of self-government beyond the limits of the Council Act of 1892, and was taking counsel with Gokhale, the most eminent Indian statesman of his time. I had known Nairoji, the first Indian member of the House of Commons, whom Salisbury contemptuously described as 'a black man', and Bhownagree, the second. In later days I was to meet Lord Sinha, the first Indian member of the House of Lords, Banerjea, 'the Gladstone of India', Tilak, the learned extremist, Lajpat Rai, the social reformer, Sastri and Sapru, Gandhi and Tagore, and indeed almost all the leading performers on the Indian stage before and after the First World War. None of them left on me such an impression of mellow wisdom and quiet strength as Gokhale. He loved his country, and the 'Servants of India' are his abiding memorial. He also understood and appreciated the West, and was therefore enabled to interpret India and England to one another. Like Tagore, but unlike Gandhi, he was not merely a great Indian but a citizen of the world.

While the Morley-Minto reform scheme was being slowly elaborated a campaign of repression was in full swing, and it was an irony of fate that the philosophic Radical in Whitehall should begin his activities with the sword instead of the olive-branch. Viceroy and Secretary of State were in agreement as to the need both for generous political concessions and for unflinching repression of violence. Great expectations were aroused among Congress politicians by the appointment of the distinguished thinker from whose writings and speeches many of them had learned the elements of Liberalism, and his refusal to modify the partition of Bengal aroused angry disappointment. When European goods were boycotted in parts of Bengal and several Europeans were murdered, the Government replied by drastic laws against seditious meetings and the press. The necessity for stern measures was generally recognized, but resort to the Bengal Regulation of 1818, under which suspected individuals could be deported without charge or trial, was too much for many of us. The revolt was led by my old friend of Boer War days, Frederick Mackarness, to whom the reign of law throughout the Empire was a religion. If a public trial seemed dangerous, why, we asked, was not the accused informed of the charges and given a chance to clear himself? To this question, repeated over and over again from the Liberal benches and echoed later by one or two prominent Conservatives, the Government rejoined that we must trust the men on the spot. We knew that such proceedings must be distasteful to Morley, who had hotly protested against similar actions and arguments in Ireland and South Africa. When I told him how strongly many of us felt about the matter, he quietly replied 'I don't wonder'. Though he felt obliged to defend the policy of the Viceroy, his letters to Minto show how he strove to limit the employment of an instrument which lent itself to abuse. Our antagonism to the practice was intensified by the fact that the Indian police were by no means above suspicion, and that Lajpat Rai and some other deportees enjoyed general respect.

Support of the men on the spot in regard to law and order was the price that the Secretary of State had to pay for his scheme of reform. The Councils Act of 1909 enlarged the membership of the Viceregal and Provincial Legislative Councils, an official majority being retained on the former alone. Communal representation was introduced for the defence of the Mohammedan majority. The Executive Councils of Madras and Bombay were to be enlarged from two to four, one member to be an Indian, and Executive Councils were foreshadowed for the other provinces. Still more important was the simultaneous appointment of Sinha, the leading Indian barrister, as Legal Member of the Viceroy's Executive Council, a post once held by Macaulay, and of two Indians, a Mohammedan and a Hindu, to the Council in Whitehall. The groundless fear that men with a dark skin could not be trusted to keep secrets was dispelled and, like other constitutional changes, the novelty faded off into a commonplace.

Lord Minto sympathized with the ideals of educated Indians, and without his steady support Morley would have been powerless. Their reforms were well calculated to 'rally the moderates', in Morley's well-known phrase. Though they failed to mollify root and branch opponents of British rule such as Tilak, they opened up a fruitful field of co-operation between the bureaucracy and responsible leaders of native opinion. While some of my Parliamentary friends were too incensed by the deportations without trial to care much about the reforms, I warmly welcomed them as a fresh example of the Liberal statesmanship which was transforming the South African scene before our eyes. Morley's Indian speeches, after he had taken time to look round, were most impressive, and they well deserved publication in book form in 1909.

The British occupation of Egypt had come to be tacitly regarded as permanent, and discussion shifted from the conditions of evacuation to schemes for constitutional advance. Since it remained in international law a Turkish province the responsible Minister was the Foreign Secretary, and it was in reference to Egypt that some of us new Members first came into contact with Grey. In the early summer of 1906 some British officers, without obtaining permission, shot pigeons belonging to the peasants of Denshawai who thereupon attacked them with sticks. In the

scuffle three peasants and a woman were accidentally shot by the
officers, of whom two ran several miles in the burning sun to the
camp, and one, weakened no doubt by the blows he had received,
died of sunstroke. Fifty villagers were tried for murder and
assault, four hanged, eight flogged, and ten others sentenced to
terms amounting to a hundred years. A special tribunal hurried
on the trial, and the executions and floggings were inflicted in the
presence of the relatives and friends of the culprits. As bad luck
would have it, Lord Cromer was at that moment on the way
home for his summer holiday. The savage retaliation sickened
the supporters of the Government, who, unlike the Foreign
Secretary, were free to say what we thought.

This deplorable incident revived general interest in Egypt, and
it dawned on the public that our position on the Nile was less
secure than we believed. The hostility of the Khedive Abbas, who
naturally hated to be a mere figure-head, was unconcealed, but he
was a light-weight and the dynasty had never enjoyed wide
popularity. Under the leadership of Mustapha Kemal, a clever
young journalist, the Nationalists, of whom little had been heard
since the defeat of Arabi in 1882, once more raised their heads.
When Cromer resigned in 1907 what he called a wave of fanaticism
was passing over the country. We were in fact witnessing the
birth of a new Egypt as well as of a new India, calling not so much
for repression as for constructive statesmanship. The country,
we argued, could not for ever be kept in leading-strings, and the
political training of the people must be taken in hand. A little
group of members was formed to keep the Egyptian question
before the House. From time to time we discussed the situation
informally with the Foreign Secretary in his private room, urging
him, busy though he was, to devote more attention to this portion
of his vast domain.

In Egyptian as in Indian matters I belonged to the left centre
of my party, not to the extreme left. I supported the vote of
£50,000 to Cromer on his resignation which was opposed by
some of our group, and I disapproved the virulence of the
pamphlets published by Wilfrid Blunt after the Denshawai
incident. It was interesting to listen to his pungent comments and
lively recollections in his London home or his beautiful seventeenth-century house near Horsham; but he was a root and branch

opponent of the Occupation, which I never was, and I felt that he undervalued Cromer's services. The revival of nationalism in 1906–7 was merely a flash in the pan, but after the First World War it found a more gifted leader in Zagloul and transformed the face of Egyptian politics.

The first Morocco crisis was in full swing when Grey succeeded Lansdowne, but we only learned later how critical was the issue at the Algeciras conference. The situation in the Near East, on the other hand, was illustrated in a flood of Blue-books which enabled us to follow every move in the game. As an original member of the Balkan Committee I was fairly well versed in Balkan politics, and my historical studies provided the necessary perspective. I was anti-Turk only in the sense that I knew the Turks to be unfit to rule over Christians. The core of the trouble was Macedonia, where the traditional antagonism of the Cross and the Crescent was complicated by ferocious rivalries between the Balkan races. The programme of reforms drawn up in 1903 at Mürzsteg by Austria and Russia, like all previous schemes, had proved utterly useless. A *gendarmerie* was instituted under officers chosen by the Great Powers, though no provision was made for financing its operations. England, alone of the Powers, really cared about the plight of the Balkan Christians. After allowing time for Austria and Russia to display their impotence, Lansdowne seized the rudder in 1905 and forced the Sultan's consent to a financial commission by a naval demonstration.

The Balkan Committee had applauded his initiative, for we knew that Turkish promises of reform had always been mere scraps of paper. Our founder was Noel Buxton, later Lord Noel-Buxton, whose mastery of the intricacies of Balkan politics was gained in numerous visits to the Near East. The story of his varied activities may be read in his own books, in *Politics from a Back Bench* by his former private secretary Dr. Conwell-Evans, and in the affectionate biography by Mosa Anderson to which I contributed a Foreword. Inheriting a distinguished name, the great-grandson of the liberator of the slaves throughout the British Empire added lustre to it by his unwearying efforts on behalf of backward and downtrodden peoples. Blessed with ample means from the family brewery, he instinctively and unselfishly dedicated himself to public service. His tall figure, perfect manners and unself-conscious dignity formed an admirable equipment. He was equally at ease with crowned heads in the Balkans and with working men. There was something spacious, restful, unhurried about him. I never saw him flurried and never heard him raise his voice. Though he had deep convictions he kept his emotions under firm control. Had he chosen diplomacy as a career he would have made a successful Ambassador. Quietly pursuing his aims, never discouraged and never embittered, he acted on the Bismarckian principle that politics are the art of the possible. When he used to say how much cleverer were some of his friends I replied that he undervalued himself. Scintillating and dynamic he was not, and he lacked the gift of speech; but in England—and above all in Parliament—character counts for most in the long run. He was to prove an energetic Minister of Agriculture in the first two Labour Governments, and, though never a Pacifist, he was an unwearying worker for peace. I regretted—and I think he regretted—that he was not appointed Under-Secretary for Foreign Affairs with Ramsay MacDonald or Arthur Henderson as his chief.

Lord Newton once observed that we were the only sentimental nation in the world. Foreigners, on the other hand, often regarded our manifestations of sympathy with the Christian subjects of the Sultan as a cloak for selfish British aims. Though the Balkan Committee was credited by friends and foes with more power than it possessed, it performed a useful work in strengthening the hands of our Government in its struggle with the obstinacy of Abdul Hamid and the indifference of the Powers. Buxton's Bulgarian sympathies were notorious, as were those of Bourchier, *The Times* Correspondent, who always addressed us on his visits to England. Bryce, our first President, was not specially committed to any of the Balkan races, and Professor Westlake, the eminent jurist who succeeded him, was equally detached. Some members of our Committee, among them Nevinson and Brailsford, had engaged in relief work after the revolt of 1903, and the latter had written a book on Macedonia which remains a classic. Our leading scholar was Sir Arthur Evans, the discoverer of Cnossus, whose personal experience of the Balkans went back to the Bosnian rising of 1875.

Lansdowne at the Foreign Office was the outstanding success

of the Balfour Ministry, and we hoped that Grey would continue the moral leadership he had assumed. Now that the secrets of the archives are revealed we can see that there was not the slightest difference in policy or zeal between the two men, but for the first two years we seemed to detect a slight fall of the temperature. In the summer of 1907 we organized an influential deputation which was introduced by the Archbishop of Canterbury and was designed to ginger the Foreign Secretary. We came hungry away, for his mind seemed more occupied with the urgent problem of the bands than with the underlying evils of Turkish rule; but Grey never wore his heart on his sleeve.

The situation in the Near East was transformed at the opening of 1908 when Aehrenthal secured from the Sultan permission to build a railway through the Sanjak of Novibazar. Though it infringed no treaty rights, this step ended the decade of Austro-Russian co-operation in the Balkans inaugurated in 1897, and broke up the Concert of Europe which at that moment was attempting to secure the assent of the Sultan to a scheme of judicial reform in Macedonia. Grey was no less incensed than Iswolsky, and now that the Austro-Russian partnership was dead he determined to take the initiative as his predecessor had done in 1905. As Noel Buxton had lost his seat in 1906, I endeavoured to represent the Balkan Committee in Parliament. By the luck of the ballot we secured one of the private members' evenings at the beginning of the session of 1908, and Masterman and I implored the Foreign Secretary to exert himself. His response exceeded our hopes, for he boldly demanded the appointment of a Christian Governor of Macedonia for a term of years. This was crying for the moon, and a Turk was installed as Inspector-General of Macedonia without power or independence: once again Abdul Hamid had snapped his fingers at the West. Further instalments of control were believed to have been planned at the meeting of King Edward and the Tsar at Reval in June, but a week or two later the Young Turks raised the flag of revolt. The old Sultan was too weak to resist his own subjects, and Turkey seemed to have been changed overnight into a modern constitutional state. The bands melted away, and the machinery installed by the Powers in Macedonia was scrapped.

Nowhere outside Turkey was the Young Turk revolution

hailed with such enthusiasm as in England. No one could be more thankful than the Foreign Secretary to be relieved of the wearisome task of attempting to secure decent government for the Balkan Christians. Our Balkan Committee shared his satisfaction, for we knew that 'the red Sultan' was incorrigible. A deputation from the Committee headed by its chairman, which an autumn session prevented me from joining, journeyed to Constantinople to convey our congratulations, and one of its members, Charles Roden Buxton, brother of the chairman, paid homage to the reformers in his book *Turkey in Revolution*. In the following year we entertained Enver Pasha to lunch on his first visit to England. His resemblance to the young Napoleon was remarkable, and at that stage of his romantic career it was impossible to detect the volcanic fires in the quiet and well-groomed little man. Talaat Pasha was a bigger and rougher type, and his looks did not commend him. The most attractive of the Young Turk leaders who visited London was Ahmed Riza, the first Speaker of the Turkish Parliament. His mother was Austrian, and, like other Young Turks, he had been compelled to live abroad. His pleasant and handsome face was an open letter of recommendation, and if he represented the new Turkey we felt that the revolution had been a deliverance. None of us could foresee that within a year or two the Young Turks would pursue an even more ruthless policy of Ottomanization than Abdul Hamid, that Armenian blood would once more flow in torrents, and that many of the worst practices of the old régime would persist behind the new constitutional façade. Some veteran Gladstonians, among them George Russell, convinced that the Turkish leopard would never change his spots, had declined to join in the plaudits which greeted the revolution; and they proved better prophets than the Foreign Office and the Balkan Committee.

The Congo problem, like the plight of Macedonia, harassed Grey as it had harassed his predecessor, and the scandals of King Leopold's rule were repeatedly brought before the House by a little band of specialists. If Dilke was the Generalissimo, the Chief of Staff was E. D. Morel. The child of a French father, born and bred in France and remaining a French subject till 1914, he had become interested in West Africa as a clerk in a Liverpool shipping firm; and he exposed the iniquities in the French and Belgian

Congo in a series of volumes of which *Red Rubber* was the best known. As secretary of the Congo Reform Association he kept the question continually before Parliament and the press, and he co-operated with Vandervelde and other reformers in Brussels. Grey moved too slowly to satisfy his passionate nature; but by 1911, two years after the death of King Leopold, the condition of the Belgian Congo allowed the British Government to recognize its transfer to the Belgian state. The winding up of the Association when its aim had been achieved was celebrated by a lunch in honour of Morel at which Lord Cromer presided and for which Vandervelde travelled to London. Morel made the best speech, for he was as fluent with his tongue as with his pen. He was a Knight Errant of Humanity, and there was a touch of genius in the man.

The most formidable missile in the attack on King Leopold was the detailed report of Consul Casement published by the British Government in 1904. With this indictment on his desk Lansdowne had taken up the matter officially, and the hideous régime never recovered from the exposure. The subsequent attitude of Casement and Morel in the World War appeared to suspicious minds to discount the value of their past testimony in regard to the Congo, but the notion that they had been German agents was ludicrous to those of us who knew them in the flesh. The simplest explanation of human motives is usually the best: they were appalled by the atrocious exploitation and they denounced it to the world. Soon after the Congo scandals had ceased a new abomination was revealed by Casement, acting once more in his Consular capacity, in the heart of Peru, where the natives of the Putumayo river were at the mercy of unscrupulous exploiters. As a member of the executive of the Anti-Slavery and Aborigines Protection Society which assisted in the campaign I saw Casement at close quarters. His evidence was confirmed by a searching Parliamentary inquiry, and on his retirement from the Consular service he was knighted. Till the storm broke in 1914 he was generally regarded with confidence and admiration.

When the Liberals returned to office in 1905, France had become a friend while Russia remained a potential foe. Most Englishmen rejoiced at the victory of Japan in the war 1904-5, and the summoning of a Duma suggested that the Tzar had learned a lesson from his defeat. Its dissolution after three months was a shock, and though we could do nothing to help the Russian people we could at any rate express our sympathy. This, to our delight, was accomplished by the Prime Minister himself. The Inter-Parliamentary Union was due to meet in London in 1906, and six representatives of the Duma had arrived when the news was flashed across Europe. C.-B. rose to the occasion, and at the last minute inserted into the text of his inaugural address the words *La Douma est morte, vive la Douma!* He had informed Grey of his intention, and no objection had been raised. Hundreds of us gathered in the Royal Gallery of the Houses of Parliament for the opening proceedings, and as I arrived I saw the Russians leaving the Conference of which they had so unexpectedly ceased to be members. It was a proud moment when the Prime Minister flung forth that message of protest and hope which infuriated the reactionaries at St. Petersburg, heartened the reformers, and echoed round the world.

When a second Duma had met the same violent fate as the first the franchise was narrowed and the third and fourth purchased survival by subservience. The system of autocracy continued unimpaired, for Ministers were responsible to the ruler alone. The Tsar found a strong man in Stolypin, who proceeded to wage war on the revolutionaries with a savagery equal to their own. British sympathies, as usual, were with the constitutional reformers, and the Mother of Parliaments was eager to help in their struggle. A Russia Committee consisting of Members of Parliament, Russian scholars and journalists was formed to collect and diffuse information, with Charles Trevelyan as Chairman and Bernard Pares as our leading expert. The publication under our auspices of a brochure entitled *The Terror in Russia* by Prince Kropotkin created a sensation by lifting the veil from a scene of horror. I visited the brave old exile and his devoted wife in their cottage in Muswell Hill, and we met at such international shrines as the Chelsea studio of Felix Moscheles, the godson of Mendelssohn. He was the most distinguished of the Russian exiles who found refuge in England before the war, and his *Memoirs of a Revolutionist* are more exciting than a detective novel. The passion of his life was Russian liberty, for which he had cheerfully suffered imprisonment and sacrificed rank, wealth and home. He was one of the most lovable of men, with the happy simplicity of a child and a heart overflowing with compassion for the poor and oppressed.

When the Russo-Japanese conflict was over England and Russia gravitated towards each other, for how could there be eternal enmity between the two friends of France? The spectre of war on the Indian frontier was banished by the Convention of August 1907 which dealt with Persia, Afghanistan and Tibet. The *rapprochement*, however, was purely official, for the man in the street, not yet obsessed by the German peril, continued to detest Tsarist rule. The issue was raised in Parliament, and the announcement that the King would visit the Tsar at Reval in June 1908 led to the most thrilling debate since the indictment of Milner in 1906. The attack was opened by Arthur Henderson, and a free vote might have carried his motion; but when Grey declared that acceptance of the critical motion would involve his resignation, several members, myself among them, abstained from the division. The Russian Liberals, he argued, desired the visit to take place, and in any case it was no part of his duty to verify the stories of atrocities or even to be aware of their existence. This ostentatious indifference to the character of Tsarist rule was a far cry not only from Gladstone's resonant denunciations of the Neapolitan prisons under Bourbon rule and of Abdul Hamid, the Great Assassin, but also from C.-B.'s recent pronouncement on the Duma. Twenty years later, when immersed in the Foreign Office archives, I discovered that the Foreign Secretary agreed with his critics more than in his official position he felt able to admit.

When the Tsar returned King Edward's visit in 1909 the Parliamentary protest was renewed, and the monarchs met at Cowes instead of London or Windsor. A warm welcome on the other hand was extended to a representative deputation from the Duma. The two most distinguished figures were Guchkoff, the Octobrist chief, and Miliukoff, the leader of the Cadets who had dominated the Dumas of 1906 and 1907. The latter had won fame as a historian before entering politics, and he was the nearest Russian counterpart to our Liberal statesmen. With his broad outlook and his faith in Parliamentary institutions he was *persona grata* in England and the United States. He spoke and wrote English astonishingly well, and to talk with him was to forget

10

the gulf between East and West. The visit of the Russian deputies was returned when Lord Weardale captained a team consisting of members of both Houses, with a sprinkling from outside. A vivid account of these occasions may be found in the *Russian Memories* of Sir Bernard Pares, whose labours in interpreting the two peoples to one another were beyond praise.

Our detestation of the Tsarist Government was intensified by the bullying of Persia. The extravagance of the Shah involved the gradual mortgaging of the country to Russia, which in turn created a demand for drastic reforms. A Parliament was reluctantly granted in 1906, the Civil List was reduced, pensions and sinecures were cut down, and the first Budget secured a surplus without fresh taxation. Persian nationalism had made a promising start when the feeble Muzaffer-ed-Din was succeeded in 1907 by his son Mohammed Ali, a cruel and dissolute despot. The new ruler carried out a *coup d'état* with the aid of the Cossack Brigade under a Russian officer, the Parliament House was bombarded, and the reformers fled for their lives. At this point the vigorous fighting tribe of the Bakhtiaris marched on Teheran and compelled the tyrant to abdicate. His youthful son was placed on the throne, the Parliament was recalled, and the urgent task of modernization was resumed. In 1911 Shuster, an American expert, was invited to assume control of the finances, and quickly won the confidence of the Constitutionalists. He proved indeed too successful, and after eight strenuous months he was chased out of the country by a Russian ultimatum. Here again the Foreign Secretary was paralysed by considerations of high policy. The British Legation in Teheran sympathized with the constitutional movement in Persia as openly as the Russian Legation frowned on the reformers. The friction between the two Great Powers was slightly diminished by the Anglo-Russian Convention, which divided the country into a large Russian and a small British sphere of influence, with a neutral zone between. Though the preamble engaged the signatories to respect the integrity and independence of Persia, the Russian Minister Hartwig snapped his fingers not merely at the treaty pledge but at his superiors in St. Petersburg. The dragooning of a weak oriental power, gallantly endeavouring to struggle to its feet after years of misrule, aroused righteous indignation in England. Grey had no liking for Russia's policy and privately strove to hold it in check; but it soon became clear that a free hand for Russia in her zone was the price we had to pay for her goodwill in Europe, and the Foreign Secretary was reduced to the argument that things would have been even worse for Persia had there been no delimitation of spheres.

The support of the constitutional movement was the object of the Persia Committee, of which Lynch was Chairman and Professor Browne—Persian Browne, as he was known to his friends—the principal expert. The former was a partner in the well-known firm which owned the Lynch steamers on the Tigris and had constructed the Lynch road over the mountains from the Persian Gulf. He knew Persia as well as Armenia, and he was the leading authority in the House on the Baghdad Railway. In Browne we possessed not only an orientalist of European renown but a personality of irresistible charm. His *A Year in Persia* is a classic, and his voluminous *Literary History of Persia* ranks among the glories of British scholarship. He used to say that he loved Persia next to his own land, and his generosity to the exiled constitutionalists was without stint. His bright eyes and rapid talk in several languages revealed the fires that burned within. I have heard him race along in Persian with Taqi Zadeh, the best of the reformers, a refined, thoughtful and attractive figure in his white garb. His book on *The History of the Persian Revolution* tells the tragic tale; if he tended to idealize his Persian friends it was a pardonable weakness. I never shared his enthusiasm for Islam, but I was heart and soul with him in his crusade against the brutalities of the Russian bear.

The worst chapter in the history of Russo-Persian relations was the eviction of Shuster. When the American Treasurer-General appointed British subjects to superintend the collection of revenue in the Russian sphere—which included the chief cities and trade routes of the country—Grey accepted the demand for his expulsion on the ground that he was infringing the spirit of the Convention of 1907 which mapped out spheres of influence. Our Committee entertained him at a public dinner on his way home and heard the distressing story of frustration from his own lips. He gave the impression of an upright and energetic business man who had done his best for the country, and there is no more discreditable tale than that which he proceeded to tell in *The Strangling of Persia*. Though Grey deplored the undiplomatic neglect of Russian susceptibilities, Russia put forward demands at Teheran which even he was unable to defend. If co-operation in Persia were to cease, he warned the Russian Ambassador, it would mean the end of the Entente and he would resign. The demands were modified sufficiently to avert a calamity, but the independence of Persia was gone. While in Macedonia and the Congo, as in India and South Africa, the Government had striven for the extension of rights and liberties, in Persia it reluctantly sacrificed our good name to Russian greed.

The reason, though never explicitly stated, was not far to seek. Though we heard more of Russia than of Germany in the opening years of the 1906 Parliament, the German peril began to loom up as its life advanced. We knew nothing of Grey's momentous conversations with the French and German Ambassadors soon after his appointment, and most of his Cabinet colleagues were equally in the dark. Our thoughts were focused on domestic problems, and we longed for a smaller expenditure on armaments. Parties of German burgomasters and theologians paid official visits to England, and we warmly welcomed them at St. Stephen's. When the Act of Algeciras was signed in 1906 the sky seemed to be clearing, and C.-B.'s article in the *Nation* in the spring of 1907 exhorted the world to make the forthcoming Hague Conference a success. Our modest building programme in the Naval Estimates of that year suggested that the Government hoped for fine weather, and the Kaiser's visit to England in the autumn seemed to restore something of the cordiality of bygone years. We were too optimistic, for the failure of the second Hague Conference to deal with armaments indicated that new storms were likely to blow up. The growth of the German fleet had been watched with increasing uneasiness since 1904 when King Edward paid an official visit to Kiel. The launching of the Dreadnought in 1905 opened a new phase of competition in which only capital ships were allowed to count: 1908 witnessed the emergence of 'the German peril' as the dominating preoccupation of British statesmanship. It opened badly with the Kaiser's letter to Lord Tweedmouth, the First Lord of the Admiralty, and though the naval estimates providing for only two Dreadnoughts testified to the conciliatory spirit of the Cabinet, no response was forth-coming from Berlin.

When the King visited his nephew at Cronberg in August on his way to Marienbad, Sir Charles Hardinge, Permanent Under-Secretary of the Foreign Office, explained our view of the dangers of naval competition and urged that friendly discussions should take place. The Kaiser, as proud of his growing fleet as a child with a new toy, impulsively rejoined that he would rather go to war than submit to foreign dictation. Three months later the publication of the *Daily Telegraph* interview increased the *malaise* which he honestly intended to dispel. While the hurricane was still raging, Lord Roberts uttered his historic warning in the House of Lords which made compulsory service a living issue. Meanwhile the construction of German battleships was pressed forward to the strident accompaniment of the Pan-German press. 'That we have eventually to fight Germany is just as sure as anything can be,' wrote Admiral Fisher, the *enfant terrible* of the British navy, to the King; and he urged that we should 'Copenhagen' the German fleet on the model of Canning's historic *coup* in 1807.

If 1908 was a bad year for European nerves, 1909 was worse. Mysterious whispers that Germany was anticipating her declared programme filled the lobbies in the opening weeks of the new session, but we were unprepared for the dramatic scene when McKenna, who had succeeded Tweedmouth at the Admiralty, rose on 16 March. For the first time the naval estimates were justified by selecting Germany as the yard-stick of our require-ments; British and German Dreadnoughts were balanced against each other down the vista of the coming years, and Balfour made our flesh creep by suggesting that our rival might possess twenty-five ships in April 1912. While rejecting such exaggerations, Asquith confessed that seventeen were a possibility and thirteen a certainty. A wave of panic swept over Parliament and our usually unemotional country, and eight Dreadnoughts were laid down during the year. War in the near future was spoken of as possible and even probable, and the legend of stealthy acceleration seemed proof of a design to wrest the trident from Britannia's hands. As a matter of fact no serious acceleration had taken place, and the forecasts of the number of German Dreadnoughts in 1912 were wide of the mark. But the mischief was done. Though Germany

had as much right to a big fleet as ourselves, the *Flottenpolitik* was
a colossal blunder, driving us ever closer into the arms of France
and Russia. While Bismarck had kept on friendly terms with
England and Russia, Germany was now on bad terms with both.
The *Einkreisung* of which she bitterly complained was entirely of
her own making.

A fresh complication was added to the troublous winter of
1908–9 by Austria's annexation of Bosnia and Herzegovina.
Hitherto our relations with Vienna had been unaffected by our
quarrels with Berlin, but now we found ourselves involved in a
first-class row with a valued friend. While the Prime Minister
and the Foreign Secretary denounced the breach of the public
law of Europe, King Edward sent a sharp reply to an autograph
letter of Francis Joseph. Since Iswolsky had concealed his
negotiations with Aehrenthal from his French allies and his
English friends, the British people were confirmed in the errone-
ous supposition that the Central Powers were the sole culprits.
Dilke declared that we were making a mountain out of a molehill,
and indeed Grey's frowns would have been more impressive had
he censured with equal severity the action of France in Morocco
and Russia in Persia. In public, at any rate, he, like other diplomatists, had one standard of conduct for our friends, another for our
potential foes.

I I

LORDS VERSUS COMMONS

Asquith's succession to the Premiership in 1908 involved significant changes. As everyone expected, Lloyd George, who had won golden opinions in the business world at the Board of Trade, succeeded to the Treasury, and Churchill stepped into his shoes. Since our new captain had been classified as a Liberal Imperialist, the ship was trimmed by promoting the leader of the radical wing. Lord Elgin was evicted from the Colonial Office to make room for Lord Crewe, whose skilful piloting of Liberal measures in the chilly atmosphere of the Upper House had brought him rapidly to the front. Two of our veterans, as the phrase goes, exchanged the green benches for the red; Sir Henry Fowler vanished from active politics behind the title of Lord Wolverhampton, and 'honest John' reappearing as Viscount Morley of Blackburn. Our new chief addressed us with graceful modesty at the Reform Club. Temperamentally he was less of a democrat than C.-B., and his relations with the rank and file were never intimate; but we all felt proud of our eminent Parliamentarian who was to prove himself equal to every emergency except a world war.

The principal item on our menu for 1908 was the Licensing Bill, which involved an autumn session and was finally lost on the rocks. The Liberal party had inscribed Local Option on its banner in the nineties, but the situation had been transformed by Balfour's Act of 1904. So long as the renewal of the annual licence of a public house was claimed as a right—though not a statutory right—it was impossible to inaugurate any of the schemes—local option, disinterested management or state purchase—dear to the heart of Temperance workers. The first task was to get back to the annual licence without claim to renewal, and this could only be done by the imposition of a time limit. The Bill fixed the close period at fourteen years, extended during the debates to twenty-one in the vain hope of saving its life. Many other changes were proposed, the ground for which had been prepared by the Peel Commission; but the heart of the fight was the time limit, which raised the question of brewery shares and other vested interests. In his last days C.-B. had foretold a real storm and the tornado duly arrived. The measure was nominally in charge of Herbert Gladstone, but the main burden was carried by the Prime Minister admirably seconded by Herbert Samuel, Under-Secretary of the Home Office. Among back-bench supporters of the bill were four experts whose contributions to debate were scarcely less significant than those from the front bench. Sir Thomas Whittaker knew more of the subject than anyone in or out of the House, and the famous Minority Report of the Peel Commission, signed by the Chairman himself, was largely his work. He combined the ardour of a Temperance reformer with the grip of an experienced business man. His comrade in the fight was Arthur Sherwell, author of the classical work *The Temperance Problem and Social Reform* and of the more technical treatise *The Taxation of the Liquor Traffic*. They argued that intemperance could never be overcome till private profit was eliminated from the sale of drink, but disinterested management could only be introduced when the community resumed unfettered control of the trade. The Temperance Legislation League was founded to foster their ideas, with Lord Peel as President, Whittaker as Chairman, and Sherwell as Secretary.

Our two other Liberal experts belonged to a more radical school. While Whittaker and Sherwell dismissed prohibition as impracticable, Leif Jones and Charles Roberts belonged to the United Kingdom Alliance for the Suppression of the Liquor Trade. I was just in time to sit in Parliament with and to know the veteran crusader, Sir Wilfrid Lawson, one of the wittiest as well as one of the most popular members of the House. No one had done so much to keep the question of Temperance before Parliament and the nation as this gallant, cheerful and lovable old man. On his death at the end of 1906 the Presidency of the U.K.A. passed to Leif Jones, the eloquent Welshman who was to end his career as Lord Rhayader. At his side stood his friend, Charles Roberts, afterwards Under-Secretary for India, who in his *Time Limit and Local Option* produced the best handbook for supporters of the bill. His wife, Lady Cecilia, was a daughter of the most forceful and, as some would say, the most fanatical warrior in the Temperance ranks. Rosalind, Countess of Carlisle, possessed a stern mouth and an iron will. We used to be told that she signalized her husband's succession to Vanbrugh's magnificent Castle Howard by emptying the contents of the wine-cellar into a hole in the ground. The contrast between husband and wife was astonishing. Lord Carlisle, a friend of Burne-Jones and himself an artist, was the gentlest of men, loving art more than politics and Italy only next to England. While Lady Carlisle was a leading light in the Women's Liberal Federation, her husband was a mild Unionist. The parental divergence was reproduced in the sons, both of whom sat in the Parliament of 1906, Lord Morpeth following the father and Geoffrey Howard the mother. The conflict of an imperious mother with her rebellious heir was amusingly depicted in *The Coryston Family*, the liveliest of the later novels of Mrs. Humphry Ward.

The Leader of the Opposition, author of the Licensing Act of 1904, was naturally in the forefront of the battle; but the weightiest antagonist was Cave, later Home Secretary and Lord Chancellor. As Chairman of the Surrey Quarter Sessions he had every detail of the licensing laws at his finger ends. With his soft voice, unfailing courtesy, and capacity for clear statement, he was a model controversialist. The Opposition fought with the utmost energy and shareholders throughout the country were mobilized for the campaign. The political connection between the public house and the Conservative party was an old story, and F. C. Gould's cartoons of Mr. Bung in the *Westminster Gazette* kept it in the public eye. To letters of protest from angry constituents I used to reply that the Archbishop of Canterbury, one of our strongest supporters, was not the man to countenance spoliation. The prestige of our bill was enhanced by the attacks of the notorious Horatio Bottomley, who, though elected as a Liberal, acted throughout as the unblushing champion of the Trade. His record made him one of the loneliest figures in the House, but he had a very thick skin. He was an excellent speaker, and had his character matched his brains he might have been a Parliamentary success. He was engaged in perpetual lawsuits in which he conducted his own case. The Attorney General, Sir William Robson, greeted me one day in the lobby with the joyful words: 'I think we've got him this time.' He was mistaken, for the plausible sinner once again wriggled through the meshes of the law. He cherished a particular aversion to supporters of the Temperance cause, and on more than one occasion I was honoured with a broadside in the columns of *John Bull*.

On our return to Westminster for the autumn debates of 1908 it was rumoured that the chances of survival for the Licensing Bill were diminishing, and when it emerged from the Commons its doom was pronounced by a gathering of Unionist peers at Lansdowne House. Though the second reading debate in the Lords revealed a good deal of weighty approval outside the Liberal ranks, it was rejected by a large majority and the main work of a laborious session was lost. It was an honest attempt to deal with an admitted evil, but Temperance legislation is never popular. No measure during my four years at Westminster aroused such a stir in my constituency, for Bath, like other old cities, was full of public houses. Maclean and I did our best by explanation and argument to commend it as a measure of social reform in which vested interests were most generously treated by a time limit of twenty-one years, but it was uphill work.

The bright spot in the session of 1908 was the inauguration of Old Age Pensions, which had been the topic of my maiden speech. The secret was revealed in the third and last budget of Asquith, who, though he had already left the Treasury, explained his handiwork before handing over to Lloyd George. Various schemes for Old Age Pensions had been worked out by Charles Booth and other experts, and the time was ripe for an advance. Five shillings a week at the age of seventy, subject to a means test, could only be a beginning, though we must remember that the value of that small sum half a century ago was roughly equivalent to that of fifteen shillings today. The Unionists, who would have preferred a contributory system, accepted our scheme without enthusiasm. Its most outspoken opponent was Harold Cox, later editor of the *Edinburgh Review*, who entered the House with the reputation of an eminent economist and proved himself a master of debate. He was the only man on the Liberal side who clung to the doctrines of *laissez-faire* in their unadulterated form. While we saw in the state an indispensable instrument for establishing a minimum standard of life for the common man, he dreaded the slackening of moral fibre as a result of getting 'something for nothing'. It was a delight to listen to his lucid expositions of an unpopular creed. Like Lord Cromer, who attacked our plan in the Upper House, he paid too little attention to the manifold maladjustments of our industrial system, and credited the average citizen with more capacity to improve his position than he possessed. Most of us stood midway between socialism and individualism, as Liberals still do, desiring to combine the best in both.

Next to Old Age Pensions no reform of the 1906 Parliament was of such outstanding significance as the creation of Trade Boards. The horrors of sweating had been brought home to the public at the opening of the new century by the Anti-Sweating League, of which Dr. Mallon, later Warden of Toynbee Hall, was the dynamic secretary. An exhibition of sweated goods was held at Queen's Hall at the beginning of my first session at which addresses were delivered on various aspects of the problem, the topic of Continental methods of dealing with underpaid labour being allotted to myself. Two years later I was invited to serve on a Select Committee to prepare the way for legislation. Our Chairman was Sir Thomas Whittaker, and the four parties in the House were represented. The witnesses included employers, employees and social workers, and it was an experience to see, hear and cross-examine the inhabitants of the industrial underworld. The representatives of the workers in the tailoring, chain-making and paper-box trades were shepherded into our committee-room by Gertrude Tuckwell and Mary Macarthur, Chairman and Secretary of the Women's Trade Union League. The former was a niece of Sir Charles Dilke who had done more than any other man in public life for the sweated worker. The latter, a bright and attractive Scottish girl, was a born organizer, whose short but fruitful career has been described in a memoir by Lady Crewe. She had sprung into notice by her campaign against the pitiable conditions of the women chain-workers at Cradley Heath, and the Trade Boards are inseparably linked with her name. Our report urged the establishment of representative bodies in sweated industries with power to fix minimum rates, and the Trade Boards Act was passed without difficulty in 1909. Since employer and employed usually pulled different ways, the impartial chairman of a Trade Board carried a heavy burden, but the pioneer bodies proved so successful that a second Act extended their power in 1918. A third piece of beneficent legislation, though less sensational than Old Age Pensions and Trade Boards, was the so-called Children's Charter, skilfully piloted through the House by Herbert Samuel in 1908. The clause which aroused most general interest was that which excluded children under fourteen from the public-house.

The admission of John Burns, the first manual worker to attain to Cabinet rank, had been one of the most popular features of C.-B.'s list. Great expectations were formed of his control of the Local Government Board, for he combined industry and eloquence with intimate knowledge of working class life. Yet his tenure of office disappointed everyone but himself. We hoped that a man who had risen from the ranks might lead a successful attack on the slums; but, though his Town Planning Act was a useful measure, his rule in Whitehall was curiously sterile. His finest hour was over. Though he must have known what his fellow-members were thinking, the sturdy member for Battersea retained his unruffled complacency to the end and his vanity was so naïve that it almost disarmed criticism. He loved to accost two or three members in the lobby, let off a story, and then walk rapidly away, turning his head a moment later to observe the effect. One of his favourite tricks was to compare the Mississippi, the Hudson and the Thames. The first, he declared, was a lot of dirty water, the second a lot of clean water, while the third was 'liquid 'istory'. In the latter case he knew what he was talking about, for he adored the city of his birth. He had read fairly widely, and his early editions of the *Utopia* were the joy of his heart. That he was physically fearless he had shown during the Boer War, and his moral courage was to be revealed by the sacrifice of his political career to his convictions in 1914. His failings were on the surface and his heart was pure gold.

Woman suffrage, like Home Rule, had to wait for the First World War, but the cause made rapid progress during the 1906

Parliament and its ultimate triumph seemed assured. I had always regarded it as an essential part of democracy: since the concession of political rights to the working man it was indefensible and humiliating to deny the vote to half the population. The case put forward long before in Mill's *Subjection of Women* was unanswerable. To the argument that they outnumbered men and would swamp them at the polls we replied that women, like men, held different views. The cry of Votes for Women never made my pulse beat faster, for I believed that their enfranchisement would involve neither the regeneration nor the ruin of the country; yet I regretted that my party, whose historic mission it had been to extend the frontiers of liberty, failed to inscribe the demand for equal citizenship upon its banner owing to disagreement among its leaders.

The majority of the Cabinet, like the majority of its Liberal rank and file, favoured woman suffrage and was anxious to concede it. Haldane and Grey were no less convinced of its merits than Lloyd George. Balfour, who had clever sisters, was an old friend of the cause, though most of his political associates were its foes. The Labour party, needless to say, was solid in support. The chief obstacle in the path was Asquith himself, an obstacle so formidable that a world war was needed to blast it away. I had the satisfaction of swelling the majority every time that the question was brought before the House by private members. My old friends Pethick-Lawrence and his wife were in the thick of the fray and went to prison for their faith. That militancy kept the subject before the public as nothing else could have done is undeniable, yet I think that the Pankhursts alienated as many people as they convinced. The steady stream of argument from the constitutional suffragists led by Mrs. Fawcett and Lady Frances Balfour outside Parliament, and from men like Lord Lytton and Sir Willoughby Dickinson within its walls, produced a deeper and more permanent effect. Mrs. Fawcett was an ideal leader, with her clarity of speech and her unemotional temperament. Our first taste of militant methods in the House occurred in 1908. The Solicitor-General, Sir Samuel Evans, the most determined antagonist in the Ministry except Lewis Harcourt, was on his legs when a shrill voice rang out from the Ladies' Gallery. We could not see what was going on behind the grille, but we learned that the crusader had tied herself to her seat. I also witnessed surging crowds of demonstrators outside the locked gates of Palace Yard, and an attack on the Prime Minister at a reception at the house of his brother-in-law Lord Glenconner in Queen Anne's Gate.

Asquith bore the strain with his usual serenity, though there can be little doubt that for a time his life was in danger. The hunger strike in prison was countered by forcible feeding, which in turn inflamed the victims and their friends to fury. I received a letter from an aggrieved husband hinting grimly at reprisals if his wife were to be forcibly fed. When I showed it to Herbert Gladstone, who as Home Secretary was officially responsible for the prisons, he quietly remarked that he received plenty of similar threats. There seemed no way out, for a divided Cabinet could not introduce a measure, and the Opposition in the Commons was strong enough to prevent the passage of a private member's bill. There was no more paradoxical feature of the struggle for the suffrage than the antagonism of Mrs. Humphry Ward. Her fame as one of the outstanding women of the time rested not only on her writings but on her public services, and when her son stood for Parliament she took an eager part in his campaign. The shaky foundation on which the Anti-Suffragists stood was revealed by Asquith's subsequent discovery that women no less than men played up in the testing time of war. His belated conversion may be paralleled by his detection of the merits of Proportional Representation when his legions in the House of Commons were melting away. No leading statesman of our time has less claim to be enrolled among the prophets and pioneers.

The four sessions of the Parliament of 1906 were mainly occupied with four great bills, only one of which became law. Even the most long-suffering Liberal grew tired of ploughing the sands when he saw the Education Bill of 1906, the Licensing Bill of 1908, and the Finance Bill of 1909 massacred by the Peers. The rejection of the Budget was the climax, and Gladstone's prophecy in his swan-song of 1894 that the struggle for mastery between the two Houses must go forward to an issue was at last to be fulfilled. Disappointing as it was to watch the stone of Sisyphus roll once more down the hill, we consoled ourselves with the resolve that it should never happen again. The merits or demerits of the Chancellor's taxes became of secondary interest in comparison with the pitched battle between the elective and the hereditary Chambers.

One of the sharpest dividing lines between right and left was their attitude towards the land. It was futile to expect land reform from the Conservatives, and it was the hope of the Liberal majority elected in 1906 that some striking advance might be made. When in 1909 money had to be found to defray the increasing expense of the navy and Old Age Pensions, Lloyd George decided to meet some portion of the bill by a group of taxes on unearned increment. The Budget speech took four hours to read, and a precedent was created by a break for tea. Everyone expected the radical Chancellor's first effort to make history, and the political situation was transformed overnight. On the rejection of the Licensing Bill in the previous autumn Asquith had declared that the veto was henceforward the dominant issue in politics. We were now to learn whether the permanent Unionist majority in the Upper House would dare to challenge the traditional control of the Commons in matters of finance; 1909 was Lloyd George's year. With his appointment to the Treasury he became *ex officio* the second man in the party. I agree with Lord Samuel's verdict that among his political contemporaries Lloyd George and Churchill alone possessed a touch of genius. On the platform he was supreme—artist, actor, magician. At Limehouse and elsewhere he delivered a series of speeches which might be described as a new Midlothian campaign. The man in the street realized with a shock how the values created by the growth of population and the expansion of industry had poured and were still pouring automatically into the pockets of the ground landlord. In his radical days Chamberlain had compared these favoured mortals to the lilies of the field 'who toil not, neither do they spin', and had scornfully inquired what 'ransom' they should pay. The role of radical leader, which had been vacant since the Home Rule split, was now filled by 'the little Welsh attorney' whose name became a battle-cry to one side and anathema to the other. He began to outshine his chief, as Ludendorff outshone Hindenburg. Massingham sang his praises in the *Nation* and Gardiner in the *Daily News*, and radicals throughout the country worshipped the rising sun.

It was a rough fight, and the Chancellor's taste was not impeccable. His opponents complained that he was not a gentleman, and the 'Slimehouse' style was angrily denounced. Though his technique was a trial to some of his Cabinet colleagues, his sincerity was beyond question and his examples of exploitation justified plain speaking. The sound principle of 'betterment' had been an axiom of the Progressives in the early days of the London County Council, and it was solely with the aim of securing for the community some portion of the increment due to its growth that the taxes of 1909 were devised. It was not his fault that our land system was too complicated for simple treatment, and that the concessions he was persuaded to make reduced the financial yield to a trickle. A few years later, when the World War had come and gone, the obnoxious imposts, which brought in a negligible revenue, were repealed.

No Liberal worthy of the name regretted the attempts of the Government to deal with Nonconformist disabilities, the liquor trade, and unearned increment, for the triumphant army of 1906 was prepared for casualties; but none of us anticipated such truculent intransigence in the Upper House. Two decades of Unionist rule seemed to have created or fortified a feeling that it was the natural right of the Conservatives to dominate the country through the Commons when they were in office and through the Lords when they were out. There were plenty of disinterested Conservative opponents of the land taxes who argued that the game was not worth the candle, but there was also a hard core of vested interests. The shrill voice of Rosebery, who had ceased even to pose as a Liberal, rose above the din. There was a lack of perspective, to put it mildly, in his panic-stricken cry: 'This is not a Budget but a revolution.' He was deeply moved, raising both arms above his head and letting them fall dramatically to his side. As we stood and listened at the bar we found it difficult to believe that he had been for a brief space our Commander-in-Chief.

The rejection of the Budget brought the chequered life of the Parliament of 1906 to an abrupt end. Liberals fought the election of January 1910 with a zeal equal to that of 1906, and a sufficient majority was returned to carry the land taxes into law; but the Unionists won back the South. The menace to Free Trade being removed, Bath decided by a majority of a little over a hundred to return to its Unionist allegiance. Having succeeded in my first attempt to enter Parliament I had no cause to complain of defeat, yet to be cut off in the middle of intense political activity was something of an amputation. The House of Commons has been called the best club in London. That it never was: it is above all an arena and a workshop. There are dull days and dull intervals on exciting days; yet no variety entertainment can compete in the wealth of its repertory, and no political assembly in the world approaches it in its atmosphere of goodwill. Foreign visitors, accustomed to a more rigorous régime and watching for instance Winston Churchill and F.E. walk away arm in arm after a hot encounter, concluded that it was a sham fight. In the dining-room of the Reichstag each party had its own table. At St. Stephen's members mix freely in the tea-room, the smoking-room, the dining-room, and on the terrace. If this levelling of political hurdles is to be regarded as a crime, the Leader of the Opposition was a notable offender. Balfour frankly enjoyed the society of Gladstone and Harcourt in one generation, of Asquith and Haldane, Morley and Birrell in the next. He was the life-long friend of Gladstone's gifted daughter, Mary Drew, and he shared memories of the Souls with the inimitable Margot. A stiffer tone set in with his successor, Bonar Law, who cared nothing for Society and little for the things of the mind. Birth and wealth count for nothing in Parliament without character and personality. No member was more universally respected than the veteran Thomas Burt, who had started life in a mine, and had grown into a man of wide culture and exquisite refinement. The Mother of Parliaments was greater than any party, and we were proud of who-ever added lustre to its fame. England without the House of Commons, the guardian of our liberties, is unthinkable.

James Lowther had been elected to the Speaker's Chair in the dying days of the Balfour Ministry, and, in accordance with precedent, we re-elected him to steer our new Parliament. Old members used to tell of the majesty of Speaker Peel and of his magnificent wrath when the dignity of the House was infringed. There was nothing of the Olympian about Lowther. As an old-fashioned Tory he detested the larger part of our policy, and most of our speeches must have grated on his ear; yet he kept his temper and his nerve, and his ready humour often averted or ended a storm. The Chairman of Committee, afterwards Lord Emmott, though an abler man, was less sure of himself; lacking the saving grace of humour he exerted less influence over the House. He dreaded a row and confided to me that he was most apprehensive when the inflammable Willie Redmond was on his feet. While my relations with the Speaker and the Chairman of Committees were pleasant but formal, I quickly learned to regard the Chief Clerk as a friend. Sir Courtenay Ilbert had won notoriety as the Legal Member of Lord Ripon's Executive Council in India, and he had long been recognized as a leading constitutional authority. He and Bryce had been intimate friends since Oxford days, and they delighted in each other's company. My chief used sometimes to slip away for tea or dinner to the Chief Clerk's hospitable house in Speaker's Court, where I was often privileged to be a guest. Lady Ilbert was a gracious hostess, and the marriage of their daughters to Herbert Fisher and Sir George Young helped to keep the old man in touch with a younger generation.

One of the privileges of members is that they can visit the House of Lords whenever they like. We all flocked into the gilded chamber at the opening of each session to hear Edward VII read the King's speech in his deep strong voice, and at the end of the session we watched the quaint ceremony by which the Lord Chancellor, in Norman-French, conveys the royal assent to bills. The House of Commons with its limited dimensions, its green benches and its lack of colour, never looks impressive. The Upper Chamber on a great occasion, with the bejewelled peeresses in the galleries, the Commons thronging the bar, the bishops in their robes and Privy Councillors standing on the steps of the throne, is an imposing spectacle. Neither of the Leaders, Lansdowne or Crewe, was equal to the best debaters in the Lower House, though the former was fluent and precise. The star performers were Rosebery, who rarely intervened, and Curzon who never feared to let himself go and as a orator was always at his best.

Naturally I heard a good deal of talk about Edward VII. After the death of C.-B., with whom he was on excellent terms, Lord Carrington, Minister of Agriculture, a friend since boyhood, was his favourite Minister. Haldane came next with Burns some little way behind. With the rest of the Asquith Cabinet his relations were scarcely more than official. He saw in Lloyd George the *enfant terrible* of the party and complained of the Limehouse speech as his mother had complained of Joseph Chamberlain. While his interest in foreign affairs was keen and intelligent, he cared little about our domestic controversies unless, as in the case of the conflict between Lords and Commons, they seemed likely to affect the structure of the State. Though nothing had been too small to escape the eye of Victoria, he was bored by legislative or administrative details. He preferred the company of old friends such as the Portuguese Ambassador, Marquis de Soveral or Lord Redesdale to that of the politicians. The Church, which had meant so much to the old Queen, meant nothing to her son. Despite his ability and activity the direct political influence of the Crown continued to decline during his reign.

As the conflict between the Chambers waxed hot a few short-sighted Conservatives headed by Lord Hugh Cecil sighed for the revival of the royal prerogative. The country as a whole, on the other hand, was well satisfied with the process by which the sovereign ceased to rule and became the symbol of unity and continuity. The King liked his job and enjoyed his popularity. The two garden parties at Windsor, to which Members of Parliament and their wives were invited, were a pleasant innovation, and we could see for ourselves that he deserved his reputation as a host, happy in the happiness of his guests. Wickham Steed described him as a great man, but I think that is going too far. Though he was never revered like his mother nor beloved like his son, he was well above the average of his royal contemporaries in ability. The official biography by Sidney Lee reveals a ruler of conventional mind, sharing to the full the prejudices of the man in the street, but free from the bitter partisanship of his mother and eager to serve his country according to his lights. The belief in Germany that he was a warmonger was a grotesque misreading of his character. Though, unlike his mother, he greatly preferred France to Germany he was not anti-German. On the other hand he was never quite at ease with his ebullient nephew whom he dismissed as the most brilliant failure in history; and the Kaiser's envious dislike of 'that old peacock' was equally unconcealed. Devoid of intellectual interests like most of his Hanoverian ancestors, delighting in travel and company, pretty women and

good food, enjoying life to the full in his own rather flashy
'Edwardian' way, wishing everyone to have a good time, he had
no use for austerity or long faces. Kipling dismissed him as a
corpulent voluptuary, but he was a good deal more than that.
We come nearest to him in the memoirs of Sir Frederick Ponsonby, who salutes him as the outstanding personality among the
crowned heads of Europe when the Kaiser and Francis Joseph
were still alive. While he was as unique as Queen Victoria,
George V, most modest and least glamorous of princes, was
Everyman—the most useful qualification for the role of a constitutional monarch who reigns but neither rules nor desires to
rule.

12

THE LAST YEARS OF PEACE

AFTER our defeat in the election of 1910 it was as natural that Donald Maclean should look out for another constituency as that I should try again at Bath. It would have been ungrateful to turn my back on the city that had elected me on my first appeal and had only rejected us by a handful of votes. I had little expectation that the verdict would be reversed, for we could hardly imagine the Conservatives, after their bitter lesson in 1906, once again stampeding Free Traders into our camp by waving the flag of Tariff Reform. Our supporters had remained faithful, and everyone with a spark of Liberalism in his soul rallied to the defence of the Commons against the Lords. Asquith came to speak for us but he kindled little enthusiasm.

The sudden death of King Edward brought a truce to political strife during which the party leaders met in conference. When the attempt to reach agreement on the relations of the two Houses broke down in November the Government dissolved Parliament and we suddenly found ourselves once more in the thick of the fight. My new colleague, George Hardy, who like myself had lost his seat at the beginning of the year, had served his apprenticeship on the London County Council. Though he lacked the personality of Donald Maclean, his Liberalism was equally ardent and sincere. Our star performer on this occasion was Lord Crewe, who had recently succeeded Lord Morley at the India Office. His unruffled courtesy suited the decorous atmosphere of the House of Lords, but he was not the man to sway a great audience. The dominant issue was the same as in January, for though the Budget was now on the statute-book the question of the veto remained. We demanded permission for a Liberal majority to do its work subject to delays which had never been imposed on Conservative bills. In other words we asked not for equality of treatment but merely for the diminution of an inequality which had become intolerable. The country responded to the appeal, and the Veto Bill became law a few months later. With an increased Conservative majority in Bath I could at last honourably withdraw from the fray. I regretted saying good-bye to the city where I had received nothing but kindness; yet, if I was ever to return to Westminster, I had to be free to accept invitations from elsewhere.

Though I often revisited the lobbies and Committee rooms at Westminster for meetings or interviews, I only climbed the staircase to the Strangers Gallery on rare occasions. The most memorable was the scene in the summer of 1911 when a letter from the Prime Minister to the Leader of the Opposition announced that he had secured the King's permission in case of need to create sufficient Peers to carry the Veto Bill. Though the election of 1910 had been fought and won on this issue, the announcement provoked a storm and Balfour denounced it as a felon blow. When Asquith rose to reply he was greeted with an organized uproar, and after standing at the box for a few minutes he resumed his seat. The speech that he was unable to make was delivered by Grey, perhaps the only Minister to whom the Opposition would listen. For the first and last time I saw the Foreign Secretary flushed and angry. His old friendship for the Prime Minister intensified his resentment at the rowdyism in which the front Opposition bench took no part. The uproar was led by F.E. and Lord Hugh Cecil, and when Grey sat down the former had the effrontery to rise. This was too much for the Liberals who treated him as he had treated Asquith. At this point the Speaker declared the sitting at an end.

The creation of peers was narrowly averted by a group of Unionists in the Upper House who preferred that the passage of the Veto Bill, which they knew was inevitable, should not involve the loss of their majority. The debate and the division are vividly described in the *Recollections* of Lord Morley, who read out the royal authorization for the creation of peers in case of necessity. The complaint has often been made that the Government should have accompanied the limitation of the powers of the Upper House by a reform of its composition. But in what way? The

Conservatives themselves had never been able to agree on a scheme. The graver charge that the Veto Act was a constitutional outrage left our withers unwrung. It was the belated rejoinder to the wrecking tactics pursued since 1906 and culminating in the rejection of a Finance Bill for the first time. No party could have been expected indefinitely to take such treatment lying down. Moreover our 'revolutionary' proceeding left our controversial measures under the handicap of having to pass three times through the Lower House in consecutive sessions while Conservative bills, however controversial, continued to reach harbour after a single voyage. The revolt against the authority of the Leader of the Opposition, who desired to avert the creation of peers, led to the resignation of his post, and with the promotion of Bonar Law the 'die-hard' section of the party gained the upper hand. The story of the prolonged crisis has recently been told once again in the official biographies of George V, Crewe and Bonar Law.

In the autumn of 1913 the appointment of the Attorney-General, Sir Rufus Isaacs, to the position of Lord Chief Justice created a vacancy at Reading, and I accepted an invitation to stand. The prospect was not enticing, for 'Rufus', a celebrity and a resident, had only held his seat in 1910 by the narrow margin of ninety-nine. Moreover I was a stranger to the constituency, whereas the Conservative candidate, Leslie Wilson, afterwards Governor of Bombay, had been 'sitting on the doorstep' for three years. It was inevitable that after eight years the pendulum should be swinging away from the Government, and the Insurance Act was too recent for its benefits to be fully appreciated. Though the new Lord Chief Justice could give me nothing but moral support, he and his wife were kindness itself. He was too popular in Reading for his opponents to make use of the recent Marconi scandal, even had they desired to do so. Though he had been guilty of an error of judgment, as he publicly confessed, the Prime Minister's decision not to withhold the Chief Justiceship on that account was generally approved. I was present when he took the chair at a lunch in the National Liberal Club after the Marconi Committee had issued its report. In moving tones he declared that his chief regret was to have involved Lloyd George, the other guest of the occasion, in his own misfortunes, and thereby perhaps to have jeopardized the career of a friend. These manly sentences impressed me much more than the self-righteous apologia of the Chancellor of the Exchequer which followed. The unexpected emergence of a Labour candidate at Reading destroyed any chances of my success. The strenuous contest lasted nearly a month and ended, as was expected, with a Conservative gain. It was my fourth and last campaign.

The Balkan wars of 1912–13 were of peculiar interest to a member of the Balkan Committee, and I gave a course of lectures at the London School of Economics on the rulers of the Balkan states. Our flirtations with the Young Turks had only lasted about a year, for we soon learned that *plus ça change, plus c'est la même chose*. The outbreak of the Tripoli war in 1911 prompted the formation of a Balkan League, and Bourchier, *The Times* Correspondent, helped to engineer a *rapprochement* between Bulgaria and Greece. In the autumn of 1912 the four little Christian states flew at the throat of their common foe and brought him down. The scholarly Greek Minister, Gennadius, was a general favourite in London, and the benevolent countenance of the venerable Madjaroff bespoke sympathy for the Bulgarian cause. Gruich, the Serbian Minister, carried less weight, for Serbia was the least popular of the Christian belligerents. When the peace negotiations brought the Balkan statesmen to London Sir Edward Boyle gave a dinner and reception in their honour. I was chiefly struck by the sparkle of Venizelos who seemed destined to realize the dream of Greater Greece. Daneff, the Bulgarian Premier, was an energetic though rather unprepossessing little man, but we all knew that the policy of his country was determined by 'foxy Ferdinand'. If the Young Turks had disappointed us in 1909, the Balkan Allies horrified their British friends still more by turning their swords against one another in the summer of 1913. Bulgaria's attack on the Greek and Serb forces in Macedonia put her formally in the wrong and brought instant punishment on her head. In vain did she argue that her late comrades were conspiring to rob her of the fruits of victory, and that her only chance of preserving them was to strike the first blow. My satisfaction at the eviction of the Turks from Albania, Macedonia and Western Thrace remained, but never again could I feel much enthusiasm for the Balkan Christians. When the Report of the Carnegie Commission on the *Causes and*

Conduct of the Balkan Wars was published in 1914 I felt still less, for there was little to choose in savagery between Christians and Turks.

The anxieties arising from the Near East were in some measure offset by a slight *détente* in the West. The Agadir crisis had ranged England and Germany against each other more sharply than ever before. I regretted the Mansion House speech, which flung a contingent declaration of war across the North Sea and stung Germany to fury; but I blamed Lloyd George, an amateur in diplomacy, less than the Foreign Secretary to whom he showed the speech in advance and who allowed him to launch a high explosive. With the signature of the Morocco and Congo treaties at the end of 1911 and the Haldane Mission at the beginning of 1912 warmer airs began to blow, for Bethmann inspired more confidence than Bülow and he was no less anxious for a *détente* than Grey. The collaboration of Downing Street and the Wilhelmstrasse in localizing the Balkan wars established a measure of good feeling unknown for years. The President of an Anglo-German Friendship Society which was now brought into being was the veteran banker, scientist and statesman, Lord Avebury, but the moving spirit was the Chairman, Sir Frank Lascelles, who had left the Berlin Embassy at the end of 1908 after twelve eventful years. No one knew better the inflammability of the German people and the clumsiness of the Wilhelmstrasse; but he understood the Kaiser as neither his predecessor Malet nor his successor Goschen ever understood him, and he was convinced that he had not the slightest desire for war. The two men liked each other, and the genial Ambassador told me many anecdotes of the temperamental ruler.

A second organization working along parallel lines was the World Alliance of the Churches. The story of Allen Baker, a Canadian Quaker who built up a successful business in England, became one of the Progressive leaders in the formative years of the London County Council, entered Parliament in 1905 and held his seat till his death, has been told in the Memoir by his widow and his brilliant son. The last decade of his life was devoted to a peace crusade, which included intimate conversations with the Kaiser, and of which the World Alliance is the abiding monument. In Söderblom, Archbishop of Upsala, he secured an ideal

President, and in Lord Dickinson he found not only an invaluable co-secretary but a worthy successor in the work. There were branches in many lands, but we were most interested in the German section, since Anglo-German tension was the problem of the hour. Its Chairman was the venerable Dr. Spiecker, the secretary Pastor Siegmund-Schulze, head of a Settlement in the east end of Berlin. Harnack came to London and gave us a spirited address in German at Queen's Hall. A meeting of the Alliance was in progress at Constance when the storm broke in 1914, and the members pledged themselves to renew their crusade after the hurricane had blown itself out.

At the height of the Veto crisis in the summer of 1911 Sir Percy Bunting, editor of the *Contemporary Review*, passed away after guiding its fortunes for thirty-five years. For some years I had been a Director of the company and for a longer period a friend of the family. Bunting and his wife had taken an active part in Josephine Butler's campaign against the state recognition of vice, and they remained in contact with Stead, Mrs. Fawcett and other fellow-workers in that cause to the end. They were also active in the crusade against the White Slave traffic and had many Continental contacts. The editor was a middle of the road Liberal with the usual Wesleyan dislike of extremes. As no provision had been made for a successor Dr. Scott Lidgett, a nephew of Lady Bunting, and I assumed control and we worked in unbroken harmony for thirty years.

Scott Lidgett was a man of many parts, and during his later years he was the chief spokesman and statesman of English Nonconformity. He was less of an orator than Dr. Clifford and less of a preacher than Hugh Price Hughes. There was no trace in him of what Matthew Arnold disdainfully described as the dissidence of dissent, and he longed for the reunion of the Churches. He knew several of the bishops and was *persona grata* at Lambeth and Bishopsthorpe. He was a Liberal rather by tradition than by temperament, and indeed in his youth it was difficult for a Nonconformist to be anything else. No one was less of a radical, and he preferred a Conservative to a Labour Government. Against the Labour Party he had something of a personal grievance, for as Leader of the Progressives on the London County Council he had seen his legions melt away till not a man was left. He was a

learned theologian, expounding his views in books and innumerable articles. That he was right centre and I left centre was
no disadvantage, for it kept the *Review* on a level keel. I was
mainly responsible for the political side, while philosophy,
theology and problems of London government fell within his
sphere. A regular feature of the *Contemporary* was Dr. Dillon's
monthly survey of foreign affairs. He had begun as a student of
theology at Munich, and his first book was on *The Sceptics of the
Old Testament*. Migrating to Russia in the seventies, he became a
teacher in the University of Kieff and began his long connection
with the *Daily Telegraph*. His range of languages, living and dead,
was astonishing, and for half a century he discussed the changing
scene with leading statesmen in the capitals of Europe in their
own tongue. I met him for the first time at the opening of the
century in Berlin where he was stationed as Correspondent of the
Daily Telegraph; but he never took root in Germany, and he
welcomed his transfer to St. Petersburg in time for the manifold
excitements which followed the war with Japan.

Dillon's first book, *Russian Characteristics*, had made a deep
impression on me at Cambridge by its unrelieved gloom. If the
picture was approximately accurate, the Russia of Alexander III
deserved the terrible verdict that it was rotten before it was ripe.
Witte's labours at the Ministry of Finance during the nineties
made a rift in the clouds, but the conflict with Japan revealed that
the colossus had feet of clay. Dillon maintained that Witte was the
only statesman the unhappy country had produced since Peter
the Great and rejoiced at his return to office in the autumn of
1905. His dispatches to the *Daily Telegraph* and his articles in the
Contemporary during the ensuing constitutional conflicts were
studied with unusual attention, for he was not only the friend but
the mouthpiece and sometimes the agent of the Premier. He had
accompanied him to America for the peace negotiations at
Portsmouth and returned under his spell. When the Japanese
adventure was liquidated and the Björkö treaty with Germany
was repudiated by Lamsdorff as incompatible with the French
alliance, Witte was ready for an understanding with England.
He dispatched Dillon to London at the opening of 1906, and his
conversations with Grey revealed an equal desire for a *rapprochement* in the new Liberal Ministry. On the fall of Witte Dillon lost

faith in reform. Though he never championed autocracy he ceased to attack it, and he surveyed the strangling of Persia through Russian rather than English spectacles. He was gorged with esoteric information, to use a phrase of Lord Acton, and the vivacious little Irishman was an admirable talker. He was also a bundle of nerves, seemed always in a hurry, and was ever on the wing. I learned much from three leading British journalistic experts in the field of foreign affairs, Dillon, Valentine Chirol and Wickham Steed, who had seen a good deal of history in the making.

The *Contemporary* could also boast of the services of Sir Edwin Pears, whose *Forty Years in Constantinople* is a precious contribution to history. Though he had revealed in the *Daily News* the atrocities committed by the Turk against his unhappy Bulgarian subjects, he settled in the Turkish capital, working as a lawyer and witnessing the whole blood-stained drama of the reign of Abdul Hamid whose life he was to write. He was also a historian, and his volumes on the Fourth Crusade and the conquest of Constantinople by the Turks are of solid worth. His conviction that the Turk was unfit to govern the Christian was the result of decades of observation, not of religious prejudice. His visits to England were always welcome, for he had more to say than he could safely put into print. Inheriting Dillon and Pears from my predecessor, I endeavoured to make the *Contemporary* the leading monthly in the field of foreign affairs. In the last three years of peace we supplied our readers with material on the Balkan wars by such experts as Noel Buxton and Sir Arthur Evans, on Persia by Lynch and Professor Browne. Perhaps the most notable of our articles was a discussion of Anglo-German relations by Sir Frank Lascelles, in which the ex-ambassador expressed his regret that the opportunity of co-operating in the Baghdad railway had been lost. Another dissertation on the same theme which aroused lively interest at home and abroad was contributed by Noel Buxton, who visited Germany immediately after the Agadir crisis. There still seemed a fair chance of averting a trial of strength.

In home affairs I occasionally turned to Sir Edward Cook, the biographer of Ruskin, Florence Nightingale and Delane, editor of the *Daily News* before it was bought by George Cadbury. A rapid worker and a writer of faultless lucidity, he could be relied on to furnish a well argued article at the shortest notice. The old cleavage between Liberal Imperialists and 'Little Englanders' had become scarcely more than a memory when I entered the office of the *Contemporary* in 1911; but the personal ties formed or strengthened during the South African war persisted, and Cook spoke for the right wing of the Cabinet as definitely as Harold Spender and Gardiner for the left. The Spender brothers were alike in their devotion to Liberalism; but while Alfred extolled the wisdom of Asquith and Grey in the *Westminster Gazette*, Harold chanted hymns of praise to Lloyd George in the *Daily News*. If the elder brother was the bigger man and possessed a calmer judgment, the younger had more fire and commanded a more vigorous style. Both have told their tale in delightful autobiographies. The third brother, Hugh, Parliamentary Correspondent of the *Westminster Gazette*, was also a competent journalist, and the *Contemporary* welcomed contributions from them all. A. G. Gardiner used sometimes to write for us on the political situation after his eviction from the *Daily News*.

The loss of my seat in 1910 restored me to my books. The first task was to write a *History of Our Time* for the Home University Library, the historical section of which was edited by Herbert Fisher. The little volumes of two hundred and fifty pages were cheap at a shilling, and some of them, including my own, sold by thousands. The survey opened in 1885, and a revised edition, published on the eve of the war, brought the story to the end of 1913. The writing of *History and Historians in the Nineteenth Century* was my main occupation during 1911 and 1912. If authors, like parents, are permitted to have favourites, that stout volume is mine. I could put more of myself into it, for my conception of history as nothing less than the record and interpretation of the life of mankind opened up a limitless field.

> The object of this work [I explained in the Preface] is to summarize and assess the manifold achievements of historical research and production during the last hundred years, to portray the masters of the craft, to trace the development of scientific method, to measure the political, religious and racial influences that have contributed to the making of celebrated books, and to analyse their effect on the life and thought of their time.

No such survey had been attempted in any language. It was a daring enterprise, and it could only be partially achieved in six hundred closely printed pages. Among my kindly reviewers was Lord Cromer, whose notice in the *Spectator* was reprinted in his *Political and Literary Essays*. The first edition was exhausted in three months, and the book continued to enjoy a steady sale and has been translated into Japanese and Italian.

A few weeks after its appearance the third International Historical Congress met in London in April 1913. The first had been held in Rome in 1903, the second in Berlin in 1908. My old chief James Bryce, who was to have presided, was far away in the British Embassy at Washington, and his place was filled by Sir Adolphus Ward. Next to our own country Germany appeared in strongest force. The most decorative figure in the German team was Wilamowitz, the German Gilbert Murray, the *doyen* of Hellenists, whose white hair, pink complexion and brilliant eyes were comely to look upon. Of equal celebrity was the gigantic Eduard Meyer, author of a monumental *History of Antiquity*. The medievalists included Gierke, the German Maitland. Among leading representatives of modern history were Schiemann, the Kaiser's friend, and Oncken, the biographer of Bennigsen and Lassalle. Lamprecht was a lonely figure, for he was despised by the pundits. I had described his voluminous *German History* and the controversy it aroused in my latest book, and he bore me no grudge for my criticisms. He was a pugnacious but likeable man, and his boyish spirits made him excellent company. An equally live wire was Pirenne, the leading historian of Belgium, who bubbled over with vivacity and wit. Rostovtsev came from Russia, Marczali from Hungary, Redlich from Austria, Blok from Holland. The United States made a fair show with the medievalist Haskins of Harvard and the veteran Charles Francis Adams as the representative of the most distinguished family in transatlantic history. France was sadly under-represented. As a member of the Reception Committee, of which Sir George Prothero was Chairman, I saw much of the delegates, and I read a paper on the Chair of Modern History at Cambridge. We were entertained at a government dinner and were shown the treasures of the Royal Library at Windsor. It was a harmonious gathering, and our visitors seemed delighted with their stay.

Ceremonial speeches are quickly forgotten, but a pregnant sentence in a private conversation was destined to travel round the world. As the guests were leaving a dinner-party given by Mr. and Mrs. Humphry Ward, Lord Haldane remarked to Oncken: 'Germany is my spiritual home.' The Professor told me of the incident on the following morning, for these words, pronounced with great deliberation, made a deep impression on him. The interpreter of Hegel, translator of Schopenhauer and lover of Goethe had every reason to speak as he did, but the phrase was to be thrown in his teeth during the stormy years that lay ahead. On the last day of the Congress the invitation to hold the next meeting in 1918 at St. Petersburg was accepted after an assurance had been asked and given that Jewish participants would be properly treated. We parted blissfully unconscious of the tornado about to break loose and of the fate of some of our guests. Who could foresee that Lappo-Danilevski, the gentle Secretary of the St. Petersburg Academy of Sciences, would starve to death, that Pirenne would spend two years in a German prison, that Lamprecht would die of a fever caught on a visit to the front, that Rostovtsev would seek refuge in America? And who could guess that Eduard Meyer would write a spiteful book on England, or that his brother Kuno Meyer, the prince of Celtic scholars and for many years a Professor at Liverpool, would denounce a country where he had many friends?

A second contribution to the Home University Library, entitled *English Political Thought from Bacon to Halifax* was the first of a series designed to sketch the evolution of our political ideas from the close of the Middle Ages. It was a pleasure to renew contact with the seventeenth century, and to supplement my youthful analysis of the champions of democracy by studies of the authoritarians, James I, Bacon and Hobbes at the beginning of my tale and of Halifax the incomparable 'Trimmer' at the end. I concluded with chapters on the relation of the state to religion and trade, tracing the evolution of the ideas of toleration and commercial controls. My last book before the war was a life of Charles, third Earl of Stanhope, which had been commenced by one of his descendants and which I was invited by the family to complete. Miss Stanhope had died after sketching the early chapters, and the book appeared in the spring of 1914 in our joint names. 'Citizen Stanhope', as he was called, narrowly missed greatness in politics and science. The grandson of the Prime Minister of George I, nephew of Chatham and brother-in-law of Pitt, seemed born for politics and promotion. He quickly distinguished himself, but his zeal for the French Revolution severed him from most of the Whigs, and his lonely closing years were mainly devoted to applied science. The champion of liberty was an autocrat in his stately home at Chevening, and his eccentric daughter, Lady Hester Stanhope, took refuge with her uncle, the younger Pitt, in Downing Street. I was welcomed by the seventh Earl among whose treasures were Chesterfield's letters to his illegitimate son and a portrait by Gainsborough of the third Earl.

The last year of peace was a time of acute tension in domestic politics, culminating in the so-called mutiny at Curragh. The Opposition was tied to the chariot wheels of Carson and 'Galloper Smith', who organized the Ulster Volunteers to resist the impending introduction of Home Rule. The eminent lawyer proclaimed that to achieve his purpose he was ready to break every law, and Bonar Law echoed his strident tones. The suffragettes had long displayed their contempt for legality: now for the first time an ex-Law Officer of the Crown incited his followers to resist an Act of Parliament. For once Alfred Spender criticized the Prime Minister for allowing the Volunteers to develop their plans without hindrance. Asquith subsequently defended himself in his autobiography, and I believe he was right. The arrest of Carson might have involved bloodshed and would certainly have stiffened the resistance of Ulster. No Liberal Government really believes in coercion as a method of dealing with strong political convictions, and if it tries its hand, as it had done in the early eighties, it soon gives up the game. The exclusion of the Protestant counties of Ulster, reluctantly conceded by the Nationalists, was right and inevitable, and a compromise on the frontier was nearly attained at the Buckingham Palace Conference on the eve of war. The story of this acute and prolonged crisis may be studied in the official biographies of Asquith, Carson and Bonar Law.

The most brilliant picture of the English scene in the last year of peace is painted in the letters of Walter Page who represented the United States at the Court of St. James's from the summer of 1913 to the end of the war. I had met his predecessors, the witty lawyer Choate and the decorative Whitelaw Reid, the latter the nearest American equivalent of a *grand seigneur*. Page lacked the conversational brilliance of the one and the Venetian magnificence of the other, but he won his way to the heart of the British people. Shrewd, observant, cultivated, he was—with the possible exception of Spring Rice—the best diplomatic letter-writer of our time. In certain die-hard circles frequented by ambassadors he was assured that England was tottering to her fall under the rule of unscrupulous demagogues. 'Somehow it reminds me of the tense days of the slavery controversy just before the Civil War', he reported to a friend. After looking round for himself he discovered that his informants were the victims of a grotesque illusion. England was not decadent and the ministers were not dangerous revolutionaries. 'You may search the world and you may search history for finer men than Lord Morley, Sir Edward Grey, Mr. Harcourt, and other members of the present Cabinet.' He continued to describe the panic of a section of the governing classes and the social boycott of Liberal statesmen with amused contempt. His admiration for Grey—'the best-balanced of them all'—ripened into a friendship that was to make history.

A European conflict appeared less likely in 1914 than in 1911, 1912 or 1913. The Moroccan question was settled and the Balkan wars were over; agreement had been reached on the Baghdad railway, and the secret Anglo-German treaty of 1898 relating to the Portuguese Colonies had been amicably revised. The grave and respected bachelor, Count Metternich, who cared nothing for Society, had been recalled in 1912 after the failure of the Haldane Mission, and the spacious mansion in Carlton House Terrace had sprung to life again with Prince Lichnowsky and his vivacious wife. No one who knew Count Metternich could doubt his sincere desire for friendly relations between his country and ours, and his dispatches, as we are now aware, were notable for their insight and foresight. Yet he never became—and indeed never attempted to become—a popular figure. Lichnowsky, on the other hand, entered on his mission with apostolic zeal. Without being a great Ambassador like Paul Cambon, he was a first-rate peace-maker. His optimism was infectious, and he was soon one of the most welcome figures of the Corps Diplomatique. He was quite unpretentious, and his admiration for England was a

12

pleasure to behold. The notion that he was a mere figure-head and that Kühlmann was plotting our ruin with the Wilhelmstrasse behind his back is a fantastic absurdity. Kühlmann was an abler diplomatist and less expansive than his chief, but their policy was the same, for they both loyally carried out the instructions of the Anglophil Bethmann. When the Archduke Franz Ferdinand was murdered the relations of the two governments were better than they had been for years.

The man in the street was unprepared for the World War because he thought of the European situation in terms of the relations of the Western Powers. He knew that the tension between England and Germany had diminished, and that the old Franco-German feud had often been more acute. On the other hand he knew little of the secular rivalry between Austria and Russia in the Near East, where well-informed observers had long regarded a conflict as probable if not actually inevitable. Russia, they argued, had turned her eyes from the Far East to the Near East after her defeat by Japan and was as determined to modify the *status quo* as Austria was to preserve it; and behind Austria stood Germany.

'I am a man of peace and I would not hurt a fly', exclaimed my old Austrian friend Professor Redlich during the Historical Congress in 1913, adding that he would fight to the death if the vital interests of Austria were challenged by Russia. I derived the same impression of acute Russophobia from intimate talks with Friedjung, the celebrated Austrian historian and publicist, during his only visit to England. When the quarrel with Serbia arising out of the annexation of Bosnia seemed likely to end in war, he was supplied with material for a campaign in the *Neue Freie Presse* portions of which turned out to have been forged. The story has been told from one side in Seton-Watson's massive treatise *The Southern Slav Question*, from the other in the second volume of Friedjung's history of the Era of Imperialism. His reputation never recovered from the exposure of his credulity, and he told me that he had broken with Aehrenthal; but his sentiments towards Russia and her Serbian *protégé* were not mellowed by this unfortunate incident.

While the Historical Congress was in session in 1913 the delimitation of the Albanian frontier was occupying the Conference of Ambassadors which sat in London throughout the

Balkan wars under the disinterested guidance of Grey. Austria
claimed two little market towns in a disputed area for her *protégé*,
the new Albanian state, while Russia stood out for their assignment to Serbia. The prestige of two Great Powers was at stake
and for some days the peace of Europe hung by a thread. I recall
Lord Morley's anxious face one day as he told me, fresh from a
meeting of the Cabinet, how alarming was the situation. It was a
tragedy that the Balkan wars, which brought London and Berlin
so much nearer to one another, kindled the antagonism between
Vienna and St. Petersburg into a devouring flame. Europe was so
full of gunpowder that as fast as the fire brigade strove to
extinguish the conflagration at one end of the continent it threatened to burst out at the other.

A final memory of the last months of peace is equally distinct.
In the Easter holidays of 1914 Schiemann revisited London to
work at the Record Office on his monumental history of Nicholas I.
He was not only Germany's leading expert on Russia in the
academic world but the author of an impressive weekly commentary in the conservative *Kreuz-Zeitung* on the international
situation. When we had met at the Historical Congress in the
previous year I found him friendly to England, though he knew
little of our methods and ideas. Russia, his *bête noire*, was rapidly
recovering her strength, and he believed she would one day
attack Germany; France he regarded as the stooge of her semi-
civilized and insatiable ally. The peace of Europe, he argued, was
threatened from Paris and St. Petersburg, where territorial
ambitions were cherished only realizable by war, not from Berlin
or Vienna, where the governments desired to keep the map of
Europe as it was. In 1914 he reiterated these convictions at a small
dinner-party given by Mr. and Mrs. Charles Trevelyan. The
Professor, with his dark and rather melancholy countenance,
spoke gravely of the virtual certainty of war in the near future.
We asked who or what was to cause the catastrophe. 'Any
incident, any trifle', he replied. Far from desiring a conflict, he
envisaged the struggle as a dread ordeal in which Germany would
have to fight for her life. I recalled those ominous words—
quelque bagatelle—when a shot rang out at Serajevo a few weeks
later and set the world aflame.

13

ARMAGEDDON

THE murder of the Archduke on 28 June 1914 found me in the grip of a nervous breakdown from overwork. While many Liberals were still searching their hearts, the invasion of Belgium brought a virtually united nation into the field. The unprovoked attack on a little State by the strongest Power in the world, which like ourselves had signed the neutrality treaty of 1839, presented a clear-cut juridical and moral issue. Yet the ravishing of Belgium was the occasion rather than the cause of our belligerence. At the opening of the century we had abandoned our tradition of 'splendid isolation' and had become entangled in the quarrels and ambitions of our friends, and it was too late to draw back. Had we remained neutral the Central Powers would have scored an easy victory and at the end we should have found ourselves alone in Europe. France and Russia would have scorned us as false friends, who, after years of diplomatic co-operation and defence agreements, deserted them in the hour of fate. Moreover the German menace, swollen to monstrous proportions by the collapse of the Triple Entente, would have compelled us to arm to the teeth on sea and land. Confronted with a choice of evils I concluded that it was impossible to stand aloof. In 1914, as in all our Continental wars, the deciding factor was the Balance of Power. Haldane, the most Germanophil member of the Cabinet, admitted that we should have been compelled by this consideration to enter the struggle even if Belgium had not been attacked.

While Morley and Burns maintained a dignified silence after their resignation, Charles Trevelyan, the third of the Ministers to lay down his office, joined with a few other neutralists to found the Union of Democratic Control. At his side stood Norman Angell who had recently sprung into fame with *The Great Illusion*. He owed his vocation to his youthful experience in America when the Venezuela crisis inflamed our Transatlantic cousins and hotheads clamoured for war. No publicist of our time had worked so intelligently and so intensively to persuade mankind that war between civilized countries is an anachronism, profiting the victor scarcely more than the vanquished, and none of my contemporaries possessed such capacity to make people think. As persuasive on the platform as with his pen, he always assumed his hearers and readers to be rational beings, not mere bundles of emotion, and no one ever caught him playing to the gallery. He has told his story in a modest autobiography.

No human being could differ more widely in temperament and method from Norman Angell than E. D. Morel, another pillar of the U.D.C. When the Congo campaign was won he turned his dynamic energies to the European situation and published *Morocco in Diplomacy*. Germany, he argued, had a good legal case which was ignored by France in her resolve to bring that country under her control. Grey was exhibited as tied to the chariot wheels of his French associates, *The Times* was branded as a public danger, and Lloyd George's Mansion House speech was denounced as an indefensible provocation. Morel had no use for *nuances*, but he was justified in demolishing the picture of France in the Agadir crisis as an injured innocent. He implored his countrymen to realize the implications of their entanglements in Continental quarrels before we were dragged into war with Germany. When the catastrophe occurred he flung himself into the work of the U.D.C. and spent the last decade of his life in crusading against secret diplomacy. In his study of war origins he was handicapped by his ignorance of German and by his lack of the critical temper, but he proclaimed earlier than most people that Germany was not the sole culprit.

The other outstanding figures of the U.D.C. were Arthur Ponsonby and Ramsay MacDonald. The former knew more of diplomacy than any of his colleagues, for his early years had been spent in the service. The policy of Continentalism had filled him with alarm, as it had scared Salisbury and Rosebery, and the vagueness of our commitments increased his apprehensions. Soon after the breaking of the storm he published a little handbook on the causes and consequences of nineteenth-century wars which passed through many editions. Ramsay MacDonald had an equally firm grasp of the unity of civilization, and he was in touch with socialist leaders all over the world. When the thunderbolt fell he argued that Grey could and should have kept us out of the tornado, and he paid for his minority views by forfeiting the party leadership. For the next four years the founders of the U.D.C. busied themselves with the dangers of secret diplomacy, the cooling of popular passion, and preparations for a durable peace. The story of their labours has been told by Mrs. Swanwick, herself an active member of the group. Though, unlike myself, they believed that we could have kept out of the war, they were joined as the struggle advanced by others who were even more interested in the future than in the past. I contributed to their series of pamphlets an analysis of the Hapsburg Empire, and in the later stages I occasionally addressed meetings on the conditions of a lasting settlement.

Unlike many of my fellow historians I abstained from pronouncements on the origins of the war till I had time to look round. My first effort was a sketch of our recent diplomacy which formed the larger half of a little book entitled *A Century of British Foreign Policy*, written in the spring of 1917 by Bishop Masterman and myself at the invitation of the Council for the Study of International Relations. Beginning with the abandonment of the tradition of 'splendid isolation', it described the alliance with Japan, the *entente* with France, the reconciliation with Russia, the successive crises of the last decade of peace, and the attempts of Great Britain and Germany to reach a naval and neutrality agreement. In interpreting the actions of the Central Powers I utilized their own presentations, such as Bülow's *Imperial Germany*, Reventlow's massive record of German foreign policy, the many volumes of Schiemann's articles reprinted from the *Kreuz-Zeitung*, and Sosnosky's spirited defence of Austria's attitude in the Balkans. For France I consulted the writings of Hanotaux, former Foreign Minister, Tardieu, Foreign Editor of the *Temps*, and André Mévil, the mouthpiece of Delcassé; for Russia the survey by Prince Trubetzkoi, an old official of the Foreign Office; for Japan the Memoirs of Hayashi, her Ambassador in London.

To understand the policy of a state the first task is to learn how it looks to its makers and their friends.

My survey closed with a few sentences expressing my conviction of the pacific character of our recent policy and my doubts as to the wisdom of certain of its features.

Alone of European statesmen the Foreign Secretary worked day and night for the preservation of peace, but he was handicapped by the undefined character of our friendship with France. It is not necessarily a condemnation of the policy of limited liability, though it suggests grave doubts as to its wisdom, that everyone was at liberty to construe it for himself, that the Cabinet was divided at a critical moment, that France counted on our naval and military aid as a debt of honour, that Russia believed that we should be dragged in, and that Germany expected us to stand out. Nor has the time come for a judicial verdict on the whole policy of Continental commitments, unaccompanied as they were by an army of Continental dimensions or by a frank explanation to Parliament and the nation of their contingent liabilities. Looking back over the crowded and anxious years, it is clear that on the one hand it increased the probability of a war with Germany by involving us in the quarrels of our friends, and that on the other it ensured that if a conflict arose we should not be left to fight alone. The risk and the premium will have to be balanced against each other by the historical actuary of the future. But whatever the judgment of posterity on its intrinsic merits or its technical skill, its foresight or its success, we may with some confidence anticipate a verdict that British policy throughout the period covered by this chapter was free from the slightest desire for territorial aggrandisement, and that the dearest wish of the British people was to maintain peace and promote goodwill among the nations of the earth.

When I explored our archives a few years later I saw no reason to alter a word of this provisional pronouncement.

My connections with Germany had in no way diminished my dislike of her system of government, for a quasi-autocracy with a second-rate actor in the title role was not at all to my taste. The army, the Junkers and the great industrialists had too much power, the *bourgeoisie* and the manual workers too little. A highly educated people was still in political leading-strings, and so long as the monstrosity of the three-class system of voting remained in Prussia there seemed no way of escape. A German victory would clearly strengthen the features of national life which I most disliked. In an address to the Sociological Society in the spring of 1915, I traced the evolution of German theories of the state from the cosmopolitanism of Lessing and Goethe to the strident nationalism of Treitschke and the Hohenzollern Empire.

> The middle decades of the century witnessed an attempt to combine liberty with authority; but the dazzling victories of Prussia ushered in a period of soulless realism in which the claims of the individual were overlooked and the partnership of nations was repudiated. The idolatry of the state reached its logical issue in the elevation of force to the sovereign principle in national life and international relations. The pendulum can swing no further in the direction that it has followed for half a century.

I concluded with the hope that defeat would set it swinging back towards the more generous inspirations of Germany's greatest teachers.

Convinced though I was that a victory for Germany would be a disaster, I never envisaged the struggle as a simple conflict between darkness and light. My knowledge of Tsarist Imperialism and Tsarist misrule did not suddenly fade away when we found ourselves allies, and the notion that the whole Triple Entente was fighting for liberty was grotesque. The omission of the Russian factor and the blind absorption in the struggle in the West must strike every reader of the fascinating correspondence of Walter Page. In his letter of resignation Lord Morley expressed his fear of a victorious Russia dominating half Europe, and in this respect I shared his apprehensions. However heartily I disliked the Young Turks I had no desire to see the Russian bear in Constantinople, for the Tsarist Empire was already much too large. No one more ardently desired the defeat of Germany in the West than myself, but in the East I hoped that none of the three Empires would emerge completely victorious. Nicholas II had shown himself hopelessly unfit to govern his subjects, and I failed to understand how it would benefit civilization or the cause of liberty to add to their number. For this reason I declined the invitation to join in the 'Fight for Right' propaganda initiated by Sir Francis Younghusband, Sir Frederick Pollock and other old friends. I owe to that group, however, the opportunity of hearing an inspiring address from Maurice Barrès on the Spirit of France, from Joan of Arc down to the *poilu* in the trenches. The famous novelist and successor of Déroulède in the leadership of militant French nationalism spoke as well as he wrote. It was a stream of eloquence perfect in form and glowing with patriotic pride. It was interesting to compare him with Anatole France, whom I had heard at a dinner given to him on his visit to London shortly before the war. Barrès seemed born for action, the author of *Penguin Island*, with his kindly eyes and slightly mocking smile, to analyse the follies of mankind.

Enthusiasm for Russia kindled like a straw fire and Russian grammars were in brisk demand. Stephen Graham's delightful books had persuaded some of his readers that Russia was Mary and that Martha was the materialistic West. We were shown a gifted, lovable, unsophisticated people, caring little for the technical triumphs of modern civilization. The experience of the next few years challenged his reading of the national character and in any case it was never true of the government. When the proclamation of the Grand Duke Nicholas at the opening of the war promised unification of the Poles of the three Empires under the Russian eagle, it was ignorantly supposed in some quarters that the announcement would rally them whole-heartedly to the cause of the Allies. Roman Dmowski, the political leader of the pro-Russian Poles, was accepted in Downing Street as their spokesman, and I listened to a lecture in which he spent the whole of his time in denouncing Germany: not a word fell from his lips as to the far worse record of Russia or of the longing of the Poles for national independence. If I had been in any doubt I should have been speedily enlightened by friends among the Polish students in London, who knew both the realities of Russian misrule and the limited value of Russian promises. Among these patriots was August Zaleski, a thoughtful young man who guessed as little as ourselves that within a few years he would be Foreign Minister of a united Republic. No race had less reason to pray, work or fight for a Russian triumph than the Poles, and the greatest of them, Pilsudski, though a Russian subject, took arms against the Tsar.

I was equally disinclined to give my name as requested to *The*

New Europe, a weekly journal founded and edited by Professor Seton-Watson, every number of which bore the legend *Pour la victoire intégrale*. The author of classical works on Hungary and Jugoslavia knew more of the Hapsburg Empire, past and present, than anyone in England except Wickham Steed. It was his conspicuous merit to differentiate between Austria, where a considerable measure of provincial autonomy prevailed, and centralized Hungary, and to emphasize the grave responsibility of the unbending Magyars for tension in South Eastern Europe. His journal, which I diligently studied from the first number to the last, stood for the dissolution of the polyglot empire and the creation or expansion of national states. He was zealously supported by Wickham Steed, Ronald Burrows, Principal of King's College, Sir Arthur Evans, the discoverer of Cnossus, Bernard Pares and other specialists. It was a powerful team, knowing precisely what they wanted and convinced that time was on their side. If a journal can be said to have a patron, that office was filled by Thomas Masaryk, who spent most of the middle period of the war in London, leaving Beneš to direct operations in Paris. When he visited me I found him the same quiet, thoughtful, unassuming scholar whom I had learned to admire many years before. He knew too much of German culture to join in shrill denunciations of 'the Hun', and too much of the rottenness of Tsarist Russia to seek salvation from the East. *The Making of a State* is one of the few great books produced by the war. While sympathizing with the aspirations of the Czechs for independence and the desire of the Southern Slavs for political unity, I felt that the Hapsburg Empire represented, however imperfectly, a unifying force in the Danubian lands, and I could not entirely rule out the possibility of a loose federation. It was the dread of some such compromise that made Masaryk desire a prolongation of the struggle till the Austro-Hungarian Empire should collapse.

While the peoples of Europe were tearing each other to pieces, the Quakers were busy as usual with their labours of love, the story of which has been told in Ruth Fry's *A Quaker Adventure*. Leaving the problem of war origins to the historian and the settlement to the politicians, they moved along the highway like the good Samaritan ministering, so far as political conditions allowed, to all in need. They hastened to Eastern France when the battle of the Marne rolled back the invader, to Russia after the revolution of 1917, to Germany and Austria when the carnage was at an end. A few days after the outbreak of war Stephen Hobhouse, himself a Conscientious Objector, set up the Friends' Emergency Committee in London to help German and Austrian subjects dismissed from their jobs or stranded within our gates. We took a German couple into our home till the sinking of the *Lusitania* removed the husband to a detention camp, and my wife visited working-class families throughout the war in most of which the woman was British born and the children could not speak German. Dozens of our German books found their way to interned civilians in the Isle of Man and the Alexandra Palace, while English books were dispatched to British internees at Ruhleben.

A second gentle influence was the Women's International League. The name of Jane Addams, head of Hull House Settlement in Chicago, was known all over the world, and John Burns humorously dubbed her the greatest man in America. Her acceptance of the office of President gave the League a good start. I never met a celebrity of either sex with less desire to shine. Some people carry you by storm, others grow on you. Jane Addams belonged to the latter class, and it was only gradually that one realized her wisdom and her strength. I could never imagine her excited or embarrassed. Her visits to Europe were an inspiration to her fellow workers, for her serenity was infinitely refreshing to war-strained nerves. The British branch of the League had Mrs. Swanwick as its Chairman, with Lady Courtney, Maude Royden and other well-known internationalists among its active members. Its object was to counterwork the passions of the strife and to prepare for the co-operation of women on the conclusion of hostilities.

The piloting of a Liberal review through the hurricane that lasted over four years was no easy task. A censorship was established with our old contributor Sir Edward Cook in control. Editors were warned off particular subjects such as the Caliphate, in addition to the general principle that nothing must enlighten our enemies or offend our allies. The latter comprehensive admonition was strictly interpreted. A sentence in Dillon's monthly survey of foreign affairs recording that Russia had put pressure on Romania to enter the war in the summer of 1916 led to the holding up and mutilation of the issue which was ready for dispatch. Our valued contributor was so incensed that he terminated his regular surveys, though in later years he offered occasional articles again. Though a monthly journal had less trouble than a weekly or a daily, the *Contemporary* specialized in foreign affairs and for that reason we skated on very thin ice. Students of the press in wartime should bear in mind how much is watered down or entirely suppressed. As Arthur Ponsonby used to say, truth is the first war casualty.

When men up to fifty were swept into the conscription net in the spring of 1918 I was placed in Class C and heard nothing more of the matter. A 'Historical Section of the Foreign Office' was created to prepare handbooks for the peace negotiations—however distant they might be—under the direction of my old Cambridge teacher Sir George Prothero, editor of the *Quarterly Review*, who invited my aid. The booklets were designed for the British Delegation, not for immediate publication, though an exception was made in the case of Professor Webster's substantial monograph on the Congress of Vienna. Our task was to revise them as they flowed in from the appointed contributors, and to write some of them ourselves. The subject of French claims in the Levant, which went back to the Crusades, was allotted to me, and I was part author of the brochure on the Anglo-French condominium in the New Hebrides. Needless to say we were not expected to suggest lines of policy. The whole series was published after the war.

Lord Lansdowne's celebrated letter in the *Daily Telegraph* in the autumn of 1917, after the rejection in *The Times*, voiced the feeling of a growing number not only of civilians but of soldiers. Since European civilization, he argued, was bleeding to death we should define the minimum for which we were prepared to fight. The letter had been drafted a year before and circulated to the first Coalition Government on the eve of its collapse. Now Russia was out of action, France crippled by the disaster at the Chemin des Dames, and the British army decimated by the butchery of Paschendael. The incident is described in the official biography of Lansdowne by Lord Newton, who approves the attitude of his friend. Though Lansdowne had rather a bad press, Lloyd George's speech to the Trade Unions in January 1918 was a partial acceptance of his counsels. The latter's modest demand for the 'reconsideration' of the problem of Alsace-Lorraine revealed how far the Second Coalition had travelled since its chief had declared for a knock-out blow in the autumn of 1916. I welcomed the Lansdowne letter. About a score of us, editors and publicists, journeyed to Lansdowne House, where our spokesman, Lord Loreburn, the former Lord Chancellor, assured the host of our support and the veteran statesman reiterated his views. His intervention came too late, for Ludendorff was preparing his 1918 offensive and was in no mood for compromise. When the tide at last turned in August it quickly swelled into a flood. General Smuts' dream of a twenty-five per cent victory was replaced first by the possibility and then by the certainty of a dictated peace. It was widely assumed that Lansdowne's pessimism had been discredited by our overwhelming victory, and that in underestimating our prospects he had been too ready to accept half a loaf. It required the subsequent convulsions of Europe, which he had so clearly foreshadowed, to vindicate his prescience.

In November 1914 the *Contemporary Review* published an article entitled 'Proposals for a League of Peace and Mutual Protection among Nations' by my old friend Aneurin Williams, an active Liberal M.P. and one of the pioneers of Letchworth Garden City. The nucleus of the League should be formed by the Allies, who, he hoped, would be joined by the neutrals, including the United States.

> What would be the attitude of Germany and Austria it is of course impossible to foresee. But if we may hope that those great nations, especially the former, will come out of the fire purified, liberated from their military masters, and recast in a democratic form, then we may hope that before long they too would join. Possibly they might join from the first if the victors were wise enough not to try to impose any unnecessary humiliations on the vanquished.

The best chance for humanity was mutual defence against attack.

In the second half of the war we looked with increasing confidence to Woodrow Wilson, and for two years we hung upon his lips. Since Lloyd George and Clemenceau were men of action and were too busy striving for victory to trouble their heads about avoiding future catastrophes, the President alone seemed to voice

the aspirations of a tormented world. Never since Abraham
Lincoln had a ruler spoken with such healing power or clothed
his message in such uplifting words. When victory was won he
emerged from the White House and crossed the sea, but the
contrast between the Fourteen Points and the Treaty of Versailles has suggested to some observers that he would have done
better to stay at home. In my view he was right to come and
wrong to stay so long: he should have delivered his message and
then recrossed the ocean. I witnessed his welcome in London
from the balcony of the Athenaeum, and on the following day
Lord Parmoor, Lord Buckmaster and I presented a short address
to him on behalf of the Fight the Famine Council. It was the face
of a scholar and a thinker, a little lacking in warmth and charm.
When Lord Parmoor had finished he made a brief reply. 'The
League of Nations is the only hope for the world', he observed
in his quiet voice, and his emphasis on this fundamental truth
goes far to outweigh his faults of temper and tactical mistakes.
Clemenceau, always thinking meanly of mankind, believed that
the war had changed nothing except the relative positions of the
combatants. Wilson, the Liberal Professor, appealed to the reason
and conscience of mankind, all too confident that we had learned
our bitter lesson at last.

'Today begins a new era in world history', observed Goethe
over the camp fire on the evening of the battle of Valmy in 1792,
'and you will be able to say that you were present at its birth.'
The same conviction was in our minds on 11 November 1918,
and the same uncertainty what was in store for mankind. The
uppermost feeling, of course, was inexpressible relief. I had
witnessed from my library window the daylight raid on the City
by a score of gleaming planes on a bright summer morning, and
the nocturnal visitations of the Zeppelins gave us a foretaste of
things to come. Tea-parties for wounded soldiers, some of whom
had to be carried into our house, kept before our eyes the sufferings of the 'cannon fodder' required by the voracious appetite of
modern war. The second reaction was profound thankfulness that
victory had fallen to our side. Since Russia had gone out of the
fight and America had come in, there was not the slightest doubt
in our minds that the best side had won. Though the Germans
are a great and gifted people, I had no wish to see Europe at their

feet. A third general sentiment was apprehension as to the use that was likely to be made of a triumph so much more spectacular than anyone had dared to conceive. Victory is a heady drink. Germany had abused her strength, France might do the same, and our own statesmen might fail to secure a fair and durable settlement. We had not long to wait before the 'coupon election' and the Treaty of Versailles proved that there was only too much reason for such fears. Keynes' devastating onslaught in *The Economic Consequences of the Peace* was a nine days' wonder, but nations are unmoved by argument, take all they can get, and have to learn by bitter experience in the course of years.

My views of the settlement were expressed in the lofty pronouncements of Field Marshal Smuts on the eve of his return to South Africa. Like Lincoln he had fought 'with charity for all, with malice for none.'

> I have signed the Peace Treaty, not because I consider it a satisfactory document, but because it is imperatively necessary to close the war; because the world needs peace above all, and nothing could be more fatal than the continuance of the state of suspense between war and peace. I say this now not in criticism but in faith; not because I wish to find fault with the work done, but rather because I feel that in the Treaty we have not yet achieved the real peace to which our peoples were looking, and because I feel that the real work of making peace will only begin after this treaty has been signed. The promise of the new life, the victory of the great human ideals for which the peoples have shed their blood and their treasure without stint, the fulfilment of their aspirations towards a new international order and a fairer better world, are not written in this treaty and could not be written in treaties. A new heart must be given not only to our enemies but also to us. A new spirit of generosity and humanity, born in the hearts of the peoples in this great hour of common suffering and sorrow, can alone heal the wounds which have been inflicted on the body of Christendom. The real peace of the peoples ought to follow, complete and amend the peace of the statesmen.

That it was not a 'Carthaginian' peace, as Keynes described it, was proved by Lloyd George's volumes on the settlement and by the fact that Germany was soon on her legs again; yet it was too severe to last.

14

TWO ELDER STATESMEN

I

URING the war years (1914–18) and the early days of uneasy
peace I was privileged to enjoy the friendship of two Elder
Statesmen whom I already knew slightly during my four
years in Parliament, and who, when their active career was over,
consoled their declining days with the imperishable things of the
mind. They belonged to a class rarely found beyond our shores.
Macaulay described Lord Chesterfield as a man of the world
among men of letters and a man of letters among men of the world.
Like Gladstone and Rosebery, Balfour and Curzon, Bryce and
Birrell, they were equally at home in the council chamber, on the
platform and among their beloved books.

Lord Morley and Lord Haldane had little use for each other.
The feud dating from the Boer War between the Gladstonians
and the Roseberyites had left deep furrows, and a fresh difference
emerged when Morley resigned from the Cabinet of 1914. To the
end of his days he never ceased to think of Haldane as an Imperialist, which in his eyes was the gravest of sins in a professed
Liberal. There was also a lack of contact outside the sphere of
politics. Morley had specialized in French thought and French
literature, and had made his name by his studies of Voltaire,
Rousseau, Diderot, Turgot, Condorcet, Joseph de Maistre and
other thinkers before he entered politics. He knew little of the
great Germans and had no taste for metaphysics. Haldane, on the
other hand, studied under Lotze at Göttingen, translated Schopenhauer and reverenced Hegel, rereading the massive treatises of
the latter to the end of his days. Since I was no less interested in

the French than in the German mind, I was equally at ease in the spacious library at Wimbledon and in the small upper room in Queen Anne's Gate overlooking St. James's Park. These veterans were blessed with warm hearts and I felt equal affection for them both. Though they were never close friends Morley declared that if he were ever in trouble it would be to Haldane that he would turn—as fine a tribute as anyone could desire.

When the outbreak of war in 1914 closed his political career at the age of seventy-six Morley sought occupation in writing his Reminiscences. On entering Lincoln College, Oxford, in 1858 he had found the influence of Mill supreme and enrolled himself among the most ardent disciples of 'the best and wisest man I have ever known'. In 'the saint of rationalism', as Gladstone called him, he discovered what he craved. Mill had freed himself from the cramping Benthamism of his youth and was compiling the treatises on *Liberty*, *The Subjection of Women* and *Representative Government* which supplied a coherent system of liberalism based on a reasoned optimism and warmed by a generous humanity. When Morley at the age of twenty-six met the oracle, his admiration for the thinker ripened into reverence for the man. He had known all the Victorian giants, Darwin, Tennyson, Carlyle, Huxley, Spencer, George Eliot, Matthew Arnold, Leslie Stephen, but he put Mill at the top of the list. The noble portrait by Watts hung over the mantelpiece in his study and his name was often on his lips. Morley's friend and biographer Francis Hirst, who had helped him with the life of Gladstone, placed him on the same level as Mill. I could not agree. Though both were Humanists of the front rank Mill possessed the more wide-ranging and original mind and powerfully affected the course of English thought.

Our intimate contact began with the publication in 1913 of my *History and Historians in the Nineteenth Century*, which he was kind enough to describe as worthy of Acton at his best. A few months later he resigned and during his remaining years he often referred to the hectic days which preceded our ultimatum to Berlin. He provided his version in a *Memorandum on Resignation* which he lent me in typescript and which was published in a slender volume after his death. He had been particularly surprised that Lulu Harcourt, who had taken an active line against intervention in a continental war, had neither resigned nor—like Lord Beauchamp

13

and Sir John Simon—attempted to resign. Though he never
regretted the decision which closed his public career he never
embarrassed his old friends and colleagues by public criticism.
He knew that I did not share his opinion as to the duty of the
Cabinet in the hour of fate, since for me the maxim of the Balance
of Power which had guided our statesmen for four centuries
decided the issue. He was quite clear, as we Pro-Boers with few
exceptions had felt in earlier days, that once engaged in the
struggle we must go through with it to the end. For this reason
he welcomed the substitution of Lloyd George for Asquith, who
was temperamentally better suited to the tasks of peace. Though
he knew that his old chief had no more desire for war than himself, he cherished a brooding resentment against him and Grey
for having involved us ever more closely in the quarrels of the
Powers. A Gladstonian in his abhorrence of Imperialism in the
far places of the earth, he remained a Cobdenite isolationist in
regard to Europe. I, on the other hand, was nearer to Gladstone
than to Cobden. For better or worse the era of 'splendid isolation'
had ended at the turn of the century, and in 1905 the Liberals
inherited the *entente cordiale* which they were powerless to change
even had they wished.

Morley used to relate how as a young man he was taken to task
by the erudite but rather arid Mark Pattison, Rector of Lincoln
College, for talking glibly about progress. Though they never
expected a millennium, Mill and Gladstone, like other Liberals,
had taken a hopeful view of human nature and the prospects of
civilization. Their disciple shared their faith in the value of wisely
directed effort, but the passions of the Boer War, the World War
and the Versailles settlement tempered his Victorian optimism.
When younger friends, myself among them, urged him to welcome the League of Nations as the best hope for a shattered
world, he rejoined that Wilson was a phrase-maker and that wars
would be prevented—if prevented at all—not by paper constitutions but by statesmen bent on peace. The horizon was still
further clouded by the murderous struggles in Ireland; but he
rejoiced when Lloyd George confessed the error of his ways and
permitted Irish Catholics to govern themselves. It was a dramatic
scene, preserved in Sir John Lavery's picture, when the almost
inaudible octogenarian Home Ruler was requested by the Prime

Minister to move the address in the House of Lords to ratify the treaty which transformed a rebellious vassal into a self-governing Dominion. He had done more for Ireland than anyone alive or dead except Gladstone. It was his last appearance, and his friends could have wished the veteran actor no more triumphant an exit from the stage.

In his early and middle years Morley was often described as a radical. In a rash moment Goschen called him the Saint-Just of the English Revolution, oblivious of the fact that no Englishman of his time or of any time less resembled that ruthless young doctrinaire than the tender-hearted humanitarian who detested cruelty and violence in every form including blood sports. Like most other elderly men he became less elastic, and the author of the Morley-Minto reforms in India feared that even the mild Montagu-Chelmsford scheme was going a little too far. That India would in any foreseeable future be granted independence was as unthinkable to him as to Curzon. Sir Almeric Fitzroy, Clerk of the Privy Council, who delighted in his mellow wisdom, emphasizes in his Memoirs how much innate conservatism, reverence for ancient institutions and respect for continuity was to be found in these Victorian Liberals, beginning with Lord John Russell, Gladstone and Bright. As Alfred Spender puts it, the Little Englander and the doctrinaire were left behind when Morley entered the India Office. He was too much of an individualist to feel enthusiasm for social reform, and he would never have described himself, like Mill in his Autobiography, as leaning towards socialism. Yet he was no hard-shelled devotee of the Manchester School, for he sympathized deeply with the 'submerged tenth' and above all with the tragedy of unemployment. Though it was not in him to supply either directions or fuel for the chariot of progress he was never a brake on the wheel. As little impressed by the Webbs as the Webbs by him, the last of the Philosophic Radicals retained the Victorian suspicion of a quasi-omnipotent state, though he never shared the extravagant individualism of Herbert Spencer. 'A charming person for a talk on literature,' wrote Beatrice Webb in her journal after a visit to Wimbledon in 1897, 'but a most depressing spectacle as a Liberal leader, in sympathy with no single progressive idea. A closed mind.' Thirty years later this patronizing critic of Victorian

liberalism saluted the Kremlin system with cheers. Each had
something of value to offer which the other missed.

During the last few years of his life Morley lacked the energy
to write books, but he retained his mental clarity to the end. A
booklet with the modest title *Notes on Politics and History*, which
he asked me to read in proof, enshrined a good deal of his experience of government and his reflections on the ways of mankind. He was full of the wisdom of the ages from Aristotle and
Lucretius to Dante and Machiavelli, Goethe and Burke, rereading
the Immortals in preference to the latest books. I always picture
him at the fireside in his spacious library with his favourite
aphorism of Bacon carved in the mantelpiece: 'The nobler a spirit,
the more objects of compassion it hath.' Anyone who imagines
that these Victorian rationalists, of whom Gilbert Murray was the
last survivor, had more brains than heart reveals his utter ignorance, for they were full of affection, sympathy and thoughtful
consideration. Everyone loved him, testifies Alfred Spender, who
often disagreed with his views. Professor Morgan's penetrating
study rightly declares loving-kindness his most salient characteristic. During the phase of rampant Germanophobia in the war
of 1914 the octogenarian statesman, who rarely left home and was
never in the least Pro-German, insisted on travelling to London
to pay his respects to my German wife. Till the end he was eager
to learn from men half his age. I used to receive affectionate little
notes before or after my visits. The little white terrier at his feet
claimed a portion of the love he would have given his children
if he had been a father. 'Cut him open,' exclaimed his devoted
friend George Meredith, 'and you will find a clergyman,' by
which he meant that at heart he was a preacher and a moralist.
Like Gladstone and Acton he regarded political problems as
moral problems. In congratulating Mackarness on his election to
Parliament in 1906 he added: 'I only care for the brave men who
fought against that insensate war in South Africa.'

It is difficult to describe the conversation of a man whom
Margot Asquith considered the best talker she ever knew. That
would not be my verdict, for I should put Birrell at the top of my
list. Garvin, Belloc and Chesterton were in the front rank, but
they were a little too full of themselves and sometimes too mani-
festly striving for effect to suit my taste. Morley never tried to

dominate, much less to monopolize, the conversation. 'His talk was wonderful when he was at his best as he usually was,' testifies Haldane; 'he was the most interesting personality I ever knew.' There was no better talk in the world, records Alfred Spender, than when he and Rosebery came together. Professor Morgan, one of the most frequent of his visitors, made copious notes which he utilized in his admirable study. The host loved to propound a large theme and collect opinions thereon—the decay of authority, the influence of the Press, the meaning of liberty and liberalism, the influence of ideas and ideals, political prophecy, lost opportunities, the achievement of Bismarck and Cavour, the future of the Labour Party. His oral reminiscences ranged over the celebrities of two generations. When I told him that Acton once described him as 'capable of all but the highest things' he accepted it as a compliment. For decades George Meredith had been very close to his heart, and the glowing portrait is one of the gems of the *Recollections*. He placed him second to Gladstone among his friends with any claim to genius. Though in early and middle life his most frequent correspondent was Frederic Harrison, the latter's Germanophobia on the eve of the war of 1914 and throughout the long struggle led him to doubt whether that pugnacious Positivist had done more harm or good with his shining literary gifts. Of his old political colleagues Birrell and John Burns were the most welcome at Wimbledon as the shadows fell. He watched the emergence of Ramsay MacDonald with sympathetic interest and enjoyed his visits: the Labour leader, at any rate, might be trusted to avoid the allurements of Imperialism.

When the end came the tired old man was more ready to go than we to say good-bye. On one occasion, in speaking of John Dillon, I remarked that I respected genuine piety. 'So do I,' he exclaimed. The militant young author of *Compromise* had long mellowed into one of the most tolerant of men, judging his fellows above all by their services to humanity. Even in his earlier years he had rebuked Voltaire for his lack of feeling for holiness. He recognized that men and women with varying backgrounds and different emotional needs had always disagreed and would continue to do so: it was for the individual, not for secular or ecclesiastical authorities, to make the choice. What men of all persuasions could do was to strive, *ohne Hast, ohne Rast*, for a gentler and kindlier world. In the glowing words of A. G. Gardiner, that prince of essayists, he was the high priest of liberty and the conscience of the political world.

II

Morley belonged to the nineteenth century, Haldane to the twentieth. His most striking characteristic was his amazing versatility: no other man of my time attained equal eminence in law, statesmanship and philosophy. Though he aroused antagonism at various stages of his career he outlived controversy, and old foes joined with old friends in recognition of a great citizen. Since it had always been his ambition to apply ideas to life, a purely political or purely academic career would have failed to satisfy him, and he declined an offer of the Chair of Philosophy at St. Andrews. Democracy without leadership, he used to say, is a mob, but leaders needed ideas. 'He does all the brainwork of the Liberal Party,' declared Asquith in 1900. He was a practical idealist, equally competent as a large-scale planner and a master of detail. The transfer of his political allegiance late in life from the Liberals to Labour, he explained, was mainly due to the indifference of his old colleagues, above all Asquith himself, to the cause of popular education at a time when universal suffrage and the rise of the Labour Party rendered it more urgent than ever to 'educate our masters'. His oldest political friend, he declared, was not a man of much imagination; Lord Oxford, echoed Keynes, created nothing. After the war his old associates, in Haldane's opinion, lacked both the energy and the originality to take a significant part in national reconstruction: the party had completed its task in the political sphere and was dying for lack of ideas.

Haldane never cared much for Lloyd George. His own special contribution was in the sphere of national education, particularly in regard to the creation of provincial universities and adult education. So strong was the sense of mission that the old crusader used to travel long distances to address meetings of no great size. Though Lady Violet Bonham Carter referred to him as Comrade Haldane, he was no more and no less a Socialist after he changed his party label than before. He had long been in close contact with the Webbs whose minds were as fertile as his own. 'What bound us together,' noted Beatrice Webb in her journal, 'was our common faith in a deliberately organized society,' and his help in the creation of the London School of Economics was particularly appreciated. Though his friendship with Asquith cooled, his affection for Grey remained intact to the end. He enjoyed his chats with Baldwin, who used to stroll round from Downing Street to exchange ideas. Neither of them cared very much about party cries or party ties: both believed in the common man and longed to give him every possible chance of securing what Aristotle called the good life. 'He is always cheerful,' declared his mother, 'never worries, and works incessantly.' In the words of A. G. Gardiner he seemed to go through life humming to himself.

Since our disagreement over the South African War lay far behind us our principal bond was our interest in Germany, past and present, German literature and German philosophy, and he read all my writings on these subjects. He had made several visits to the Weimar country with Professor Hume Brown, author of the best English biography of Goethe to which after the author's death he contributed a chapter on the Second Part of *Faust*. After the war he revisited Göttingen and invited some teachers to a good meal at his hotel at a time when food and money were scarce in a land of ruinous inflation. He enjoyed his trip and liked to hear my impressions whenever I crossed the Rhine. Both of us sympathized with the efforts of the Weimar Republic in very discouraging circumstances to operate a system of democracy for which the nation had shown little desire and for which it had been so imperfectly trained. Both of us devoured the biographies, autobiographies and diaries which poured from the German press, above all those relating to the Kaiser, Bülow, Bethmann, Tirpitz and other protagonists in the drama whom he had met. Though he had never accepted the legend that Germany had deliberately unleashed a struggle for the conquest of Europe and the world, he deplored the blind folly of the *Flottenpolitik* which drove England into the Franco-Russian camp, bringing Italy in her train. While William II had not the slightest desire for war with England or anyone else, that vain and ebullient potentate had no notion how to keep the peace. The 'Haldane Mission' of 1912 convinced him that Bethmann was as anxious as Grey to avoid a clash, but also that the high-minded Chancellor was not master in his own house since Tirpitz possessed the ear of their master. In the best organized of European states, he used to say, there was anarchy at the top. The more he learned about the Kaiser the less he admired him. When I lent him Count Zedlitz's book *Twelve Years at the Kaiser's Court* he commented that he had never fully realized how superficial he was. 'What an Emperor and what a Government! No wonder that both ended in colossal disaster.' He deplored the total break in personal relations between the grandsons of Queen Victoria and would have welcomed a message of sympathy from Buckingham Palace when the ailing Empress passed away. It was fortunate that he died in the belief that German democracy had come to stay and that the sinister shadow of Hitler did not fall across his closing years. Delighted to welcome German scholars to his home, he was disappointed that Tröltsch, one of the finest intellects in Europe, died on the eve of a visit which he had helped to arrange. Always ready to devote time and thought to the needs of German friends who had fallen on evil days, he was particularly incensed by the hardships inflicted on innocent aliens through the confiscation of their property as one method of securing reparations, leaving the German Government to indemnify the sufferers if so inclined.

Haldane's interest in philosophy remained as keen as in his student days at Edinburgh and Göttingen. He was the only statesman of his time except Balfour to deliver Gifford Lectures, and *The Pathway to Reality* was the most comprehensive of his books. Wells, though no authority on philosophy, compared the book, which he had certainly not studied, to a big soap bubble. Among contemporary thinkers he chiefly admired Whitehead. Unlike most professional philosophers he had some knowledge of science, and he attempted to relate the discoveries of Einstein to his own Hegelian creed. The remarkable success of *The Reign of Relativity*, published in 1922, gave him keen pleasure, and his acquaintance with the great physicist was one of the delights of his closing years. His third large work, *The Philosophy of Humanism*, and the little book *Human Experience*, designed for the general reader, summarized his message and were widely read. A still briefer outline of his creed appeared with the title *Affirmations* a few months before his death in 1928 at the age of seventy-six.

Though he regarded the Christian and all other creeds merely as guesses at truth, he enjoyed the society of divines such as his fellow Scots Archbishop Davidson and Archbishop Lang, the two scholarly Deans Rashdall and Inge, and the Unitarian Dr. Jacks, editor of the *Hibbert Journal*.

Haldane accepted with alacrity the invitation to become President of the English Goethe Society. Founded in 1886 under the auspices of Max Muller, its first President, it had continued its activities under his successors Edward Dowden and Sir Adolphus Ward till its voice was silenced by the roar of the guns in 1914. On the death of our third President in 1924 Professor J. G. Robertson, the *doyen* of British Germanists, felt that the passions of the conflict had cooled sufficiently to resume our activities, since even Germanophobes could scarcely quarrel with the most cosmopolitan of sages. I had the pleasure of hearing and publishing his inaugural address on Goethe and Modern Thought in the *Contemporary Review*. On one occasion he presided at a lecture delivered in German and commented on it in the tongue he had learned at Göttingen fifty years before. In Goethe he found the universal outlook, the broad humanity, and the wealth of ideas which he so greatly prized.

No one who knew Haldane intimately could fail to realize the warmth of his affections. To his wonderful old mother he wrote every evening of his busy life. A picture of her lying in bed as she approached her centenary hung over his mantelpiece, and his contribution to the memorial volume entitled *Charlotte Elizabeth Haldane* enshrines a unique relationship. To his sister Elizabeth, the biographer of Descartes, who kept house for him after their mother's death, he was closely bound by their common interest in philosophy. In his last address to students he advised them to read the Gospel of St. John and Plato's story of the trial and death of Socrates, breathing the spirit of love and tolerance which should guide them through life. The last time I visited him, a few days before he travelled north to the family home at Cloan to die, he produced a volume of Browning and read me some of his favourite poems. I paid my tribute in the *Contemporary Review*. He had fulfilled himself, and that alone is happiness. He had won some of the richest prizes of life, not merely fame and fortune but admiration and love. The hardest blow of his career—the sudden

and unexplained breaking off of his engagement one month before
the wedding day—increased his sympathy with suffering in every
form. 'He longed to help anyone in trouble,' testifies Lady Horner,
his closest friend outside the family. He was the first to visit
Oscar Wilde in prison and procured him books to read. His heart
was as large as his head, and he was as generous with his purse as
with his time. His posthumous Autobiography summarizes an
honourable and fruitful career. Goethe, declared Matthew
Arnold in a memorable phrase, saw life steadily and saw it whole.
That was also the ideal and in large measure the achievement of
Haldane.

15

THE NEW EUROPE

THE old Europe had disappeared and with it the complacent England of Victoria and Edward VII. The 'governing classes' who had steered the country since 1688 had reached the end of their term. Huge families became a memory of an almost tax-free past. Society, with its lavish week-end parties, swollen staffs and interminable dinners which Arthur Ponsonby had pilloried in *The Camel and the Needle's Eye*, was a war casualty. Vanity Fair had packed up and disappeared. It was not merely on the social plane that far-reaching changes had occurred. There was a chill in the air. Though John Bull never despairs, he was in a chastened and critical mood. We had shed our superiority complex. The war was won in the sense that we could point to the captured cannon in the Mall, but there was no sense of elation. Stanley Baldwin, soon to be summoned to the helm, lamented that he had never known such bad feeling in the country. Bruised in body and soul, we mourned our million dead; the uncertain outlook weighed on our spirits, and the prevailing pessimism was mirrored in Aldous Huxley's *Brave New World*. The Bloomsbury set, captained by Lytton Strachey and Virginia Woolf, dwelt apart in fastidious isolation from the common herd and enjoyed debunking Victorian reputations. No one now spoke of 'the war to end war', a slogan which may have brought a fleeting consolation to a few stricken souls during the long agony. How could anyone forget that great wars and dictated settlements breed fresh conflicts? The friends of today often become actual or potential foes almost as soon as the ink of the signatures to peace treaties is dry, since the *status quo* at any moment never suits everybody. It speaks well for our manual workers that communism, which thrives on frustration and discontent, made little appeal.

The Lloyd George coalition contributed little to the convalescence of Europe. It was a colossal error to furnish moral and material support to Russian generals of the Tsarist régime who endeavoured to overthrow the Bolshevists. There were only two practicable policies towards the men who had evicted Kerensky in the autumn of 1917—to attack in overwhelming force or to leave them alone. We did neither. Our pin-pricks riveted their yoke on the neck of their countrymen and compelled them to rebuild a formidable army. A second blunder was the encouragement of Greece to occupy Smyrna in 1919, an adventure which transformed Mustapha Kemal into a national hero and caused the violent expulsion of the Greeks from Asia Minor.

Nearer home the performances of the Black and Tans in Ireland sickened us of the sterile game of coercion. At last the supple Prime Minister made a *volte-face*, and the Irish Treaty set the Sinn Feiners in the saddle. No one could forget his resourceful leadership during the war, but the four years of quasi-dictatorship which followed convinced most Englishmen in all parties that he was hardly the man to reconstruct a shattered world. He seemed to have shed his Liberalism as completely as Joseph Chamberlain a generation before. With his rise to power he had developed the dualism inherent in his complicated Celtic nature, so brilliantly analysed by Harold Begbie in *The Gentleman with a Duster* and in Alfred Spender's autobiography. To most Liberals the post-war chapter of the Coalition was a nightmare. Even the faithful C. P. Scott of the *Manchester Guardian*, who might be described as Lloyd George's conscience, turned against him on Irish coercion, and Garvin, who fought his battles at the Genoa Conference, gave him up when the Greek *débâcle* threatened a Turkish war. I felt no enthusiasm for Asquith, but like most Liberals I served under his banner since no alternative was in sight. The 'Coalies' drifted ever further away from the main Liberal army, following their unpredictable chief wherever he went. The Welsh wizard was finally dislodged not by disgruntled Liberals, who were too few to decide the issue, but by mutinous Conservatives. The Prime Minister, argued Baldwin, Bonar Law and the Conservative Chief Whip, had broken one party and must not be allowed to destroy the other.

Asquith had a golden opportunity when the war was over and failed to seize it, for he was growing old and weary. The contention that he was right to leave the entire responsibility for the settlement to the man who had dethroned him is unconvincing: he should have summoned his countrymen to work for a moderate peace and denounced our futile policy towards Russia. The routing of his troops in the *coupon* election of 1918 sickened him of politics, though he bore it with his usual serenity. My old colleague Sir Donald Maclean led the little remnant of Independent Liberals in the House of Commons with courage and tact, but he never carried heavy guns. The most outspoken Liberal critic of the government was Grey, but he never relished a fight. Asquith's passivity in foreign affairs was matched by his *immobilisme* at home. The war ended the period in which our main problems were political, and with the return of peace economic issues became paramount. Here the old Liberal leader, the last of the Whigs, had no contribution to make; he thoroughly understood constitutional issues and the Free Trade case, but he had no burning interest in social reform. His inertia seemed to exert a paralysing effect on some of his colleagues, and many Liberals concluded that the party had finished its work. Several of my old Parliamentary friends, among them Arthur Ponsonby, the Buxton brothers, Charles Trevelyan, Percy Alden and Joseph King, had transferred their allegiance to Labour on grounds connected with the war. A further exodus occurred when it seemed that even in the domestic sphere the Liberal oracles were dumb. The hungry sheep looked up and were not fed. I have never felt the slightest temptation to join the Labour Party, for I was no more attracted to wholesale nationalization than to *laissez-faire* individualism. The Conservative Party, with its die-hard record in Ireland and South Africa and its devotion to tariffs, attracted me just as little.

For a Liberal discontented with the intellectual inertia of his leaders the Summer School movement—the Liberal equivalent of the Fabian Society—seemed like a breath of spring. In the annual gatherings at Oxford or Cambridge fresh problems were discussed and old questions handled in a new way. The enterprise was launched by a number of experienced publicists, economists and administrators. The leading spirit was Ramsay Muir, who had exchanged his chair of History at Manchester for the rough and tumble of public life. No one except Sidney Webb equalled his capacity for clear and rapid formulation by tongue and pen of arguments and ideas. In lectures, on political platforms, in the press, in books and pamphlets, he expounded the up-to-date Liberalism which he helped to formulate. His colleagues included Sir E. D. Simon, ex-Lord Mayor of Manchester and a specialist on Housing, now Lord Simon of Wythenshawe, Seebohm Rowntree, England's leading authority since Charles Booth on the condition of the workers, Sir Walter Layton, editor of the *Economist*, now Lord Layton; Philip Kerr, afterwards Lord Lothian; Charles Masterman, Professor Graham Wallas, Sir William Beveridge and Maynard Keynes. The latter's brochure, *The End of Laissez-faire*, set forth some of the leading ideas of the movement, including the control of industry by semi-autonomous corporations. Portions of the field were intensively studied by teams of specialists, and reports were published on Coal and Power, Agriculture, and Industry. The latter, a mine of constructive ideas, went by the name of the Yellow Book. The series embodied the most fruitful and systematic thinking on domestic problems that had been attempted in any quarter since the return of peace. Lloyd George, still full of life and vigour, was in full sympathy, but his patronage was hardly an asset.

The three outstanding features of our domestic politics in the post-war years were the rise of Labour, the decline of the Liberals, and the official adoption of Protection by the Conservatives. Since Labour could offer the most tempting bait to manual workers, it naturally received increasing support. Debarred by their principles from the class appeal of their rivals, Liberals were ground between the upper and nether millstones. Conservatives, most of whom since 1903 had always been as Protectionist as they dared, found a new argument for tariffs in a decade of unemployment. No one could recall a period of such frequent elections, sweeping victories, and catastrophic defeats. The ship was still rocking after the great storm.

While Great Britain enjoyed a fictitious prosperity for a short space after the return of peace when stocks had to be replaced, large portions of the Continent were at the last gasp. The famine in Russia was merely the most spectacular aspect of the Calvary of the peoples. America, under the inspiring guidance of Hoover, shouldered the main burden, but in private works of mercy England was not far behind. Eglantyne Jebb and her sister Dorothy Buxton established the Save the Children Fund which appealed for the little victims of war and has survived the emergency which called it into being; and the Fight the Famine Council was formed to focus attention on the problem as a whole. The leading spirit was Lord Parmoor whom the war had stirred to the depths. The successful lawyer and Conservative landowner emerged from the conflict a changed man. 'I belong to no party,' he confided to me; 'I am a Christian Internationalist, not a pacifist but a peacemaker.' He longed to heal the running sores of Europe and to assuage the vindictive passions of the strife. His path crossed that of the Quakers among whom he found his second wife. I had known John Ellis and his daughters since the South African war, and it was a delight to watch the happiness of the newly wedded pair. Though nearing seventy, Lord Parmoor advanced into the firing line with his very capable wife as Chief of Staff. Next in importance to our Chairman was Lord Buckmaster. We had entered the House together in 1906, and he had succeeded Haldane on the Woolsack for a short time in the middle of the war. He had always been an eloquent speaker, and the horrors of the conflict inspired him to a deeper note. I recall a gathering in the Central Hall towards the end of the war on the conditions of permanent peace which was addressed by Archbishop Davidson, Lord Bryce, General Smuts, Lord Hugh Cecil and Buckmaster. All the stars were at their best, but to my mind the latter was the most impressive. The third member of our ruling triumvirate was Sir George Paish, who supplied the knowledge of international finance which the rest of us lacked. Among our tasks was the organization of Conferences in London, in which leading publicists from Germany, Austria, Italy and other countries took part. The most urgent need was to preach and practise co-operation between victors and vanquished.

The *Contemporary Review* had a modest share in the campaign for reconciliation. We published an address delivered at the first Fight the Famine Conference in 1920 by Professor von Schulze-Gaevernitz, a cousin of my wife and a Democratic Member of the Reichstag, which discussed for the first time from a German point of view in a leading English journal the reconstruction of

Europe. Shortly afterwards I learned that the veteran Professor
Delbrück, the successor of Treitschke at the University of Berlin
and editor of the *Preussische Jahrbücher*, desired to explain how the
origins of the war looked to a leading German historian. I accepted
his article, accompanying it with a reply by Headlam-Morley,
author of the weightiest defence of Grey's policy in 1914, first
and last Historical Adviser to the Foreign Office. The two articles
were reprinted in a German translation as a brochure with a
Preface by Delbrück. The Professor, though no uncritical
admirer of German policy, denied the existence of a will to war.
The British historian replied that by encouraging her ally to
attack Serbia instead of holding her back, and by refusing support
to Grey's mediatory efforts, Germany rendered herself responsible
for the catastrophe. These articles aided readers of each country
to understand the position of the other and to realize that no
single state had been exclusively responsible.

No British monthly could boast of such an array of specialists in
foreign affairs. I always kept in mind Palmerston's maxim that
England has no eternal friendships and no eternal enmities, only
eternal interests, the greatest of which is peace. While Leo Maxse
in the *National Review* dismissed such innovations as the League
of Nations as scornfully as Clemenceau himself, our contributors
proclaimed the gospel of political and economic interdependence,
reduction of armaments and tariffs, and support of the League.
The monthly survey of foreign affairs which had been contributed
for many years by Dr. Dillon was resumed by Leonard Woolf
and later by George Glasgow. The latter, who had served his
apprenticeship as sub-editor of Seton-Watson's *The New Europe*,
followed the problems of reparations and inter-allied debts with
particular care, and his articles were worked up into a series of
instructive little books. Every autumn our readers were instructed
in the achievements of the Assembly at Geneva by Wilson Harris,
later editor of the *Spectator* and M.P. for Cambridge University,
whose experience of the League was unique among British
journalists. Sir George Paish frequently drew attention to the
economic chaos, analysed the Dawes and Young plans, and
foretold the world-wide collapse of 1929. Sisley Huddleston,
successively Paris correspondent of the *Westminster Gazette*, *The
Times* and the *Christian Science Monitor*, kept us in touch with

French opinion. S. K. Ratcliffe, a pillar of the *Manchester Guardian*, described the changing scene in the United States during his annual sojourn in the New World; and Lord Meston, one of the most modest and lovable of men, commented on the political adolescence of India where he had spent the best part of his life. The Spender brothers and Charles Masterman kept the Liberal flag flying, and Wickham Steed supplied a couple of articles yearly on world politics till his sight began to fail. Looking back on the eminent journalists I have known I should put Dillon and Chirol at the top of the list for their grasp of international affairs, Alfred Spender and C. P. Scott for balanced judgment on our domestic controversies. Garvin, the emotional Irishman, had more sails than ballast. For distinction of style no one excelled Massingham and Brailsford, while A. G. Gardiner's pen portraits of celebrities in the *Daily News*, later gathered into volumes, form a precious contribution to the history of the English post-Edwardian age.

The problem of neutral rights at sea in time of war had been brought up informally during the peace negotiations by Colonel House, who met with no response from British statesmen. He returned to the charge in a widely discussed article in the *Contemporary Review* arguing that our island position since the invention of submarines had been changed from a fortress to a trap, and that our interest was now to be found in the freedom of the seas. His annual visits to London were a delight. I was attracted from the first by his open, smiling face, bright eyes and quiet distinction. It was easy to realize how Wilson, at heart a rather lonely man, found in him the understanding friend and counsellor whom he sought. The publication of the four volumes of his *Papers*, sympathetically edited by Professor Charles Seymour, revealed him as the partner rather than the mouthpiece of the President, and in certain departments of foreign affairs he was at times more the teacher than the pupil. It was impossible to know him without realizing his disinterestedness, wide sympathies, and tact. His friendship with Wilson was the romance of his life, its termination the most grievous of his regrets.

From the point of view of suffering humanity the neglect of Turkish Armenia was the gravest blot on the settlement, for the victors shirked the task of saving the remnants of a gifted race by

14

a mandate to one of the Powers or a scheme of international
control. I joined an Armenian Committee of which Aneurin
Williams was Chairman and the veteran T. P. O'Connor an active
member. We were in touch with the Armenian colony in London
and with Boghos Pasha, the son of Nubar who had been Prime
Minister in Egypt in the early days of the British Occupation.
The old man, an impressive figure, did his best in London and
Paris, the two capitals whence alone help could be expected; but
our efforts were fruitless, for Mustapha Kemal put an end to all
thought of external supervision. While the Russian Armenians in
Transcaucasia lived on under the yoke of the Bolshevists, the
Turkish Armenians almost disappeared.

I had welcomed the dethronement of the Tsar who had mis-
governed his subjects in peace and paralysed their energies in the
grim ordeal of war: if any twentieth-century régime deserved to
perish it was the empire of the Tsars. Dynastic autocracy is at best
a gamble, at worst a catastrophe. The Romanoffs produced few
able men, and the last was one of the weakest. Inefficiency,
favouritism, corruption, callous cruelty and obscurantism blighted
the life of the largest nation in Europe. The Provisional Government which seemed to promise a far happier era was only a brief
interlude, Kerensky merely a nine days' wonder. A few months
after the collapse of the old régime Russia was ready for the
Bolshevists, not because she wanted communism but because she
needed peace. Kerensky, who turned up in London, struck me as
a sincere patriot and reformer who lacked the capacity to co-
operate. As a loyal ally of the Western Powers he had faced an
impossible task, for the Russian people, like a tired horse, could
go no further. His apologia entitled *The Catastrophe* is a spirited
performance, and he was not solely responsible for the failure to
hold his ground. A doctor can do nothing if he is called in too late.
The story of the revolution was told in vivid detail by Trotsky
in a book which was read all over the world.

Supporters and critics alike of the old régime were scattered
over the face of the earth when Lenin seized power in the autumn
of 1917. Sazonoff, Kokovtseff and Miliukoff settled in France, and
the latter paid occasional visits to London. The veteran leader of
the Cadets, who had done more than anyone to expose the 'dark
forces' of the Court and had been Foreign Minister for a few

weeks in the Coalition Government of 1917, displayed surprising resilience. His faith in the emergence of his country from its purgatorial fires was unshakeable. From time to time I asked him to write for the *Contemporary Review*, and he was always ready to oblige. That he was not *persona grata* with his fellow exiles was not necessarily his fault, for such orphans of the storm proverbially disagree. Part of the strength of the Bolshevists in their early days derived from the disunion of their opponents. The Grand Dukes sulked on the extreme right. Kokovtseff and Sazonoff, who had been too liberal for the Tsar, were too conservative for Miliukoff who, in turn, was not radical enough for Kerensky. Russia, like Germany, was paying dearly for her lack of political education. Though somewhat less inefficient the new masters were as despotic and ruthless as the old. Before very long the free world discovered with regret that the long-suffering Russian people had exchanged the frying-pan for the fire. Lenin had restored peace but he had not created a happy country.

Though London counted fewer Russian refugees than Paris and Berlin, Constantinople and Prague, many of them had a struggle to live. I sympathized with the Royalists as deeply as I had sympathized with Prince Kropotkin and his friends before the war, for they too had lost all they possessed. The old Prince returned to Russia when the Bolshevists seized the helm, but he had lived too long in the tolerant West to be happy under their despotic sway. I was glad to render some slight assistance to Constantine Nabokoff, Baron Meyendorff and Prince Mirsky by taking articles for the *Contemporary Review*. Nabokoff, who had served as Russian Consul in India and in the Embassy at Washington, was Chargé d'Affaires in London from the death of Count Benckendorff at the opening of 1917 till the November revolution ended his diplomatic career. His brother had been murdered in Berlin, and he always spoke with passionate detestation of the Bolshevists. He supported himself with difficulty by lectures and articles on Russian literature. His command of idiomatic English was amazing, and his readings from Chekhov and other Russian dramatists were a delight. He would have made a first-rate actor; Duse was his goddess and he became quite lyrical in recalling her visit to St. Petersburg. His *Ordeal of a Diplomat*, a useful contribution to the history of the war, gives only the political facet of a man whose soul was dedicated to literature and the arts. His death after an operation in 1927 cannot have been wholly unwelcome to him, for the bondage of his country oppressed him even more than the struggle for his daily bread.

The fate of Baron Meyendorff, formerly a Vice-President of the Duma, and Prince Mirsky, son of a former well-known Minister of the Interior, was less melancholy, for after a period of anxiety they received small lectureships in the University of London. Both were men of wide erudition, the former specializing in economic history, the latter in Slavonic literature. With his touching modesty and gentle nature, Meyendorff was as nearly a saint as the frailty of human nature permits. Mirsky, with his dark enigmatic face, was more of a fighter. Ten years after the revolution which had made him a penniless exile he surprised his friends by a eulogistic biography of Lenin and a return to his native land. Though I approved the resumption of diplomatic relations with Moscow by the Labour Ministry in 1924 and had no desire for the return of the Romanoffs, I declined invitations to the Russian Embassy. I agreed with the Webbs that it was a new civilization, but no Liberal could share the delight of the elderly couple who travelled to the Promised Land and chanted a hymn of praise on their return. Not all Bolshevists, of course, were alike. Krassin, the well-groomed Trade Commissioner, was extremely pleasant, and indeed one did not feel sure if he was a revolutionary at all. Litvinov, soon to become Foreign Minister, struck me as singularly unattractive, for there seemed little warmth in him, but his ability was to be displayed at Geneva and elsewhere. When I asked Sir Hagberg Wright, the learned Librarian of the London Library, who knew him well, what he thought of him I received the reply: 'I neither like him nor dislike him.' The selections from his diaries published long after his death would be more interesting if we could be certain of their authenticity. Ambassador Maisky played his difficult part with tact and success. He liked England and we liked him.

Having welcomed the reunion and independence of Poland I was disappointed with the use to which she put her new-found liberty. The rape of Vilna by General Zeligowski in 1920 was an outrage, whatever one might think of Polish claims to the old Lithuanian capital. Pilsudski's *coup* in 1926 ended the feeble democratic experiment without putting a better system in its place, and the treatment of the Ruthenes in Eastern Galicia provoked the censure of the Council of the League. It was distressing to witness the Poles treating some of their fellow-citizens almost as roughly as they themselves had been treated by the Tsars for a hundred years. I told the Polish Ambassador, Skirmunt, a kindly and cultivated old man, that if he wished for our goodwill they must cease to throw the sword into the scales. Mme Pilsudski's Memoirs made out the best case she could for her husband, whose conspicuous services to his country before and during the war were recognized by his political opponents and by his critics abroad; but dictators are never popular in the free world.

The emergence of Finland from the grip of Russian autocracy was equally welcome to Englishmen. When the formidable Communist rising was suppressed, the problems of the land of forests and lakes were far simpler than those of Poland. From the Finnish Minister in London, Sastamoinen, who had risked his life and damaged his health in the civil war, I used to hear periodical reports of the progress of the industrious and highly educated little state. He regarded the Bolshevist régime with loathing and thought England the best friend of his country, though he realized we could do nothing to help. Similar Anglophil views were held by the Estonian Minister, one of the most attractive members of the diplomatic corps. The heart of Dr. Kallas was in folk-lore, on which he was a recognized authority; but when the infant Republic needed the services of its few Intellectuals he obeyed the call. His wife, Aino Kallas, herself a Finn, shared his passion for the study of the customs and superstitions of the Baltic peoples, and recalled the past to life in a series of tales—*The White Ship, Eros the Slayer,* and *The Werewolf* —which impress the reader with their grim realism. No other couple united such intellectual distinction with so much personal charm.

Baron Palmstierna and his wife entertained on a generous scale in their spacious eighteenth-century mansion in Portland Place, and the eager little man followed every phase of our national life —cultural as well as political—with the keenest interest. The Crown Prince of Sweden, now King, whom I met at a small luncheon party, struck me as an admirable specimen of the thoughtful, unpretentious, unselfish, duty-doing royalties who alone have survived the war, and he possessed the additional attraction of intellectual interests. The Norwegian Minister, who represented a smaller and poorer land, was less in the limelight; yet there was no more popular diplomatist in London than Dr. Vogt, who had represented his country at Stockholm during the years that followed the separation in 1905. He told us of his social and spiritual isolation in the capital of the dynasty whose sway he had helped to repudiate, and he was thankful to be transferred to the warmer atmosphere of London. He had been a schoolfellow of Nansen and was no less ardent a champion of the League of Nations. Little nations find some compensation for their minor role on the European chessboard in the stature of their citizens.

The Balkan Committee continued to function, and when Noel Buxton entered the Labour Cabinet as Minister of Agriculture in 1923 his place as Chairman was efficiently filled by Sir Edward Boyle. After vainly pleading the cause of his beloved Bulgaria at the Peace Conference, our old comrade Bourchier of *The Times* returned to Sofia to die. Whatever her errors no one can deny her capacity for gratitude to her British champions from Gladstone onwards: though we had been enemies in the war Bulgarians never lost their admiration for England. Foxy Ferdinand had abdicated, and no country could desire a better constitutional monarch than his son Boris. When Bulgaria surrendered, Stambulisky, who had courageously opposed intervention in the war, emerged from prison and grasped the reins in his rough peasant hands. I have never seen a more formidable-looking human being than the Bulgarian Premier whom I met on his visit to London. He had a dark and forbidding countenance, and his square shoulders suggested enormous physical strength. Conversation was interpreted by Nadeija Stancioff, the polyglot daughter of the popular Bulgarian Minister in London, who had vainly warned his master in 1915 not to invite defeat by joining the Central Powers. Stambulisky's head seemed to be turned by his sudden rise, and it was no surprise when his career was cut short by a violent death. The Balkan states specialize in political assassination.

The Romanian Minister in London, Titulesco, afterwards Foreign Minister and a familiar figure at Geneva, was a lively and intelligent man, with a curiously Mongolian face and a flow of talk in impeccable French. As we walked away from a luncheon party at the Romanian Legation Professor Seton-Watson remarked to me: 'At any rate he is not corrupt'—a high compliment to a leading politician from the Near East. But no Balkan statesman of the twentieth century compared with Venizelos in the brilliance of his abilities, the range of his achievements, and the vicissitudes of his career. Though I had rejoiced in the victories of Greece over Turkey in the Balkan wars, I was shocked by the seizure of Smyrna in 1919. I was aware that the city and its environs had been Greek since classical times, but there was a danger of the Greeks being tempted into the interior and of the far stronger Turks retaliating and driving the invaders into the sea. My fears were well founded, and the gamble ended with the catastrophe of 1922: if Greece deliberately stuck her hand into the hornets' nest she could only expect to be stung. In an address to the Anglo-Hellenic Society some years later I concluded a tribute to the work of the outstanding statesman of modern Greece with a mild censure of the Smyrna enterprise. The Greek Minister Caclamanos, who was present, and other members of the Greek colony took my criticism in good part, for they knew it came from a friend. No Balkan state, however, keeps such a vigilant eye on foreign opinion or strives so intensively for a good press. A report of my talk was sent to Venizelos, and on his next visit to London he asked me to call on him at the Ritz. In a lengthy *tête-à-tête* he poured forth an eloquent defence of his policy. His plan, he explained in fluent French, had been to occupy the Smyrna zone, which was easily defensible, and he had never dreamed of going further. His overthrow at the general election of 1920 was followed by the return of Constantine, who, with his Royalist advisers, pushed rashly forward towards Angora: the entire responsibility rested on his political rivals. The youthful vigour of the veteran statesman, without a wrinkle on his brow, was remarkable. Bourchier, who had known him since his rebel days in the mountains of Crete and had seen him at work during the peace negotiations of 1919, used to lament that he was irresistible. That he was an outstanding personality no one who met him could doubt. No public figure of my time except Lloyd George has aroused more passionate admiration and incurred more vitriolic abuse. How the Greek Royal Family hated him we may read in the vivid Memoirs of Prince Christopher, youngest brother of King Constantine.

Little Serbia had grown into big Jugoslavia as Piedmont had grown into Italy. I heard good accounts of her peasant soldiers from Mrs. St. Clair Stobart who had nursed the sick and wounded in their terrible retreat across the Albanian mountains, and from Sir Edward Boyle who helped to sustain the physique and morale of the refugees in Corsica. I was invited to a small reception to the Crown Prince—later King—Alexander and the omnipotent Pasich, who visited London during the lull between the conquest and the liberation of their country. They formed a striking contrast. The Crown Prince, a dark young man of earnest expression, spoke briefly in French of his desire to unite the different sections of the Southern Slavs—*une race, une langue*—under his sway. Pasich, with his benevolent countenance and patriarchal beard, might have passed for a venerable Nonconformist minister; but his disarming innocence was only the outer shell, for he could claim the title of the Fox of the Balkans with as much right as Ferdinand himself. The short-sighted policy of subordinating the new provinces to the centralized rule of Belgrade produced its inevitable results. Catholic Croatia, which had long enjoyed partial autonomy within the Hapsburg Empire, found its Parnell in Radich, who, like other celebrities from the Near East, was invited to address our Balkan Committee. The impression was not particularly favourable. His address in halting French was a rambling performance, and he seemed to shirk direct replies to searching questions. As an old Home Ruler I sympathized with his aims, but I could understand that he was regarded as an *enfant terrible* at Belgrade. His assassination as he sat in his place in the Chamber led to the substitution of a Royal dictatorship for a Constitution which had ceased to work; but King Alexander was soon to follow him to a bloody grave. In the Balkans one murder usually leads to another, for east of Vienna life is cheap.

Hungary forfeited two-thirds of her territory and population, but none of her sons regarded the new frontiers as more than a temporary disgrace. Magyar visitors would whip a card from their pocket with the old and the new boundaries indicated on the two sides, and ask indignantly whether we would accept such

humiliation. The Magyars are a governing race, and like an eagle
in its cage they beat their wings against the bars. Rarely have I
found a Hungarian willing to admit that the treatment of racial
minorities had been open to criticism. An exception was Count
Michael Karolyi, who had steered the ship during the distracting
winter between the revolution of 1918 and the brief Communist
dictatorship of Bela Kun and told the story in his spirited apologia
Against the Whole World. When his short reign was over and his
country was once again ruled by the Magnates, one of Hungary's
largest landowners found himself an almost penniless exile in
London. Next to Stambulisky he was the most formidable-
looking of Balkan Premiers. A squint in one of his eyes gave the
face a rather sinister expression, and a cleft in his palate rendered
his voice thick and hoarse. His name was execrated by the
nobility, who regarded him as a traitor to their caste, and hardly
less by the conservative *bourgeoisie*. When I mentioned him to a
former Hungarian official living in London I received the reply:
'If he entered my house I would kick him downstairs.' Still more
drastic was the reaction of a titled Austrian lady whom I met at a
lunch party in Vienna: 'I should like to shoot him in the stomach.'
His foes depicted him as an unscrupulous adventurer, destitute
of public and private morals. He was certainly ambitious, yet I
never believed that his course was shaped by ambition alone. He
had advanced by stages towards radical and international principles and sacrificed everything on their behalf. His plucky wife
was more attractive. Accustomed from childhood to every
luxury in the household of Count Julius Andrassy, she stood
loyally by her husband in exile and was maid of all work in their
little Pimlico flat. They were a curious contrast—the dark face of
the rebel aristocrat and the charm of the pretty little woman.

For several years after the collapse of the Hapsburg Empire
the sufferings of Vienna were even more poignant than those of
Budapest. While the land of the rolling plains could at any rate
feed itself, the mountainous rump which was all that was left of
the old Austria, cut off from its minerals and its food supply, was
doomed to semi-starvation if its manufactures failed to scale the
surrounding tariff walls. There was no more pathetic spectacle in
the new Europe than the little Republic with a capital of two
millions in an agricultural community smaller than Belgium—a

giant's head on a dwarfish trunk. The spacious embassy in Belgrave Square seemed like a mockery of departed greatness, and I used to wonder how Count Mensdorff could bear to return as a visitor to the scene of his former dignity. The new Austrian Minister, who has painted his own portrait in a delightful auto-biography, was just the man for the post. Baron Franckenstein, who had served under Mensdorff before the war, belonged to one of the oldest families in the land, and every feature testified to the quality of his blood. His extreme refinement, his gentle voice, and a touching air of resignation seemed to fit him for the task of representing a country which had shrunk from a Great Power to the position of one of the smallest and least regarded members of Dame Europa's school. Quickly winning the sympathy and respect both of official and unofficial circles, he gallantly strove to popu-larize Vienna and the Austrian Alps as a holiday resort. How he rejoiced when the League came to the rescue in 1922! Deeply as he loved his country he was no less devoted to art. Members of the Anglo-Austrian Society, in the foundation of which he was backed by Herbert Fisher, at that time Minister of Education, and Sir Maurice de Bunsen, our last Ambassador at the Court of Francis Joseph, were privileged to hear at the Embassy not only some of the best musicians of Austria but expert lectures on history and architecture. Even in defeat the venerable *Kaiserstadt* remained the home of the arts. When Hitler ravished Austria in 1938 and thereby terminated the official mission of her repre-sentative, King George conferred a knighthood on him and he was promptly naturalized. Many years later he and his Scottish wife, unlucky to the last, perished together in an aeroplane accident.

Of all the Succession States Czechoslovakia made the quickest recovery. The impressive figure of the President conferred in-comparable prestige on the young republic, and uninterrupted tenure of the Foreign Office by his favourite disciple seemed to emphasize its stability. The reception of Masaryk and Beneš, when they paid an official visit to London soon after the liberation, was cordial in the extreme. I was a guest at the lunch in their honour in the Mansion House. Plato's philosopher-king remained the same grave and unassuming person I had known as a private citizen. Beneš made an impression of remarkable vivacity and quickness of mind; that he also possessed steadfast courage and endurance we know from his elaborate record of his activities during the war. The Czechoslovak Minister, Jan Masaryk, whom everyone liked, had followed his father's example in marrying an American and shared his liking for Anglo-Saxon civilization. On that sunny day no one dreamed of the tragedies, both personal and national, which lay ahead.

With the Fascist authorities I declined all contact, for the march on Rome robbed the country of its constitutional rights. For the first two years the Duce collaborated with other parties, and a certain measure of liberty remained to the press; but when the Matteotti murder threatened his authority he tightened up the machinery of the totalitarian state. All parties except his own were dissolved, local self-government was abolished, opposition by tongue and pen exposed the critic to the peril of physical assault. The country swarmed with spies and informers, families had to control their talk in the presence of their staff, children of tender age were enrolled in the party and schooled in the doctrines of a chief who declared that war was to man what maternity was to woman—the fulfilment of his destiny. Unlike Hitler, Mussolini was an intellectual, but their methods were much the same; though he shed less blood he was equally unfettered by moral scruples. His theory of government was that a Man of Destiny has a right to do what he likes since he knows what is best for his countrymen. That the national economy was out of joint, that communism was spreading in the cities of the north, that there was sporadic rowdyism and a brief occupation of the factories by the workers in 1920, and that after the resignation of Giolitti there was no firm hand at the helm, is undeniable; but that Mussolini rescued Italy from utter anarchy is an exaggeration as the evidence summarized in Salvemini's indictment *The Fascist Dictatorship* seems to prove. By 1922 the worst was over. A second excuse for the revolution—that the country was unfitted for self-government—was equally unconvincing. If we admit that the Latin races are less apt pupils than the cooler Teutons of the north, can any reader of Benedetto Croce's masterly record of united Italy maintain that her Parliamentary performance was inferior to that of France? The Duce diminished the number of beggars, improved the railway services, accelerated the draining of the Campagna, and terminated the old feud with the Vatican; but he also dragged Italy into the Second World War, lost her colonial empire, destroyed the Monarchy, and condemned his countrymen to the horrors of invasion. Moreover, dictators always rob their country of the services of many of its leading citizens, for they cannot tolerate criticism. Nitti, an ex-Premier, fled to Switzerland; Count Sforza, Giolitti's Foreign Minister, settled first in Belgium, then in the United States; Turati, the Socialist leader, escaped to France in an open boat; Don Sturzo, a courageous priest, founder of the *Partito Populare*, sought refuge in London where we often met. In the academic world the ravages were equally severe. Croce, possessing private means, purchased immunity from anything worse than a raid on his house in Naples by abstention from public censure of the régime. Ferrero, the historian of Rome, was welcomed to a chair at Geneva. Less eminent opponents were spirited away to the islands to eat out their hearts as *Confinati*. A few bold spirits made a dash for liberty, among them Carlo Roselli, whom I was to know in later years and whose cowardly murder in a country lane near Paris by hired Fascists every lover of liberty was to mourn. His unpolitical brother Nello, Professor of History at Florence, shared his fate.

It was a privilege to be of the slightest assistance to the victims of tyranny in every land. No one could fail to be attracted by Gaetano Salvemini, who had quitted his chair of history at Florence for the sake of his independence, had suffered imprisonment, and had saved his life by flight. He was an ardent politician as well as a scholar, and from his place in Parliament had opposed the cry for Dalmatia. On his arrival in England he used to pour forth torrents of eloquence in French; but English was quickly mastered and he was installed as a Professor at Harvard. He was full of warm humanity and, despite public and private sorrows, bubbled over with boyish fun. He was as sure that Italy would regain her liberty as Victor Hugo had been that he would witness the downfall of Napoleon III. He always maintained that firm action, as recommended by General Badoglio, would have repulsed the Fascist assault in 1922, and that Victor Emmanuel might have overthrown his gaoler with the applause of the nation after the murder of Matteotti. It was easier for an Englishman like myself than for the temperamental Professor who had been in the thick of the fight to understand the passive attitude of the King. Victor Emmanuel had always been respected for his physical courage and for the simplicity of his life, and he had never attempted to transcend his role of constitutional monarch. He may be fairly described as an Italian counterpart of George V, though with wider intellectual interests, and he believed that self-effacement provided the best chance of saving the dynasty. Neither opposing nor flattering the superman, he stood aloof, waiting patiently on events. He knew enough history to realize that dictators are essentially birds of passage. His toleration of the dictatorship made Salvemini a Republican, as Alfonso's patronage of Primo converted millions to republicanism in Spain. It was a satisfaction to accept articles for the *Contemporary Review* from Salvemini, Sforza, Don Sturzo, and others who were bravely struggling to earn their daily bread, to save their souls, and to keep the flickering torch of liberty alight.

Bolshevists, Fascists and Nazis despised democracy and pro-claimed an authoritarian philosophy to buttress their power. For Communists liberty is a bourgeois invention, invented by and serving the interests of the comfortable middle class, oblivious of the manual worker who needs social justice, not political self-determination. To Nazis and near-Nazis, such as Möller von den Brück, Liberalism seemed the gospel of anarchy, everyone thinking exclusively of his own interests and caring nothing for society or the state. Mussolini's ideology was explained in a striking article on Fascism written for a new edition of the Italian Encyclopedia. Liberalism, he declared, had only flourished for half a century; it was born in 1830 in reaction against the Holy Alliance. It is the logical and indeed the historical forerunner of anarchy. Today the Liberal faith must close the doors of its deserted temples, for the peoples of the world realize that its worship will lead, as it has already led, to certain ruin. Liberalism implies individualism, Fascism implies the state. The author was unaware that British Liberalism went back to Lilburne and Locke, Tom Paine and Bentham. The Rule of Law, which forms the framework of ordered liberty, is beyond the mental grasp of Dictators, whether Communist or anti-Communist.

No feature of the victory of the Allies caused deeper satisfaction than the return of King Albert to his throne. Though the Belgian refugees as a whole had not left a particularly fragrant memory in England, everyone admired the heroic steadfastness of the royal pair whom I saw at close quarters when the King presided in the Guildhall at the Annual Dinner of the Royal Literary Fund. The Wittelsbach Queen, small and dark, might well have been a Walloon. The King, tall, blond, and with a slight suggestion of clumsiness in his build, looked a Teuton from head to foot and might have come from Hanover or Mecklenburg. His Ambassador in London, Baron de Cartier de Marchienne, was one of the most popular, cultivated and hospitable members of the Diplomatic Corps. It was a pleasure to meet Pirenne again at his table, and to find that Belgium's leading historian seemed none the worse for his long imprisonment. What Emile Cammaerts, poet, professor, historian, did for his country during his long residence among us is known to all.

The reconciliation of England and Germany was assisted by Lloyd George's appointment of Lord d'Abernon to Berlin and the nomination of Dr. Sthamer to London. The former was one of our elder Statesmen, and his delightful Diaries furnish the best English account of the Weimar Republic. Few of us, on the other hand, had heard of the elderly Hamburg Senator when he arrived at the opening of 1920. His position as the representative of a defeated nation was difficult, and for the first year or two he led rather a lonely life; but he was wise enough not to force the pace and to trust to the healing power of time. Though the bitter memories of the struggle died slowly, the *rapprochement* was accelerated by the blunders of French policy in the fostering of separatism in the Rhineland and the invasion of the Ruhr. Long before the end of his ten years in Carlton House Terrace the Ambassador had become not only a respected but a popular figure: his quiet dignity, unfailing tact and genuine kindliness had earned their reward. His wife, a German American, was an ideal helpmate; neither as hosts nor as guests did the Sthamers give themselves airs. They fitted into the simpler habits of post-war England as perfectly as the Lichnowskys had suited our colourful society before the flood.

Next to the beloved Ambassador no German in England took a larger share in rebuilding the bridges than the Councillor of Embassy Dufour-Feronce. He had inherited from his Huguenot

ancestors a Gallic vivacity which formed a contrast and com-
plement to the reserve of his chief. He had lived in England till
his seventeenth year and had been educated at Dulwich College.
He was bilingual, and his attachment to our country survived the
loss of his only son in the war. He was a man with a mission, for
his great sorrow led him to exchange a business career for
diplomacy. Henceforth his life was dedicated to reconciliation.
Both his head and his heart told him that friendship with England
was the best policy, for the hostility of France appeared incurable
and Bolshevist Russia made no appeal to a prosperous Leipzig
industrialist. Despite his French ancestry and his Anglophil
sympathies, he remained a patriotic German to the core. Soon
after their arrival we gave a small reception for Sthamer and
Dufour; Ramsay MacDonald was among our guests, and the
newcomers made an excellent impression on all who met them.
We remained in close touch with the two families till Dufour
was transferred to Geneva in 1927 and Sthamer resigned in
1930.

Dufour's successor Dieckhoff came to London from Washington and left us for a high post in the German Foreign Office. He,
too, was as charming as he was Anglophil, and his three years in
London assisted the healing process. Equally zealous in the good
cause was Count Albrecht von Bernstorff, whose grandfather had
represented Prussia at the Court of St. James's in the middle of
the nineteenth century, and whose uncle had vainly striven to
avert a breach with the United States. He had been one of the
earliest Rhodes scholars, was keenly interested in every aspect of
English life, and had wider English contacts than any member
of the Embassy. Little did he or we dream that he would die on
the gallows in the purge which followed the attempt on Hitler's
life in 1944. When Neurath succeeded Sthamer and Dieckhoff
was called to Berlin, Bernstorff became Councillor of Legation,
and young Bismarck moved up from the fourth to the third place.
The Prince was justly proud of his name, and his admiration for
his grandfather was boundless. He loved to talk about him and
gobbled up the biographies and monographs as they appeared;
but he had no intention of living on the family record, for he
possessed brains and energy for a career of his own.

At the Embassy and elsewhere I met most of the German

celebrities who visited London after the war—Einstein, Emil Ludwig, Count Metternich, Dr. Solf and Dr. Rosen, ex-Foreign Ministers, Schubert and Bülow, nephew of the Chancellor, successively heads of the Berlin Foreign Office, and—last but not least—Rathenau. Massingham had made the acquaintance of the latter at Wiesbaden, and he invited me to lunch when the Foreign Minister came to take soundings in the City. He was a citizen of the world, and as a Jew it was easy for him to embrace the larger patriotism. No German of his time could compare with him in the range of his interests and achievements—in business, invention, politics, authorship, science and art. He was kind enough to send me *Von Kommenden Dingen*, his favourite among his books. His style was involved but he had a great deal to say. It was a shock to hear not long afterwards of the cowardly murder of the statesman who ranks with Stresemann among the ornaments of the Weimar régime. The impression that he was an exceptionally gifted human being was confirmed by Count Kessler's biography.

Ten years after the war the bridges had been rebuilt, and Anglo-German Societies were founded in London and Berlin. Our President was Lord Reading, who spoke German, and our first function was a dinner at Claridge's to Cuno, his opposite number in Berlin. The head of the Hamburg-America line, who had been Chancellor during the invasion of the Ruhr, looked a typical Nordic with a strong but not unsympathetic face. The speech of the evening was made by Sir Ian Hamilton, who presided in the absence of Lord Reading. The old General, who had always been much more than a soldier, had devoted himself since the war to the reconciliation of the combatants. Our second function was a farewell lunch to Sthamer, who spoke with his usual attractive modesty of the work he had tried to do. It was in every sense a farewell, for he died within a year. Soon afterwards we were greeting Neurath, his successor, later still Brüning and his Foreign Minister Curtius. The last Weimar Chancellor suggested refinement rather than strength and seemed insufficiently tough to weather the gathering storm.

16

CONTINENTAL CONTACTS

MUCH could be learned of the new Europe from our foreign visitors, from British travellers and from the written word, but the atmosphere of a country at any given moment can only be sensed on the spot. Visiting her parents in Saxony in 1919 my wife found her countrymen stunned by the shock of defeat, and little change had occurred when I accompanied her in the spring of 1920. The visa for entering Germany had to be procured in Rotterdam, and the journey from London to Zittau, a picturesque old town on the Bohemian frontier, claimed four days. It was something of an adventure to travel in the country which I had last seen in rude health and strength in 1913.

The first ocular demonstration of collapse was to be found in the refreshment room at the frontier, its almost incredible austerity contrasting poignantly with the opulent display on the Dutch side of the barrier. We were in a land of scarcity and soaring prices. Tea and coffee were luxuries reserved for great occasions. *Ersatz* coffee was made from roasted acorns, *Ersatz* tea from dried lime-blossoms. At the big Leipzig station the American ham tasted as nasty as it looked, but the waiter was only too thankful to be allowed to finish the plate. The meat ration was a pound in three weeks, the butter ration for breakfast at the hotels almost invisible, and 'jam' was a courtesy title. On the other hand, with the mark at 270 to the pound, we travelled all the way from the Dutch frontier for a few shillings. Though some hotels trebled their charges for visitors from more favoured lands, the gain on the pound in Germany more than compensated for the loss in Holland. Nothing more forcibly illustrated the plight of Europe than the variations in the value of our Treasury notes on passing from country to country.

The recent war was generally regarded in Germany as an unprovoked struggle for existence against a ring of foes spurred on by Russia. That England had sided with the Slav against the Teuton seemed incomprehensible and almost unpardonable to a nation whose political thinking had recently run so largely on racial lines: that our policy had always been and always had to be shaped by the principle of the Balance of Power was beyond their comprehension. No tears were shed over the fate of the Hapsburg Empire, which had dragged its loyal ally into the disastrous conflict, and the only small consolation was found in the collapse of Tsarist Russia, 'the land of the knout'. At any rate the Teuton had beaten the despised Slav, and it was believed that with better leadership he would have won the battle of the Marne. I heard no word of sympathy with the Kaiser whose flight had shocked the circles of the Right, and contemptuous regrets were expressed that he lacked the courage to seek a soldier's death. 'Little Willie', the frivolous Crown Prince, had long ceased to count. The *bourgeoisie* were like sheep without a shepherd: having lost their faith in the Kaiser and retained their horror of socialism, they saw nothing ahead but the abyss. They were suffering from political inexperience, for in the days of prosperity they had left policy to the government. The Socialists, on the other hand, were full of self-confidence, for they had always proclaimed the right and capacity of the masses to govern themselves: at last their hour seemed to have come. The only elements which displayed resilience were the organized town workers, who forced up their wages as prices soared, and the great industrialists of whom the dynamic Stinnes was spokesman and chief.

The lack of a Thiers or a Gambetta to conduct the national orchestra was a serious handicap. Ebert, the Socialist President, impressed the Diplomatic Corps with his patriotism and sound sense, but there was nothing about him suggestive of epic or romance. With the exception of Erzberger, the mention of whose name sometimes provoked a snort of contempt, no Minister had struck the public imagination, and the republican régime received no encouragement from the victorious Allies. The Spartacist and Communist risings had been suppressed with an iron hand by the socialist Noske, who was so obsessed with the danger from the Left that he ignored the mounting peril from the Right. I was waiting at Hanover station for the train to the Hook on the way home when a newsboy appeared on the platform with papers and a large poster bearing the words *Revolution in Berlin*. After a *mauvais quart d'heure* spent in reading the telegrams it was a relief to see the express roll into the station—the last to run till the rebellion was suppressed.

A visit to Austria in 1923 revealed a more pathetic casualty of the war. The early years of peace in Vienna had been a nightmare of inflation, starvation and disease. I was told the *ben trovato* story of two sons who had inherited equal portions from their father. While the sober elder brother had invested in state securities and lost every penny, the younger, who had wasted his fortune in riotous living, joyfully discovered that his empty champagne bottles found a ready sale. The downward course was arrested in 1922 when Dr. Seipel threw himself on the mercy of the League of Nations at Geneva. An international loan was authorized and promptly taken up, a League supervisor was installed at Vienna, and the krone was stabilised at the rate of about 320,000 (instead of 25) to the pound. Though the unemployed and the pensioned officials constituted an almost intolerable burden, the people were striving to be cheerful once more. I had been invited to lecture at the recently instituted International Summer School, which was open to the public for a small fee and drew teachers and learners from many lands. The old city looked at its best in the bright September sunshine, and though the picture gallery had been compelled to surrender some of its treasures to Italy it remained an unending delight. The Hofburg and Schönbrunn, which I had only seen from outside in 1900, were now open to the public. In the former the Spartan simplicity of the suite of Francis Joseph was a striking contrast to the splendour of the state apartments. Most interesting of all was the bedroom of Maria Theresa, the one radiant figure in the six centuries of Hapsburg rule. Schönbrunn spoke not only of Francis Joseph but of the ill-fated son of Napoleon, and of the last hectic hours of the reign of Karl, the well-meaning young ruler who never had his chance.

The Summer School was opened in the aula of the University

in the presence of Hainisch, President of the Republic, and Seipel, the Chancellor. The former was a general favourite, and during my visit I had many opportunities of appreciating his kindliness and tact. The latter, with his priestly garb and commanding nose, would have arrested attention in any gathering, and Austria was grateful to the man who had saved her at the eleventh hour. He looked like a Prince of the Church in the *ancien régime* or a Papal Secretary of State in the days of the Temporal Power. No one would have guessed that he, any more than Masaryk, was of humble birth. Being asked to speak for the British contingent, I expressed the sympathy of my countrymen with the young Republic and paid tribute to the services of Baron Franckenstein. My addresses on British foreign policy before and during the war attracted large audiences, for the causes of the catastrophe seemed of keener interest to the vanquished than to the victors.

Among old friends whom it was a pleasure to meet was Professor Pribram, the most eloquent lecturer in the historical department of the University and editor of *The Austro-Hungarian Secret Treaties from 1879 to 1914*. His view of the background of the war was much the same as my own. He invited leading authorities on war origins, among them Srbik, the interpreter of Metternich, Uebersberger, the hammer of the Slavs, and Molden, the biographer of Aehrenthal, to meet me for a symposium on the policies of our respective countries. I heard once again how deep had been the dread of the Russian colossus. To the West it had been a struggle to avert German domination of Europe, to the Austrians a war to defend Western civilization against semi-Asiatic barbarism. In Pribram's view it had been right to send the ultimatum to Serbia, wrong to declare war after the partially submissive reply.

There was no more brilliant intellect in Vienna than Professor Joseph Redlich, well known in England by his frequent visits and his treatises on our Local Government and Parliamentary Procedure. He had been an active Member of Parliament before the war and, like his friend Baernreither, had striven for an understanding with the Jugoslavs despite the fact that he was violently Russophobe. When the Empire was cracking in the autumn of 1918 he was called to the Ministry of Finance in the Cabinet of Professors formed by Lammasch, the revered jurist and pacifist.

A fortnight later the last Ministry of the Hapsburgs was swept away by the revolutionary flood, and power passed to the Socialists. Redlich talked with affection of Lammasch and with respect of Seipel who entered politics in this short-lived combination. He had hotter blood than Pribram and always spoke of Prussia with curious bitterness.

A third old friend, whom I had not seen since 1900, was Sigmund Münz, for many years a pillar of the *Neue Freie Presse* and author of chatty books on the statesmen and countries of Europe. He was in bad odour in England owing to his connection with the Cartwright incident at Marienbad in 1911, for he was supposed either to have embroidered the interview or to have betrayed the confidence of the British Ambassador. He repudiated both charges and laid the blame on his paper for presenting his report in a form which revealed the identity of the diplomatist. He was an experienced journalist, and no one who knew him believed him capable of dishonourable conduct. His bachelor tea-parties were an institution, and his visitors' book, which he showed me with pride, would be a treasure for the collector of autographs. At his tea-table I heard something of the military side of the war from General Auffenberg and of the new order from diplomatists of the Succession States. The host was strongly Anglophil, and his study of Bülow shows that he could be on friendly terms with a statesman without approving all his ways.

A fourth friend was Dr. Friedrich Hertz, who had been made a Hofrat for his services to the Ministry of Finance. Since the death of Alfred Fried and Baroness Suttner he had been the leading spirit among Austrian Pacifists. At that time a *Privatgelehrter*, possessing independent means, he was free to say what he liked, and he assailed nationalist and racial prejudices with unflagging zeal. His well known book *Race and Civilization* was at once a sociological treatise and a political manifesto. Some years later he was called to the Chair of Sociology at Halle, leaving behind him an Anglo-Austrian Society in Vienna for cultural contacts. Like all Continental Liberals he was an admirer of England.

That Pribram and Redlich, Münz and Hertz were Jews was characteristic of the position occupied by that indomitable race in the academic and social life of Vienna. Freud was as famous as

Ford, and Schnitzler, author of *Liebelei*, was read and played all over the world. Finance was largely in Jewish hands, and the *Neue Freie Presse* was their property. It used to be said in jest that 'next to Benedikt' Francis Joseph was the most important person in Austria. He had occupied the same sort of position as Delane of *The Times*, and his organ was regarded abroad as the voice of Austria. His son, who inherited his devotion to the paper, was a less dominating personality but a man of wider intellectual and artistic tastes. He envied us Lloyd George, whom he regarded as a born leader of men, and asked my opinion of him. I replied that the ex-Premier was a complex Celtic personality, not very easy for a plain Englishman to understand. When the news of Lord Morley's death was telegraphed from London Dr. Benedikt invited me to write an obituary, and I had the melancholy satisfaction of paying homage to my old friend in the leading Austrian organ.

Visiting lecturers were overwhelmed with kindness. The President of the Republic gave us a reception at the Ballplatz, where Kaunitz and Metternich had made history, in which the Congress of Vienna had sat, from which the fateful ultimatum to Serbia had been launched, and where Dollfuss was soon to be murdered by Nazi thugs. We were invited to the Presidential box at the Opera and the Burgtheater, and I had the unexpected experience of occupying the seat of Francis Joseph. We were shown the treasures of Melk by the Abbot. Lordly Göttweih, perched on its hill above the Danube, and Kloster Neuburg, a few miles from the capital, were equally full of Napoleonic memories. These immense baroque palaces suggested both the power and the worldliness of the Church before Joseph II thinned out the monasteries. Very different emotions were evoked by a visit to Heiligenkreuz, where the body of Marie Vetsera was hurriedly buried after the tragedy at Mayerling.

In addition to the Austrian Professors German scholarship was worthily represented at the Summer School, and I had my first opportunity of discussing the origins of the war with German experts. Hermann Oncken, the leading authority on the Bismarckian empire, whom I had met at the Historical Congress of 1913, remained a National Liberal. The more philosophic Meinecke had moved towards the Left, joining Delbrück,

Harnack, Tröltsch, and other colleagues at Berlin in counter-working Tirpitz and the *Vaterlandspartei*. Though convinced that their government had never wished for war, neither Oncken nor Meinecke suggested that it had been free from blame. The latter, in particular, recognized the estrangement of England by the *Flottenpolitik* to have been a blunder of the first magnitude. None of the German scholars expected or desired the return of the Hohenzollerns.

There was much to see and hear in Vienna apart from the activities of the Summer School. The praises of Dr. Schober, President of Police, were on all lips. He had been Chancellor once already and it was expected that his turn would come again. A talk with him left the impression of a capable and tactful man who would employ force only in the last resort. Though the Socialists would naturally have liked to see one of themselves in his strategic position, they preferred him to any other bourgeois official. Except for the police they dominated the administration of the capital, and had much to show for their so-called extravagance. The working-class dwellings were the admiration of the world, and their care for the welfare of children was beyond praise. There was still acute suffering among the middle classes who had lost their all in the inflation and received neither pension nor dole, but a good deal was being done for their relief. We were some-times told that the Viennese ask little more from life than to sip their coffee and whipped cream in an open-air café in the Wiener Wald and listen to the waltz music of Johann Strauss: they are certainly much less political than the citizens of some other capitals. Viennese children are said to possess exceptional artistic gifts, and I witnessed the hunger for adult education in the huge classes at the People's University whither I was taken by Professor Ludo Hartmann. The learned historian of Medieval Italy, who had adopted socialism in middle life and had represented the Republic in Berlin, was fired by the ideal of an educated democracy. My visit to Austria occurred at perhaps the happiest moment in the life of the little Republic. I was warned by some financial experts that it could not live under the new economic conditions and that union with Germany or a Danubian federation was essential, but the experiment was young and there was hope in the air.

A summer in Saxony in 1925 enabled me to sample the atmosphere five years after my last visit. The catastrophe of the mark in 1923 was spoken of with the same horror as the 'Turnip Winter' of 1916–17. The savings and investments of a thrifty people had melted away, leaving little except land and houses above the flood. It was a shattering blow to the professional classes, but the stabilization of the currency had begun to revive confidence, savings were resumed, and the unemployment figures were low. Stresemann was at the helm and the Locarno Pact was within sight. The Communists were weak and the moderate parties in control. Germany was slowly recovering, thanks to the national tradition of hard work, and the Weimar system appeared fairly safe. The Hitler *putsch* of 1923 seemed to have been a storm in a tea-cup and on this visit I never heard his name.

A week in Munich was followed by two months in Zürich, where our stay in a sanatorium was enlivened by the society of two old friends. Professor Alfred Stern, a Frankfurt Jew, had taught history for half a century in Switzerland, the neutral atmosphere of which facilitated the cool detachment of his ten big volumes on Europe in the Nineteenth Century. No French, German or Austrian historian has written so dispassionately on the creation of the Hohenzollern Empire as the veteran scholar who at eighty remained as active in body as in mind. A greater contrast could not be imagined than Friedrich Wilhelm Förster, who had played much the same role in Germany during the war as Bertrand Russell and Morel in England or Romain Rolland in France. He had been deprived of his Chair at Munich, and even when the Bismarckian edifice was a memory he preferred to live abroad. We had met in London at Toynbee Hall thirty years before, and I had followed his career with interest. His books on ethics, pedagogy and the Youth Movement revealed a teacher of rare nobility. He was filled with the significance of his mission and convinced of the sinfulness of his foes. Though a Prussian himself, he believed that the Prussian spirit had not been changed by the war, and concluded that France had a right to be afraid. The sunshine of Locarno left him cold. He defended French policy in the press and welcomed Emil Ludwig's vivisection of the Kaiser. He was an earnest and able man, ready at any moment to go to the stake for his principles, but his shrill indictment of German policy damaged the cause it was intended to serve.

Three years later, in 1928, the International Historical Congress met in Oslo. When the last quinquennial meeting had been held at Brussels in 1923, the bitter memories of the war forbade the participation of German and Austrian scholars, and I was not tempted to attend a Congress international only in name. Ten years had now passed since the restoration of peace, and a neutral capital enabled ex-combatants to meet at last. The sovereigns were kind enough to invite some of us to tea at the palace and received us with the unpretentious simplicity which the Norwegians prefer. The insecurity of the new state, it was believed in 1905, could be overcome by the choice of a well-connected prince, and we had learned from the official biography of King Edward how eagerly he supported the Danish husband of his daughter Maud. Yet Norway was republican at heart, and in 1928 there was not much romance in the relationship between dynasty and people. King Haakon was the ideal figure-head, and Prince Olaf, who had been transplanted as a child, was regarded as virtually a native. The Queen, on the other hand, had never entirely won the hearts of the people, and her lengthy sojourns in England revealed her unchanging preference for the land of her birth. She had inherited her mother's outspoken dislike for Germany.

Historians had gathered in hundreds, and the fifth International Congress was opened in the spacious aula of the University. We were welcomed by the Prime Minister, but the main burden of a crowded week was borne by Professor Koht, soon to become Foreign Minister. His tact, friendliness and knowledge of languages made him an ideal chief, and the atmosphere was never seriously ruffled. A few Germans complained of coolness in the attitude of some of their late British enemies, but the presence of neutrals eased the situation. I was glad to make the acquaintance of Pierre Renouvin, then and now the best French authority on the origins of the First World War. With Pirenne, vivacious as ever, I discussed the growth of the Flemish movement which was transforming his own University of Ghent. The German Delegation was headed by Oncken, the Austrian by Srbik. Dembinski, fluent in four languages besides his own, and Handelsman spoke for Poland; Yorga, formerly tutor of King Carol and before long to be Prime Minister of Romania, came from Bucharest. Pokrovsky, the loneliest figure in the Congress, symbolized the revolution in Russia. His lecture on the Russian Autocracy expounded the new orthodoxy of Marx, and the historical drama revolved round the conception of the class war. He had returned from exile in France when Lenin seized power and had been appointed head of the archives, producing at intervals tit-bits of secret diplomacy in the *Krasny Archiv*; now he was busy with a large-scale publication of Foreign Office documents. His erudition was incontestable, but he was the slave of his formulae. He struck me as an efficient Marxist machine without much warm blood in his veins. My first conversation with a leading Bolshevist scholar proved that there was even less opening in Russia for critical historians under the new dispensation than under the Tsars.

The contrast between the two halves of the Scandinavian peninsula strikes every visitor. While Norway is among the most democratic communities in Europe, Sweden is the aristocrat of the north. The King possesses more influence than most of his tribe, the old noble families are still in evidence, and the Social Democrats coo like doves. It is a land of political equilibrium, culture and tradition, and I was assured by Professor Hecksher, the eminent economist, that Sweden was the most prosperous country in the Old World. The vast rectangular palace breathes strength and self-confidence, and in the Riddarholm Church lie the heroes of the house of Vasa. None of the smaller European states except Holland can boast such rulers as Gustavus Vasa, Gustavus Adolphus and Charles XII. Swedish Imperialism died with the latter, but its trophies adorn the churches, museums and palaces. No public building of our time has received so many compliments as the Town Hall, but I was more impressed by Gripsholm, some forty miles away, its dark red Vasa towers mirrored in the lake. Amalienholm, a few miles up the broad Mälar, is purely French. Uppsala on its hill is a place of memories, and in the Gothic manuscript of Ulfilas it possesses the earliest specimen of any Teutonic tongue.

Among the manifold activities of the Carnegie Peace Endowment was the establishment of a Chair of International Politics in the newly founded Hochschule für Politik at Berlin. The original intention was that foreign scholars should reside for a term or a year, and I was invited to be its first occupant. Since a long absence from home was impossible for others as well as for myself, the Carnegie Chair was transformed into Carnegie Lectures. At the opening of 1929 I gave two addresses on Grey's foreign policy from 1905 to 1909, the latter date being determined by the fact that the *British Documents on the Origins of the War*, edited by Professor Temperley and myself, had only reached that point. I prepared myself for the task by a talk with Lord Grey at Brooks's Club on February 14.

I. Your policy, as I understand it, was based on three principles—two old, one new. The first was supremacy at sea.

G. Yes, but leaving the United States out of account. I never regarded the Two-Power standard as applying to them.

I. The second was the Balance of Power.

G. I don't like that phrase.

I. I mean by it what you have expressed as follows: 'England has always drifted or deliberately gone into opposition to any Power which establishes a hegemony in Europe.'

G. Thus interpreted, I accept it.

I. Your third principle was friendship with France.

G. Yes.

I. You also took over from Lansdowne the policy of a *rapprochement* with Russia. Nearly all foreign and some English writers make you responsible for the great change over from isolation to what I call Continentalism. It seems to me that the new lines were laid down by Lansdowne rather than by you.

G. That is so.

I. You said during the war that you believed there were no records here of Bernardiston's conversations in Brussels.

G. They were purely academic.

I. They have been found in the War Office. The men who may have known about them had all gone to the war.

G. Are you going to publish them?

I. They were published in our third volume last December. Did you read any parts of that volume?

G. No, I can read so little.

I. If you had consulted the Cabinet in January 1906 about your conversations with Cambon, as you now admit would have been wise, would you have met with opposition? In other words, would it have made any real difference to history?

G. I don't think so. Campbell-Bannerman and Ripon, as well as Asquith and Haldane, knew and approved. We should doubtless have had criticism but not, I should say, opposition. It was impossible to refuse the French request for military consultations: that would have been to undo all the work of 1904–5. Besides, we made it clear that we were to remain absolutely uncommitted.

I. General Huguet, in his book, says that you, Haldane and Campbell-Bannerman were too clever not to realize that these conversations and arrangements constituted something like a moral engagement.

G. If that had been the case, Cambon would have said so in 1914, whereas he only appealed to our interests.

I. Cambon spoke very differently to Wickham Steed when he asked if the word honour was to be blotted out of the English language.

G. We always made it clear that the conversations left the Governments absolutely free, and we stated it in the letters of 1912, which I think reassured some of my colleagues.

I. Cambon thought that the Liberal maximum might have been only a Conservative minimum. Would the Conservatives have gone further to meet French wishes and been ready to make an alliance?

G. Some Conservatives would have liked to do so, but it would have been impossible. Public opinion would have been opposed to it.

I. The more I study the documents the more I feel that our friendship with France, once made, rendered real friendship with Germany impossible. Bülow admits in his book that the gulf between France and Germany was too wide to be bridged. France was suspicious of all our approaches to Germany; and German policy in Morocco and in regard to the fleet made friendly relations with us difficult. Your task was pretty hopeless.

G. As long as Holstein was there, nothing could be done.

I. Holstein was half cracked.

G. And Bülow was false. Look at his treatment of Chamberlain.

I. I should prefer the word slippery.

G. Yes, slippery is better.

I. There were difficulties on this side also. I am impressed by Eyre Crowe's intense hostility to Germany.

G. Crowe was anti-German. But I don't think the Minutes of officials ought to be published, or they will be afraid to write them.

I. They add greatly to the interest and value of diplomatic publications. Sir Austen Chamberlain has given us a free hand, except as regards obviously hasty and unconsidered Minutes, which we have no desire to publish.

I. I have always regretted that you authorized Lloyd George's Mansion House speech and did not keep the Agadir issue in your own hands.

G. But Germany had sent me no reply; and did it not prevent war?

I. Possibly, though I don't think it was so near as that. The Kaiser and Bethmann were opposed to war over Morocco. But it made very bad blood, played into the hands of Tirpitz and the militarists, and led to the increase of armaments.

G. That is very interesting. If it is the case, it shows how bad the situation in Europe was. They began it by sending a ship to Agadir.

I. The Germans think that France began it by the occupation of Fez.

I. Foreigners find it difficult to believe that you never inquired about the details of the naval discussions with Russia.

G. I did not, and I believe very little was actually done. In any case there could have been nothing affecting naval strategy like the Mediterranean agreement of 1912, which was important.

I. In July 1914 the ideal would have been for you to state in good time what we should do. But I know that was impossible, as the Cabinet was divided.

G. Quite impossible.

I. You were widely blamed for not urging Russia to abstain from any irrevocable step which might start hostilities.

G. I resent that criticism. After Germany refused the Conference I could not put pressure on Russia. She was far less prepared for war than Germany. If I had tried to hold back her military preparations, Sazonoff would at once have said: 'Then will you help us if war comes?' It was for Germany to hold back Austria, who was her ally, and to whom therefore she had a right to speak. She should have pressed Berchtold to accept the Conference.

I. She dared not do so. The German Government did not want war, but it had given Austria *carte blanche* and could not regain control of the situation. And it was genuinely afraid of losing its only dependable ally. The Austrians did not want a patched up settlement with Serbia, and they had such bitter memories of the Ambassadors' Conference during the Balkan wars that they would not look at the idea. This was thoroughly understood at Berlin.

G. I agree that neither the Kaiser nor Bethmann nor Jagow wanted war. But why should they be afraid of losing Austria? What could she do?

I. Germany was convinced that the alliance was at stake if she declined to play up, and she dreaded isolation.

I. Many writers, here and abroad, while fully recognizing your desire for peace, argue that you allowed our friends to make the pace. We were a satiated Power; they were not. We had indeed made up our quarrels with them, but in doing so we got mixed up in their quarrels with other people.

G. That is only partially true. We should never have supported France in aggression.

I. Of course not, and she knew it. But she was tied to Russia, who was both ambitious and untrustworthy.

G. Russia was like a big ship without a rudder. There was no real control. Think of Hartwig at Teheran. War was not inevitable in 1914, but it was almost inevitable some time on account of the state of Europe with its balance of power, alliances and armaments. That is why I am so keen on the League, Locarno, and disarmament. It was a very bad mistake to attribute the whole responsibility for the war to the Central Power in the Treaty of Versailles, as I have said in the Preface to the cheap edition of my book.

My views on war origins were known to German specialists, but no English historian had as yet explained the broad outlines of our policy to a mixed audience in German and in the German capital. The Hochschule für Politik was unable to accommodate the six hundred ticket-holders, and the ceremony was transferred to the University. In addition to the students many members of the staffs of the Hochschule and the University were present, as well as the British Ambassador. The policy of a statesman, I began, could only be understood in relation to the tradition of his country. The two governing principles of British policy for centuries had been the command of our home waters and the preservation of the Balance of Power. These were the key to Grey's activities and to those of his predecessors. The notion that commercial envy had decided our course was fantastic, and a plan for isolating Germany had never entered his head. The causes of the lamentable estrangement were the construction of a formidable fleet and the menace to France in Morocco in 1905 and 1911. The former, as Count Metternich had repeatedly emphasized in his dispatches from London, was bound to alarm an island people dependent for its daily bread on its exports and imports; the latter inevitably strengthened the ties between the signatories of the Treaty of 1904. Though the legal right of Germany to take these steps was incontestable, the result had proved disastrous to her interests. The Franco-Russian alliance was an annoyance rather than a danger, for the Triple Alliance could look after itself. The formation of the Triple Entente, on the other hand, transformed the European situation by the addition of England to Germany's potential antagonists, and no one expected Italy to expose her long coastline to the guns of the British fleet for the sake of Vienna and Berlin. I presented the policy of Lansdowne and Grey as an automatic reaction to the policy of the Wilhelmstrasse: possessing all we desired, our supreme interest was the maintenance of peace. Satiated Powers do not make wars.

It was a pleasure to renew acquaintance with old friends like Meinecke and Oncken, and to meet academic veterans such as Max Lenz and Erich Marcks, the biographers of Bismarck, and Delbrück, historian of the art of war. The latter, then in his eighty-first year, was wonderfully vigorous, and his mind had moved with the times. He had fought in 1870, tutored Waldemar, a younger brother of the Kaiser, sat in the Reichstag as an Independent Conservative, edited the *Preussische Jahrbücher*, and accepted the Weimar Republic without a pang. He admitted the mistakes of William II and his Chancellors, while stoutly denying that they had ever desired a war; and in resounding attacks on Ludendorff he denounced the man who in the spring offensive of 1918 had staked the national cause on a gambler's throw. In addition to the Carnegie Lectures in German on Grey, I was invited to address the students of the English Department in my own tongue. I attempted to explain our policy in the Dominions, India and Ireland, our relations with the Great Powers and the League, the decline of the Liberal Party, the rise of Labour, the burden of the unemployed. As Professor Dibelius, the head of the Department, had lauded our political instinct in his well-known volumes on England, I reminded my hearers that we had enjoyed centuries of experience, and I saw no reason why Germany should not acquire the art of self-government with time and patience. Before the war most Germans had trusted their government: now they must have confidence in themselves.

At parties kindly given for me by the British Ambassador,

Dr. Becker, Minister for Education, the Hochschule für Politik
and by personal friends I was enabled to meet most of the leading
figures in public life. Dr. Becker, one of Germany's leading
Orientalists, I had known since the Historical Congress of 1913,
and I rejoiced at the promotion of this enlightened scholar. An
equally attractive figure was the venerable Dr. Schmidt-Ott, head
of the Notgemeinschaft der Deutschen Wissenschaft created to
sustain learning and learned institutions during the lean years.
Among the politicians I was glad to make the acquaintance of
Breitscheid, the orator of the Socialists, and Severing, the working-class Minister of the Interior. The former, a refined Intellectual, always saw the difficulties of a situation more clearly
than the way out. The latter reminded me of certain figures in the
British Labour movement. Quiet and self-possessed in manner, he
was regarded as one of the pillars of the Republic. I was still more
impressed by the quiet strength of General von Seekt, the Scharn-
horst of the new German army which the Allies vainly expected
to keep within the limits imposed at Versailles. Since the monkey
tricks of Ludendorff and his second wife had sickened his
followers, Seekt had emerged as the hope of the Right. One heard
that he had Presidential ambitions, and in his book *The Future of
Germany* he expressed his conviction that Presidents should not
be afraid of responsibility. Combining military prestige with a
powerful will, the General, I felt, might well make history. A very
different figure was Meissner, Political Secretary successively of
Ebert and Hindenburg. An experienced official of the Foreign
Office, he had the slightly impersonal manner of the Civil Servant,
and no one could foresee what an important part he was to play
in the overthrow of the Republic.

Herr von Schubert, whom I had met in London, was now
Permanent Under-Secretary of the Foreign Office. We know from
Lord d'Abernon's diaries how helpful he had been in fashioning
the Locarno Pact, and what a high opinion our Ambassador
entertained of Stresemann's right hand man. He likened him to a
heavy cavalry dragoon, and indeed the burly figure was curiously
unlike the prim official type. He possessed large private means,
and no one in Berlin entertained so lavishly. I was invited to one
of his monster dinner-parties, forty-eight people sitting down at
three large circular tables. He hoped to succeed Sthamer at the

Court of St. James's, but he was appointed to Rome instead. The waiters stood in a row as we all trooped away, expecting and receiving tips from the guests. I was familiar with the difference of national habit, but this authorized mendicancy always jars on British notions of hospitality.

Among my hosts was Dr. von Wegerer, Director of the Zentralstelle für Erforschung der Kriegsursachen. I had studied *Die Kriegsschuldfrage*, his monthly organ, from the beginning, and I sympathized with the effort to disprove the charge that Germany was solely responsible for the war. Wegerer, an ex-officer, was assisted by experts, several of whom were gathered to meet me. The President of the society and the *doyen* of our company was Raschdau, the last survivor of the Bismarckian Foreign Office, one of Holstein's many victims and the author of delightful reminiscences. The most indefatigable champion of the German cause was Count Montgelas, grandson of the Savoyard Minister who had transformed Bavaria into a modern state a century before. A general on active service at the outbreak of hostilities, he had resigned his command in 1915 in disapproval of certain methods of waging war and had devoted himself to the study of the causes of the catastrophe. His principal work, translated into English as *The Case for the Central Powers*, was familiar to students, and a little volume on Grey, a much slighter performance, appeared in America. I had more to learn from Jagow who had succeeded Kiderlen at the Foreign Office at the opening of 1913 and had helped Bethmann to shape German policy in 1914. His views were familiar from his book, and I remembered the friendly reference to him in the *Reminiscences* of Sir Rennell Rodd, his old colleague in Rome. He condemned Bülow as a man without principle who dared not tell the Kaiser the truth; repudiated the assertion that Tirpitz or Moltke had any share in the control of policy; and argued that Austria would have regarded a German refusal of her appeal for support in July 1914 as a rupture of the alliance. I reminded him of Szögenyi's statement that, in telling him of Grey's proposal for a Conference, he (Jagow) added that the German Government was not in favour of it and only passed it on out of necessity; and I ventured to remark that most Englishmen believed the statement of the Austrian Ambassador. Jagow replied that Szögenyi was really past work; he

(Jagow) had merely said that Germany would not leave her ally in the lurch.

A talk with Kühlmann in his sumptuous flat in the Wilhelm-strasse was far more interesting. He looked hardly a day older than when I had seen him in London before the war. Since his eviction from the Foreign Office in 1917 by Hindenburg and Ludendorff for declaring that the war could not be won by arms alone he had devoted himself to business. It seemed a pity that a man of such ability, energy and long diplomatic experience should not have been employed by the Republic. Like most people from the Kaiser downwards he despised Bülow, had a friendly word for the exile at Doorn, and deplored the influence of Tirpitz. He had never believed war to be inevitable. Grey sought peace, he declared, and the cry of *revanche* was dying down in France as the older generation left the stage. A naval agreement might perhaps have followed the colonial agreements completed on the eve of the war. Unfortunately while Anglo-German relations had improved, Vienna had wrested the control of the Austro-German alliance from the feeble hands of Berlin and war with Russia became difficult to avert. If Kiderlen had lived he would never have given Berchtold a blank cheque and would probably have kept the peace. History, he believed, would speak of the conflict as the war of the dissolution of the Austrian Empire.

In the autumn of the same year (1929) I paid my first visit to Geneva since it became the international capital of the world. The Tenth Assembly of the League was a memorable gathering. The British Delegation, led by Ramsay MacDonald and Arthur Henderson, William Graham and Lord Cecil, obviously meant business. Sir Austen Chamberlain, I learned, had been called 'the Everlasting No', and there was general rejoicing when Great Britain seemed about to assert her moral leadership. The Prime Minister announced our signature of the so-called Optional Clause pledging us to submit justiciable disputes to the Permanent Court at the Hague. A few minor Powers had already signed, but it was not till we gave the signal that the rest came trooping in. Not less constructive and sincere were the speeches of the Foreign Secretary and the President of the Board of Trade. It was Willie Graham's first appearance at Geneva, where his modesty and mastery of economic problems were universally recognized. He outlined a plan for a tariff holiday, but the demon of economic nationalism proved too powerful to be exorcized. Arthur Henderson's proposal to transform the officials of the League into permanent Civil Servants was a welcome indication that it had come to stay. The Foreign Secretary, who was in the best of spirits, had come straight from the Hague, where he had spent a *mauvais quart d'heure* at the side of his unbending colleague Philip Snowden in settling details of the Young Plan, and he was relieved that the discussion with France had ended without a break.

I had heard so much of Briand for over twenty years that I watched the old statesman mount the platform with keen anticipation. He spoke for three-quarters of an hour without a note, and every word was in its place, though as a dramatic performance it could not compare with the oration in which he had welcomed Germany into the League and declared that both nations had had enough of glory. His plan for a United States of Europe, though merely outlined, struck the imagination of the Assembly and for the rest of my stay it became the main topic of conversation. Was he the mouthpiece of Count Coudenhove-Kalergi and the Pan-Europa school? Was he out to construct a new bulwark for the *status quo* which suited France? Was the plan primarily economic or mainly political? Was it to be a rival or a supplement to the League? That such questions could be asked was a proof of the vagueness of the project. Though its author diffused a little more light at a lunch-hour address to journalists in his hotel, it was months before the promised memorandum was dispatched and the replies, including our own, were so negative that the project was dropped.

The leader of the German Delegation presented a striking contrast to the eloquent Frenchman. Stresemann's ugly face and bull neck had been familiar for years, and Locarno had made him a world figure, but the reality was different from expectation. We knew that he was ill, but the shrunken frame and ashen face were a shock. He pulled himself together for his speech, but he was a dying man, and a slight stroke in the previous year was a warning. He travelled with his doctor, his nurse and his cook, declined all social invitations, and went backwards and forwards to the Assembly from his bed. It was his swan-song to which I had listened and a month later he was dead. The story of his gallant fight for life was told a year later in Antonina Vallentin's biography of the greatest German statesman of the Weimar era. The German Delegation regretted that the spirit of Thoiry had borne so little fruit, but none of them questioned the wisdom of the Locarno policy. Among other old acquaintances at Geneva were Count Mensdorff and August Zaleski. The ex-Ambassador bore the collapse of the Hapsburg Empire with simple dignity; the latter was the same quiet and thoughtful man I had known in London during the war. When I remarked on the incredible change in his fortunes since our last meeting, the Polish Foreign Secretary replied: 'Yes, even now I sometimes wake up in the night and ask myself if it is not all a dream.' The Grand Old Man of the Assembly was Count Albert Apponyi. His hair had whitened since I heard him in Westminster Hall in 1906, for he was now over eighty; but he was still vigorous in mind and body, and his towering stature made him the most decorative figure on the crowded stage.

In August 1932 I took part for the first time in the annual Summer School in Geneva organized by the League of Nations Union. My tasks were to open the proceedings by a survey of the world situation during the previous year, and at a later stage to assess the first results of the Japanese attack on China. Sir George Paish reviewed the economic situation; Lees-Smith, ex-Minister of Education, spoke on India; Professor Rappard, co-founder with Professor Paul Mantoux of the Institut des Etudes Internationales, summarized the recent work of the League; William Martin, the influential editor of the *Journal de Genève*, criticized projects for a European union as inimical to the wider interests of the League; Dr. Sherwood Eddy, the indefatigable organizer of American travel parties, spoke from direct experience of the seizure of Mukden by the Japanese troops in September 1931; Professor Manley Hudson, the Harvard jurist, concluded a sketch of the relations of the United States with the League by the forecast that his country would in due course become a member as was hoped by numerous Americans in the audience. Some of the addresses, according to custom, were published in the well-known series entitled *Problems of Peace*. Many of the British contingent were teachers, several of whom were paying their first visit to

Geneva. To such young men and women—for most of them were young—these summer schools were an inspiration. Our meetings were held in the hall where the Council of the League met three times a year. A few yards away was the room in which the Disarmament Conference held its first ineffectual sessions. Within a short walk was the International Labour Office, standing in its beautiful grounds on the edge of the lake, in which the furniture and decorations had been presented by the members of the League, each contributing some characteristic specimen of its national art. In so far as the post-war world had a capital it was here.

The atmospheric difference between 1929 and 1932, the date of my second visit, was felt at once. The barometer had fallen: there was less faith, less hope, less drive. The rape of Manchuria had revealed the impotence of the League in dealing with a powerful offender. Geneva was waiting for the Lytton Report, but even if it contained the anticipated condemnation of Japanese aggression what could be done? It had no force of its own and none of its members was ready to take risks. Japan had chosen the moment of the great slump to strike her felon blow. I found the Chinese plenipotentiary a little less pessimistic than the members of the Secretariat. Though Japan was militarily invulnerable, he argued, her Achilles heel was finance; she was a poor country and China's passive resistance would wear her out. She had gained the first round, as aggressors usually do, but she need not win the game.

The Geneva sky was darkened not only by the conflict in the Far East but by the disappointments of the Disarmament Conference. It had met in February and adjourned in July without positive result. Arthur Henderson's courage and skill as Chairman were gratefully recognized, but I heard a good deal of criticism of the British Government. Great Britain, it was complained, sought only the reductions which suited her needs. If, as we are often told, there is a 'Geneva spirit', there is also a Geneva opinion, and in this case it was clear enough: we lost the opportunity of giving the vigorous push with which the Americans had launched the Washington Conference in 1922. British prestige stood as low in the summer of 1932 as it had been high in the summer of 1929. Our Foreign Secretary Sir John Simon lacked

Henderson's gift of making friends, and in some quarters he was unjustly suspected of a certain sympathy with Japan and a lukewarm zeal for disarmament. Ramsay MacDonald, the titular head of a predominantly Conservative team, was regarded as no longer an effective champion of the League, and was believed to prefer direct settlements between the Great Powers if they could be achieved. The 'sunshine of Locarno' had faded, for Japan was on the war path, Mussolini was speaking of the Mediterranean as *mare nostrum*, and Hitler was impatiently awaiting his call. Storm signals were out all over the globe. Though no one talked openly of a second world war there was little sign of confidence in an enduring peace.

APPENDIX TO CHAPTER 16

CONVERSATION WITH KÜHLMANN, 22 FEBRUARY, 1929
(In English)

K. Grey was a great gentleman and he sought peace, but he was not a strong man. I doubt if he was always his own master.

I. Of whom are you thinking?

K. Tyrrell. He was the strongest influence in the Foreign Office.

I. But do you consider he was anti-German?

K. No. He saw the danger of being tied too closely to France.

I. May I ask your opinion of Bülow and the Kaiser?

K. I have no respect for Bülow. He was a *Kleber*: he had no system or principles, except that he wanted to stay in office. I have always liked the Kaiser, and I wrote to him a week or two ago on his seventieth birthday.

I. I know that you deplored the Tirpitz policy.

K. Yes. I agreed with Metternich in deploring that policy, but I did not share his belief that failure to reach a naval agreement involved a total failure to improve Anglo-German relations. I preferred the discussion of concrete colonial problems. Lulu Harcourt and I sketched out a satisfactory African settlement. A naval agreement might have been possible after a colonial agreement. I always regarded the German desire for a neutrality formula as hopeless.

I. Grey inherited the commitment to France and therefore could not make real friends with Germany.

K. Not at once. But with time the older French generation would die out and the younger would think less and less about Alsace-

Lorraine. I was in close touch with Paris all those pre-war years, and several influential Frenchmen told me privately that they regarded Alsace-Lorraine as a closed question.

I. They never dared to say so publicly.

K. Time would have helped. Bethmann's Constitution of 1911 was a step. The gradual cessation of complaints from Alsace-Lorraine to Paris would have made a *rapprochement* possible. I was at Tangier in 1905. I wished to get a good price for consenting to France having a free hand in Morocco. I was for hard bargaining but not for threatening. I was asked by French friends to suggest an arrangement. I replied that I thought Germany should yield on Morocco in return for the whole of the French Congo and the pre-emption of the Belgian Congo.

I. You anticipated Kiderlen's idea of concentrating on a Central African Empire?

K. Yes. Holstein prevented such a bargain. He was the real author of the first Morocco crisis and Bülow could not stand up against him.

K. What did Sazonoff say to Grey at Balmoral in 1912?

I. I am afraid I must not quote our documents after 1909 before they are published.

K. He must have thoroughly alarmed Grey about a Balkan explosion, for the Foreign Office then became extremely anxious for Anglo-German co-operation.

K. I was spending a week-end at Polesden Lacy (Mrs. Ronald Greville's country house) about 1913. The visitors' book there would give the date. Iswolsky was there. I shall never forget our conversation. He said Russia would give any terms to Germany if she would desert Austria and allow Russia to smash her. He was not anti-German, but he was passionately anxious for war with Austria.

I. What a curious legend it was that you were mischief-making in Ulster just before the war!

K. Yes. I was recalled from my leave in Germany at the end of July, 1914. On reaching London I went to Haldane's house on the afternoon of Sunday, 2 August. I advised England to stand out at first, and then, after the first shock of arms, to dictate peace by a threat of intervention. Only thus could the war be localized and shortened, and the complete exhaustion of one side or the other be prevented. Haldane was interested, seemed to sympathize with the idea, and said he would bring it before the Cabinet for discussion. Grey now appeared, and I restated my view. He replied in effect that he had an honourable obligation to France. I was surprised by the picture of Haldane as warlike in Morley's Memorandum on Resignation. His talk on 2 August with me was quite the reverse.

K. The world war, in my view, was the war of the dissolution of the Austrian Empire. Franco-German relations would probably have improved with time, and Anglo-German relations were over the worst. Both these problems were infinitely simpler than the Austro-Russian antagonism. War was difficult to avert if Vienna, not Berlin, was in control.

I. As she was from the coming of Aehrenthal till 1914.

K. Yes, except when Kiderlen was in command. Had he lived he would not have given Austria a blank cheque on 5 July 1914, and he would probably have prevented war.

I. Lichnowsky also thought that the war was caused by Berlin surrendering the leadership to Vienna.

K. Lichnowsky had family reasons (through his father) as well as political conviction for his hostility to Austria.

I. Jagow denies that Berlin was taken in tow by Vienna.

K. That is because he was in office himself, but it is true.

CONVERSATION WITH JAGOW, 27 FEBRUARY, 1929
(*In German*)

I. Have you seen Sir Rennell Rodd's very friendly references to you in the third volume of his *Reminiscences*?

J. Yes. I was always for good relations with England, and so was the Kaiser. He used to talk loudly and wildly, but I could always tell him what I thought when we were alone together. When I pointed out the objections to any policy or proposal, he was very reasonable. Tirpitz had great influence, but Bülow is chiefly to blame for the estrangement with England. He had no political principles, no system, except to stay in power. He did not dare to tell the Kaiser the truth.

I. He had fallen from power before your appointment as Foreign Minister. Did you know him well?

J. Very well indeed.

I. I fear Bethmann's task was hopeless, and yours too. You were both called in too late. The harm was done. Equally I feel that Grey could not be friends with France and Germany at the same time. The choice had been made before he took office.

J. Yes, the situation was pretty hopeless. War was practically inevitable, not necessarily in 1914 but some time.

I. I regret Germany gave Austria *carte blanche* on 5 July, 1914. Of course you had to stand by her, but why did you not insist on her consulting you at every step?

J. We did not give her *carte blanche*. We expected she would tell us about the ultimatum in good time. I was continually asking Szögenyi for news.

I. I think you ought to have asked not only to be informed but to have been consulted about the ultimatum, for it was obviously a dangerous path. Yet the Kaiser always said that the matter was entirely one for Francis Joseph to decide. And many believe that Tschirschky was a firebrand. What do you think of his role?

J. Tschirschky carried out his instructions and did not exceed them, but he was a pessimist. He did not work or wish for war, but he expected it.

I. Szögenyi reported to Vienna that, in telling him of Grey's proposal for a conference, you said that the German Government was not in favour of it, and only handed it on because you had to do so. You have denied this, but most people in England prefer Szögenyi's report to your subsequent denial.

J. I know that, but I never said anything of the sort. Szögenyi was really past work. Some time before Serajevo one of the Foreign Office officials said to me: 'Somebody must always look through Szögenyi's reports before they go to Vienna.' I never said more to him than that we would not leave Austria in the lurch.

I. Grey believes that you, Bethmann and the Kaiser desired peace, but he thinks the military element wanted war and pushed you on.

J. Nothing of the sort. Tirpitz was on holiday and was not consulted. Nor was Moltke consulted till the end. The control of our policy was entirely in civilian hands.

I. I regret that you only put pressure on Austria so late.

J. That would have been time enough if Russia had not made war inevitable. We had warned Russia of the effects of such a step. We did put pressure on Austria, but Grey never tried to hold Russia back.

I. Grey says he had no *locus standi*. We were not allies, and he could do nothing more after the rejection of his plan for a conference. He says you were the people to hold Austria back, as you were allies. He thinks there was no danger of you losing Austria if you had taken a strong line, for she could not do without you.

J. That is not the case. She could make friends with France, and then reach some agreement with Russia about the Near East.

I. Any such arrangement would have been a triumph for Russia. We think you could and should have pressed Austria more than Russia. Each of us feared the loss of our friend or ally. The European system was the main cause of the war. Germany was dragged in by Austria, England and France by Russia. It was an East European quarrel.

J. That is so.

17

AMERICAN INTERLUDE

INVITATIONS reached me before and since the war of 1914 to teach history for a term in one or other American University, but in 1925 a call to lecture at the Lowell Institute in Boston proved irresistible. A prolonged breakdown in health postponed the visit till the spring of 1927 when I crossed in the congenial company of Professor Graham Wallas. He had visited America at intervals during a period of thirty years, and I could have desired no better chaperon. We stayed for a week at the Harvard Club in New York, which had been Theodore Roosevelt's headquarters in New York and which was filled with portraits of 'the Colonel'. No traveller can forget the overwhelming impression as the skyscrapers of Manhattan and Brooklyn loom up out of the sea on a misty morning. A house dating from before the Civil War was regarded as an antiquity, and modern dwellings of four, five and six floors were being torn down to make way for their giant successors. It is fortunate that Central Park was laid out before the northward trend raised the value of land to astronomical heights. The Art Museum could not compare with the treasures of our European capitals, but the priceless Pierpont Morgan Library, housed in McKim's exquisite little marble palace, can hold its own against the world. Invited to name some author I drew a bow at a venture and said 'Keats', a monosyllable which produced an array of portraits, manuscripts and first editions.

Thirty years ago it was something of a novelty to receive a wireless invitation to lunch from Colonel House in mid-Atlantic and to dispatch a reply. His beautiful flat in New York was full of Wilson memories, and Professor Charles Seymour of Yale, the editor of his papers, was there with a dozen others to meet me.

Our host's annual visits to Europe, where he looked up his former Paris comrades, Balfour and Cecil, Clemenceau and Orlando, kept him in touch with the Old World, and his belief that the United States would eventually enter the League was unchanged. During my tour I received several first-hand accounts of the personality of the late President. In New York, next to Colonel House himself, my chief informants were David Houston, his Minister of Agriculture, and Henry Morgenthau, his Ambassador at Constantinople. The sharpest criticism came from an old friend who shared his ideals and maintained that he had betrayed them. I had known Oswald Garrison Villard for many years and admired his work for international understanding. I felt, however, that the editor of the *Nation* did not always make sufficient allowance for the difficulties of statesmen, and that with a little executive experience he might have been a milder judge. He reminded me of my old friends Mackarness and Friedrich Wilhelm Förster in the loftiness of his principles and the severity of his verdicts. There had been no greater admirer of Wilson's early years at the White House, but the decision to enter the world war transformed the disciple into an angry foe. The grandson of Garrison the abolitionist was a born crusader, and he sensed dangers ahead in unchecked capitalism and Imperialist temptations in Central America.

I heard the same sort of talk from the staff of the *New Republic*, the rival Liberal weekly, which was a good deal less radical than the *Nation*. The editor, Herbert Croly, was one of the most thoughtful of American journalists, and the historian Charles Beard was at the height of his fame. Walter Lippmann, the youngest and most influential of the team, today the *doyen* of American publicists, used to drop in at the Harvard Club for a talk. All these men were the enemies of Imperialism and plutocracy in the New as well as the Old World. While the leading articles in the best papers were well up to our British standard, I starved for full knowledge of the life of Europe and the wider world till the belated arrival of my copy of *The Times*. Some of my American friends took the *Christian Science Monitor* for its excellent foreign intelligence. The Hearst journals proved even more lowbrow than I expected.

Intellectuals in the Atlantic States seemed as anxious to hear the

comments of an Englishman on the problems of the Old World
as I to learn their views of the New. I was entertained by the
Foreign Policy Association, a non-party organization, and at a
dinner presided over by Professor Coolidge, editor of *Foreign
Affairs*, at both of which I spoke on British foreign policy. It was
easier for such audiences than for the average American citizen to
realize that the days of isolation were gone, and I found the same
wide-minded concern for the fate of Europe in Columbia University. I had often met the President, Dr. Nicholas Murray Butler,
Chairman of the Carnegie Peace Endowment, Professor Shotwell,
the editor of the vast Carnegie series on the Social and Economic
History of the War, and other members of the staff. It was a relief
to pass from the noisy streets to the heights crowned by the
University buildings and McKim's noble library. Grant's tomb
is close at hand, and beneath flows the broad Hudson between
lofty banks. Here at last there seemed room to breathe.

A visit to Henry Street Settlement, perhaps the best known of
its class after Hull House, Chicago, revealed another aspect of
the teeming city. No social worker in New York possessed more
experience than Miss Wald, who had lived and laboured so long
and so faithfully in the slums of East Side. Wedged in between
the towering magnificence of the twentieth century and the imposing sky-line of Brooklyn across the bridges in Long Island, the
tangle of mean streets spoke of an earlier age. Except for the
negroes, who lived to the north, every race seemed to be represented. Here was the capacious 'melting-pot' into which immigrants were dropped and assimilated as wave after wave surged
across the Atlantic. The rationing of immigration was among the
most important and most generally welcomed results of the war,
and many were the lamentations that the door had stood too wide
open for so long. A more controversial consequence was Prohibition. Even when all allowances were made for the evils of
boot-legging and the violation of the law, Miss Wald and her
fellow-workers were convinced that it was a blessing, at any rate
on East Side, a verdict confirmed by social workers in other
cities.

Boston is a haven of peace after the clatter of New York, and
nowhere in America does an Englishman feel so much at home.
There is something restful about the Common, the shining expanse

of the Charles river, the broad streets and squares, the comfortable houses, the blessed absence of skyscrapers. In the old quarters lie memories of three centuries. A few miles down the coast is Plymouth Rock, a few miles inland are Lexington and Concord. The old State House had echoed to the harangues of Samuel Adams, in the harbour was staged 'the Boston tea-party', across the river is Bunker Hill, and to the south are the low summits where Washington encamped. A couple of miles to the west stands the earliest and greatest of transatlantic universities. Now that the history of our old quarrel has been rewritten by Osgood, Beer and a host of conscientious American scholars, the bitterness is gone. The revolt of the colonies was due, not to the 'tyranny' of George III, but to the logic of events. Our fellow-subjects, as liberty loving and law-abiding as ourselves, were growing up and wanted their own way, and it was a blessing for us all that they got it.

The lectures I had come to deliver had been endowed by a member of the Lowell family nearly a century before. The town of Lowell, Massachusetts, perpetuates the name of the clan which took the largest share in developing the textile industries of the north, and which produced in James Russell Lowell one of the glories of American literature. The endowment was controlled by Lawrence Lowell, President of Harvard, from whom the invitation had come. The lectures are open to the public without fee. My discourses, later developed into two large volumes, delivered at the rate of two a week, dealt with eight of the statesmen who had shaped the fortunes of Europe during the last years of peace, and related them to the political tradition of their respective lands. Having no thesis of guilt or innocence to establish, my task was a venture in interpretation, and nearly ten years after the war educated circles seemed ready for a cool analysis.

The widening of the curriculum by President Eliot had raised Harvard to the standard of the leading European shrines of teaching and research. The President of an American University of the first rank is a national figure, and Eliot's successor was fully equal to his responsibilities. Having met Lawrence Lowell on his visits to England and studied his solid treatises on the constitutions of the Old World, I learned to know him as a host. He had built a roomy house close to the University which the childless and generous scholar designed to be the home of his successors. Bursting with energy despite his seventy years, he was delightful company. No after-dinner speech in America is complete without its anecdotes, and here was a star performer. Though a Republican, like most of the old families of New England, he had shared with Root and Taft the desire to create a League of Nations in which their country would play a leading part. His sister, Amy Lowell, the gifted biographer of Keats, had died shortly before my arrival.

The Harvard Faculty of History was the first in the land and I already knew most of its leading lights. Samuel Morison, who had been the first occupant of the chair of American history founded at Oxford after the war, was soon to publish the best political history of his country of medium size, and later to describe the work of the Navy in the Second World War. He lived at Concord, half an hour from Cambridge by train, and in his company I visited the little bridge at Lexington where the first shots were fired in the War of Independence. But Concord also speaks of Emerson and Thoreau. Emerson's Essays with their serene undogmatic idealism had meant much to me as a young man, and I was glad to see his home and library which contained presentation copies from his life-long friend Carlyle. Of scarcely less interest was a visit to Salem, with Hawthorne's *House of the Seven Gables* on the shore, and the hill outside the town where pitiful victims of the witchcraft craze were hung in 1687. The story of Puritan New England, like that of Anglo-American relations, has been rewritten by the descendants of John Adams, by James Truslow Adams (a namesake but not a relative), and other students who have no axe to grind. Massachusetts in the seventeenth century, like Geneva under Calvin, was a theocracy, not a democracy, still less a paradise. No historical narrative dating from the middle decades of the nineteenth century required and received more drastic revision than that of Bancroft on which generations of American citizens had been reared.

The leading Harvard authority on contemporary history was Archibald Cary Coolidge, who had begun his career in the diplomatic service. His lectures on the United States as a World Power, published in 1907, showed what he could do, but he never produced a comprehensive work. His *métier* was to inspire young

students to research, particularly in the field of Slavonic languages.
In addition to his academic duties he was in charge of the magnificent Widener Library, and the wealthy bachelor spent the whole
of his salary as librarian on enriching the shrine he loved, buying
largely as he moved about Europe after the war. As editor of the
new quarterly *Foreign Affairs* he secured articles from men who
were making or had made history. He was one of the first
American scholars to realize the complexity of the problem of
'war-guilt', and on the publication of my *History of Modern Europe*
he wrote to tell me that his view of the background of the struggle
was much the same as mine. His kindness and hospitality
sharpened the regret with which I heard of his premature death
at the close of the same year.

The most distinguished ornament of the Historical Faculty was
Haskins, the leading medievalist of the New World since the
death of Henry Charles Lea, historian of the Spanish Inquisition.
The robust figure I had known before the war was now an
invalid, though the quality of his writings was unimpaired.
Among new acquaintances I may mention Taussig, the *doyen* of
American economists, and Kuno Francke, historian of German
culture. The latter was typical of the numberless German immigrants who had become loyal citizens of the United States without
forgetting the land of their birth. Unlike his colleague Munster-
berg, the celebrated psychologist who had defended the German
case on the outbreak of war, Francke had discreetly retired into
the country till the storm had blown itself out. The ailing old man
was now back again, no longer as Professor, but as Curator of the
Germanic Museum which contained reproductions of masterpieces of German art.

No department at Harvard enjoyed a higher reputation than the
Law School. Felix Frankfurter had migrated with his parents from
Austria at the age of twelve and was soon to become a Justice of
the Supreme Court. At the moment he was much in the public
eye owing to his scathing attack on the judicial methods of
Massachusetts in the Sacco-Vanzetti case. In the Harvard Club
in Boston, where I lived until I became the guest of President
Lowell, I heard both sides warmly espoused. A colourful *roman à
thèse* by Upton Sinclair narrated the story of the two Italians who
were electrocuted seven years after sentence of death, and painted

a repulsive picture of the callous materialism of the Boston *bourgeoisie*. Reading the little book which Frankfurter presented to me I concluded that the case for a fresh trial was made out. His appeal was in vain, but a committee of three, among them President Lowell, was invited to look into the matter and reported against the prisoners. Another eminent Austrian jurist, my old friend Joseph Redlich, accepted a call to the Law School with a high salary and a minimum of academic burdens. He was busy with his biography of Francis Joseph, and his annual visits to Vienna kept him in touch with his countrymen. In a circle where so many able men were to be found he was perhaps the most brilliant talker of them all.

A pleasant practice exists in the classic land of hospitality by which a foreign scholar is occasionally invited to lecture to a class in place of the Professor, and Faculties meet for lunch when such birds of passage as Lowell Lecturers are invited to speak. In Boston itself every cause and every movement has its representatives. In the course of a month I discoursed to womens' clubs, the English-speaking Union and the Ethical Society as well as to various conferences on British policy. The most controversial issue was Russia. I addressed a lunch meeting in which the case for the Kremlin was voiced by Louis Fischer, author of a useful work on Russia's foreign relations, and the opposing argument was advanced with equal vigour. My task was to describe the phases of British sentiment since the war. Hundreds of people listened with eager interest to the discussion from different angles of a system which appeared to many to threaten the stability of American institutions. Uncle Sam is more easily rattled than John Bull.

On Sundays I sampled the churches, beginning with episcopalian Holy Trinity, where the social *élite* of Boston once flocked to hear Philipps Brooks. At the time of my visit there was no divine in Boston with such a following as Fosdick in New York. Christian Science, on the other hand, like the Society of Friends, is independent of clergy, sermons and creeds. The great dome of the Mother Church dominates the west end of the city, and well-dressed citizens thronged the spacious edifice. I had attended one or two services in London without exhilaration, and I was no more thrilled in the Mecca of the new faith. As I walked away a

17

member of the congregation, guessing that I was a visitor, volunteered the information that a new church was opened on an average once a week in some quarter of the world. If Philadelphia stands for the Quakers and Salt Lake City for the Mormons, Boston embodies in its history the evolution of religious life in the New World. The home of Puritanism and Unitarianism had become with the Irish immigration a largely Catholic city, and with the emergence of Mrs. Eddy the headquarters of a new gospel.

I found nothing in America more charming than Williamstown, nestling among the hills of Western Massachusetts in early spring. It had sprung into fame after the war with its Institute of Politics and the summer Conferences on International affairs. I had received an invitation to lecture a year or two before but had felt unable to accept. My delightful host Dr. Garfield, President of the College, who asked me to run over from Boston for a single lecture, was the son of the President whose murder I had heard discussed in my youth. On my way back I broke my journey at Northampton and lectured at Smith College with its two thousand women students. No two men in the United States had done so much to destroy the myth of Germany's sole guilt as Fay and Barnes, yet no two writers could be more different in temperament and method. The former, my kind host, had won the confidence of historical students in both hemispheres by his mastery of the evidence and his serenity of judgment. The latter fought with the gloves off, arguing that the statesmen of the Triple Entente were the real villains of the piece. Fay's classical volumes on the origins of the war, which he interpreted as primarily an Austro-Russian quarrel, were nearing completion, and it was reassuring to discover that our views were almost identical.

When my duties in Boston were over I travelled slowly south. My first halt was at Providence, the capital of Rhode Island, the smallest of the forty-eight states. The city of Roger Williams, Baptist champion of religious toleration about whom I had written in my earliest book, was now a bustling centre of industry, but there was an air of academic peace in Brown University. At New Haven, Connecticut, my next stage, I was still in Puritan territory, and Yale stood next to Harvard in antiquity and prestige. Professor Seymour showed me some tit-bits from the forthcoming

final volumes of Colonel House's Papers, which I vainly hoped
would explain the termination of his intimacy with Wilson. The
affectionate letters from Washington, it appeared, had become
rarer and had finally ceased without a hint of ruffled feathers or
blame, but silence told its own tale. Among the luminaries of the
Yale Historical Faculty it was a pleasure to renew acquaintance
with Rostovtsev, and to discover that the revolution had in no
way paralysed the energies of the greatest Russian historian of the
ancient world.

Princeton, the next halt on the journey south, is the nearest
equivalent of Oxford and Cambridge, and its rural tranquillity
and eighteenth-century buildings suggest an ideal atmosphere for
study and research. Memories of the War of Independence are all
around us. For me it also possessed a more recent interest, for it
had witnessed the emergence of Woodrow Wilson. From
Professor to President of the University, from President to
Governor of New Jersey, from Governor to the White House—
such were the stages in the rapid ascent. My kind host, Philip
Marshall Brown, Professor of International Law and former
member of the Diplomatic Service, lived in Wilson's old home.
The latter's attempt to make Princeton a working University had
caused sparks to fly, for it raised in acute form the problem of the
relation between learning and wealth. No one contested his
courage or the purity of his motives, and it was this revelation of
reforming zeal which suggested to the Democratic managers that
he might be presidential timber.

Philadelphia cannot compare with the dynamism of New York,
the dignity of Boston, and the smiling charm of Washington.
Dingy little dwellings of two storeys jostled imposing stores,
though skyscrapers were still unknown. The city of William
Penn looked rather unkempt, and austere citizens grumbled that
it was no less corrupt than Chicago. Nothing, however, can rob
it of its memories. Here stands the old City Hall where the
Declaration of Independence was signed, and here was the seat of
government till Washington was built after the death of the first
President. Penn's statue crowns the towering steeple of the Town
Hall, and Philadelphia was the home, though not the birthplace,
of Benjamin Franklin. I visited Haverford, the Quaker College,
with Rufus Jones the historian of mystical religion as its star

performer, and Bryn Mawr with its beautiful buildings and its throng of happy girls.

Washington makes up for its youth by the beauty of its situation and the dignity of its official buildings. The Capitol with its terraced slopes dominates the landscape as the Dome of St. Peter's towers over Rome. Since Congress had dispersed a few days before my arrival I could wander through the Senate, the House of Representatives and the Supreme Court and climb the dome which unifies the grand architectural design. Among the memorials of American statesmen it was a pleasant surprise to find the bust of my old chief Lord Bryce, the only Englishman in a distinguished company. A hundred yards away stands the Library of Congress, connected by an underground corridor, the most sumptuous storehouse of books in the world. And here is the greatest documentary treasure in America, the Declaration of Independence with the original signatures. Its Director kindly showed me the gigantic institution at work. In no other library of its size, I was proudly informed, could books be so speedily produced, and the rapid mobilization of one of my own confirmed the claim.

On landing in America I found people talking of a new book *Revelry*, in which President Harding and 'the Ohio Gang' were held up to scorn. No political novel had made such a stir since Henry Adams's *Democracy* denounced the noisome vapours of the capital forty years before. The substitution of Vice-President Coolidge had been like a breath of air in a stuffy room, for everyone was thankful to have a man of unblemished character in the White House. I heard occasional lamentations that such a mediocrity should be in control, but while prosperity lasted the average American felt no need of a superman. Business had taken the place of politics. Frank Simonds, perhaps the most influential of American journalists in the field of foreign affairs, invited me to meet Kellogg and Hoover, both of whom I had known in London before their political careers began. No one ever suggested that the Secretary of State had ranked among the great Ambassadors to the Court of St. James's; but his name was soon to be enshrined in the Kellogg Pact, though the movement for 'the outlawry of war' was initiated by Dr. Murray Butler, Professor Shotwell and other academic lights.

The outstanding figure in Washington in 1927 was neither the President nor the Secretary of State but the Minister of Commerce. Herbert Hoover, who was to tell his own story in three volumes twenty years later, had won world-wide fame as the relieving officer of Europe. The massive head and square shoulders spoke of the strength and self-confidence of the man once humorously described as looking like a reformed prize-fighter. The mining engineer who made his fortune before he was thirty had become Minister of Commerce under Harding and Coolidge, and for the last six years had displayed on American soil the aptitude for large-scale organization hitherto at the service of the Old World. He rarely dined out, and our host warned us that he was not always willing to talk. On this occasion, however, Graham Wallas and I found no difficulty in mobilizing the oracle. Though neither of us was a pessimist his robust optimism sounded strange in our ears. We suggested that America was still in a stage roughly corresponding to our Victorian era: so long as there was enough cake to go round, a political Labour movement was impossible and socialism made no appeal. But might not a day be coming, as it had come to us, when the supply of labour would—at any rate for a time—outrun demand, unemployment stalk through the land, and capitalism be as sharply challenged for its insufficiency as it was now applauded for its success? These spectres had no terrors for the Minister, though he admitted that agriculture was in difficulties and the textile industry of the north less prosperous than of old. American capitalism, he explained, had learned to avoid the errors committed in the Old World. It had made its peace with Labour by high wages and with the public by low prices; mass production and instalment purchase had solved the problem of combining the two principles to the advantage of all concerned. So long as employers operated the industrial machine with reasonable intelligence, sharing its mounting benefits with the community as a whole, there was no probability either of a serious economic crisis or of political discontent. We listened without conviction to this sturdy individualist who saw no cracks in the system under which his countrymen were flourishing as they had never flourished before and he himself had won wealth, office and fame. Yet the greatest slump in American history lay only two years ahead.

Though Congress had dispersed the Supreme Court remained in session. I watched the nine judges troop in, with the burly figure of Chief Justice Taft at their head. The ex-President was happier on the bench than he had been in the White House. The proceedings were as quiet and almost as informal as in our House of Lords when sitting as a judicial body, but its decisions had often made history. In 1927 the burning constitutional issues of State Rights, in which Chief Justice Marshall had pulled one way and Chief Justice Taney the other, had fallen into the background, and economic problems filled the stage. The two outstanding figures after Taft were Holmes and Brandeis, the most politically progressive members of the Court. I had brought introductions to them both from their devoted friend Harold Laski, and I visited them in their homes. Justice Holmes was the Grand Old Man of Washington, and his eighty-seven years sat lightly on him. With his handsome face, warm colouring and bright eyes he looked like a man in the sixties. His writings on the Common Law revealed the philosophic background of his thought, and his generous desire that Labour should get fair play made him the vigilant guardian of its interests. I was to make closer acquaintance with him many years later in the four substantial volumes of his correspondence with Sir Frederick Pollock and Harold Laski on almost every topic of the day. Justice Brandeis seemed to look deeper into the problems of the times than anyone I met in the United States. While Hoover saw nothing ahead but a beckoning vista of achievement, he disliked the virtually unchallenged domination of Capitalism and there was a shade of melancholy in his thoughtful face.

The Democrats in Washington and elsewhere were waiting for the emergence of a new leader. Though the name of Al Smith, the penniless East Side Irish lad who had risen to be Governor of New York, was on all lips, few people believed that a Roman Catholic would ever enter the White House. I never heard Franklin Roosevelt mentioned as a candidate. Isolationism had survived the war, and the world had to suffer a second blood bath before the United States realized the impossibility of its continuance. There were, moreover, differences even in the ranks of those who approved the idea of a League. 'Does the Covenant guarantee effective action against an aggressor?' I was asked by

Dr. David Jayne Hill, the veteran jurist and historian who had been Ambassador to Berlin before the war. I replied that, as he was well aware, the decision remained with the individual Powers. 'Then it is a sham,' he rejoined. I argued that a larger surrender of sovereignty had been impracticable in 1919 when the Covenant was drawn up; but lawyers crave for sanctions, and Republican lawyers looked with greater favour on a League to enforce peace. The League in its actual form found few admirers.

Washington is the gate to the South, and the traveller crosses the Potomac into historic Virginia. Who can forget the tranquil beauty of the National Cemetery at Arlington, the graves scattered in thousands among the trees with the white marble monument in the midst? A few miles down the river lies Mount Vernon, the home of George Washington, 'first in war, first in peace, first in the hearts of his countrymen'. While the names of Hamilton and Jefferson remain the battle-cries of warring schools, the first President, like Benjamin Franklin, stands above the battle. Too reserved to become a popular figure like Lincoln, Washington is best understood if we transplant General Botha into a Virginian of the eighteenth century. Next to Mount Vernon no shrine attracts more pilgrims than Monticello, the home of Jefferson. Friends motored me to Charlottesville in the heart of Virginia, one hundred and thirty miles from the White House. The view over the hills, with the University of Virginia, the child of his old age, a mile or two away, was a perfect setting for the home of the scholar-statesman who loved books as much as politics and agriculture no less than philosophy. Here Lafayette had visited his old friend half a century after the Declaration of Independence.

The road from Washington to Charlottesville took us through Fredericksburg and the Wilderness with their memories of carnage, and from Charlottesville I journeyed to Richmond. To a student of the Civil War the capital of Virginia is of absorbing interest. Here the Confederate Government had been installed. Here was the State House with Houdon's fine statue of Washington of which a replica stands in Trafalgar Square. Close by was the White House where Jefferson Davis toiled through four agonizing years. The former Executive Mansion is now a museum of the war in which a room is allotted to each of the Confederate States. It seemed astonishing to a foreigner that the wounds of this fratricidal struggle should have healed so quickly, but the process has been facilitated by the rapid expansion of the nation across the boundless West. The new America no longer consisted exclusively of the victorious North and the vanquished South, for the old antagonists found themselves units in a mighty community which spans the continent from sea to sea. On entering the museum we are back among the tense passions of the fray. Here is pride, not penitence, gratitude to the men who fought and died for State Rights, not remorse that their cause was linked with slavery. For the few surviving veterans it was all very real. In Boston Professor Burgess, the expert on Constitutional Law, recalled to me his experiences more than sixty years after the event and referred to the Confederates as 'the rebels'. It has been the task of historians, with James Ford Rhodes at their head, to depict the most tragic event of American history as a struggle less between slave-owners and abolitionists than between rival doctrines of federal government.

My final speaking engagement was at Vassar, the Women's College seventy miles up the Hudson, and on the voyage home I had time to reflect on the experiences of two crowded months. When John Morley was asked what had impressed him most during his visit in 1904, he replied: 'Niagara and President Roosevelt.' I should have had to give a less epigrammatic response, for no superman was in sight. The dominant impression was the abundant kindness I had received. The second was the diffused prosperity of the country. The pulse of life beat strongly and the standard of comfort was the highest in the world. Every private carried a Field Marshal's *bâton* in his knapsack, as in Napoleonic France. On all sides were men who had made their way or felt confident of making it. The bracing climate and the sunshine were a perpetual tonic. Here was a community, the first in the history of mankind, which seemed able to live its life without external dangers. There was nothing to prevent its citizens developing their vast estate in their own way. The world war had left the buoyancy of over one hundred million human beings unimpaired and a second world war appeared as unthinkable as a slump.

The brilliant scene, needless to say, was not without some shadows. Prohibition, like woman suffrage, was a child of the war, and society was divided into drys and wets. I had heard so much of the violation of the law that as an abstainer I was agreeably surprised to find so little liquor wherever I went. Spacious houses like those of President Lowell and Professor Coolidge were using up old stock as they were legally entitled to do, but otherwise it was unusual to see anyone drinking wine. My wettest experience was a dinner arranged for me in a well-known Washington Club—not the Cosmos where I was staying—when the wine was served by the host while the waiters discreetly withdrew. I knew that the academic world of which I saw a good deal was merely a section of the picture, and in Irish Boston I heard of bootleggers who had made their fortune in a year or two and left for the land of their fathers. Discussing the problem with all sorts of men and women, I gathered that nobody wished for the return of the saloon, that everyone recognized the advantage of Prohibition to industrial efficiency, and that the violation of the law was generally deplored. The negro problem rarely came up in conversation in the North, but in Washington it was in the air. In the Cosmos Club the only white faces to be seen among the staff were in the office. The parlour-maids in private houses were black, the trains were full of dusky citizens, and a notice in the trams requested 'coloured' passengers to take the back seats. The memory of their services in the war and of the lack of colour prejudice in France rendered political and social frustration more difficult for them than ever to bear, but the Deep South proves difficult to convert and impossible to coerce. In the phrase of André Siegfried, the observant author of *America comes of Age*, it is like gazing into a bottomless abyss.

There are various Americas, and I had only sampled the oldest, the most cultured, the most European variety. Had I struck into the interior I should have found myself in Main Street and Zenith City, rubbing shoulders with the Philistine Babbitts of the Middle West. Yet even there the complacency for which American citizens used to be celebrated was being challenged, Sinclair Lewis campaigning by pungent satire, Upton Sinclair by frontal attack. Mencken, the American Bernard Shaw, was more than a mere cynic when he held up the mirror to the cultural crudities of his countrymen in the *American Mercury*. Educationalists lamented the superficiality of the training received at hundreds of the newer

Universities, some of them scarcely worthy of the name, with their swollen classes and the resulting lack of contact between the overworked teacher and the rough diamonds below his desk. Opinion seemed to be moving towards a limitation of numbers by raising the standard of entrance, just as the rationing of immigrants had come to be regarded as an overdue reform. Quality was beginning to count for more, quantity for less.

18

HOURS IN A LIBRARY

M Y main occupation, after the war as before it, was the writing of books. *Germany and the French Revolution*, published in the spring of 1920, had been my companion during the later years of the conflict, and I found some consolation amid airraids and casualties in the company of the titans of the Augustan age. Beginning with a sketch of political decrepitude and intellectual rejuvenescence during the eighteenth century, I described the impact of events in France on publicists, philosophers, poets and statesmen. For Mme de Staël Germany was above all a nation of thinkers and poets, and there was not one of them on whom the Revolution failed to leave its mark. The chapters on Goethe and Kant gave me special satisfaction, for the two greatest German writers of their time were good Europeans and therefore deeply stirred by the stupendous drama staged beyond the Rhine. Though the main theme was the analysis of opinion, the closing chapters explored the impact of the cataclysm on the Holy Roman Empire and its units with the aid of our Ambassadors' dispatches in the Record Office. As a study of international contacts and an example of the interaction of ideas and events it was a theme after my own heart.

In the same year I published a substantial biography of Lord Courtney which his widow invited me to write after his death in 1918 at the age of eighty-six. It was a labour of love, for I knew him as intimately as a younger man can ever know his seniors. For twenty years I was a frequent guest in Cheyne Walk, and we had discussed every phase of the war till within a week or two of the end. He was too well informed to swallow the popular delusion that Germany was solely responsible for the catastrophe, and he agreed with Smuts that a crushing victory for either side would be a disaster for civilization. Detesting German militarism like the rest of us, he realized that it was only one example of the Imperialist fetish which he had always abhorred. Had he lived to witness the birth of the League of Nations he would have greeted it with a cheer.

While allowing me unrestricted use of his correspondence and her journals, Lady Courtney left me a free hand in the selection of letters and the expression of my views. The rich family material was supplemented from outside sources. Lord Rosebery alone refused permission to publish his letters on the unconvincing pretext that they were not worth printing; but as he declined similar requests I felt no personal grievance. Lord Morley, his oldest political friend, allowed me to use the correspondence of forty years, and his approval of the book was a reward for my pains. *The Times* permitted me to reveal his authorship of many leading articles in the sixties and seventies when Delane helped to rule England from Printing-House Square. In a chapter entitled 'Cheyne Walk' I collected intimate studies of his home life and personality by such devoted friends as his former secretary Professor George Unwin, the economic historian, and Professor Basil Williams, biographer of Chatham; and I analysed his thoughtful *Diary of a Churchgoer*, the authorship of which was only revealed after his death. The outstanding activities of his career were his life-long struggle against Imperialism and his crusade for Proportional Representation. The narrative threw light on the Home Rule, Egyptian and other controversies of the time as well as on the South African war. He could have held high office had he wished, but, like Cobden and Bright, he was happiest on the back benches, where he felt it was not merely his right but his duty to say exactly what he thought. A Parliament of Courtneys would lack cohesion, but a legislature without independents would resemble a stagnant pond. Men of all parties acclaimed his unique contribution to our national life. 'He was one of the greatest figures of our time', wrote Lord Bryce, 'in his absolute independence of mind and his absolute courage in thought and action.' 'One of the bravest and finest figures of our time', echoed Lord Haldane; 'such a combination of heart and brain is rare at all times.' 'His intellect, his independence, his courage, his character', testified Lloyd George, 'were a national asset.' South Africa, cabled another Prime Minister, General Botha, owed him an irredeemable debt of gratitude. Some time afterwards a volume of selections from his writings, with an Introduction by Sir Arthur Quiller-Couch, was published with the title of *Cornish Granite*.

Two years later, in 1922, I compiled a brief Memoir of his old comrade Frederic Mackarness, who died in 1920. Convinced that the most modest of men would have frowned on an official biography, I accepted the request of his friends on condition that the volume should be privately printed. It contains material that may be of use to historians of the South African war and of the movement for Indian reform, but the justification of such a tribute was to be found less in his public services than in his personality. He was a miniature Courtney, in no way inferior in courage and in his passion for national righteousness. The little book concluded with appreciations by various friends, among them Lord Loreburn, who had made him a County Court Judge. The cessation of political activities on his promotion to the bench was a sore trial, and at times the temptation to regain his freedom by resignation was almost irresistible. He found scope for his broad humanity in Court, where his heart went out to the victims of the house famine which followed the war. From time to time he engaged a solicitor at his own expense to appear for some poor man who was unrepresented, fearing that otherwise the points in his favour might not be adequately presented. Such citizens are the conscience of democracy, and there are never as many of them as we need.

My biography of Courtney found favour with Lord Harcourt, better known as Lulu, who invited me to discuss the possibility of writing his father's life. I was flattered by the suggestion though it made no appeal. I had seen and heard the formidable old warrior, but I had never met him and he was never one of my heroes. Moreover I doubted whether I should have the necessary independence with the most devoted of sons continually looking over my shoulder. The task was admirably performed by A. G. Gardiner in two stout volumes which reveal a powerful but irascible personality with a vein of tenderness that made him more attractive in private than in public life. Lulu, unlike his father, preferred the rapier to the bludgeon. His brief political career, which ended with the formation of the First Coalition in 1915, was unquestionably a success; but he was too tall to be robust, and he had virtually retired from public life before his premature death. He had many interests, literary and artistic, and was full of *arcana imperii*.

Both in *Germany and the French Revolution* and the *Life of Courtney* the problem of nationalism was frequently cropping up, and in the same year that the larger works appeared I published a brief study of this controversial theme. My old Cambridge friend Lowes Dickinson, who had felt the war as deeply as any man in England, planned a series of half-crown handbooks designed to instruct the general reader. He himself wrote on Causes of War; Sir George Young, with twenty years of official experience, on Diplomacy; Leonard Woolf on Economic Imperialism. Nationalism I defined as:

> the resolve of a group of human beings to share their fortunes and to exercise exclusive control over their own actions. Where such a conscious determination exists there should be a state, and there will be no abiding peace until there is a state. Where there is a soul there should be a body in which it can dwell.

I sketched national movements and the diffusion of the idea of nationality from the French Revolution onwards, not in Europe alone but in Egypt, Persia, India and the Far East. A final chapter, welcoming the new states into the comity of nations, ended with a warning:

> The gospel that a people with a distinct national culture and self-consciousness should be allowed to live its own life shows no sign of losing its power, for it is the expression of a profound and legitimate human instinct. Yet the doctrine of nationality, like its twin the sovereignty of the people, has had a chequered career. Its explosive force has torn unjust treaties to shreds and shattered despotic empires. It has also fostered savage racial passion and repulsive national arrogance, and the cult of 'sacred egotism' has almost obliterated the sense that civilization is a collective achievement and a common responsibility. Only when each nation respects the rights and aspirations of its fellows as its own, and recognizes in theory and practice its subordination to the welfare of humanity, can a league of contented peoples bring healing to a distracted world.

If this sounded utopian I could shelter myself behind Mazzini, the greatest prophet of nationalism in the nineteenth century, who proclaimed that it is not enough.

In 1918 Sir Adolphus Ward, Master of Peterhouse, chief editor of the *Cambridge Modern History* and the *Cambridge History of English Literature*, finished the third volume of his *History of Germany in the Nineteenth Century*. At eighty his powers of work were undiminished and his thoughts turned towards fresh activities. 'A History of British Diplomacy is very much needed,' he wrote to me, 'and I am trying to persuade the Cambridge Press to undertake it. Of course it must be done by younger hands than my own and by more competent.' Six weeks later he reported that the Press approved the idea, and proposed that I should shoulder the task.

> It would no doubt occupy some years—something like five years is in my mind—and would absorb during its production a great part of the energy even of so active a mind as yours. But, if adequately accomplished, it would be a work worthy of yourself and of the University. My co-operation in the scheme would be cordially given, but I am too old to think of any further part in the work.

I replied that a history of modern British foreign policy based on the archives would require not five years but the remainder of my life; that England possessed scholars who had specialized in particular sections of the vast territory; that the only way of producing an authoritative narrative was to follow the precedent of the *Cambridge Modern History*; that he was the man to take the lead in the enterprise, and that I would gladly assist as joint editor. These considerations produced their effect, and we were soon discussing the number of volumes, the chronological limits, the scheme of chapters and the list of contributors. We started with the younger Pitt, but the terminal date was less easy to settle. He desired that I should deal with the latest phase of the story, and I pleaded to be allowed to lay down my pen on the outbreak of the World War. The University Press, however, expressed a wish that the survey should be continued to the treaties of peace, and we finally agreed that the years 1914–18 should be outlined in an Epilogue.

The experts played up, and when we met with refusals the

grounds were generally convincing, Lord Fitzmaurice, imprisoned in his Wiltshire home by ill-health, was unable to consult the archives. Lord Newton explained that he had given his secrets to the world in the *Life of Lord Lyons*. Sir George Prothero, after undertaking the years 1902–7, was compelled by illness to withdraw. We were allowed by Lord Curzon to consult the archives of the Foreign Office till the close of 1885, twenty-five years later than the official limit at that time. The first volume (1783–1815) was published in 1922, the second (1815–66) in the spring of 1923, the third (1866–1919) in the autumn of the same year. The work contained two thousand large pages and was written by twenty scholars. The senior editor's contributions appeared in the first two volumes, mine in the last. My task was to describe British policy from 1902 to the Treaty of Versailles within the limits of two hundred and fifty pages. On particular points I consulted Ministers and officials of the Foreign Office, but the judgments were my own.

My Parliamentary experiences were a help, as I had listened to many debates and met many leading actors on the world stage. I discovered that there was no recognizable difference between the Unionist Lansdowne and the Liberal Grey; that their governing aim was the maintenance of peace; that the fine humanitarian tradition in British policy appealed with equal strength to both, and that the Balance of Power was kept continually in view. In reading the Blue-books and White Papers I was struck by the patchiness of our available knowledge. Official information on Macedonia, the Congo and Persia, for instance, was almost overwhelming in bulk. Great crises and events on the other hand, such as the making of the Anglo-Japanese alliance, the Anglo-French and Anglo-Russian treaties, the Conference of Algeciras, the Bosnian crisis, Agadir and the Balkan wars, remained in shadow. I had to fill in the gaps as best I could from Hansard, the press and other sources, oral, printed and unprinted.

The most authoritative portion of my survey was the brief account of the peace negotiations, which was revised by Headlam-Morley, Historical Adviser to the Foreign Office. The most novel chapter in the whole work was the masterly sketch of the working of the Foreign Office since its institution in 1782 by Algernon Cecil, a nephew of Lord Salisbury, which embodied a good deal of inside information. The only item that incurred criticism on the score of partiality was Sir Valentine Chirol's survey of the years of the South African war, in which he gave free vein to the Germanophobia which he had acquired in the Berlin office of *The Times*. Sir Adolphus Ward lived long enough to witness the completion of the latest of his enterprises, and passed away a year later at the ripe age of eighty-six, respected and beloved by pupils and friends.

Shortly before the war of 1914 I was invited by Cassell to attempt a survey of European history since the Congress of Berlin. Fyffe's *History of Modern Europe* began with 1792 and ended with 1878, and it was the desire of the publisher that his scholarly narrative should be continued. The invitation, which I had declined at the time, was renewed and accepted after the war. My *History of Modern Europe 1878–1919*, published in 1923, was the first attempt in any language to utilize the mass of new material which had come to light during and after the conflict. The first six volumes from the German archives, revealing the secrets of the Wilhelmstrasse from 1871 to the fall of Bismarck, were published just in time, and Pribram's *Secret Treaties of Austria-Hungary* enabled me to reconstruct essential portions of the diplomatic framework of Continental history. 'The theme of the book', I wrote in the Preface, 'is the relations of the Great Powers of Europe to one another.' There was no room, even in a volume of seven hundred pages, to deal with the domestic problems of the various European states. Regarding Europe as a family, though a very quarrelsome family, I endeavoured to write, as Fyffe had written, like a 'good European'.

My chapter on The Breaking of the Storm analysed the case of each of the Great Powers, and I concluded that they acted in what seemed to them the most natural way.

To explain the conduct of the statesmen of Europe in July and August, 1914, is not necessarily to justify it on the grounds either of morality or expediency, or to approve the policy pursued by them and their predecessors out of which the crisis arose. The root of the evil lay in the division of Europe into two armed camps, which dated from 1871, and the conflict was the offspring of fear no less than of ambition. The Old World had degenerated into a powder magazine in which the dropping of a lighted match whether by

18

accident or design was almost certain to produce a conflagration. No war, strictly speaking, is inevitable, but it requires rulers of exceptional foresight and self-control in every country to avoid catastrophes. It is a mistake to imagine that the conflict of 1914 took Europe unawares, for statesmen and soldiers had been expecting and preparing for it for many years. It is also a mistake to attribute exceptional wickedness to the governments which, in the words of Lloyd George, stumbled and staggered into war. Blind to danger and deaf to advice as were the civilian leaders of the three despotic empires, not one of them, when it came to the point, desired to set the world alight. But though they may be acquitted of the supreme offence of deliberately starting the avalanche, they must bear the reproach of having chosen paths which led straight to the abyss. The outbreak of the Great War is the condemnation not only of the clumsy performers who strutted for a brief hour across the stage, but of the international anarchy which they inherited and which they did nothing to abate.

Three chapters on the war and the settlement completed the record. The opportunity for a new international order had come with the urgent need.

If some Rip van Winkle had closed his eyes in 1914 and opened them in 1919, he would scarcely have recognized the Europe in which he was born. Germany was a Republic with a Socialist President, the Kaiser and the Crown Prince in exile, the fleet at the bottom of the sea, Alsace-Lorraine in the hands of France. The Tsar and his family had been murdered and a Communist dictator ruled the Russian Empire from the Kremlin. The proud realm of the Hapsburgs had been shattered into fragments and its last ruler was an exile. Poland, Lithuania and Bohemia had risen from the grave. Finland was free. Estonia and Latvia were independent States. Serbia had grown into Jugoslavia. Montenegro had disappeared. Hungary was halved and Romania doubled. Italy was in Trieste, Greece in Smyrna. Turkey had shrunk to a shadow of her former self. The Balance of Power had ceased to exist. France was supreme on land and Great Britain on the seas. The Triple Alliance and the Triple Entente were dead and buried. In a new world where familiar landmarks have been swept away by the storm and the earthquake, the beginning of wisdom is to recognize that the survival of European civilization is bound up with the vitality and authority of a League of Nations embracing victors and vanquished alike within its sheltering arms.

The book met with the same success that had greeted Fyffe's volumes more than a generation before, and an American edition was used as a text-book in many Universities of the New World. It was translated into Russian and Serbian, and has recently been republished in India. Reprinted again and again, its financial reward exceeded that of all my previous writings put together.

In 1923, the year of the publication of the *History of Modern Europe*, I was invited to deliver the annual Creighton Lecture in the University of London. I chose for my subject *Franco-German Relations 1871–1914*, and published the address in an expanded form in a slender volume of sixty pages. Now that the French were in the Ruhr and the tension between the two great nations was at its height, it appeared to me that a bird's-eye view of the drama by an English observer might be of use since the ashes of the conflict were still too hot for a French or German historian to do full justice to the other's case.

The war of 1914 [I began] was the outcome of three separate and simultaneous antagonisms. The oldest was the quarrel of France and Germany over Alsace and Lorraine. Second in order of time was the competition of Russia and Austria for hegemony in the Near East. The most recent was the rivalry between Great Britain and Germany for the command of the seas. Of these problems two have already been solved. The Anglo-German feud ended at Scapa Flow. The Austro-Russian duel terminated with the dissolution of the Haps-burg Empire. The Franco-German conflict, on the other hand, has not only survived but been intensified by the Great War. The Rhine Provinces, the Challenge Cup of Europe, have changed hands once again, but the Treaty of Versailles possesses no more moral authority for Germany than the Treaty of Frankfurt possessed for Frenchmen. The quarrel of Paris and Berlin, which dominated and poisoned the life of the Continent after 1870, dominates and poisons it today.

I was writing before Locarno, and Poincaré's foot was on the neck of his prostrate foe. I proceeded to sketch the relations of the two countries through the war scare of 1875, the *détente* under Jules Ferry, the threatening Boulanger episode and the two Moroccan crises. The super-patriot school of opinion was illustrated from the poems of Déroulède and the novels of Maurice Barrès, while Marcel Sembat spoke for the little group of Socialists and

Internationalists who tacitly accepted the verdict of Sedan. *Faites un Roi, sinon faites la Paix*, he cried in 1913, but his countrymen rejected both monarchy and renunciation. When the call came from St. Petersburg in 1914 France's unhesitating response was due not merely to her loyalty to the Russian alliance but to her hope that the sword of the Entente would restore the children of the Rhineland she had lost in 1871.

In 1924 Herbert Fisher, who had added to his stature by six years at the Board of Education, invited me to undertake Germany in the series he was planning under the general title *The Modern World*. The object of these volumes, of which mine was the second, was to describe the political, economic and intellectual life of the nations in the twentieth century. The book was published early in 1925, with a brief Introduction by the editor, who described it as surprisingly dispassionate. 'Certainly we are here a thousand miles removed from the heat and dust of the conflict.' A German translation appeared with an Introduction by Kühlmann, who welcomed the attempt at objective handling of a highly controversial theme. The book was soon in a fourth impression, and an American edition also sold well.

> The military machine [I wrote of the situation on the eve of the war] was the most perfect in the world, and the High Sea Fleet was growing apace; the widening of the Kiel Canal was almost completed; the country was rich, the people well educated and fully employed; the broad clean streets of the cities spoke of order and prosperity; the rhythm of the national pulse was clear and strong. Germany, in the proud image of Prince Bülow, was like a well-tended garden. It was a glittering vision of mind and muscle, of large-scale organization, of intoxicating self-confidence, of metallic brilliancy, such as Europe had never seen. Yet the country was restless, its appetite for power unappeased; and here and there a voice was heard to ask whither it was being led, and what it would profit a nation if it gained the whole world and lost its own soul.

Two chapters on the war were followed by surveys of the Revolution, the Weimar Constitution, the Treaty of Versailles, the execution of the Treaty, Reparations, Capital and Labour, Education and the Youth Movement, the German Mind, social changes and foreign affairs. I analysed the thought of Rathenau and Spengler, Rudolph Steiner and Keyserling, then at the height of their fame, and described the 'expressionist' dramas of Toller, Kaiser and Unruh. Though Germany was recovering, I closed on a note of apprehension which the next decade was to prove fully justified.

A rare opportunity for securing the peace of the world was lost when the victorious Allies preferred a vindictive to a moderate settlement, and critics have not been wanting who argue that the 'Carthaginian peace' doomed the young Republic which was forced to accept it to an early death. The battle of democracy at any rate is not yet won, and the destiny of the Republic depends far more on the attitude of its neighbours than on the theoretical principles of its citizens. If the new Germany obtains reasonable consideration at the hands of the victorious Powers, it may survive and take root in the national consciousness. If it fails to secure the ordinary amenities of life for the mass of the people, if it is crushed by political and economic servitudes, if it comes to be generally identified with humiliation and suffering, it will assuredly be overthrown. New institutions must derive from success the prestige which older structures inherit from the past. Self-government has never formed part of the religion of the German people. The thrones were overturned by the sword of the enemy and the arrows of President Wilson. If they are re-erected, it will be because the nation is convinced by bitter experience that a tame Parliamentary Republic is incompatible with the strength and prosperity of the realm. Thus the future of Germany is inextricably linked to the fortunes of Europe; and the fate of victors and vanquished alike will depend on the capacity of rulers and people to perceive and pursue the abiding interests of our common civilization.

Hitler's name occurred only in a passing reference to the Munich *putsch*.

In the autumn of the same year, 1925, I edited *The Later Correspondence of Lord John Russell*. Two volumes published by his son Rollo in 1913 brought the story down to 1839, and his widow invited me to deal with the far greater mass of material extending from 1840 to his death. The correspondence during the six years of his first Premiership, the Crimean war, and the six years at the Foreign Office in the last Palmerston Ministry, is of importance not only for English but for European history. Lord John was Grey's right hand man in carrying the first Reform Bill and the chief associate of Palmerston in fostering the unification of Italy.

No British statesman played a larger part in facilitating the peaceful transfer of power from the landed aristocracy to the *bourgeoisie*. My Introduction discussed his later career in the light of the papers consigned to my charge and of new evidence which had come to light since Spencer Walpole's official biography was published in 1889. If he lacked the wistful charm of Melbourne, the *panache* of Palmerston and the magniloquence of Gladstone, he carried on the fine tradition of Fox, and his career of public service, extending over half a century, is inseparably connected with the greatness of England. Among my difficulties was that of deciphering the writing of some of the principal actors. Palmerston's flowing hand is a delight, and Lord John himself, like Queen Victoria, is always legible. Melbourne's physical decline was only too obvious, and Wellington's letters became more and more of a riddle as he approached and passed his eightieth year. Perhaps the blackest sheep in the flock from the point of view of calligraphy was the irrepressible Brougham who, though withdrawn from the party fight to the sunshine of Cannes, kept up a lively commentary on men and events. I was rewarded by the approval of Lady Agatha Russell who wrote: 'I to whom everything concerning my father is more precious than to anyone now living can only express my gratitude.'

When the Hohenzollern Empire collapsed in Germany the Republican Government decided to reveal the secrets of the Wilhelmstrasse from 1871 to 1914, beginning with the documents on the outbreak of the World War. The plan was condemned by Bülow among others as a perilous concession to the craze for open diplomacy, and it was widely believed that the victors would never follow suit. The first six volumes of *Die Grosse Politik* appeared in 1922, and in 1924 the faith that the example of Germany would one day be copied by her conquerors was justified. In the summer of that year Ramsay MacDonald, Foreign Secretary as well as Prime Minister, informed me of his desire to open the British archives and invited me to shoulder the burden. 'I want to produce a sound historical narrative, properly documented and honestly done,' he wrote, 'and I wish you would take it up yourself. I am sure your name would carry the weight that is necessary.' I replied that it was too heavy a burden for one pair of shoulders, but I would do my best if I had an experienced colleague such as Harold Temperley. The condition was accepted, and in November Austen Chamberlain, the new Foreign Secretary, announced that a collection of documents bearing on the general European situation out of which the war arose would be edited by Dr. Temperley and myself. The reputation of the editors, he added, offered the best guarantee of the historical accuracy and impartiality of their work. It was regrettable that, owing to the defeat of the Labour Government, the announcement was not made by the statesman to whom the decision was due. The British initiative was followed at intervals by the opening of the French, Austrian, Russian and Italian archives.

'The characters of Mr. Gooch and Mr. Temperley', wrote *The Times* in a leading article, 'are such that students all over the world need fear no partial or unfair selection.' This confidence we endeavoured to deserve, not only by scrupulous impartiality on our own part but by a clear intimation in the Prefaces to successive volumes that we should resign if forbidden to publish any document which we judged of vital importance. Such a veto we never anticipated from the British side; but the Foreign Office maintained its usual practice of submitting certain documents to the foreign governments concerned, excepting in this case not only our enemies in the World War but Russia as well. We were always ready to omit a phrase or a sentence reflecting on the private life of public men, but from time to time a difficulty arose about matters of substance, and a volume might be held up for months. The Foreign Office gave us steady support, and on one occasion Sir Austen addressed a personal and successful request to Paris to lift the ban on a particular document. When asked, as I often was, whether we had a free hand, I replied that until our resignations were announced the public might rest assured that nothing of importance was suppressed. We were, of course, in a strong strategic position. The Foreign Office had entrusted the task to two independent scholars, and the prestige of the whole undertaking was bound up with unimpaired confidence in our *bona fides*.

The Foreign Office suggested that we should begin with the year 1904, when our old quarrel with France was made up. There was no question of going much further back, for the starting-point had obviously to be chosen at the time that we began to abandon our policy of splendid isolation, or, as I prefer to call it, the free hand. I pointed out, however, that the change would not be understood unless we could throw light on the years of transition. It was therefore agreed that two preliminary volumes of moderate size should be devoted to 1898–1904, covering the period of Anglo-German negotiations, the alliance with Japan, and the discussions leading up to the Anglo-French Treaty of 8 April 1904. The papers of this period were kept in the Record Office in Chancery Lane, but a few documents of a particularly secret character had been retained in the Foreign Office. The most important of our revelations related to the Anglo-German negotiations in 1901 for an alliance or an understanding, of which the German version was already available in the *Grosse Politik*. A second plum in the pudding was the so-called Windsor Treaty with Portugal of 1899.

After the signing of the Anglo-French Treaty we allowed ourselves more latitude. Our third volume, which described the first Morocco crisis, demolished the legend that we had offered an alliance to France in 1905. The fourth was devoted to the *rapprochement* with Russia in 1907, the fifth to the Bosnian crisis in 1908–9, the sixth to our relations with Berlin from 1907 to the Haldane Mission in 1912, the seventh to the Agadir crisis in 1911, the eighth, which we called the omnibus volume, embraced such items as the second Hague Conference, the renewal of the Japanese alliance, and the neutrality of Belgium. The ninth, in two parts, illustrated the affairs of Eastern Europe from the close of the Bosnian crisis to the end of the Balkan wars in 1913. The tenth, also in two parts, was devoted to the Baghdad railway and the excitements of the last year of peace. The eleventh, dealing with the outbreak of war, had been edited by Headlam-Morley and appeared first. Our task had been merely to confirm its *bona fides*, and in our brief Preface we disclaimed responsibility for his editorial Introduction. The value of the whole enterprise was enhanced by copious extracts from the vast collections of private papers of Grey and Nicolson, Permanent Under-Secretary from 1910 to 1916, bound up in over a hundred large volumes, which they had presented to the Foreign Office on quitting their respective posts.

Our work resembled the German publication in grouping the

materials into chapters dealing with particular issues, and though the French, Austrian and Russian editors adopted the rival method of strict chronological sequence we never regretted our decision. On the other hand we departed from the German precedent by abstaining from all comment. Thimme's annotations in *Die Grosse Politik* are always interesting, but their controversial character aroused sharp criticism in Germany as well as abroad. We were assisted throughout by Professor Lillian Penson, now Dame Lillian, our obligations to whom it is impossible to exaggerate. I found no single document or letter, official, semi-official or private, which as a patriotic Englishman I should have blushed to reveal. Opinions naturally differ as to the wisdom of this or that aspect of British policy during the sixteen eventful years whose secrets we brought to light; but Salisbury, Lansdowne and Grey were men of the highest principle, and the honour of England was safe in their hands. Party politics never exerted the slightest influence on their decisions. Living as I did for several years in the company of the men who had stood at the helm, reading not only their official dispatches but their private correspondence and their numberless minutes, I learned to realize more fully the enormous responsibility and complexity of their task. Never had British historians enjoyed such an opportunity of watching our policy in the making, for never had such a mass of first-hand material been at their disposal. Professor Temperley, who never wore his heart on his sleeve, wrote to me that he felt a solemn and deep sense of thankfulness that we had been able to complete our task, and generously added that our association had been one of the most memorable things in his life. We could at any rate claim that we had kept faith with our readers, and none of our reviewers in many lands ever accused us of partisanship or concealment.

In 1922 I read a paper entitled *Recent Revelations of European Diplomacy* to the British Institute of International Affairs. Lord Oxford, who was in the chair, described as a travesty of history my assertion that in 1914 our hands were no longer free since we had become enmeshed in the quarrels and ambitions of our Continental friends. I replied by quoting Lloyd George's description of our relation to France as an obligation of honour. It was an interesting discussion in which Sir Valentine Chirol, General

Sir Frederick Maurice, Sir Francis Acland, Under-Secretary for Foreign Affairs in 1914, and Percy Molteno, an active Parliamentary critic of Grey's policy, took part. The latter reminded the audience of our naval agreement with France in 1912 by which the French fleet was withdrawn from the Channel in tacit reliance on British support in that quarter, and inquired how the claim of a free hand could be reconciled with such a vital strategic arrangement. I expressed no opinion as to the wisdom or necessity of our abandonment of 'splendid isolation', but I argued that the inescapable price was the loss of unfettered control over our policy. The address, reprinted as a *brochure* by the Institute of International Affairs, met with a considerable demand and I was pressed to bring the survey up to date. The resulting volume, bearing the same title, which appeared in 1927, surveyed publications subsequent to the outbreak of war which illustrated the period from the accession of William II in 1888 to the Treaty of Versailles. The revelations were described under the countries of their origin, beginning with Germany as the principal contributor of material and ending with the United States.

A brief concluding chapter opened with an exhortation to students to stand above the battle and to remember Hegel's pregnant aphorism: 'Tragedy is the conflict not of right with wrong but of right with right.' The time had come to abandon the division of the contending parties into sheep and goats. Though the conduct of each of the belligerents appeared to its enemies to indicate a double dose of original sin, it was in every case what might have been expected.

It was natural that Serbia should aspire to unite under her sceptre the discontented Jugoslav subjects of her neighbour, should use their undoubted grievances in Croatia to foster the Pan-Serb idea, and should look to Russia for assistance, as Cavour in similar circumstances had looked to France. It was equally natural that Austria should resolve to defend herself against the openly proclaimed ambition to rob her of provinces which she had held for centuries. The ultimatum to Serbia was at best a gambler's throw; but it was envisaged by the statesmen of Vienna and Budapest as a strictly defensive action, offering the best chance of escape from a danger which was certain to increase and which threatened the existence of Austria as a Great Power. The conduct of Germany was no less shortsighted but no less intelligible. Austria had set her heart on abating the Serbian nuisance; and she was the only Power, large or small, on whom Germany could rely, since Italy and Romania were allies in nothing but name. If Austria ceased to be a Great Power through the loss of her southern provinces, Germany would stand alone in Europe, wedged in between a hostile Russia and a France bent on revenge.

Turned into a gramophone record this chapter found its way into circles which the volume was unlikely to penetrate. The book was quickly reprinted, and a second edition, with a supplement on the revelations of 1927, appeared at the opening of 1928. A third edition, with a supplement on the revelations of 1928–9, was published in 1930, and a fourth enlarged edition in 1940.

For some years I had toyed with the idea of collecting and revising a few minor writings, and the plan was fulfilled in 1931. The principal item in *Studies in Modern History* was a full-length portrait of Baron von Holstein, expanded from a sketch contributed to the *Cambridge Historical Journal*. 'The Mystery Man of the Wilhelmstrasse' was an interesting pathological study, and since he was largely responsible for German policy from the fall of Bismarck in 1890 till his resignation in 1906, some of the most important scenes of contemporary history pass before our eyes. A *brochure* written in 1920 for the series *Helps to Students of History* was brought up to date with the title *The Study of the French Revolution*. An address on *The Political Background of Goethe's Life*, delivered to the Goethe Society and published in its *Transactions*, reappeared without change, as did an article on *Germany's Debt to the French Revolution*, written for the *Quarterly Review* in 1918. An address to the Sociological Society in 1915 on *German Political Ideas* was brought up to date with a sketch of the Weimar Constitution and of the ideology of its main author, Hugo Preuss. *The Study of Bismarck*, the only new item in the volume, embodied some of the reflections suggested by the reading of forty years. *German Historical Studies since the War* was written for the German number of *The Times Literary Supplement* of 18 April 1929, and was brought up to date. The *Cambridge Chair of Modern History* grew out of a paper read at the Historical Congress in 1913, and was likewise brought up to date by comments on Bury and George Trevelyan. *The Study of Foreign Affairs* was an expansion of a Presidential Address to the Social and Political Education League. The volume concluded with an address on Historical Novels to the National Home Reading Union.

When the completion of the *British Documents* was in sight I summarized the mass of new material released from our own and other archives in my longest book, *Before the War: Studies in Diplomacy.* The first volume, devoted to Lansdowne, Delcassé, Bülow, Iswolsky and Aehrenthal, appeared in 1936; the second, concerning Grey, Poincaré, Bethmann, Sazonoff and Berchtold, in 1938. Since the chronological development of the European situation during the opening years of the century had by this time been traced by Sidney Fay, myself and other writers, I surveyed the drama from a fresh angle, reconstructing events as they appeared to the principal actors and their fellow-countrymen. Though the personality of a Foreign Minister may well be a factor of importance, the main element in the determination of policy is the national tradition. The chapters were neither miniature biographies nor essays in psychological interpretation but studies in diplomacy. None of the ten wanted war, but nobody dreamed of renouncing it as an instrument of policy. The rattle of arms was never far away, for Europe was merely a geographical expression. Though the dangers of international anarchy were recognized, attempts to remove or diminish them at the Hague Conferences were half-hearted and the Hague Court was only employed for minor affairs. The ultimate cause of the conflagration in 1914 was the traditional doctrine of unfettered sovereignty and the universal assumption that the graver disputes between nations could be settled only by the sword.

Though none of the statesmen described in these volumes was a superman, I felt entitled to allot them different marks for competence and character. Lansdowne and Grey were depicted as cool, honourable and peace-loving men with nothing to conceal.

To stand by France, first in regard to Morocco as by treaty bound, and later in the whole field of international politics so long as her policy was unaggressive; to complete the *rapprochement* with Russia which Lansdowne had begun; to strive for a naval agreement and neighbourly relations with Germany; to maintain our traditions of an invincible navy and a small voluntary army; to be friends with the United States; to keep the alliance with Japan in repair; to carry on the humanitarian efforts of his predecessor in Macedonia and the Belgian Congo; to labour for peace without for a moment forgetting the dread possibilities of war: here were the outlines of a programme of which Grey saw no reason to be ashamed.

Delcassé is presented as the man who changed Britain and Italy into friends. Poincaré is absolved of the charge that he plotted with Iswolsky for war. Bülow, the most brilliant of the team, sometimes though not always spurred on by his impulsive master, threw away the friendship of England, which Bethmann, a great gentleman but never master in his own house, vainly strove to regain. Iswolsky is praised for winning the confidence of England and Japan but censured for his blunders in the Near East. Sazonoff, a man of high character, emerges as the weakest on the list, encouraging Pan-Serb ambitions which the Hapsburg Empire was certain to resist. While Aehrenthal appears as a brilliant failure, Berchtold is defended against the charge of being, as Masaryk used to maintain, a mere dilettante, chiefly interested in his racehorses and his clothes; behind the veil of aristocratic nonchalance were the heart and brain of an Austrian patriot.

Professor Sidney Fay, the leading transatlantic scholar on the origins of the war, wrote that some critics—though not himself—might perhaps feel that I had been a little too lenient in my verdicts. After such floods of bitter and over-condemnatory war-guilt literature, he added, it was pleasant to see the leading actors presented with the aims and motives which they conscientiously tried to follow. If a recorder of contemporary history cannot hope to stand like a god above the raging battle, however earnestly he may strive to do so, he can at any rate afford the foes of his country the same privilege of telling their story as he allows to its friends. The two volumes were translated and about to appear in German dress when the outbreak of war in 1939 switched public interest from the past to the present and prevented publication.

Though historical scholarship is its own reward every writer is grateful for the approval of his peers. During the inter-war years I received the degree of Hon. D.Litt. at Oxford and Durham, was appointed President of the Historical Association for the usual three-year term, and was elected a Fellow of the British Academy. Trinity College made me an Honorary Fellow, and I succeeded Professor Robertson as President of the English Goethe Society. The Academies of Göttingen, Prague and Vienna and various American institutions enrolled me as a Corresponding Member. The greatest surprises were the C.H. conferred in 1939 and the German Order *Pour le Mérite* in 1955.

19

THE NAZI REVOLUTION

WHEN Hitler's standard-bearers in the Reichstag jumped from 12 to 107 in the election of September 1930, some observers foretold the doom of the Weimar experiment. I was not among the prophets, for it was only when Brüning was evicted in May 1932 that I began to worry. The spectacle of Papen, a brainless cavalry officer, expelling the Prussian Government and ruling without popular support in the Reichstag or the Reich filled me with disgust. My feelings at this moment were expressed in a brilliant book, *Germany puts the Clock Back*, by Edgar Mowrer, the leading American journalist in Berlin. Neither the aged President, nor the ambitious Papen, nor the intriguing Schleicher, wanted Hitler, but they all unwittingly played his game. He was lucky to have such clumsy antagonists, and when they opened the flood-gates the bitter waters of revolution gushed forth. I recalled Heine's grim prophecy that one day the old pagan gods would descend from their thrones and smash Christian civilization with their hammer blows.

In the afternoon of 30 January 1933, I read on the London placards the ominous words in bold type: *Hitler Chancellor*, and recalled Spengler's recent forecast that Germany was more likely to see another Caesar than another Goethe. The Third Reich had begun, bringing in its train disgrace, devastation and defeat to Germany and measureless misery to the world. Like the Munster Anabaptists, the Jacobins, the Communards of 1871 and other fanatics throughout the ages, the Nazis blared forth the thread-bare formula that they destroyed in order to rebuild. For the first time since the fall of Bismarck Germany had a master, and millions of her citizens, particularly among inexperienced youth, rallied

279

to his call. To a people accustomed to courts and uniforms the Weimar system seemed drab and nerveless, and there was a fierce resentment at the fetters of Versailles: the brighter the glories of the past, the greater seemed the humiliation of defeat. Judging by the elections of 1932 and the final test of March 1933, nearly half the nation saw in the Führer the captain who would stand up to France, restore self-confidence, vindicate the authority of the state, and find work for the unemployed. Once again a minority under a new Pied Piper of Hamelin triumphed over a leaderless crowd. The outlook was bleak, and so far from making the world safe for democracy the war had paved the way for dictators in many lands. Was it merely a transient illness, we wondered, or had we, as Mussolini argued, passed out of one era into another, exchanging the Liberal illusions of the nineteenth century for the 'discipline' of the twentieth? Republics, declared Victor Hugo, were crowns for white hairs, by which he meant that successful self-government demands a certain political maturity; but no one could seriously claim that Germany, Poland and other young states passed that exacting test.

The term Dictator comes to us from Rome, the type it denotes from Greece, where the feverish politics of the City States threw up the *Tyrannos* as a recurring phenomenon, an authentic or presumed superman who seized power in an emergency and was tolerated or welcomed by his fellow-citizens. He was the man of the moment, the saviour of society, disappearing as suddenly as he came when his task was done or his incapacity exposed. He was always regarded as something exceptional, provisional, irregular. The greatest of the class in the ancient world was Julius Caesar; in modern times Cromwell and Napoleon. Lacking anchorage in the stabilized society of the pre-war world, the younger generation of Germans, many of them unemployed or under-employed, was ripe for experiments. Democracy became widely identified with surrender and distress, instability and irresolution, inefficiency and delay.

As Bismarck found his model in Cavour, so Hitler copied Mussolini. The soil had been prepared by the severity of the dictated treaty, the ill-judged encouragement of separatism in the Rhineland, the humiliation of African troops in the occupied zone, the burden of reparations, the invasion of the Ruhr, the collapse of the mark—here was a sequence of shocks and sufferings very difficult for a proud nation to endure without losing its balance. When Briand succeeded Poincaré and Stresemann brought Germany into the League of Nations it was too late to eradicate these bitter memories. Their savings and familiar landmarks gone, the middle and lower middle classes felt like sheep without a shepherd. Despite the ability and devotion of Rathenau, Stresemann, Brüning and a host of lesser men, the Republic never took root; compromises, coalitions and dissolutions robbed the Reichstag of such prestige as it possessed. The supporters of democratic institutions were deeply divided; though Socialists, Liberals and Catholics sat together in various Cabinets, the old gulf between the *bourgeoisie* and the manual worker was never bridged. And all the time the Communists, offspring of suffering and frustration and fortified by the sympathies of the Kremlin, were at work, weakening the Socialists by incessant attacks and frightening timid citizens out of their wits.

It only required a dynamic demagogue to fan the smouldering discontents into a flame. For years there had been a growing call for a Man, and at last he appeared. Germany, screamed Hitler, had not been defeated in the field but stabbed in the back by traitors at home, and had been misruled by Jews and Marxists ever since; the old quarrelsome factions must be swept away. Henceforth, announced Goebbels, one party would suffice—his own party, combining a spirited foreign policy with an advanced social programme for the common man. No more colourless Reichstags nor transient Cabinets nor anaemic Chancellors, but a Leader, with red blood in his veins, risen from the people and therefore aware of their needs, grasping the helm firmly in his hands, standing up to Germany's foes abroad, regaining for the Fatherland its rightful place in the sun and rearming for the inevitable conflict to come! The shrill denunciations of their recent rulers, combined with roseate visions of strength and prosperity, swept millions off their feet. Caring nothing for birth, titles or wealth, preaching the gospel of discipline and national unity, the greatest mob-orator of modern times made a powerful appeal to the little man who had nothing to lose and to the idealism of the young. 'We Nazis', wrote Goering in his book *Germany Reborn*, 'believe that in political matters Adolf Hitler is

19

infallible, just as the Roman Catholic believes that in religious matters the Pope is infallible. His will is my law.' After trampling down all opposition and removing the curse of unemployment by large scale rearmament and public works, the new régime proudly announced that it would endure for a thousand years.

In a lecture in the Senate House of the University of London with Sir Horace Rumbold, former British Ambassador, in the chair, I gave my audience the only comfort I could offer.

The Bolshevists have probably come to stay, for Russia is accustomed to autocracy and Stalin can easily be replaced. It is difficult, however, to believe that the Nazi and Fascist régimes will long survive their founders. When Mussolini and Hitler are gone, there are no leaders to take their place. Their unique personalities suggest a time-limit for their experiments. Before Cromwell's body was in the grave the Restoration was in sight. It is a fairly safe prophecy that millions who are today content with their bondage will weary of it and cast it off.

Though my forecast was correct I failed to foresee that the price of liberation would be a second world war.

The summer of 1933 was devoted to studying the new Germany and her neighbours. In Berlin I was visited by some young historians who had lost their posts on account of their Jewish blood and were planning a flight to happier lands. The brutal purge of the Universities, the schools, the public services and the professions had begun. The writings of Jewish authors had disappeared from the shop windows, which were filled with copies of *Mein Kampf* and biographies of the Nazi chiefs. Frederick the Great had supplanted Bismarck as the national hero, Potsdam had displaced Weimar. I noted the Nazi interest in Cromwell, the man of destiny who emerged to save and rule the state.

Next to the Brownshirts in the streets, the Swastika flag on houses and portraits of the Leader in the shops, visitors were struck by the black-out in the press. Socialist as well as Communist papers had disappeared. The *Berliner Tageblatt* had been compelled to change its tune, and Theodor Wolff, its accomplished Jewish editor, had fled to France. Rosenberg's *Völkischer Beobachter*, the official organ of the party, and the *Angriff*, into which Goebbels spewed his venom, were read or at any rate bought by all who desired to stand well with the new masters. Next to the *Frankfurter Zeitung*, which still retained faint traces of independence, the best of the dailies was the *Deutsche Allgemeine Zeitung*, a Conservative though not a Nazi publication. Its respected editor Klein having been dismissed for describing Hitler's propaganda against the Austrian Government as a civil war, the more pliable Dr. Silex was summoned to Berlin. He had spent four years as its correspondent in London, where he had visited me, had written a book on Ramsay MacDonald, and passed for an Anglophil. When he called at my hotel in Berlin I expressed my horror at the cruelty and intolerance of the new régime. Though not a member of the ruling party, he replied, he was convinced that it was the only way: the democratic experiment had failed and Germany needed a strong hand. 'You will get used to it, as you have got used to Mussolini, and then we shall be able to do business.' I rejoined that, so far as I was concerned, I had not got used to Mussolini. Like so many Germans he failed to grasp that an Englishman, with the rule of law in his blood, abhorred dictators of every kind. Did not Herder call Germany the land of obedience? Had not Hegel and Treitschke deified the state? Brüning had dismissed the eruption of the Nazi volcano with the contemptuous words: *Das ist die kranke Jugend*, but he was too civilized to understand its wide appeal. After fifteen years of bodily and mental suffering millions rejoiced that they could once again speak with the enemy in the gate. Among the causes of the Nazi triumph the lifting of the inferiority complex claims high place, and the racial doctrine, unscientific though it was, emphasized the virtues of a stock to which a citizen might be proud to belong. At last the lads in brown felt they were needed and had something to live for. Bidden to think with their blood, they obeyed the Führer's command. France had tired of dictators, but their inflammable neighbour had to learn its lesson.

After a visit to Zittau in Saxony, my wife's old home, where the revolution seemed less challenging than in Berlin, I crossed the frontier into Czechoslovakia. My old friend Marvin had organized the earliest 'Unity School' amid the turmoil of the First World War, for the author of *The Living Past* and *The Century of Hope* was an incurable optimist. His aim was to remind us of the many things we have in common and to survey our joint efforts to build a civilized world. The experiment was a success, and the addresses were published each year in a volume by the Oxford University Press. I lectured to three of the gatherings at home before the venue was changed to Vienna, Stockholm and Danzig. In 1933 the choice fell on Prague, and I accepted the invitation to visit that glorious old city on the way to Warsaw for the International Historical Congress. Each School had a special theme, and this time it was Liberty. I undertook the topic of National Liberty; but as Marvin was laid low by an operation at the last moment, I had also to deliver the inaugural address and to preside over the meetings. The main aspects—political, religious, economic—were reviewed by British, French, Austrian and Czech specialists. We were proud to meet under the auspices of a community which had recovered the blessings of external and internal freedom. It was thirty-three years since my previous visit. When the Hapsburg Empire broke up in 1918 the Czechs regained their independence three centuries after the battle of the White Mountain, and the Austrian garrison withdrew without firing a shot. The rule of Vienna had long ceased to be oppressive, but it remained an alien influence, and the country possessed a ready-made ruler in the person of its most illustrious citizen. The octogenarian President was on holiday, but it was good to hear of his excellent health and to observe the respect he inspired. Holding aloof from party strife, *pater patriae*, he was the ideal head of a virile and liberty-loving people.

No more perfect partnership has existed in twentieth-century Europe than that of Masaryk and Beneš. Master and pupil lived side by side in the Hradschin, towering above the winding river, the one in the Presidential suite, the other in the Foreign Office. Hearing I was in Prague Dr. Beneš kindly invited me for a talk. When I congratulated him on the recent consolidation of the Little Entente he agreed as to its significance, emphasizing that the new treaty was only the formal embodiment of an existing relationship. He did not believe that territorial changes would occur in Europe without war, since small modifications would be useless and large concessions were ruled out by public opinion. He remained unyielding in regard to the new territorial and political *status quo* on the middle Danube. In reply to my question as to the return of a Hapsburg to the throne at Budapest he exclaimed that it would be worse than the *Anschluss*, since it might pave the way for the reunion of Hungary and Austria. Within the existing limits, however, he was ready to help Austria in any way he could, 'in spite of all the harm she has done us'. When I suggested that the maintenance of Austrian independence was a Czechoslovak as well as a European interest he cordially concurred. He showed no sign of apprehension that the new masters in Berlin might one day gobble up his country, and seemed in all respects a carefree man.

During my week in Prague I learned something about internal conditions. The best sign was that since 1926 German Ministers had sat in every Cabinet and irredentism appeared to be unknown, but there were bitter memories of the past. The views of the German element in regard to the Nazi revolution were divided. The Socialists, needless to say, found a new reason for contentment with their Czechoslovak citizenship which guaranteed their civic rights; but the German districts in the north, being the most industrialized, suffered more from the slump than the Czech peasants, and the unemployed were a grievous burden for the state. I found the Commercial Secretary to the British Legation more optimistic than the official spokesmen of the Government Departments, but they agreed that the management of the finances had been admirable. English visitors appeared to be welcome, and I was invited to broadcast on the problems of the British Empire.

To cross the Polish frontier was to enter a country which, like Bohemia, had risen from the tomb but was confronted with graver difficulties at home and abroad. Kattowitz was in the heart of the industrial zone of Upper Silesia, a province developed by German brains, German capital and Polish muscles, but cut in half by the plebiscite in 1921. Most of the German residents had migrated, and it was now a Polish town in blood as well as in law. From noisy Kattowitz to the tranquil dignity of Cracow was only an hour's journey. The old capital with its palace and cathedral on the hill above the Vistula recalls the centuries when Poland was a Great Power. The city never recovered its prestige after Sigismund Vasa moved to Warsaw, but the palace had been frequently occupied and the spirit of the gallant Sobieski haunts its courts. Poles thrill with pride as they gaze at the luxurious tent of the

Sultan captured when their cavalry drove the Turks from the walls of beleaguered Vienna in 1683, and every Pole looks across the river to the gigantic mound of Kosciusko with a song in his heart. Cracow speaks not less of culture than of glory. The statue of Copernicus adorns the court of the University, and in the picture gallery the vast historical canvases of Matejko reminded one of Verestchagin. With their long hair, dark skin and black frocks the Galician Jews who angered Hitler in Vienna introduced an oriental note.

Though Warsaw had been in Russian hands for more than a century there was little to remind one of the fact. The Citadel where so many patriots had been shot at dawn stands on the river bank outside the town. The Orthodox Cathedral, dumped down in the largest square of a Catholic city, was destroyed by the Poles when they regained their independence, and the site became Pilsudski Square. The Belvedere Palace had become Pilsudski's home, but the old Marshal was away. Warsaw is one of the least rewarding capitals in Europe. The country is flat, the Vistula small and shallow, the architecture commonplace. There are no old churches and the picture gallery is third-rate. The Palace is mainly the work of Stanislas Augustus, one of the earliest lovers of Catherine the Great and the last of the Polish kings. Far more attractive is the Lazienki palace built by the same cultivated monarch in a quiet park on the outskirts of the city, a little French gem filled with the portraits of his friends.

Poland gave the Historical Congress a cordial welcome. We travelled at half price on the railways and were free of the museums. Receptions were held by the President in the Palace, by the Prime Minister in the old Radziwill mansion, by the Municipality, and by the British Legation. Polish scholarship was represented among many others by Dembinski, the Nestor of the Congress over which he presided, a friend from Oslo and London; by Handelsman, another friend well known in Western capitals, and by Halecki, author of the best short history of his country. Their fluency in French, German and English was a marvel. There had been some fear that the old antagonism between the Teuton and the Slav might keep German scholars away, but they turned up in force. Almost every University from Königsberg to Freiburg was represented, and I learned of the changes enforced or threatened by the Nazi purge. The most distinguished of the German delegates was Brandenburg, author of an admirable book on recent German foreign policy which has appeared in English dress. None of them, needless to say, was a Nazi, for Hitler and his rabble had no use for history except as an instrument of propaganda. The Russians, represented as usual by the dominant clique, once again focused attention on the relations of classes. Dr. Koht, the future Norwegian Foreign Minister, came from Oslo, Friis from Copenhagen, Yorga from Bucharest, Rostovtzev all the way from Yale. My own contribution was an address on Hobbes, happily the sole champion among British thinkers of the totalitarian state.

After the Congress I travelled north to Danzig and the Corridor, the focus of Polish-German antagonism. Though severed from the Fatherland by the Treaty of Versailles, the fine old Hanseatic city remained German to the core. The local Nazis were in control, and the massive brick tower of the Marienkirche was defiled by huge Swastika flags. There were plenty of Nationalists, Socialists and Liberals who detested the new ideology, but as usual they were unable to combine. I had never joined in the denunciation of the Danzig Statute, which was mainly the work of Harvard Professors at Paris, for I could not improvise a solution acceptable to both races. It was easy to understand the resentment that a historic German city was severed from the Reich; yet the case for the Poles was equally strong, for Dansk had been a Polish city for centuries before it passed to Prussia in the Second Partition and it stood at the mouth of Poland's longest river. It was the task of the High Commissioner, representing the League of Nations, to smooth away administrative difficulties as best he could. The all-out Nazi attack had not begun in 1933, but there was thunder in the air. The blue and yellow post-boxes placed side by side symbolized the division between the two camps. No one dreamed that four months later Hitler and Pilsudski would sign a Ten Years Pact, a Nazi stratagem for postponing the reckoning till the Führer felt strong enough to pounce. The magnificent castle of the Teutonic Knights at Marienburg a few miles beyond the boundary of the Free City, restored at great expense by the Kaiser, spoke of the historic German claim to dominate the Eastern marshes.

The construction of a port with the largest trade in the Baltic was the most impressive symbol of Poland's resurrection. I was motored to Gdynia, which had grown from a little fishing village to a town of 40,000 inhabitants and was soon to double its size. A railway connected the coalfields of Polish Upper Silesia with the sea, and the docks and warehouses were planned on a generous scale. I was taken from wharf to wharf in a motor launch and entertained on a Polish passenger steamer about to sail for England. Though few ships were to be seen my hosts assured me they would come, for this grandiose enterprise was designed to be a naval base as well as a commercial port. My last day in Poland was spent in Posen, renamed Posnan, only a hundred miles from Berlin. I left the country rejoicing in its liberation but anxious about its security. It was desperately poor despite its coal and timber; one third of the population was of non-Polish blood, and it was wedged in between two large and unfriendly states who might one day combine in a sudden attack. The strict investigation of my bag at the German custom-house on my way to Breslau indicated strained relations, for a dozen books were taken out and scrutinized. The volumes containing summaries of the lectures delivered at the Warsaw Historical Congress seemed to excite suspicion, and the official spent a considerable time scanning the pages for ideological contraband.

My travels in 1933 ended at the earthly paradise of Baden-Baden, where the liberal tradition of South Germany was reflected in the widespread disapproval of the anti-Semitic crusade. Hotel keepers openly deplored the absence of their Jewish *clientèle* from within and without the Reich, but material reasons were not the only ones. The little town prided itself on the orchestra which played at the spa and which had been worked up by a Jewish conductor. We learned with horror that he was under notice to quit, and I shall never forget his farewell concert. The hall was packed and the applause amounted to a political demonstration. Words were unnecessary. The Nazis had not yet shown their whole hand against the Jews, the churches, or the smaller neighbours of Germany, but I had seen enough to vow that I would not revisit the country so long as these thugs were in control. Innocent men were being tortured and murdered in concentration camps, and the secret police, an abominable import from Russia, were at work. The Reichstag fire trial was in progress, and it was revealing to compare Douglas Reed's vivid reports in *The Times* with the doctored version in the muzzled German press. The exchanges between Dimitroff, the Bulgarian Communist, and Goering, bellowing forth threats of vengeance, were a drama in themselves. The new masters had turned their backs not only on law and liberty but on civilization itself.

How long would it last and what should be our attitude in England? My wife and I felt that we were confronted with a revolution of the most sinister kind and that social contact with its official representatives was unthinkable. When invited to lunch by a member of the German Embassy I had to explain as politely as possible that I must decline. 'Do you feel as strongly about it as that?' he inquired. 'Yes, I am afraid I do.' I burned my boats in an article in the *Contemporary Review*, inspired by the bloody purge on 30 June 1934, in which scores of Hitler's old associates were shot by his orders and many more slaughtered without them. This new Bartholomew Massacre would have disgraced a Balkan state, and I let myself go. The original title, 'The Butchers of Berlin', was abandoned in proof as unsuitable to the dignified traditions of the journal, and I contented myself with 'The Terror in Germany'. The Nazis had revealed their true character, and I foretold that they would come to a violent end. As Camille Desmoulins had exclaimed, *La Révolution dévore ses enfants*. After this open declaration of war it would have been impossible to cross the German frontier again even had I desired. Careful note was taken of all such offences, as Dorothy Thompson, Elizabeth Wiskemann and Norman Angell discovered when they were bundled out of the country which they had incautiously revisited.

The blood-bath of 1934 shattered our Anglo-German Society. Since the coming of Hitler we had lain low, but some of our members thought it a mistake to boycott the new régime, however little they liked its ways. At a meeting at the House of Commons Sir Ian Hamilton pleaded for the resumption of our activities, including the entertainment of Nazi officials. No one had worked harder to restore friendly relations between the two peoples, and his appeal carried great weight. The other side was put by Harold Nicolson, speaking with the authority of a former official of the British Embassy at Berlin, and by myself. The régime, we argued, was so cruel and so incorrigibly uncivilized that nothing should be done to enhance its prestige: as admirers of the better Germany, temporarily submerged by the raging flood, we felt we must not let our old friends down. How could we sit at table with defenders of the Gestapo and the Concentration Camps, thereby appearing to indicate that we did not greatly care? A week later the news of the massacre blew the Society to pieces. The vacuum was only partially filled by the creation of an Anglo-German Fellowship which avowed enemies of the Nazi régime like myself declined to join.

Soon after the horrors of 30 June I received a letter from our old friend Dufour-Feronce who, after representing his country in London, Geneva and Belgrade, was living in retirement at Berlin. Baron Werner von Rheinbaben, I was informed, was coming to London and desired a heart to heart talk. I had met him in Berlin in 1929 at a lunch party given for me by Professor Moritz Bonn, had heard him at Chatham House, and had read his admiring biography of his old leader Stresemann. He was not a Nazi, I was told, but he wanted us to be friends with the new team. He fortified himself with a second introduction from Lord Lothian. It was understood that this pleasant-mannered former naval officer was in close touch with the Wilhelmstrasse and would report his conversations. 'I know you are pro-German and anti-Nazi', he began. He proceeded to argue, as Silex had done, that German democracy had failed: he had been a National Liberal member of the Reichstag for ten years and could speak from experience. The German people, he assured me, were happy enough. 'Take a car and drive about the country, and you will see for yourself.' Unemployment had been abolished. Germany wanted the peaceful revision of the Treaty of Versailles, fair play and nothing else: there was no thought of war.

When I spoke of Nazi crimes as an obstacle to friendship he interjected: 'Crimes! That is a strong word. What crimes?' First the outlawry of the Jews, I replied; second, the concentration camps; third, the butcheries of 30 June. If Germany substituted autocracy for democracy that was her affair, but we expected a minimum standard of conduct from a nation claiming to be civilized. He reminded me of the different tradition of his country and pleaded that it was politically immature. When I pronounced the persecution of the Jews to be a crime even worse than the flaying of the Huguenots by Louis XIV because our standards had risen in the last two centuries, he questioned whether there had been much of a change. He admitted that the Nazis were rough customers and made no attempt to defend all their abominations. His thesis was that we made too much fuss about such things, judged Germany by too austere a test, and overlooked the good work that was being done. When I mentioned the ravings of *Mein Kampf* he pleaded that Hitler deserved to be treated as a responsible statesman and leader of his people, not reproached for a book written many years earlier when he was a private citizen and when the French were in the Ruhr. Despite my plain speaking he came again to see me when he revisited England and wrote two striking articles on German foreign policy for the *Contemporary Review*. The second, published directly after the Munich crisis, admitted that Hitler's methods had been unconventional, but welcomed the settlement of the Sudeten problem as an example of revision by consent. I retorted that it would be more accurately described as revision by ultimatum. His assurance that German territorial ambitions were now satisfied, and that there was nothing more to prevent friendly relations with England, sounded plausible enough till the Dictator gobbled up what was left of Czechoslovakia a few months later. Whether he approved this fresh outrage which made nonsense of his assurances I do not know, for he never wrote to me again. The difference between a professing Nazi and a 'fellow-traveller' like the Baron was evidently not very wide. National Liberals had always been more national than liberal.

I may illustrate the failure of Nazi propaganda in England by the discomfiture of another and less eminent German visitor. Dr. Wolfgang Schwarz, a former leader-writer on the staff of *Vorwärts*, a refined young man with an English wife, introduced himself to me at the annual Congress of the National Peace Council held at Oxford in 1933, at which I was presiding. Having asked and obtained permission to speak he proceeded to defend the anti-Semitic campaign by quoting statistics of Jewish over-representation in the professions. The indignation of the hundreds of delegates waxed hot as he proceeded to roll off the figures, as if a cruel wrong could be explained away by percentages. Happily there was a far more distinguished Socialist at our Congress who preferred exile and poverty to apostasy. Dr. Breitscheid had been the orator of his party in the Reichstag for many years and had represented the German Government at Geneva. This tall and distinguished looking Intellectual was reputed to be lacking in decision, but his speech, superbly translated by Charles Roden Buxton who had acted as interpreter at many international conferences, created a deep impression. He had fled to Paris when the Nazis came to power and was struggling to maintain himself and his wife by his pen. It was an honour to open the pages of the *Contemporary* to a man who wrote almost as well as he spoke. His modest bank balance had been confiscated and a box of clothes forwarded by a friend in Berlin was seized at the frontier when the customs official discovered to whom they belonged. Shortly afterwards he was deprived of his German citizenship. The best rejoinder to the clumsy sophistries of Dr. Schwarz was the appearance of Dr. Breitscheid as a penniless refugee.

My experience as President of the National Peace Council, 1933–36, revealed the confusion of thought on fundamental issues which prevailed between the wars and which goes far to explain the vacillations of successive British Ministries. Our forty affiliated societies were working for peace according to their lights, but that was their only bond of union. What was to be done if a powerful nation ran amok? One section, to which I belonged, believed in resisting naked aggression, if necessary at the risk of war; the other, represented by Quakers and pacifists, refused to contemplate even an economic boycott which might lead to serious trouble. Interminable debates took place without changing anybody's views. 'You will get us into war,' cried the pacifists; 'anything is better than that.' 'To do nothing is to encourage the aggressor', was our reply.

Italy's invasion of Abyssinia during my term of office raised the issue in an even more challenging form than the rape of Manchuria. Both countries were members of the League, but Japan was far away and the Mediterranean close at hand. I had favoured economic sanctions against Japan in 1931 if the United States were willing to collaborate, which unhappily was not the case.

In 1935 the problem seemed simpler. Italy's supplies for the distant campaign had to pass through the Suez Canal, and the mountainous country in the heart of Africa coveted by the brigand Duce could only be conquered with the aid of oil for his bombers. Like most Englishmen I welcomed Sir Samuel Hoare's definition of our policy at Geneva in September as steady and collective opposition to unprovoked aggression, and rejoiced when we took the lead in a partial boycott of the aggressor. Many people shied at the word sanctions, which was not to be found in the Covenant, and I prefer the word non-assistance. If we could not help the victim why should we aid the criminal by buying his goods and meeting his vital needs? Never since 1918 had our prestige sunk so low as during the winter of 1935-6, when the Hoare-Laval scheme proposed to reward the burglar, and when, while supporting the oil sanction in principle, we consented to delay its application till it was too late to be of use. I shall always regret that the Anglo-Persian Oil Company, in which the British Government held the majority of shares, supported the aggressor throughout the war. That Laval preferred the rape of Abyssinia and the sabotage of the League to the estrangement of Mussolini was known to the British Government and should have been considered before raising false hopes at Geneva and Addis Ababa. If we really believed in the utility of sanctions we should have added petrol to the list and faced the risk. If, on the contrary, we were resolved to avoid the possible risk of war we should not have moved at all. *Sauter pour mieux reculer* does not make sense. In a spirited defence of his policy in *Nine Troubled Years* Sir Samuel Hoare maintains that he could have done nothing else in the existing circumstances.

The most notable incidents in the life of the National Peace Council were our annual congresses, over four of which I was called to preside. I have mentioned the Oxford meeting in 1933, when the addresses were published in a volume entitled *In Pursuit of Peace*. Our lecturers included Sir Arthur Salter, Dr. Hugh Dalton and Sir Frederick Whyte. At our usual public meeting in the Town Hall the chief orators were Sir Stafford Cripps and Dick Sheppard, a curious contrast of types, the former precise, lawyer-like and self-possessed; the pacifist parson speaking with the fervour of an evangelist on the subject nearest his heart. Our 1934

Congress, an even more remarkable gathering, was held at Birmingham, with Lord Cecil, Lord Ponsonby and Vera Brittain as our star performers. One session had been devoted to a survey of Russian policy by the Russian Ambassador which attracted wide attention in the press. Maisky's appearance on the platform in the Town Hall produced an ovation, not because people liked Communism but because they believed his assertion that Russia stood for peace. The honours of the evening, so far as applause was concerned, were shared with my old Trinity friend and host, Bishop Barnes, who had preached the Congress sermon in the cathedral on the previous day. The sight of a middle class audience in the city of Joseph Chamberlain loudly cheering the Russian Ambassador and the Liberal Bishop was an unusual experience.

In 1935 we met in London at Friends' House, where Lord Cecil and Arthur Henderson spoke at the opening session. I was shocked by the haggard appearance of the former Foreign Secretary and a few weeks later he was dead. What a gallant struggle for disarmament the dying man had made we were soon to read in Mrs. Hamilton's biography. In 1936 we met in Leeds, where Lord Lothian pleaded for the pooling of sovereignty as the only solution, and George Lansbury, vigorous as ever despite his years, preached his familiar gospel of loving our neighbour to a crowded audience in the Town Hall. If Mill was 'the saint of rationalism', Lansbury was the saint of pacifism: to know him was to love him. It used to be said that he invariably made the same speech, but his message, like the Sermon on the Mount, was always in season. At all these Congresses, attended by hundreds of delegates from every part of England, a few Communists reiterated their parrot cry that if capitalism were overthrown war would disappear. They could not anticipate that a year or two later Russia would overrun Poland and Finland and gobble up three little Baltic states. No one dealt more skilfully and patiently with this childish nonsense than Sir Norman Angell, one of the best debaters and one of the best psychologists of our time, always master of his subject and himself. Lansbury appealed to the emotions, Norman Angell to the head.

On becoming President of the National Peace Council in 1933 I was invited by Gilbert Murray to join the Executive Committee of the League of Nations Union, then at the height of its influence, and I agreed to serve for a year. At our weekly meeting the same sort of subjects came up as were being discussed in the body which I represented. The sunshine of Locarno had gone, Japan had opened a new chapter of unprovoked aggression in China, and the Disarmament Conference had failed, but in England belief in the League was as strong as ever. There were similar associations in other countries, but none compared with ours in energy and inspiring leadership. Gilbert Murray was the ideal Chairman, infinitely patient, exquisitely courteous, knowing instinctively when and how to end a debate. At his side sat Lord Cecil, his predecessor in the Chair, the most impressive figure in any company, combining the intellectual precision of a lawyer with the crusader's unquenchable zeal. Among the veterans round the long table sat Lord Dickinson, the honoured co-founder with Allen Baker of the World Alliance of the Churches, Lord Rhayader, better known as Leif Jones, who specialized in finance, and Sir Norman Angell. Among our younger members Philip Noel-Baker occupied a place apart, his gift of speech rendering his interventions a delight. The interests of coloured races were represented by the former missionary Sir John Harris, secretary and soul of the Anti-Slavery Society. Sir Geoffrey Mander was always ready to put our questions in Parliament and to follow them up by supplementaries. Our women members included Lady Gladstone, widow of the Governor-General of South Africa, Mrs. Dugdale, niece and biographer of Lord Balfour, and Megan Lloyd George. Last but not least may be mentioned our indefatigable Secretary, Dr. Maxwell Garnett, who sat at the Chairman's right.

Though all political parties were represented on the Executive there was never the slightest trace of party feeling, for we tried to judge statesmen and their policies by the letter and spirit of the Covenant. The many branches of the L.N.U., the itinerant lecturers, Albert Hall meetings, publications, Easter and Summer Schools kept the great experiment before the country. The Peace Ballot afforded millions of citizens the opportunity to say what they wished the Government to do in certain circumstances, and the Abyssinian outrage deprived it of an exclusively academic character. In England, as elsewhere, there has never been a majority for peace at any price. Our Kensington branch, one of the

largest and most active in the kingdom, was lucky enough to have
Lord Phillimore and Lord Meston as its first and second Presi-
dents, busy men who were never too busy to attend to its affairs.
Every spring I gave a course of three addresses on the European
situation which filled the Town Hall. Among the stars at our
annual meetings, usually held at Armistice time, I recall Lord
Cecil and Duff Cooper. Debates always attracted an audience, and
I remember a duel between Gilbert Murray and Leo Maxse, the
die-hard editor of the *National Review* who had no use for the
League. Shortly before the Second World War I presided at a
debate between two ornaments of the Labour Party, Lord
Ponsonby and Mr. Zilliacus, a former official of the League. It
was no surprise to my old friend the champion of the Peace
Pledge Union that the vote went against him. The aggressors
were at work, cried his opponent; what are you going to do about
it? Aggression by the strong against the weak would continue till
aggressors discovered that it did not pay.

Visits to Geneva to lecture at the annual Summer School
organized by the League of Nations Union enabled me to feel the
international pulse as the European situation changed from year
to year. One of the attractions of the city of Calvin and Rousseau
was the veteran Count Bernstorff, formerly German Ambassador
to the United States, who detested the Nazi régime so heartily
that he spent his closing years in Switzerland. When I suggested
that Hitler was about five per cent abnormal he exclaimed: 'You
mean ninety-five per cent.' It has been a misfortune for herself
and for the world that Germany has produced so few Liberals of
the Bernstorff type. The gleaming Palais des Nations embodied
the faith of its builders in the ultimate sanity of mankind, and
there was no place like Geneva for fostering the larger patriotism.
An admirable training for budding statesmen, diplomats, international lawyers and publicists was provided at the Ecole des
Etudes Internationales under the joint direction of Professor
Rappard and Professor Mantoux and staffed by specialists from
many lands. Professor Burckhardt was taken from his lecture
room to fill the post of High Commissioner of the League at
Danzig. Professor Ferrero, author of a best-seller study of
economic Imperialism in ancient Rome, had left his Italian home
where liberals could scarcely breathe in the sultry atmosphere of

Fascism. It was a privilege to deliver five lectures in 1936 on British Foreign Policy since the First World War to an audience of the School representing many nationalities.

My last international gathering before the second conflagration was the seventh Historical Congress held at Zürich at the end of August 1938. Our Swiss hosts were as hospitable as ever, but there were dark clouds overhead. At the Warsaw Congress in 1933 there were no Nazis; at Zürich there were a few, none of them scholars of the first rank, and the champions and victims of the Third Reich kept out of each other's way. That little Austria, with her gracious culture, had ceased to exist, was deplored by most of our members whatever their nationality. 'You must feel it', I remarked to Ritter von Srbik, the most eminent of Austrian historians. 'Yes,' he replied, 'but I never regarded the Republic as viable.' The Poles appeared in good spirits, but the French seemed depressed and regarded another life and death struggle with Germany as a virtual certainty.

Where was the next quinquennial Congress to meet in 1943? An invitation reached us in Zürich from Rome, but should we accept it? Opinions were divided. My answer was no. How could I accept hospitality from a régime which had deprived eminent scholars like Gaetano de Sanctis, the historian of ancient Rome, of their chairs, had driven my friends Professor Salvemini and Don Luigi Sturzo into exile, and had evicted Jewish officials in order to curry favour with the German dictator? The discussion was postponed, and the question was answered by the outbreak of World War II in the following year. I had refused an official invitation to take part in a meeting of the Volta Society in Italy some years before, and I declined an invitation to a reception at the Italian Embassy in London. Apparently our well-intentioned policy of appeasement, as was to be expected, encouraged the Dictators to believe that we did not much care how they bullied their subjects and menaced their neighbours. The distinction between Hitler and Mussolini sometimes drawn in England seemed to me to be fallacious: one used the sledge-hammer, the other the stiletto. Anything more than correct official relations with such malefactors I felt to be impossible.

A stream of refugees began to flow into our home on Campden Hill after the accession of the Nazis to power in 1933. Few

20

Englishmen, I imagine, received more of these unhappy victims, whose affairs henceforth claimed a considerable share of my time. Lord Wedgwood, as good a European as he was a British patriot, kept a list of his suppliants who amounted to over two hundred. Some fled directly Hitler took office, others after the Reichstag fire: a certain number only lost their posts during the summer and autumn of 1933. The vicissitudes even of those personally known to me would fill a volume. Most of them were Jews, but the Liberal Professor Veit Valentin, an 'Aryan' of Huguenot descent, historian of the German Revolution of 1848–9, lost his position in the Reichsarchiv at Potsdam on the pretext of 'political unreliability'. Professor Friedrich Hertz fled from Halle, where he held the chair of Sociology, to Prague just in time to escape a search of his house. A third, Professor Rothfels, was allowed to retain his chair at Königsberg a little longer than most Jewish scholars because he had lost a leg in the war, but he was evicted when the anti-Semitic fanatics warmed to their work. A fourth, Professor Moritz Bonn, one of the keenest intellects in Germany and an ornament of the Handelshochschule at Charlottenburg, was welcomed to the London School of Economics. A fifth, Professor Gustav Mayer of Berlin, the biographer of Engels, assured me that his ancestors had lived in Germany for four hundred years. A sixth, Professor Mendelssohn-Bartholdy, grandson of the composer and Director of the Institut für auswärtige Politik at Hamburg, found refuge at Oxford where he died of cancer. A seventh, Professor Kantorowicz, an expert on medieval law and author of a courageous book entitled *The Myth of Encirclement*, fled from Kiel and settled in Cambridge. Our Universities played up magnificently by making openings for teachers and by the collection of funds. The first practical step was taken when Sir William Beveridge, Director of the London School of Economics, opened a register of refugee scholars and founded the Academic Assistance Council with Lord Rutherford as its President. Thousands of pounds were gathered in yearly appeals, and hundreds of posts were filled in the British Commonwealth and the United States. Many applicants had to wait for months, some for years, some appointments were temporary; but new hope was given to many a scholar who had lost everything except his self-respect.

It was more difficult for non-academic refugees to find their feet. One of the most striking personalities in this class was Rudolf Olden, a lawyer by training, who had fought in the war and had been on the staff of the *Berliner Tageblatt*. While its brilliant editor, Theodor Wolff, like Georg Bernhard, editor of the *Vossische Zeitung*, had sought refuge in France, Olden preferred England. He quickly mastered our language and wrote a series of books which attracted some attention. His biography of Hitler was less highly coloured than that of Conrad Heiden, but I disapproved his title, *Hitler the Pawn*. He maintained that the Führer inherited the evil tradition of Prussia, both in its policy of aggression and its hatred of democracy, and that the revolution of 1918 was merely a storm in a tea-cup. This thesis was worked out in his biography of Hindenburg, who carried the Junker tradition into the Weimar era and helped to sabotage a promising experiment. His last book, *Is Germany a hopeless Case?*, written at the suggestion of Gilbert Murray, sketched German history from his peculiar angle. The only hope, he argued, lay in the elimination of the Prussian Generals and the establishment of genuine democracy. Much the same gospel was preached by another gifted publicist, Dr. Edgar Stern-Rubarth, formerly the friend and colleague of Stresemann. German Liberals of the type of Olden, Moritz Bonn, Stern-Rubarth and Valentin, however, were *rari nantes in gurgite vasto*. Though Prussia was not Germany it formed the larger part and the mainspring of the Reich, standing for the unchallengeable authority of the state as the Liberal stands for the primacy of the citizen. Despite his notorious anti-Nazi convictions and activities Olden was interned when a wave of panic swept over England in the anxious summer of 1940. Released on receiving a call to lecture in America, he was torpedoed with his wife on the way across. Hitler had got him after all.

The liberalism of Prince Hubertus Loewenstein sprang from different roots but was equally vigorous and sincere. Liberal Catholics, like Acton in England, Lamennais in France, and Don Sturzo in Italy, have always been rare birds. Prince Hubertus, a member of one of the oldest families in Germany, co-operated wholeheartedly with Liberals and Socialists who strove to save the tottering Weimar edifice, and described his work for the Reichsbanner in a moving Autobiography. Had the Ministers in

Prussia and the Reich possessed something of his zeal and courage liberty might have been preserved, for it was leadership, not numbers, that was lacking when the hour struck. His first book, *The Tragedy of a Nation*, which I reviewed in the *Spectator* before meeting the author, analysed the causes of the collapse, emphasizing the lack of understanding shown by the authorities for the needs and aspirations of youth. He started a paper at Saarbrücken on the eve of the Saar plebiscite, was disgusted when Cardinal Innitzer, the professed friend of Dollfuss and Schuschnigg, welcomed the ravisher of Austria, and saw in Franco, not the Christian knight and dragon-slayer depicted in the Catholic press, but a tool of the Dictators. He realized that anti-clericalism in Spain was the result not of Russian propaganda, for it had existed long before Lenin was born, but of the simple fact that the Church usually sided with the enemies of political, agrarian and educational reform.

A no less arresting personality among the refugees was Dr. Rauschning, ex-President of the Danzig Senate, who had once been a member of the Nazi party and on closer acquaintance withdrew in disgust. His name became widely known soon after the Munich crisis through his book *The Revolution of Nihilism*, which declared open war on Nazi ideology. Though clumsily written and much too long, it revealed a man of ardent patriotism and sturdy Protestant convictions. While nearly all the refugees were men of the Left, most of them Jews, here was a Conservative landowner of Aryan blood. His thesis was that we were confronted with a revolution which challenged the foundations of morality and religion. His second and far more readable work *Hitler Speaks*, based on conversations between 1931 and 1934, was held back till war broke out. When he visited me in London early in 1939, he spoke of war as close at hand, and a week or two later Czechoslovakia was wiped off the map. I noted his forecast that when the storm burst Hitler would invade Holland. He made the impression of an able and high-minded man who had dedicated his life to the fight against the new paganism and might perhaps play a leading part when the Nazi régime had been overthrown, a forecast which has not been realized.

To an old student of international affairs Chatham House was a perpetual feast. As a member of the Meetings Committee I was able to witness its rapid growth at close quarters. The stately eighteenth-century mansion in St. James's Square welcomed makers of history from all over the world, for though membership of the Royal Institute is confined to British subjects the list of our foreign speakers is impressive. Usually we invited them, sometimes they proposed themselves. They could count on a courteous hearing from an audience including experts in every field. Dissent was almost always decorously expressed and very rarely did the slumbering embers burst into flame. Count Bethlen, after ten years as Premier of Hungary, pleaded for the revision of her truncated frontiers in a series of addresses in England afterwards published in a volume. He came to see me and discoursed in excellent English on his country's claims. Knowing him to represent the old feudal tradition I ventured to remark that Englishmen hoped to see the end of open voting in the rural districts which rendered the franchise a farce. He replied that it would soon be done. Men of the Right often make themselves out more progressive and men of the Left less radical when they visit England, the classic land of the *juste milieu*. The discreet omissions in Count Bethlen's address on Hungary at Chatham House provoked Wickham Steed to an attack in the ensuing debate so fierce as to provoke loud protests. The only other time I witnessed an explosion was when Harold Spender, an ardent Gladstonian Philhellene, accused Professor Arnold Toynbee of transferring his sympathies from the Greek to the Turkish side after the *débâcle* in Asia Minor in 1922.

Between the wars Chatham House had more visitors from France than from any other foreign country. None of them excited my curiosity more than Colonel de la Rocque, the founder of the Croix de Feu, then at the height of his influence. Was he perhaps the new Boulanger, the future dictator of whom many a rightwing Frenchman dreamed? I asked Wickham Steed, who had met him, what to expect. 'He's a fool', was the prompt reply, and after listening to his address I understood what he meant. For nearly an hour he described in moving terms the patriotism and personal devotion of his followers, the *anciens combattants*, united by the sacred memories of the conflict. He had no use for existing parties, and I gathered that he would forcibly resist the establishment of a Communist régime, but he gave no indication of what he would do if he came to power. While preaching the gospel of discipline, unity and service with unmistakeable sincerity, he was evidently not cut out for leadership. Another French soldier, General Faucher, for many years military adviser in Prague, came after the rape of Czechoslovakia and the refusal of France to implement her alliance. He was so incensed that he exchanged his French citizenship for that of the state which he had served and whose army he warmly praised. Most leading French journalists also found their way to St. James's Square. 'Pertinax' impressed me by his quiet mastery. Unlike Briand, but like Clemenceau and Poincaré, he had no belief in the latest plans for keeping the world at peace. 'The Covenant of the League,' he exclaimed (lifting his right hand and letting it fall), 'a piece of paper.' 'The Kellogg Pact (lifting his hand a second time and letting it fall) a piece of paper.' He was a true prophet. Jacques Bardoux, who knew England best of them all for he had studied at Oxford, spoke for Conservatives who were loyal to the Republic. Mme Tabouis, whom I heard and met elsewhere, was credited with a somewhat exuberant imagination, but her knowledge and womanly charm made her welcome everywhere. Vladimir d'Ormesson, on the other hand, author of the best brief sketch of French policy since the First World War, was a model of discretion. On one occasion at Chatham House we strayed far afield from politics when Jacques Maritain, the eminent Catholic philosopher, discoursed on tendencies in French thought.

No issue divided British opinion so profoundly before the Munich crisis as the fratricidal struggle in Spain unleashed by Franco's rebellion. Our Meetings Committee felt that the best plan would be for each side to have an innings to itself. Ex-King Alfonso's former Ambassador, Marquis de Merry del Val, the handsomest member of the *Corps Diplomatique*, asserted that Franco had rescued his country from Bolshevist domination and thereby saved the lives of many leading Spaniards from massacre. Supporters of the Republic retaliated by pointing to Mussolini's legions and Hitler's bombers at Guernica. The nearest approach to a balanced estimate came from Professor Castillejo, the eminent educationalist, who had sought refuge in England from the waring factions. Salvador de Madariaga, scholar, diplomatist and former official of the League of Nations, complained that if he returned to his country he would be shot in front by one side and in the back by the other. I never idealized the Republican Government, which contained no Communists, but I wished it to survive. It was supported by the working classes who had never had a fair deal and were miserably poor. The storm clouds were gathering in the Mediterranean and a Fascist Dictator in Madrid might threaten our Imperial interests. As the correspondent of the *Daily Express* tersely remarked: 'All Spaniards are mad, but the people over here are less dangerous to England.' A Republican Government would never have sent 'volunteers' to fight under Hitler's banner against our Russian ally.

Among other visitors to Chatham House whom it was interesting to see and to hear were Dr. Schacht, reputed to be the financial wizard of Germany; Otto Bauer, leader of the Austrian Socialists, who discoursed in German on the achievements and ideals of his party shortly before its brutal suppression by Dollfuss in 1934; Dr. Hodza, afterwards Prime Minister of Czechoslovakia at the time of the Munich crisis; Avenol, the uninspiring successor of Sir Eric Drummond as Secretary of the League of Nations, who analysed the proposed modification of the Covenant and concluded that no weakening of its obligations, already weak enough, should be allowed. No foreigner attracted a larger audience than Emil Ludwig, who had become a Swiss citizen long before the Nazi régime. I have never known an *emigré* who had more entirely shed his sympathies with the land of his birth. On his latest visit, when I was in the chair, his theme was the tragic contrast between Weimar and Potsdam, the former admirable but ineffectual, the second detestable but efficient. He quoted Goethe's scathing verdict on his countrymen—so admirable as individuals, so miserable in the mass. He delighted in his fame and was proud of the vast circulation of his books, some of which, including his Autobiography, he presented to me. Interested in everything, he used to produce a note-book in which he recorded anything in conversation which struck his fancy. When Imperial Conferences brought Dominion and Indian statesmen to London, we sampled them at Chatham House. No one drew such a crowd as Gandhi, but Nehru and Sapru were scarcely less impressive. Indians, I have often noticed with admiration, seem to master our language more completely than other foreigners.

Two hardy annuals were of outstanding interest at Chatham House. The first was a report on the September Assembly of the League by some leading member of the British Delegation, the second the dinner at which the Foreign Secretary was the principal guest. The most memorable of the latter festivities was in June 1939 when Lord Halifax announced that we should keep our promise to fight if Poland were attacked, and he added that he and his colleagues were well aware what that pledge involved. We had had a series of discussions in recent years at Chatham House on the principles of our foreign policy, champions of limited liability, such as Lord Lothian, arguing against the crusaders for collective security led by Lord Cecil. Now, in the summer of 1939, we had closed our ranks. I cannot exaggerate my debt to the Institute of International Affairs, to its Library and Reading room, to Professor Toynbee's annual surveys of Inrernational Affairs, to the Journal, the public meetings, the group discussions, the monographs, the co-operative volumes on world problems. When the Second World War broke out a volume on the principles of British foreign policy was in active preparation by a group of which I was a member under the chairmanship of Sir George Clerk, formerly Ambassador at Paris. Two of our members, General Temperley, brother of the historian, and Herbert Sidebotham, 'Scrutator' of the *Sunday Times*, passed away in the early part of the war and the project dropped.

I agreed with Neville Chamberlain's frank admission that we had treated Germany without wisdom or magnanimity and that the Treaty of Versailles was as imperfect as most dictated settlements, though her own abuse of victory at Brest-Litovsk had been infinitely worse. I was not surprised when German troops marched into the Rhineland in March 1936, since the inequality of status between a fully armed France and a largely disarmed Germany permanently open to invasion was too paradoxical to endure. A few shrewd observers sensed that it was the first step towards German domination of Europe, as we now know it to have been, but I was not among them. The rape of Austria, on the other hand, filled me with a sense of impending doom. Here, alas, those short-sighted patriots Dollfuss and Schuschnigg had helped to dig her grave, the former by his insensate attack on the Social Democrats who dominated the capital, the latter by his refusal to co-operate with them till the Nazi hordes were thundering at the gate. The lamentable story of the collapse of the little Republic has been told by my old friend Gedye, at that time Vienna correspondent of the *Daily Telegraph*, in the burning pages of *Fallen Bastions*.

During the Munich crisis I stood midway between the champions and the critics of Neville Chamberlain. I grieved over the ravishing of Czechoslovakia as much as anyone, but how could we save her when her French ally shirked a fight and public opinion throughout the Commonwealth abhorred the notion of another struggle? That Hitler was bluffing no one could believe who listened to his denunciation of Beneš on 26 September 1938. We had often heard his rasping voice, but that evening we were horrified by the vitriolic hate with which he hissed out the name again and again: we felt he was out for blood and would stick at nothing. Chamberlain, like Baldwin, was an amateur in foreign affairs, but he gave his whole mind to them when called to the helm. He could not know—as we have learned from the captured German documents—that in the autumn of 1937 the Führer revealed to a few intimates his programme of aggression against Austria, Czechoslovakia and Poland in that order, which, if successful, would render him the virtual master of the Continent. He dismissed Chamberlain and Halifax as two old hens who could only cackle. 'I saw those two worms (Chamberlain and Daladier) at Munich. Too cowardly to fight, they won't go beyond a blockade.' If Chamberlain is to be blamed for anything, it is for failing to detect at an earlier stage the immeasurable perfidy of the two Dictators; but it is only fair to remember that this myopia was shared by most of his countrymen. The case for 'appeasement' has been argued in Keith Feiling's biography of the Prime Minister, the apologias of Lord Simon and Lord Templewood, and Sir Evelyn Wrench's life of Geoffrey Dawson, editor of *The Times*. The other side is presented in the first volume of Churchill's War Memoirs and the third volume of Amery's recollections. No agreed verdict can ever be expected.

When the weary Prime Minister announced to the cheering crowd in Downing Street that, like Disraeli, he had brought home from Munich 'peace with honour', I could not agree. Czechoslovakia had been thrown to the wolves, so where was the honour? And peace? Hitler was only sharpening his sword. With such adventurers *l'appétit vient en mangeant*. When the Führer devoured what remained of Czechoslovakia five months later and we listened to Chamberlain's speech in Birmingham Town Hall we knew that the policy of appeasement had failed. England returned to her traditional policy of the Balance of Power, our time-honoured method of seeking security through coalitions, and the pendulum swung from one extreme to the other. After years of humiliating retreat in Abyssinia, the Rhineland and the Danubian basin, we bounded forward, scattering guarantees in our path. The agreement with Turkey was a solid gain, and we could help Greece with our ships, but what could we do for Poland or Romania in case of attack? Was everything possible done to secure the support or neutrality of Russia in the probable event of Nazi aggression? Here our task was complicated by the refusal of the Poles to allow Russian troops on their soil, and we could not in honour surrender the little Baltic states to the deadly hug of the Russian bear. If Russia was to risk her blood and treasure in a desperate encounter she would demand a very substantial reward, and such a bribe we could not supply. Putting himself up to auction Stalin naturally closed with the highest bidder. The signature of the fateful Russo-German pact gave the all-clear to the megalomaniac in Berlin and doomed millions to a violent death. I had always thought of the Napoleonic era as the worst European ordeal since the Thirty Years War, but it yields pride of place to the first half of our blood-stained century.

20

HITLER'S WAR AND AFTER

I

WHILE the war of 1914 belonged to the familiar type of conflicts between the Great Powers, that of 1939 was also a clash of ideologies. The formal reason for our belligerence was our pledge to Poland, but our compelling motive was the Nazi challenge to principles dearer to us than life. 'We are fighting evil things,' exclaimed Neville Chamberlain, who on this occasion at least spoke for us all. We fought, as we have always fought, for the Balance of Power, but also for a still greater cause. Combatants always depict their foes as devils incarnate, but my estimate of the Nazis had been formed long before we heard the thunder of the guns. Never have we been so united. There was no flinching, for John Bull with his back to the wall is a stubborn animal. Hitler and Mussolini, like Tirpitz and Ludendorff, underestimated the staying power of the British Commonwealth. The only suggestion for a compromise came from the ageing Lloyd George after the collapse of Poland in the first month of the war, and it aroused no echo.

Gilbert Murray expressed the general mood in one of his finest utterances entitled *The Great Challenge* which I invited him to write for the *Contemporary Review*. The building of a World Order, he admitted, had proved a harder task than we thought. Unlike the war of 1914 the new challenge was not unexpected, and we should not be surprised by any devilry; far worse men were now in power in Germany though more precariously enthroned. Why was an undistinguished, raucous, verbose, mendacious and half insane Austrian mystic accepted as the adored Leader of a great nation? The answer was clear enough: he represented with paranoic intensity the prevailing emotion of a proud and warlike people maddened by military defeat. When a British visitor asked him to explain his policy he shouted *Deutschland!*—a cry which awoke an echo in every German heart. No easy enterprise lay before us. We must ask the French and British peoples to endure hardships and perils almost unexampled in history, and at the end to emerge with their heads clear and their hearts unsoiled by bitterness. 'The challenge seems almost too hard for average human nature to meet, yet it must be met.' A similar policy was urged in the *Contemporary Review* throughout the five years of conflict—the decisive defeat of the aggressor to be followed by as statesmanlike a settlement as the emotions of the conflict and the memory of unspeakable crimes would allow. However discouraging the news from the various fronts, however remote the prospect of victory, never for a moment was I tempted to abandon the slogan: No peace or parley with the Nazis! Though there were plenty of fine young men among the Brownshirts, full of idealism and ready to give their lives for the Fatherland, their leaders, baleful architects of ruin, were beyond the pale.

Our peril began in May 1940 when Hitler stormed into Norway and Denmark, Holland and Belgium, and forced the French to their knees in three weeks. It was the end of France as a Great Power. The stout-hearted country of Clemenceau and Poincaré seemed like a dim memory, for the feeble octogenarian Pétain reigned in their place. 'We need a statue on a pedestal,' explained Laval, who found what he sought in the faded hero of Verdun. His nerve had failed in the Ludendorff offensive in 1918 and now it failed again. While de Gaulle kept the torch alight in a foreign land, Laval announced that he confidently expected and ardently desired a German victory. I shall never forget how in the one o'clock news we heard Pétain's declaration: 'il faut cesser les hostilités', and sensed that our gravest hour since the Armada was at hand. While power in France had passed from Paul Reynaud to Pétain, the helm in England was transferred from Neville Chamberlain to 'the pilot who weathered the storm', under whom Labour and Liberals were proud to serve without the slightest friction through five testing years. Churchill's record of the Second World War ranks in historical importance with Lloyd

George's narrative of the First and surpasses all other political apologias except that of Bismarck.

Our new captain fought without rancour, as Abraham Lincoln had waged the American Civil War, detesting the Nazi régime like the rest of us but refusing to indict a whole nation. This time there was no wrecking of innocent little German shops. Churchill has never hated Germany, Russia or any other nation. That the example of the Prime Minister should be universally followed was too much to expect, as the popularity of Sir Robert Vansittart's *Black Record*, published in January 1941, was to prove. The Permanent Under-Secretary of the Foreign Office had been removed from his responsible post by Neville Chamberlain for his opposition to the policy of appeasement, and was relegated to a new position as Chief Diplomatic Adviser to the British Government; but his advice was never asked.

> These talks are designed to show that the German has not really altered since Tacitus' day [ran the publisher's announcement on the back page of the brochure]. He has always been a barbarian and war-lover, the enemy—furtive or avowed—of humanitarianism, liberalism and Christian civilization; and the Hitler régime is no accidental phenomenom but a logical fruit of German history, the German *in excelsis*.

That was a fair summary of a work containing such passages as the following:

> Germans in the plural are the Brazen Horde. The Brazen Horde has not changed down the ages. To mankind as a whole Germans have brought nothing but misery in all its forms. Hitler, the ex-Kaiser, Bismarck, away back into the dank record, you will find nothing but a procession of mirthless braggarts ruling over dreary robots. The lust of world domination has been working in them for generations. Force and fraud, fraud and force: that is the old German gospel.

Declining a publisher's invitation to attempt a detailed rejoinder to this pathological denunciation of 'the butcher-bird of Europe', I contented myself with a critical notice in the *Contemporary Review*.

> Few if any of Sir Robert's numerous readers will dissent from his verdict on the fanatically efficient gangsters who hold the unhappy German people—and today many others as well—in their deadly

grip. It would indeed be difficult to exaggerate the cruelty, the intolerance, the corruption, the spiritual darkness of the Nazi régime which has plunged Europe into war and which must be utterly destroyed if civilization as we know it is to survive. The chief fault of the book is that he overdoes his case. His voice is unvaryingly shrill. If we accept him as our guide through German history and our interpreter of German character there is very little hope for the world. Yet perhaps *Black Record* is not the whole story after all. He should lay to heart the profound aphorism of Renan, *La vérité est dans les nuances*.

A septuagenarian living in the country could do little for the war effort except lecture to wounded soldiers and trainees and take part in an occasional Brains Trust. Night after night during the autumn of 1940 we watched the bursting of our anti-aircraft shells over London twenty miles away. Bombs were dropped on our village, one of them missing us by forty yards. The burning of the stock of four of my books and the destruction of the office of the *Contemporary Review* a few months later with all the furniture and files were a trifle compared with the tribulations of many friends. The wholesale slaughter of civilians in London and the 'Baedeker' raids, far from breaking our national spirit, rendered it as strong as tempered steel. 'Who lives if England dies? Who dies if England lives?' One night we heard dozens of planes fly overhead and learned a few hours later that they were on their way to Coventry.

Evil communications corrupt good manners, and in the final stages of the conflict the allies stooped to the level of their enemies in the obliteration of historic Dresden and the launching of the Hiroshima bomb. The Second World War brought home the realities of war to almost every corner of our crowded island. When the V1 and V2 were hurled at us in 1944 they were in one respect a little easier to bear than the bombardment of 1940–1, for the tide had turned at Alamein and Stalingrad and we knew that the end could not be very far away. The fall of Mussolini was the writing on the wall. He had dragged an unwilling and unprepared nation into a conflict which he believed to be nearly over and paid the just penalty with his life. Garibaldi, who had loved England as much as England admired him, had pronounced a curse on any Italian who forfeited our friendship, and now 'the curse of Garibaldi' was dramatically fulfilled. The belligerence of Italy, which Palmerston, Russell and Gladstone had indirectly helped to unite, was one of the most painful experiences of the struggle. Yet since 'one man and one man only', in Churchill's phrase, was responsible, we knew we should soon be friends again. In the twenties and thirties the Duce had appeared to a few un-thinking Englishmen as the efficient autocrat who had made the trains run on time; but the legend of the superman had faded by the time of his death, and what was left of it was destroyed by the posthumous publication of Ciano's diaries. If it be argued that the Italians, like the Spaniards, cannot work Parliamentary govern-ment, the reply is that the French are hardly if at all better and that the alternative of dictatorship proved infinitely worse. No one has ever maintained that democratic institutions are easy to run.

Our dislike of Bolshevist theory and practice—another variety of the totalitarianism which Englishmen abhor—was intensified by the pact with Hitler and the invasion of Poland and Finland; but when the Führer threw off the mask and invaded Russia in 1941 we obeyed the instinct of self-preservation. In Churchill's lapidary formula, Hitler's friends were our enemies, Hitler's enemies our friends. Some later critics have censured him for sustaining a régime which he detested and which was to dis-appoint our expectations of co-operation after the war; but there was no real choice, for our countries had to swim or sink together. The only sound maxim for statesmen in such emergencies is First Things First. For the next three years we mourned the trials of our ally and rejoiced when the tide turned. That Russia was a difficult and exacting ally we discovered soon enough, but not till the struggle was over did we learn from Churchill's thrilling narrative the depth of his anxieties in the closing phase.

While the Russians were repeating the miracle of 1812, France forfeited part of the sympathy we had extended to her in 1940. The most grievous incident in the whole desperate struggle was the bombardment of a squadron of the French fleet off the African coast when our proposals to save it from the Germans were ignored. Whether or not we were prudent to sever diplomatic relations with Vichy while the United States remained in contact, the decision was in accord with public opinion since Pétain had let us down without apology or apparent regret. Here was our main difference with the Roosevelt Administration which scoffed at the claim of de Gaulle to speak for France, but the friction was cushioned by the affectionate comradeship of Churchill and Roosevelt. No British statesman had enjoyed such popularity in the United States as our valiant son of an American mother, and no President before Eisenhower has been so fully trusted in England. Without their historic friendship the war might have been lost.

While fully sharing the gratitude for Churchill's incomparable leadership in our darkest hours, I welcomed the verdict of the election of 1945. Disraeli's aphorism—'England does not love coalitions'—is as true as ever. When the purpose of the historic partnership of 1940 was achieved by the unconditional surrender of Germany it was time to part without waiting, as the Prime Minister desired, for the surrender of Japan. The resounding triumph of Labour proved how unrepresentative the House of Commons with its large Conservative majority had become. Though the party truce had been loyally observed it was at the cost of shelving urgent Labour demands. The greatest Englishman of our time could speak for his countrymen in the years of war but not on the return of peace. Moreover it is undesirable for any party to remain in office over a very long period, for the 'ins' tend to think themselves indispensable and the 'outs' to become disgruntled. In the homely words of old John Selden, the father of the Whigs, Parliaments, like cats, grow cursed with age. But there was also a specific reason in 1945 for ending the partnership. The stoutest bulwark against Communism in England is not a Conservative Government but a powerful and as responsible Labour Party, pledged by sincere conviction to the maintenance of free institutions.

As an impenitent Liberal, abstaining if no Liberal candidate was available, I could claim for the first time in my life to stand above or at any rate at some distance from the battle. I had never been alarmed by the fear of 'Socialism' so widely entertained in what used to be called the ruling classes, for no section of the community is less doctrinaire than the trade unions which form the backbone and supply the funds of the Labour Party. Throughout the free world, where the power of the central government is continually increasing, the choice is not between socialism and individualism but between a larger or smaller measure of control in the sphere of industry. Whether we confess it or not, we are all both socialists and individualists. The wisest course is to

consider every proposal on what appears to us to be its practical
merits and not to worry about labels. Such was the attitude of the
Liberal Party in its prime, and such it remains in the days of its
eclipse. Formerly the party of the Left, it is now the voice of the
centre. Most of its old working class supporters have transferred
their allegiance to Labour, and 'the Nonconformist Conscience'
which furnished valued support to Gladstone is only a memory.
Now that political democracy, the child of the Liberal Party, has
been achieved, the creation of economic democracy—a far more
complicated issue—is the problem of the age. The case for the
nationalization of the mines seemed to me overwhelming, for that
of the railways very strong, for that of road transport doubtful,
for that of iron and steel weak. My instinct is to leave industries
alone which are doing reasonably well.

I have never dreamed that the elimination of private profit
would automatically create industrial peace, for human nature
remains unchanged and all classes have shown themselves equally
selfish. The slacker does not grow less lazy or the urge to squeeze
every ounce of advantage out of employers and consumers less
peremptory. While small companies may plead that they cannot
afford increases in wages and amenities, the state possesses no
such excuse, for it can borrow what is needed to meet legitimate
or irresistible demands. Except among the Bevanites there is less
enthusiasm for the principle of nationalization and less demand
for a litter of further experiments now that the country has had
time to observe its rather disappointing results. The bright sun-
rise vision of 'the people's railways' and 'the people's mines'
has faded into the light of common day. Profits, it is true, no
longer flow into private pockets, but it is equally true that the
balance sheets reveal not profits but deficits. To such complaints
champions of nationalization may retort that the situation would
have been even worse under private ownership, and that the
costly and inescapable modernization of basic industries is impracticable without the resources of the state.

The Labour Parliamant of 1945–50 proved itself, as I anticipated, left centre, not extreme left. The foundations of the
Welfare State had been laid by the Liberals before the First World
War, the Beveridge plan had focused attention on its development, and the system of national insurance, whatever its defects,

implemented many aspirations of the workers. There was scarcely
less unanimity for collaboration with the United States in the
economic rehabilitation of Europe and the erection of bulwarks
in the West against the menace from Moscow culminating in the
rape of Czechoslovakia and the equally iniquitous blockade of
Berlin. The broad-shouldered figure of Ernest Bevin at the
Foreign Office commanded the confidence of the Opposition, and
no one could seriously describe Attlee and Herbert Morrison as
dangerous revolutionaries.

The courageous decision to terminate our three centuries of rule
in India, the second historic achievement of the Labour Government, provoked inevitable disagreement. Churchill seemed to
me as wrong-headed on this issue as he was statesmanlike
in foreign policy. 'That picturesque survival of eighteenth-
century imperialism,' as Laski classified him, had vehemently
opposed Sir Samuel Hoare's cautious extension of self-government, and the transfer of control of the largest of our possessions
to its inhabitants filled him with anger and grief. The Conservatives had successively opposed Home Rule for Ireland and self-
government for South Africa: now they resisted the decision to
leave India before we were pushed out. Lord Halifax, alone of
their leaders, speaking with the authority of an ex-Viceroy,
declared in the House of Lords that he could not oppose this
momentous resolve. Its wisdom was soon to be confirmed by the
humiliating experience of France in Indo-China and of Holland
in Indonesia. The Attlee Cabinet wisely recognized the irresistible
appeal of the slogan 'Asia for the Asiatics'. 'The patient East' of
Matthew Arnold's poem had become impatient, and the principle
of self-determination popularized by President Wilson had
fostered the ambitions generated by Japan's victory over Russia
in 1905. Ideas do not recognize frontiers.

The federal plan recommended by the British Government
would have averted the horrors arising from the partition of the
Punjab and the dangerous friction in Kashmir; but I was not
surprised by the conviction of Pakistan that the Moslem minority
could not count on fair treatment by a three to one Hindu majority
in an all-India system. Ulster had used a similar argument when
Eire was established, and the Jews when the Turkish withdrawal
from Syria and Palestine left the Arabs in general control. That a

condominium is difficult to work we had learned when Norway broke away from Sweden and by the chronic friction between Vienna and Budapest under the Ausgleich of 1867. Communities with different traditions and languages naturally view things from different angles; and when, as in the Indian peninsula, fundamental religious differences exist as well the conditions of success were lacking. The Prime Minister received his reward when both the new states decided to remain members of the Commonwealth. 'I like the English,' Gandhi used to say, 'but I do not want to be ruled by them.' Nehru's sentiments were precisely the same. Though he had learned our English way of life during his formative years at Harrow and Cambridge, he threw himself into the campaign for independence and spent many years in prison as the result of successive sentences. Once again the old Liberal principle of self-determination exerted its healing influence. As Campbell-Bannerman had turned Botha and Smuts into friends, so the Attlee Government and Lord Mountbatten, the last of our Viceroys, transformed the Congress Party and its leaders into valued colleagues. The story of Nehru's struggle to terminate a foreign yoke is told in his moving autobiography which may be described without exaggeration as the voice of India.

The transfer of votes in the elections of 1950 and 1951, slight though it was, showed that the tidal wave of 1945 had spent its force. Such is the familiar rhythm of British politics. Neither party was strong enough to make drastic constitutional or economic changes even had it desired to do so, and foreign observers detected little difference between the diplomacy of the Front Benches. That such unofficial collaboration was sapping the dynamism of the Labour Party was the cry of the Bevanites, and the increased Conservative majority in 1955, due above all to 'good times', was no surprise. Like Lord Samuel and most of my Liberal friends, I welcomed the verdict, partly because the two-party system requires a working majority if members are not to be worn out by fatigue. So long as the two main armies oppose not merely Proportional Representation but the Alternative Vote, Liberals remain under-represented. Meanwhile the little band carried on the tradition of the Independents before the University seats disappeared. In contrast to the notorious indiscipline within the parties in Congress and the customary anarchy of the French

Chamber, the power of the machine in England is a boon to the party leaders and a legitimate grievance for the holders of minority opinions.

The keenest disappointment in the post-war years has been the unsleeping hostility of Russia to the nations of the free world which had helped her to survive. After our brief but by no means cloudless honeymoon old suspicions of the West revived in un-diminished strength, and Churchill voiced our pained astonish-ment that our valiant ally should cast away such a precious store of friendship and goodwill. Once again we learned the bitter lesson that any Westerner who claims to understand the Russian mind and predict its course is riding for a fall. The emergence of formidable Communist parties for the first time in the French and Italian Parliaments sounded the alarm, but not till the lights went out in Czechoslovakia and Berlin was severed from the West did we realize that we were living on the slopes of an active volcano. A third rude shock, the invasion of South Korea, extended the area of conflict to the Far East. Since the armed strength of France was locked up in Indo-China and North Africa, we were driven to the paradoxical—some would say the desperate—expedient of rearming our late German enemies. Mindful of the brief span of the Weimar experiment, no one could help wondering what might happen when the aged Adenauer, the trusted friend of the Western Powers, should disappear. It will be easier for those who come after us to pronounce on the wisdom or folly of that decision. As Bismarck, the maker of many treaties, observed, every agreement contains the unwritten clause *rebus sic stantibus*— provided there is no change in the situation. And the situation is always changing. The only forecast I can make in the inter-national sphere with full assurance is the permanence of our ties with the United States, not because we love one another but because we need each other's support and feel a joint responsibility for the maintenance of values of Western civilization.

II

Migration from London in 1939 to the peace of the Home Counties provided more leisure for literary work than I had ever enjoyed. The first task was to bring *Recent Revelations of European*

Diplomacy up to date by comments on the documents and diaries, biographies and autobiographies which had appeared since the latest edition in 1930. The chronological terminus—the First World War and the peace treaties—remained, for the new era which opened in 1919 could best be surveyed as the prologue to Hitler's war and was a task for Sir Lewis Namier and other hands. With this enlargement of a volume of two hundred pages to double its original size I took leave of Bismarckian and post-Bismarckian Europe which had been my principal literary occupation for twenty years.

A second enterprise was the republication of a dozen essays and addresses under the title *Studies in Diplomacy and Statecraft* dealing mainly with the nature and use of power. A British Academy Master Mind lecture on Hobbes voiced my lifelong detestation of the Absolute State, a detestation intensified by the repulsive performances of Mussolini and Hitler. As a grateful disciple of Locke, Burke and Mill I had little use for the author of the *Leviathan* who has always seemed to me rather a continental than a British type. If, like Taine, we regard *homo sapiens* as a gorilla we clamour for a warder to keep him behind thick bars. If, on the other hand, we feel that we can in some degree tame his primeval instincts and build the good life with the unforced aid of our fellow-citizens, we press for a measure of self-determination. The deeper issues of community life were further discussed in an address entitled *Politics and Morals*, which explained why moral principles are so much easier to apply within a state than beyond the frontiers where differing traditions and standards may prevail. The dilemma tormented Machiavelli, not a heartless cynic but a disillusioned moralist, reluctantly convinced by experience and by study of the past that to apply the Sermon on the Mount in a lawless world spells national suicide. For him, as for Nietzsche, politics are 'beyond good and evil'.

A survey of political autobiographies in *Studies in Diplomacy and Statecraft* led to a volume entitled *Courts and Cabinets* which dealt with writers whose testimony is of value for what they witnessed, not for what they achieved. That memoirs require to be microscopically examined in the light of the author's character, ideology, opportunities of observation, and the interval between the events described and the date of composition, has been a commonplace since Ranke's first work appeared in 1824. Yet even when *Quellenkritik* has done its worst the testimony of men and women who have stood close to events is indispensable. Of my authors eight were French, four were English, and only one was German, the inequality arising from the fact that in the quantity and quality of historical memoirs France holds the first place. Saint-Simon carries off the first prize, but Mme de Motteville and La Grande Mademoiselle, Mme Campan and Mme de Rémusat, Queen Hortense, Caulaincourt and Juliette Adam do not lag too far behind. England was represented by Burnet and Lord Hervey, Horace Walpole and Fanny Burney. Wilhelmina, the favourite sister of Frederick the Great, emerges as the least reliable of my team of thirteen. The sub-title, I suggested, might have been *Studies in Human Nature*.

The great ones of the earth live in glass-houses where we watch them in dress and undress, at work and at play. Whatever the country or the century, the picture of human nature in the dramas here briefly described is strikingly similar. There are the same glaring contrasts of good and evil, the same hectic scramble for power and place, the same jealousies and backbiting, the same repulsive greed. It is not a pretty picture, but we should beware of identifying White-hall or Kensington Palace with England, the Tuileries or Versailles with France, Potsdam with Germany. While kings, queens and princesses, emperors and ministers, mighty soldiers and scheming *arrivistes* sat at their card-tables or busied themselves with love and war, ordinary men and women were performing their unrecorded tasks and creating the wealth which their superiors felt themselves entitled to waste.

The next volume, *Studies in German History*, contained a dozen items, old and new. The longest was the expanded study of Holstein, widely regarded as the master-builder of German policy from the fall of Bismarck in 1890 to his resignation in 1906. It was the first detailed study in any language of that slightly patho-logical figure who was credited with the power to make or mar the career of ministers and diplomatists alike. Donna Laura Minghetti, the witty mother of Princess Bülow, declared that it was for men like Holstein that the Bastille had been built. That he was undisputed master of the situation is nonsense, for he dis-approved both the Kruger telegram and the *Flottenpolitik*; but he was partly responsible for the lapse of Bismarck's secret treaty with Russia, for the rejection of Joseph Chamberlain's approaches at the turn of the century, and for the first Moroccan crisis. Neither the Kaiser, nor Bülow, nor Holstein desired war with France; but the latter was playing with fire and had to go, leaving behind him the spectre of the Triple Entente. Among the minor results of the Second World War was the capture of the Holstein papers and the publication of his fragmentary Memoirs, which portray him rather unconvincingly as merely a conscientious official. Among other items in a substantial volume were studies of German political ideas from Luther to Hitler, Germany in the eighteenth century, Prince Henry, the gifted brother of Frederick the Great, Mirabeau's analysis of the Prussian Monarchy, Goethe's political ideology, Ranke's interpretation of German history, Bismarck in his Table talk, and Treitschke in his correspondence. I had more to say of German scholars in a revised edition of my *History and Historians* with an Introduction on the work of the last forty years.

The most ambitious undertaking of my later years was a study of the Enlightened Autocrats of the eighteenth century, Frederick the Great and Catherine the Great, Maria Theresa and Joseph II. Since excellent English biographies of them all were available, my object was to paint their portraits and explain their system. The Patron Saint of Prussia, as Lord Rosebery called Old Fritz, the obscure German princess who ruled Russia for thirty-four years, the pious Hapsburg Empress and her reforming son, differed widely in character, but they shared the conviction that their paramount duty was to be the first servant of the state. Everything for the people, nothing by the people! That any method of collaboration, any division of authority as advocated by Locke and Montesquieu, was desirable never entered their heads. Their model was Louis XIV, with his gospel of the concentration of power and unremitting industry, but two new features were added to the august tradition of Le Roi Soleil. Frederick and Joseph established direct contact with their subjects by frequent journeyings through their dominions and by seeing everything with their own eyes, the former halting his carriage for talk in the village street, the latter travelling incognito as Count Falkenstein and sleeping at the village inn. The second departure

from the Versailles precedent was in the attitude of all the Enlightened Autocrats except Maria Theresa towards the Churches.
Frederick and Catherine were sceptics, Joseph a believer, but they
were equally determined to be masters in their own house, regarding religious persecution not merely as a relic of the Dark Ages,
but as damaging to the interests of the state. All that these children
of the *Aufklärung* demanded—and all that any ruler had a right to
require—was good citizenship. If that essential condition were
fulfilled, everyone, as the Philosopher of *Sans Souci* phrased it,
could find his own way to heaven. Every law-abiding and able-
bodied subject was an asset, for the best ruler could do nothing
without plenty of sturdy hands. That Frederick's policy of toleration was not merely the fruit of religious indifference was
demonstrated by sheltering the Jesuits when the Catholic
monarchs drove them in hundreds from their dominions and
compelled the Pope to suppress the most unpopular Order in the
Church.

The Enlightened Autocrats made a fair success of their system
because they combined a sense of duty with exceptional gifts. It
was a great advance on the seventeenth century when the doctrine
of responsibility to God alone was proclaimed by the early
Stuarts and Louis XIV and tacitly accepted by many of their
subjects. In countries which possessed neither the institutions nor
the tradition of representative government, efficient autocracy
seemed the best available system, but it could hardly be expected
to last. Though it was good enough for Voltaire, the climate of
political opinion was changing in Western Europe with the rise
of the *bourgeoisie*. A régime which had suited predominantly
illiterate agricultural communities failed to satisfy an epoch in
which industry and commerce were increasing the importance of
the cities, the lawyers were becoming an influential factor, and the
Encyclopédistes were challenging traditional institutions and
beliefs. The prosperity of England told its own tale, and the
creation of the United States, without King, nobility or Established Church, indicated that a practicable alternative to dynastic
autocracy had been discovered.

To round off my story of eighteenth-century Enlightened
Despots I added a fourth volume on their unenlightened contemporary, Louis XV, since autocracy without an efficient

autocrat is a sorry farce. Though he took a lively interest in foreign affairs, on the home front he was a *roi fainéant*, by no means unintelligent, but indolent, an incorrigible voluptuary and totally unfitted to rule. I attempted to hold the balance between radical historians like Michelet, who left him hardly a rag to cover his nakedness, and neo-royalist authors like Gaxotte with their pail of whitewash. His virtues were negative: there was no strain of cruelty in him and he had not the slightest craving for military glory. Lacking energy, self-confidence, relish for his task and all sense of responsibility—the qualities which rendered Louis XIV a great if not a wise monarch—he allowed things to slide. 'I have done no one any harm,' he exclaimed when Damiens struck his blow, and in a strictly limited sense it was true: it escaped his perception that his reign inflicted on the Monarchy a mortal wound. To the charge that he was its principal grave-digger there is no reply. While the Intelligentsia of Europe flocked to *La Ville Lumière*, spiritual darkness brooded over the palace of Versailles. His fateful legacy was a discredited dynasty and a disillusioned people. 'I found the crown of France in the mud,' declared Napoleon. 'I picked it up and put it on my head.' It was Louis XV who had let it fall. Had he returned to earth in 1789 he would have felt little surprise at the spectacle. Though he never said *Après moi le déluge* that was what he thought.

21

JOURNEY'S END

An octogenarian historian can look back with deep satisfaction at the progress achieved during his lifetime in every sphere of academic study. We survey the evolution of mankind with wider knowledge, clearer vision and cooler heads than in the far off days of my apprenticeship. If we produce fewer literary masterpieces than in the Age of the Amateurs, the general standard of scholarship, above all the critical use of authorities, is infinitely higher. We are less cock-sure, less tempted to glittering generalizations. Such tendentious narratives as those of Macaulay and Michelet, Bancroft and Motley, Droysen and Treitschke are no longer compiled by scholars worthy of the name. Our ideal—our paramount obligation—is to deserve the unstinted confidence of our readers. As Ranke remarked, the writing of history is a matter of conscience. No strident advocate of his race or his country, his party or his Church, has a claim to enter the temple of Clio. The next outstanding achievement is that today we cast our net ever further into the waters. 'What men have done and said,' declared Maitland, 'above all what they have thought: that is history.' Our domain is the totality of human experience. Among the most important developments of the last hundred years have been the discovery of ancient civilizations, the revelation of the pre-historic background which we call anthropology, the patient study of comparative religion, the recognition of the immense significance of economic factors and the majestic panorama of Asia. So long as we were mentally tethered to our base in Europe historical perspective on a grand scale remained impossible. Voltaire's appeal in his *Essai sur les Moeurs* to begin our quest with Asia, the mother of civilization, has been

322

impressively reiterated in our own day by Toynbee. To understand the life of man we must study it and think of it as a whole.

Though our knowledge of the past accumulates from year to year, we are not a step nearer agreement on the deeper problems of human destiny. Is there a meaning, a purpose, a guiding hand in the vast welter of world history? We should like to think so. From Augustine and Bossuet to Hegel and Comte, Buckle and Gobineau, Spengler, Croce and Toynbee, philosophers, theologians and sociologists have offered us a bewildering choice of master-keys to lead us through the labyrinth: whom—if any of them—shall we follow? The pundits, like the amateurs, can only guess and they all guess differently. There is no 'verdict of history', only a babel of voices; no agreed philosophy, only competing philosophies. 'We must consider how very little history there is,' remarked Dr. Johnson with his usual robust good sense, 'I mean real authentic history. That certain kings reigned and certain battles were fought we can depend upon as true; but all the colouring, all the philosophy of history, is conjecture.' Froude said much the same in a striking phrase: 'History is like a child's box of letters; you can spell with them any word you will.' All history is contemporary history, declared Croce, by which he meant that we witness the procession of the ages through the coloured spectacles of our own time. When Bury warned us against 'the illusion of finality' he was merely repeating the aphorism of Heraclitus that everything is in flux. Our view of individuals and institutions, ideologies, movements and events, however honestly we strive to stand above the battle, must always remain in large measure subjective. There is and there can be no court of final appeal, for scholars and publicists differ and will continue to differ in their scale of values and their angle of approach. Christians and Moslems have fought for centuries and contemptuously dismiss each other as infidels. China has always looked down on Europe and till recently Europeans have looked down on China. To the Lutheran Ranke the Reformation was a liberation, the supreme achievement of the German race; to Catholics it is an apostasy and a crime. The radiant hero of George Trevelyan's Garibaldian trilogy was recently denounced by a Catholic writer as a blasphemous brigand. *Quot homines*, *tot sententiae*. Such shrill antagonisms caution us not to swallow the first or last book on controversial topics which comes to hand, and it is a safe rule to distrust writers who cannot control their emotions and are always waving a flag.

Decades of study have confirmed my congenital distaste for over-simplifications and pocket formulas of every kind. My attitude is concisely expressed in Herbert Fisher's oft-quoted declaration in the Preface to his *History of Europe*. 'Men wiser and more learned than myself have found in history a plan, a rhythm, a predestined pattern: such harmonies are hidden from me. I only see one emergency following another, like the waves.' 'As a great poem,' writes George Trevelyan, 'an epic without beginning or end, I read history and never tire, but I can find in it no philosophy of history.' 'I do not believe that any future consummation could make sense of all the irrationalities of the preceding ages,' confesses Sir George Clark, his successor in the Cambridge Chair; 'if it could not explain, still less could it justify.' Frederick the Great, who was continually ruminating on the past, used to speak with awe of *Sa majesté le hasard* of which he had his full share, for instance the opportune death of the Tsarina Elizabeth when he was at his last gasp in the Seven Years War. In the catastrophes of nature, the holocaust of wars and pestilence, in accidents on land, at sea and in the air, in sickness and murder, the one is taken, the other left. Where does Fate or Providence come in? Certain things, which we may think good and bad, happen at certain times to certain people; that is all we know. What we call evil triumphs as often as what we call good. We lose ourselves in a web of casuistry if we try to fit the chances, changes and tragedies of daily experience into a pre-ordained pattern. If a bullet had killed Hitler in the Munich *putsch*, when several of his comrades fell at his side, there would probably have been no second world war and millions of Jews would be alive today.

'A mighty maze but not without a plan,' sings Pope in the *Essay on Man*. Perhaps, but what is the plan?

> One far-off divine event
> To which the whole creation moves

echoes Tennyson. Perhaps, but where is the evidence? Wishful thinking can neither be proved nor disproved. *C'est magnifique mais ce n'est pas l'histoire.* Like Lessing, if compelled to choose, I should prefer the quest for truth to its integral possession. It is this bracing challenge to our faculties which has raised us above the animal world from which we spring, exchanging perfection in a limited sphere for imperfection in a field of boundless possibilities. The Sphinx smiles at our audacious attempts to penetrate her secrets. Though all philosophies of history have been splendid failures, bold spirits try and try again, refusing to recognize defeat, and it is right that they should.

The rival interpretations of history—the teleological and the empirical—are as strongly entrenched and as deeply divided as the world religions. That a single ideology, political or theological, will ever prevail is a dream—as Moltke said of perpetual peace, not even a beautiful dream. Our best hope is that the zealots for uniformity will gradually abandon the futile idea of universal domination and will reconcile themselves, however reluctantly, to the practical necessity of co-existence. The history of philosophy reveals that to think is to disagree. In my long life I have seen half a dozen systems—Hegelian idealism, logical positivism, existentialism and the rest—rise and fall. Individuals, like communities, have widely differing traditions, varying types of mind, dissimilar emotional needs. Some of us crave for authoritative direction of their lives and thoughts, others prefer to find their own way. George Eliot exhorted us to live with clear-eyed endurance and not take opiates. Rome, like Islam, is monolithic, Protestantism fundamentally individualist. In a free community everyone has a right—and should exercise his right—to fulfil the law of his being. The Index of Prohibited Books illustrates the gulf between the Churches: preferring to select my own intellectual nourishment, I dislike spoon-feeding whoever administers the dose. Happily there is room for us all in the vast army of humanity whatever banners we carry. It is wiser for ourselves and the world to emphasize our human affinities than our ideological antagonisms.

Nature furnished me with a questioning and critical mind which has been useful in my profession and which I could not change if I wished. *Nullius addictus jurare in verba magistri*, I can no more believe to order than I can love to order. My convictions are no less profound than those of friends securely anchored in traditional faiths. In confessing his ever increasing wonder at the starry heavens above and the moral law within Kant spoke for us all. Man, he added in a noble aphorism, cannot get away from the idea of right. The three ultimates—truth, beauty and goodness—are older than the creeds and beyond the reach of iconoclasts. While many aspire to soar into the sky, others prefer solid earth under their feet. I belong to the latter class. Though not in the least mystical, I have a keen and abiding sense of all-encompassing and unfathomable mystery. No system which professes to give all the answers has ever claimed my allegiance. Papal infallibility and Fundamentalism repel me as strongly as they attract certain other types of mind. Lord Acton spent his life fighting the concentration of power in church and state and in exalting the Christian conscience as the final court of appeal; and to no one did the stern Catholic moralist allot higher marks than to the Quakers with their hatred of political and spiritual regimentation and their simple gospel of the inner light.

The worst treason a historian can commit is to pretend to higher authority, profounder wisdom and greater certainty than he possesses. Mindful of his responsibility, he should be content distinterestedly to seek for truth, to contribute his mite to the reconstruction and interpretation of the manifold experiences of mankind. Nature is largely predictable, man wholly unpredictable: all we can do is to apply the patient methods of science to our challenging task. We must start by striving—*sine ira et studio*—to ascertain, in Ranke's lapidary phrase, how things actually were. 'The fall of man' is a theological dogma with which historians have no concern. There are only a few generalizations on which we may venture without peril, for instance, that the satisfaction of primary physical needs has led to migrations, collisions, inventions, organizations; that small units tend by compulsion or consent to grow into larger ones; that, as Prince Kropotkin argued in a memorable book, mutual aid is as primordial and almost as powerful an instinct as self-preservation; that with the advance of civilization the activities of mind and heart find expression in the arts and sciences, philosophies and religions, in a word, the pursuit of what Aristotle called the good life. I agree with General Smuts that an urge to integration lies at the heart of the historical process. How that urge originated is a question which the historian is as incapable of answering as his readers.

History and philosophy move along parallel lines which never meet. Spengler's doctrine of periodicity—inescapable as the seasons and the tides—appeals to me as little as that of Calvinist predestination. I reject determinism in every form for the simple reason that I see no evidence to support the belief. I cannot regard myself or anyone else as a robot or a marionette of which the strings are pulled by some unseen hand; for the whole conception of law, punishment and citizenship rests on the assumption of direct personal responsibility.

The more I learn about the past the more I am impressed by the unchanging character of the human heart. So far as public and private morals are concerned the Age of Faith was certainly no better than the Age of Inquiry which dawned in western Europe in the sixteenth century and has dominated western thought ever since. As Pascal declared three centuries ago: *Les révolutions changent tout sauf le coeur humain*, and we who have witnessed dozens of revolutions in our own time can only draw the same conclusion. Here and here alone, as I see it, is to be found what we used to call the unity of history.

The first article in the Liberal creed to which I adhere is the uniqueness of every individual, and the more we develop our faculties the more differentiated we become. Every Liberal, it has been said, is something of an optimist: were it otherwise he would not plead for the maximum of opportunity and the minimum of constraint both for individuals and communities. As Mill, that oracle of individualists, observed, if the schoolmaster does all their sums for them his pupils will never get on. Though born in what Marvin in an inspiring little book described as the Century of Hope, I feel equally at home in the more critical climate of the Century of the Common Man. All around us are loss and gain, unhoped for triumphs and grievous disappointments. Long ago Disraeli spoke of the two nations in England, the rich and the poor; today, as the result of education and the Welfare State, of levelling up and levelling down, there is only one. I rejoice that more persons have wider opportunities and better prospects than ever before. Yet the common man who has pushed his way— with a good deal of assistance from the privileged classes—to the centre of the stage has a great deal to learn. He is as selfish, short-sighted and quarrelsome as those who used to be called his betters, no better and no worse. Exhortation is resented or ignored, and, like the rest of us, he is only taught by bitter experience. When Metternich heard the ominous roar of the mob in the streets of Vienna in 1848 which drove him into exile he bitterly exclaimed: 'That is what they call the voice of God.' *Vox populi vox Dei* is as much an affront to common sense as the old claim of Divine Right by Stuart and Bourbon Kings or Mussolini's fatuous slogan which Italian schoolchildren were taught to repeat like parrots: *Il Duce ha sempre ragione*. Acton used to say that the tyranny of a majority is even worse than that of a minority because it is more difficult to remove. Worthwhile democracy means very much more than 'counting heads instead of breaking them': it means above all the sharing of responsibility. The acid test of an epoch, a régime or a civilization is the importance it attaches to the body and soul of every citizen, old and young, rich and poor, and to the free formation and expression of opinion.

Tried by this searching test we feel justified in placing our western way of life, despite its imperfections, at the top of the list. Democracy, as Montesquieu pointed out, demands more from the citizen than any other system: to authoritarians like Hobbes that is its fundamental weakness, to libertarians like Mill the core of its appeal. In one of our last conversations my old chief the octogenarian Lord Bryce, who had recently published two massive volumes on *Modern Democracies*, lamented the eclipse of the more sanguine hopes of his youth; yet he never dreamed of putting back the hands of the clock. Compelled to learn by trial and error we must expect some hard knocks in the process. Democracy, he proclaimed, would never perish till hope had expired. I do not share the apprehension that we shall be bossed and bullied by Civil Servants or by some Big Brother in 1984. I see no reason to believe that John Bull is becoming less disinclined to lie down on a bed of Procrustes and be elongated or shortened to the required length.

In a well-known work Emile Faguet dismisses democracy as 'the cult of incompetence'. The Latin races of which he was chiefly thinking have had less time and appear to possess less aptitude for the daring experiment than the cooler sons of the north. In any case where are we Anglo-Saxons to find a political philosophy which ensures happier results? 'The general inclination of all mankind,' declared old Thomas Hobbes, 'is a perpetual and restless desire after power which ceaseth only in death'. If this is the case we must never forget that 'the price of liberty is eternal vigilance'. The epidemic of dictatorship which swept across the Continent like a rash after the First World War was the natural result of the material and spiritual upheaval, and we may hope the worst is over for the present. From the days of the Greek *Tyrannos* emergencies have bred dynamic adventurers—the human equivalent of quack remedies—who have hurled their unfortunate countrymen into the furnace of war. Mussolini and Hitler found a few admirers in England, happily only a few, for Cromwell cured us for ever of the craving for a superman. Even a dictatorship in Sunday clothes, as in the Portugal of Salazar, is at most a tonic, not a diet. The spiritual damage it inflicts—mass production of citizens, the stunting of individuality, the negation of civic responsibility, the affront to human dignity—outweighs spectacular material achievements. Our stout seventeenth-century ancestors proved that the ultimate choice is between responsible and irresponsible government, and we have wisely chosen the former. For the flowering of personality, to which we look for the enrichment of the community, we need abundance of light and air. The truest happiness lies in self-realization and the filling of our lives. Democracy is at all times a venture of faith, demanding endless patience, unresting endeavour, horse sense, cool heads, steady nerves, tolerance, a minimum standard of civic conduct and a distaste for pushing things to extremes. The Englishman, to use the expression of Halifax, is a Trimmer. In the absence of such qualities, as in Central and South America, it is a squalid farce. *Corruptio optimi pessima.* The perfect society on earth, like the perfect citizen, remains a dream, but we can always follow the gleam.

Le cœur a ses raisons que la raison ne connait pas. Pascal was right, yet our hearts can no more unlock the ultimate mysteries than our brains. That certain beliefs comfort millions of souls is no demonstration of their truth. One man's food is another man's poison. The Moslem recoils in horror from what seems to him the blasphemous notion of the Mother and the Son of God, and religious images are anathema. That Christ was born of a virgin, walked on the water and raised Lazarus from the dead can neither be proved nor disproved. Argument is futile: certain types of mind are able to believe such assertions, others are not. Perhaps the Christian mystics like St. Theresa and St. John of the Cross, and the Eastern sages who fascinate Aldous Huxley, find the most unalloyed spiritual satisfaction in their sense—whether theistic or pantheistic—of union with God. No Englishman of my generation laboured more devotedly and more fruitfully in the cause of mutual understanding and mutual respect than my old friend Sir Francis Younghusband, soldier and diplomat, scholar and traveller, founder of the Congress of Faiths. While Catholics boycott mixed gatherings, speak with pitying disdain of their fellow-Christians as heretics or schismatics, talk of the 'poison of Protestantism', and pray for 'the conversion of England' as if we were a pagan tribe, he found himself at home in churches and chapels, mosques and temples in every land. Believing in the fatherhood of God and the brotherhood of man, he respected all sincere beliefs. 'Live and let live' was his slogan. Like old Tom Paine he could say: 'All religions are good which make man good.' He never suggested that they were all equally good, for each of us thinks his own is the best; but he regarded them—and I regard them—as branches of a single tree. Like Toynbee he rejected both the notion that Christianity is 'the only true religion' and the arrogant claim that within the Christian fold there is only one true Church. Confronted by Tertullian's peremptory pronouncement *Extra ecclesiam nulla salus* and Belloc's frowning formula 'Outside the Church is darkness' we may murmur gently: 'In my Father's house there are many mansions.'

In the familiar aphorism of William James, the expositor of Pragmatism, 'that is true which is true for me, and that is true which is true for you'. The orthodoxy of the one always has been and doubtless always will be the heresy of the other. The principle of friendly co-existence in which I have always believed is illustrated in my own family. I was bred in the Church of England, my wife in the Roman communion, and our eldest son finds just what he needs in the Society of Friends. That the preservation of morals depends on the acceptance of certain specific doctrines seems to me not merely a repudiation of what is called natural religion but a confession of despair, since the percentage of Christians diminishes day by day owing to family limitation in the

West and to the unchecked surge of population throughout Asia
which already contains the half of mankind. Conscience is older
than any existing Church or creed. Breasted, the eminent American Egyptologist, traces its dawn to ancient Egypt, and Socrates,
like numberless other martyrs, died happy in obeying his *daimon*.
Though I have known too many noble and helpful people of
widely differing faiths in my own and other lands—to say nothing
of the saints and sages of the past—ever to despair of mankind,
I anticipate a marked improvement of human nature as little as a
mass retrogression. Despite our rapidly increasing mastery over
nature we seem likely to stumble along in much the same way as
we have done through countless aeons, sometimes reaching for the
stars, often wallowing unashamedly in the primeval slime. There
has never been peace on earth or a Golden Age and I do not
expect any such happy consummation.

I have found the evening of life a time of tranquil happiness.
Youthful ambitions have been realized or proved unrealizable.
If an octogenarian has not learned serenity he has lived in vain.
Old age brings—or ought to bring—wider perspectives, greater
tolerance of everything except cruelty and intolerance, calmer and
therefore fairer judgments of men and things, past and present.
If the lamp burns less brightly there is less flickering of the flame.
I await the fall of the curtain with a quiet mind. I have never felt
the slightest fear of death, any more than a tired child dreads the
hour of rest. The sting of death is when it comes too soon to make
our special contribution, however humble, to the life of the community, and to repay part of the debt we owe to those who have
gone before us. As an old member of the Psychical Research
Society and a grateful student of Myers on *Human Immortality*, I
keep an open mind on the problem of survival. In view of our
descent from animals, to whom no one concedes immortality, I
think it improbable that conscious continuity will be my lot.
Perhaps 'our little life is rounded with a sleep'. That something
may persist, however tenuous and earthbound, is suggested by a
good deal of evidence, though it does not take us very far.
Messages from 'the other side', as in *Raymond*, do not seem
particularly edifying, but to some stricken souls they may appear
better than nothing. I have known friends who await the end in
confidence that they will enjoy an eternity of bliss with those they

loved and are in consequence eager for the reunion; others who hope without any certainty, still others who have no hope at all. In Buddhist India, far from desiring survival, the weary millions long for Nirvana, a return to the ocean of being where consciousness, the source of all suffering, is no more. Europe, it has been declared, says Yes to life, India says No. I am content to make my last voyage in ignorance of my destination. We see through a glass darkly. Dogmatic assurances about the shape of things to come, elaborate doctrines of rewards and punishments, leave me unconvinced. If consolation is needed at journey's end may it not be sought in my favourite beatitude: 'Blessed are the pure in heart, for they shall see God'?

INDEX